Effective
Secondary Teaching

Effective Secondary Teaching

GOING BEYOND THE BELL CURVE

JAMES QUINA

Wayne State University

1817

HARPER & ROW, PUBLISHERS, New York

*Cambridge, Philadelphia, St. Louis, San Francisco,
London, Singapore, Sydney, Tokyo*

PHOTO CREDITS: All photos appear by courtesy of James Quina, with the following exceptions: p. 3: AP/Wide World; p. 9: Forsyth, Monkmeyer Press Photo; p. 15: © 1985, Clay, Jeroboam; pp. 18 (top), 311: © Antman/The Image Works; p. 18 (bottom): © Arms, Jeroboam; p. 33: NASA; p. 57 (right): Dejean/Sygma; p. 101: Strickler, Monkmeyer Press Photo; pp. 162, 163, 225: Collection Haags Gementemuseum—The Hague © 1988, M. C. Escher, c/o Cordon Art, Baarn, Holland; pp. 173, 180, 249: Conklin, Monkmeyer Press Photo; p. 189: Scala/Art Resource, El Greco, *View and Plan of Toledo,* Toledo, Casa di El Greco; p. 206: Carey/The Image Works; p. 221: Bettmann Archive, p. 277; Rotker, Taurus; p. 299: © Berlinger/The Image Works; p. 328: Zimbel, Monkmeyer Press Photo; p. 371: Kagan, Monkmeyer Press Photo; p. 389: Heron, Monkmeyer Press Photo; p. 406: Ruben, Monkmeyer Press Photo.

Sponsoring Editor: Alan McClare
Project Editor: Jo-Ann Goldfarb
Text Design: Joan Greenfield Design
Cover Design: Edward Smith Design, Inc.
Text Art: Pamela J. Nilis; Fine Line Illustrations, Inc.
Photo Research: Mira Schachne
Production Manager: Jeanie Berke
Production Assistant: Beth Maglione
Compositor: ComCom Division of Haddon Craftsmen
Printer and Binder: R. R. Donnelley & Sons Company
Cover Printer: Phoenix Color Corp.

EFFECTIVE SECONDARY TEACHING: Going Beyond the Bell Curve

Library of Congress Cataloging in Publication Data

Quina, James.
    Effective secondary teaching : going beyond the bell curve / James Quina.
        p.   cm.
    Includes index.
    ISBN 0–06–045473–3
    1. High school teaching—United States.   I. Title.
    LB1737.U6Q56   1989   88–24530
    371.1'007'1273—dc19   CIP

88 89 90 91 9 8 7 6 5 4 3 2 1

In memory of my father and my mother

For years we have assumed that only a few in each class could be outstanding and that some must fail. We used the bell curve to describe the distribution of classroom achievement. Now we know that it is possible to go beyond the bell curve . . . possible for every student in every class to do outstanding work.

Peter Kline
Super-Accelerative-Learning Workshop
Wayne State University

Contents

Preface xv

PART ONE · DEFINITIONS, STANDARDS, AND TRENDS

■ **CHAPTER 1**

What Is Effective Teaching?   3

Teaching According to Sally, Mark, and John   4

Teacher Definitions of Effective Teaching   5

Dictionary Definitions of Effective Teaching   6

Professional Views of Effective Teaching   7

Recall of Ideal Teachers   8

Documentaries   10

Synthesis   11

■ **CHAPTER 2**

The High School Teacher Today: The Myth, The Reality, The Vision   15

Popular Views of Teaching   16

Realities of Teaching   16

Academic Expectations   19

Minimum Competency Movement   20

The Dropout Problem   22

A Vision of Excellence   23

PART TWO · PLANNING

■ **CHAPTER 3**

Planning I: Defining Educational Values, Purposes, Goals, and Objectives   33

Purposes and Objectives   34

The Seven Cardinal Principles of Secondary Education   38

The Educational Policies Commission   40

Sources of Educational Purposes   41

■ **CHAPTER 4**

Planning II: Creating Effective Instructional Objectives/Cognitive Domain   44

Planning as Decision Making   45

Stating Objectives   46

Bloom's Taxonomy of Educational Objectives   52

Use of the Taxonomy   54

■ **CHAPTER 5**

Planning III: Creating Effective
Instructional Objectives/Affective
Psychomotor Domains   57

Feelings and Values in Learning   58
Affective Domain of Bloom's Taxonomy   59
Identifying Feelings and Values   61
Resistance to Affective Teaching   63
Relationships Between Domains   63
Stating Affective Objectives   65
The Fusion of Affect and Cognition   65
The Psychomotor Domain   66

■ **CHAPTER 6**

Planning IV: Designing Effective
Lesson Plans   70

Lesson Plan Format   71
The Same Format/Different Content   73

Some Alternative Formats for Lesson
Planning   84
Design Your Own Plan   88
A Teacher's View of Planning   88
Myths About Lesson Plans   90
Sources for the Lesson Plan   91
Course Syllabus: College Prep
Chemistry   92

■ **CHAPTER 7**

Creating Units and Courses   101

The Unit as Relationship   102
Science Sample Unit: Patterns of
Heredity   104
The Unit and the Course   109
Humanities Sample Unit: The
Crucible   112

PART THREE · INSTRUCTION AND EVALUATION

■ **CHAPTER 8**

Teaching Styles and Strategies   139

Traditional Methods   140
Nonverbal Methods   147
Questions as Method   154
Critical Thinking as a Method   155
Self-Instructional Packages   158
Games and Puzzles as Method   159
Integrative Approaches   161

■ **CHAPTER 9**

The Teacher and Technology   173

Instructional Technology Application: In a
Place Called School   175
Current and Future Teaching
Technology   181

■ **CHAPTER 10**

Multicultural Education for an Urban
Society   189

Values and Education   190
The Meaning of Culture   190
The Challenge of Unity Versus Cultural
Pluralism   192
Globalization of Culture   192
Multicultural Methods   194
Encounter Teaching   194
Fantasy and Cultural Exploration   196
Lesson Plan: A Fantasy of Culture Based
on Katherine Anne Porter's Maria
Concepcion   197
Lesson Plan: A Fantasy of Culture Based
on Gloria Naylor's The Women of
Brewster Place   202
Music and Culture   204

■ **CHAPTER 11**

Identifying Special Learning Problems   206

Diagnostic Categories   209

Your Role in the Special Education
Process   216

General Classroom Adaptations and
Procedures   217

■ **CHAPTER 12**

Metaphor as Method   221

Metaphor as a Way of Knowing   222

Root Metaphors in Science   227

Root Metaphors in Literature   231

Teaching Root Metaphor Suggestopedically   235

Rational Extension of Root Metaphor:
World Hypotheses   237

Lesson Plan: A Pluralistic Approach
Based on John Knowles's A Separate
Peace   237

Critical Pluralism   243

■ **CHAPTER 13**

Homework as Multiple Skills
Mastery   249

The Status of Homework   250

Purposes of Homework   251

Studying for Tests and Exams   255

The Homework Plan and Parents   259

Internalization of Broad Purpose   262

Homework as Expansion of Creativity   263

■ **CHAPTER 14**

Instructional Testing and
Evaluation   265

Test Development   266

Domain   266

Table of Specifications   267

Item Types   269

Supply and Completion Item Types   269

PART FOUR · MANAGEMENT SKILLS

■ **CHAPTER 15**

Motivation of Self and Student   277

Overcoming Resistance   278

Classroom Practices   281

Modeling   283

Vocation/Avocation: Selected Profiles   284

Teaching Self-Motivation   292

NLP and Motivation   293

Suggestopedic and Optimalearning
Approaches to Motivation   294

Individual Differences   296

■ **CHAPTER 16**

The Organized Teacher: Time
Management   299

Your Time-Management Habits   300

Goals for the Week, Month, and Year   302

Daily Objectives   303

Working Faster   303

Using Wait Time   304

Overcoming Blocks   304

Organizing Your Work Space   304

Creating Projects   306

Systems That Support You   306

Eliminating Work: The Art of Delegating   306

Increasing Energy Sources   307

Create Your Own Time-Savers   307

Effective Communication   308

■ **CHAPTER 17**

Communication as a Rhetoric of
Inquiry   311

Communication and Teaching   312

Conference Planning and Preparation   317

General Guidelines for
  Conferencing   322

■ CHAPTER 18
Classroom Management   328

Assertive Discipline   329
Behavior Modification   332
Operant Conditioning   334
Reality Therapy   335
Cooperative Learning/Control Theory   336
Use of Humor as Behavioral Control   337
Organizational Strategies   340

Suggestopedic Integrative Learning, and
  Optimalearning Techniques   342
Synthesis: A Teacher's View   344

■ CHAPTER 19
Stress Management for Teachers   351

Physiological Basis of Stress   352
Reducing Stress in the Environment   355
Contextual Shifts   356
Stress Reduction for Teachers and
  Students   356
The Control of Stress   365

PART FIVE · PROFESSIONAL DEVELOPMENT

■ CHAPTER 20
Getting Hired   371

Preparing for Employment   372
Substitute Teaching   374
Preparing a Resume   375
The Audio-Video Portfolio   384
The Interview   386

■ CHAPTER 21
Legal Rights and Responsibilities   389

Teachers' Legal Responsibilities to
  Students   390
Jurisdiction of School Authorities   391
Records and Freedom of Information   392
Search and Seizure   393
Educational Malpractice: Fact or Fallacy?   395
Teachers, Schools, and Boards of
  Education   397
Legal-Risk Management   398
Due Process and Equal Protection   399

Teachers and the Collective Bargaining
  Process   401
Future Perspectives   403

■ CHAPTER 22
Professional Goals and Development   406

Areas of Professional Development   407
Professional Well-Being   407
Setting Professional Goals   408
Exploring Current Methods   409
Professional Reading   409
Professional Organizations   409
Professional Conferences, Workshops, and
  Seminars   410
Networking   410
Study Grants   412
Committee Work   412
Self-Assessment Instruments   412
Ethical Issues   414
Motivational Workshops and Tapes   415

Appendix A: Teaching to the Whole Brain 419
Appendix B: Music for Learning and Teaching 436

Appendix C: Instrumentation of Bloom's Taxonomy: Cognitive and Affective Domains 446

Appendix D: Self-Management Charts 452

Glossary 455

Bibliography 467

Name Index 481

Subject Index 484

Preface

Effective Secondary Teaching: Going Beyond the Bell Curve is an introductory text-book for secondary teaching. It is both a teaching text and a reference to support teachers during their first years of teaching.

The underlying philosophy of this text is pluralistic and stresses multiple modes of knowing—the quantitative and the qualitative, the left brain and the right brain, the cortical and the subcortical, the formistic and the contextual, the mechanistic and the organic, the theoretical and the practical, the analytic and the synthetic. The aim of this philosophy is to promote excellence in all its forms. To carry this out, the beginning teacher is invited to go beyond the bell curve, a metaphor for breaking out of the limits of linear thinking.

One can go beyond the bell curve in many ways—by taking individual differences seriously, thereby refusing to pigeonhole students in convenient categories; by staying open to the possibilities of new modes of evidence; and by using whatever means available to bring forth the experience and practice of excellence for all students.

Today's schools place broad and varied demands on new teachers. National and local legislation now mandates training in the teaching of the early adolescent, the handicapped, and the culturally diverse. The demand for computer literacy is but part of a much larger cultural mandate—that teachers take leadership in high-tech literacy.

New teachers will enter schools in the wake of an accountability movement that now demands increased skill not only in planning, but also in all stages of instructional delivery and evaluation. At the same time, the schools are under attack for emphasizing skills at the expense of content. Writers like Allan Bloom and E. D. Hirsch and national commissions like that of the Carnegie Foundation press for a return to a strong academic foundation. This text provides strategies for meeting such demands. Throughout, a variety of methods is illustrated with examples from the arts and the sciences.

Recent developments in brain research and the cognitive sciences have spawned new methods that are no longer based on simple behavioral models of human learning. Traditional methods can now be used in concert with new technologies or transformed into new ways of teaching and managing. Appendix A, "Teaching to the Whole Brain," provides a summary of the new research and its application to teaching. This research and methodology are used throughout the text. Appendix A may be studied in its own right or used as an augmentative supplement to relevant chapters.

Many people contributed to the development of this book. Chapters written by specialists have been provided to meet specific needs: Chapter 9, "The Teacher and Technology," by John W. Childs, addresses the need for training in high-tech literacy. Chapter 10, "Multicultural Education for an Urban Society," written with Rodolfo Martinez and Ricardo Marin Ibañez, provides a methodology for increasing awareness of cultural diversity and appreciation of differences in cultural values. Minority views and modes of behavior of blacks and Hispanics are addressed in the context of global culture and multiple values. Chapter 11, "Identifying Special Learning Problems," by Paula Wood, spells out specific guidelines for working with mainstreaming. Chapter 14, "Instructional Testing and Evaluation," by Donald Marcotte, explores both the creative and scientific aspects of test design; Chapter 17, "Communication as a Rhetoric of Inquiry," by Mary C. Furlette, examines techniques of conflict resolution and effective conferencing with students, teachers, parents, and administrators. Chapter 21, "Legal Rights and Responsibilities," by Joseph Wright, contains practical legal guidelines and references for the new teacher.

I am indebted to my graduate and undergraduate students and to their diligent work in the field and in the classroom—work that gave me a concrete, practical, and living dimension to the methods developed in this text. Some methods are adaptations from SALT (Society for Accelerative Learning and Teaching), the Lozanov Learning Institute, and the Barzak Educational Institute. Others were created and used regularly in classrooms throughout the inner-city schools of Detroit and the suburbs. To the many teachers and students, too numerous to mention by name, who made valuable contributions to this work, my sincere thanks.

Without the thoughtful efforts of the following reviewers, this book would not have been possible:

> Burton Boxerman, University of Missouri–St. Louis
> Anne Lally, University of Missouri–St. Louis
> James Migaki, Washington State University
> Frank Olson, Pacific Lutheran University
> Fred Rodriquez, University of Kansas
> Richard Schwab, University of New Hampshire
> Ed Smith, Longwood College
> Dale Young, Texas Christian University

I would also like to thank Alan McClare, Donald Hadd, and Jo-Ann Goldfarb of Harper & Row for their suggestions and encouragement.

Special thanks go to Harun-Ur Rashid of the Philosophy Department at Wayne State University, who made a substantial contribution to Chapter 8, "Teaching Styles and Strategies"; and to James Hand, Assistant Dean of Medical Education, University of Illinois, who provided me with current research on the brain and learning and made significant contributions to Appendix A, "Teaching to the Whole Brain." Sallyann Poinsett's and Bill Hammond's "Managing in the Information Age: Whole Brain Approaches" provided direction for linking theory and practice. Ivan Barzakov, Peter

Kline, and Ocie Woodyear supplied valuable information on suggestology and suggestopedia. Ivan Barzakov, Barzak Educational Institute, San Rafael, California, was the chief consultant on Georgi Lozanov's theories and on the technical skills of suggestology and optimalearning.

I am thankful to Pamela Nilis for illustrating the entire book. I thank Janet Bobby, Mary C. Furlette, and Jeanette H. Piccirelli for reading the manuscript and making useful editorial suggestions.

Finally, I want to thank those who stood by me throughout the project—my sister and brother-in-law, A. F. Parker and T. A. Parker, and my dear and trusted friends Otis Nelson and Sharon Carlton.

James Quina

P A R T O N E

Definitions, Standards, and Trends

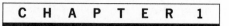
What Is Effective Teaching?

A model of excellence: Annie Sullivan teaching Helen Keller.

Teaching is an applied science derived from research in human learning and human behavior: an applied science that utilizes the findings of psychology, neurology, sociology, and anthropology. The science of teaching is based on cause-effect relationships... Teaching... is the constant stream of professional decisions that affect the probability of learning: decisions that are made and implemented before, during, and after interaction with the student.

—Madeline Hunter

Teaching, like all other forms of human interface with environmental phenomena, is a dynamic interaction between both exterior and interior forces—the exterior world of the classroom and the interior world of the teacher. Teaching is an inseparable science/art alliance, which is unified only when the ultimate reality without is identical to the reality within. It is that search for unity that transcends either the art or the science.

—Arthur L. Costa

Literature and science are replete with statements about teaching. Most everyone beyond school age has experienced being taught and will voice an opinion on teaching. But what is it, really? And what constitutes good teaching? In short, what is effective teaching?

A clue here is that our answer may depend on whom we ask, so let us ask a variety of persons. After all, if teaching is to become our chosen profession, it only makes good sense to find out what we are getting ourselves in for and formulate an accurate idea of what constitutes effective teaching. Isn't this reasonable? Let us begin our survey with high school students themselves. These are the people we are purportedly going to teach. What do they say teaching is? What do they say good teaching is?

Teaching According to Sally, Mark, and John

Students in both senior and junior high schools in western and midwestern states were asked the question "What makes a good teacher?" Here are some of their responses:

1. They help you individually. Some are really nice.
2. They are clear. You can understand them.
3. They know their subject and are willing to explain things . . .
4. They have control of their class.
5. They show that they care.
6. They are fair.
7. They have a sense of humor; they are not so straight-faced.
8. They can explain things in different ways.
9. They are firm, but not too strict.

10. They know your parents
11. They make learning fun.
12. They help you individually.
13. They are good disciplinarians.
14. They don't have to discipline; the students behave on their own volition.
15. They teach relevant topics.
16. They make the class interesting.
17. They are willing to explain assignments.

Some themes emerged again and again. Discipline was a recurrent theme. The full continuum showed up—from students who rejected discipline to those who rated it as the supreme virtue of a teacher. Many students attempted a distinction between class control and harshness or punitive teacher behavior—"You have to be smart but cool!"—and between being friendly at the expense of losing control: "When you goof around a little that's fine, but when they want business to get done—you work."

PROBE Review the list of responses and write a composite definition of effective teaching that represents the students' point of view.

The research of Kounin indicates that high school students value a highly organized teacher—not in the sense of being rigid, but in the sense of knowing what he or she is about moment by moment.[1] Preparedness, a sense of order, and what Kounin calls "withitness" (an awareness of everything going on in the class) rated high on his list for excellence in teaching.[2] Can you see a relationship between Kounin's findings and the students' responses above?

Teacher Definitions of Effective Teaching

Let us now turn our attention to a consideration of what teachers themselves think constitutes effective instruction. Here is a sample list from teachers' responses in my university classes over a period of six years. Good teaching is:

1. A shared experience between students and the teacher
2. Imparting information and critical thinking skills to others
3. Facilitation of the learning process
4. Practicing the art of analyzing content and distributing the information to others
5. Guiding students to be critical thinkers and enabling them to evaluate their world
6. Conveying facts or information through a machine or person
7. The art of showing, sharing, and exploring aspects of life
8. Guidance designed to motivate students to use their full potential
9. Helping students to find knowledge within themselves
10. An art—a performing art

PROBE

1. Are there any commonalities here? Are some definitions too narrow? Some too broad?
2. Notice the definitions that are in conflict. Is one right; the other wrong? Or is it possible that the teachers are stressing different aspects of teaching?
3. A common definition of teaching is that it is a planned process resulting in a change of behavior for the student. Which of the listed teachers' definitions fit this description?
4. How many of the definitions assume that teaching is something which goes on in school?
5. And what about self-teaching? When Malcom X was in prison, he taught himself to read, and Aldous Huxley taught himself to play the piano during an interim of nearly total blindness. How could you rephrase one of the listed definitions (or your own) to account for such possibilities?
6. The Latin word for educate is *educare,* meaning "to bring up." Do any of the listed definitions echo this idea?

Dictionary Definitions of Effective Teaching

In working with these problems you may have noticed that in the process of defining teaching several other terms may be introduced, such as educate, instruct, and train. The *American Heritage Dictionary* makes these distinctions in its definitions of "teach":

1. To impart knowledge or skill; give instruction to
2. To provide knowledge of; instruct in
3. To cause to learn by example or experience
4. To advocate; preach

Synonyms are instruct, educate, tutor, train, school, discipline, and drill. These verbs mean to impart knowledge or skill. *Teach* is the most widely applicable since it can reflect any such act of communicating. *Instruct* usually suggests methodical direction in a specific subject or area. *Educate* is comprehensive and implies a wide area of learning, achieved either by experience or, more often, by formal instruction in many subjects. *Tutor* usually refers to private instruction of one student or a small group. *Train* generally implies concentration on particular skills intended to fit a person or sometimes an animal for a desired role. *School* and *discipline* now usually refer to training in modes of behavior. *School* often implies indoctrination, not necessarily in an unfavorable sense, and an arduous learning process. *Discipline* usually refers to teaching control, especially self-control. *Drill* implies rigorous instruction or training, often by repetition of a routine.

Even with all of these distinctions there is one major distinction we have not made and that is the distinction between teaching (whatever it is) and "good" teaching. Since this entire text is an exploration of excellence in teaching, it will not be defined at the outset. Rather, we will engage in a *quest* for effective teaching. That quest begins with this chapter. You have already seen how teaching is multifaceted. When you try to define it, you discover that it is related to many other concepts.

PROBE   Look up definitions of "effective" and "good" in *Webster's New International Dictionary* and *The Oxford English Dictionary.* How will you determine which definition to apply? (See Figure 1.1.)

In this text we will explore communication, the effective use of time, planning, handling stress, styles and methods of instruction, uses of computers, and even legal responsibilities—all as they relate to effective teaching.

Professional Views of Effective Teaching

Let us now turn our attention to professional educators to explore yet another dimension of what effective teaching may be like. We will find that the researchers whose ideas also influence educational policy are often at opposite ends of a theoretical spectrum. Madeline Hunter, Academic Ad-

Figure 1.1   The method of Socrates included attempts to define the good.

ministrator, University of California at Los Angeles, says that effective teaching is that

> constant stream of professional decisions that affect the probability of learning: decisions that are made and implemented before, during and after interaction with the student . . . Teaching involves factor-analyzing those goals into dependent and independent sequences of learning, diagnosing students to determine what each has achieved in that sequence, and employing psychological principles that contribute to the speed and effectiveness with which each student acquires new learning in those sequences. Both science and art are essential to effective teaching.[3]

This professional interpretation of effective teaching stresses conscious analysis of cause-and-effect relationships between the teacher's and the learner's behavior. In short, feedback is emphasized. Rational analysis is stressed. For example, Hunter argues that intuition in teaching is not replicable. Having once been used to create a good learning environment, it cannot be re-created in a new situation. In this sense, Hunter compares intuition to a sterile animal that cannot re-create itself. Contrast this view of what constitutes effective teaching with that of another prominent educator, Arthur L. Costa, Professor of Education, California State University, Sacramento.

> Teaching . . . is a synthesis, not a separation—a synthesis of the human mind's rational *and* intuitive capabilities. Neither is comprehended in the other, nor can either be reduced to the other. Both of them are necessary; supplementing one another for a fuller understanding of the realities of teaching and of learning. We need to transform our conception of teaching to encompass this dynamic interplay between mystical intuition and scientific analysis.[4]

Costa continues in his direct disagreement with Hunter by arguing that task analysis is a dated reductionist concept like the "smallest particle" concept of an outmoded physics. A modern scientific view would reveal teaching as a "complicated work: an infinite number of interactions between learning probabilities, teaching processes and environmental conditions."[5] In this view our present concepts of teaching are "too absolute, too rational, too aggressive." What is needed, according to Costa, is less yang (absolute, rational, aggressive) and more yin (intuitive, sensuous, subtle) to "bring back a delicate balance. Children might then learn those other basics: the wholeness and unity of existence—the art of living in harmonious balance with nature and with each other."

We have in the foregoing summaries two diametrically opposed views of what constitutes effective teaching, both presented by respected educators. Do you favor one interpretation over the other? Can you envision possibilities not presented in these views?

Recall of Ideal Teachers

This kind of conflict provides us with yet another clue in our investigation—that definitions of teaching are reflections of broader assumptions about human beings and the nature of reality. As we move through this book, you are asked to note

Many persons in the 1960s thought that Montessori schools provided an ideal form of teaching.

that many educators hold to a "scientific" view of evidence, others to a "rational" view, and still others to an "experimental" view. You as a person electing to become an educator are encouraged to formulate your own views. As a matter of fact, where are you right now in respect to defining effective teaching?

PROBE   Recall your own high school experience. Think back to a time when you were learning at a very productive level. Perhaps ideas were flooding your mind and you were making connections in rapid fire. Perhaps you quietly worked your way through a problem and suddenly with a flash of insight solved the problem. Perhaps you had immediate recall of the facts or principles you needed to solve the problem or to create a more interesting problem. Perhaps it was none of these ways. Only you know how learning was for you when you were very productive and really enjoyed it. Recall that now. (Give yourself 5–10 minutes.) Now visualize the teacher who provided the background for this experience. Imagine that you see that teacher and zero in on him or her. What specifically is the teacher doing that makes learning work for you? Notice the teacher's behavior very carefully. What does the teacher say? How does the teacher respond to students in general? To you? What is the total environment like? Now get clearly in your mind the qualities, behavior, style, and approaches that you think contributed to your learning experience. When you have done this, make a list of those characteristics and/or behaviors and from this list create a definition of effective teaching.

Documentaries

The preceding process of recall is yet another way to get a handle on what constitutes excellence in teaching. It is a personal look at what effective teaching is. But perhaps there are other ways of discovering what it is from what it looks like. Aside from specific behaviors associated with effective teaching are there certain attitudes, certain contextual qualities inherent in good teaching that are readily recognizable? Consider the following documentary interpretation of effectiveness from a study of American high schools conducted by President Ernest L Boyer of the Carnegie Foundation for the Advancement of Teaching:

> Rosemont High School is a large suburban high school in the Northeast. When you walk through the halls during class periods and peer through open doors, students are attentive and busy. Most teachers feel confident enough to leave their doors open. The educational setting seems lively—and highly assessable. Teachers share ideas with other teachers and often work together on curriculum projects across disciplines. Teachers here have a shared sense of purpose . . .
>
> At Rosemont, there are many types of teachers with many different styles of teaching. A typing class is energetically engaged in pounding the keys, working against a teacher's stopwatch. In a physics laboratory, small groups of students work collectively on an experiment, while the teacher circulates around the room offering encouragement and clarification. Students in a U.S. history class lead a lively discussion, with the teacher in the background.[6]

Boyer goes on to comment on the total environment—on the absence of bells, for example:

> The visitor at Rosemont is surprised not to hear the harsh sound of bells signaling the beginning and end of class periods. Despite the absence of bells, classes start on time. Rosemont students show surprise when asked about the lack of bells. Says one, in mock alarm, "This isn't a prison, you know! We're not Pavlov's dogs!"[7]

Classrooms at Rosemont are also free of noise:

> . . . . In a reading class for those with learning disabilities the room is noiseless as students work individually at their seats. The teacher insists upon quiet and helps students focus on their assignments. When their attention wanders, she directs them back to the task; when they become discouraged and begin to turn off, she supports them and re-engages them in their work.[8]

And there are the star teachers:

> . . . The Constitutional History teacher who has developed an innovative curriculum using primary sources and original documents . . . ; an English teacher who has developed a course called "The Art of the Essay" in which students write and critique each other's work. . . . In an American Literature class . . . the discussion is on *Death of a Salesman;* the focus is on Willie's decision to commit suicide, and the teacher encourages students to talk to one another rather than direct all their comments to her.[9]

When one girl holds back, the teacher says, "Assert yourself . . . get in there . . . you have something to say." When the conversation loses direction, the teacher says: "We have a whole lot of separate ideas on the floor. Let's take a few minutes and sort them out . . . If you can't remember anyone's ideas except your own, you haven't been listening . . . I have heard at least fifteen explanations for Willie's suicide. See if you can reconstruct it."[10]

The teacher then asks the students to reflect on some very hard questions: "What happens when a dream you've lived by turns out to be a lie? How do you feel about that? Or are you too young?" The students respond:

> "People shouldn't circle their lives around one idea."
> "But it is not just one idea, it is their whole reason for being."
> "There is always a danger in being too committed, too closed. You don't have to die with one ideal."[11]

The teacher, says Boyer, encourages the struggle. She wants them to struggle with profound determination to recognize Willie's pain. She does not direct them toward a tidy conclusion.

PROBE Review the section just quoted, noting the qualities and the behaviors Boyer alludes to that constitute effectiveness. Make a list of the qualities and behaviors and include them in a definition of effective teaching.

| Synthesis |

Many educators argue that the curriculum of the high school needs complete reorganization, that no matter how effective methods are, they will do no good if we are not teaching worthwhile content. Allan Bloom, in *The Closing of the American Mind,* urges that university teachers return to the primary mission of the university—the search for truth. If Bloom is correct, the supermarket curriculum found in high schools throughout the nation is but symptomatic of the malaise that infects all education on a grand scale.

Extreme relativism, cynicism, loss of innocence, and loss of the quest for what is good in life can only be remedied, says Bloom, by a return to a serious study of the humanities (Plato, Shakespeare, perhaps the Great Books) and to a practice of the rational principles embodied in the Declaration of Independence and the Constitution. This would mean more rigorous liberal arts requirements for teachers.

In *Cultural Literacy* E. D. Hirsch says high school graduates have lost the ability to communicate via a common language—a language based on a knowledge of history, science, and literature. Our youth can no longer be expected to comprehend written or spoken allusions to "fighting windmills," "Grant and Lee," "free and indivisible," "There is a tide in the affairs of men . . . ," "Big Ben," "Gone with the wind," and many other cultural references. Hirsch says these are but samples of basic knowledge that every American should possess to be able to read a newspaper or a mainstream book intelligently. And yet we can no longer depend on high school graduates to comprehend these allusions. The solution, says Hirsch, is to return to a strong liberal arts curriculum in the schools: "We will be able to achieve a just and prosperous society only when our schools ensure that everyone commands enough shared background knowledge to be able to communicate effectively with everyone else."[12]

National commissions, such as the Carnegie Foundation and the Holmes Group, which set standards for the high schools and teacher education, also recommend a return to a strong content base for improving the quality of instruction. An old argument has returned in force: You can't separate good teaching from the teaching of good content. To attempt to do so results in teaching skills in a vacuum. And according to Hirsch this is precisely what has happened with the skills approach to teaching.

Neither Hirsch nor Bloom recommends a specific methodology for accomplishing their ends. How are students to be assessed to find out what they can learn and when? How are they to be motivated? Hirsch recommends memorization, but he does not say how memorization can be maximized or how memorized facts are to be integrated with concept formation, analysis, and judging. Bloom recommends a return to the classics, but he does not say what is going to revitalize students' interest in the classics—only that such study is desirable.

We have returned to the old debate of content versus method. Content without method is inert: method without content is vacuous. A linear approach to the problem suggests building a strong content foundation in the liberal arts, then studying pedagogical technique, psychology of education, curriculum development and philosophy of education. Finally, we apply what we know; we put the pieces together; we assemble. But how?

Consider, however, another possibility: a way of being that goes beyond a mere mechanical performance of teaching tasks and the dispensing of knowledge—a total way of engaging yourself which creates intended results. It is called being effective. No formula for action can produce effectiveness. Learning content, the skills of planning, instructional delivery, management, and professional decision making are but the seeds of teaching effectiveness. The effective teacher transforms knowledge and skill into a personal synthesis. This takes commitment to a personal vision. In the process of studying and exploring the content of this text, you are invited to develop a personal vision of teaching, to create your own personal synthesis—to transform the seeds.

■ *SUMMARY*

The purpose of this chapter is to engage you in an intellectual and experiential quest—the quest for excellence in teaching. What is it? What are its discernible characteristics and how do teachers behave when they are being effective. We can examine the definitions of what teaching is, or should be when it is effective, according to students, teachers, and researchers in education. And yet we must realize that expert knowledge is preconditioned by the philosophical bias of the researcher—behaviorists will find behavioral evidence to support their descriptions and cognitivists will find cognitive evidence to support their claims. If we turn to a dictionary, we may discover current usage (but perhaps not even that if the dictionary is not current). We can turn back the clock, recall our memorable learning experiences—our effectiveness owing to the influence of a teacher—and we can look to a current description of excellent teaching in research literature, like Boyer's *High School.* Ultimately, you are thrown back on your own resources. Even if you use all of the foregoing modes of analysis and inquiry, you will still have to synthesize your own definition of effective teaching.

As you progress through this book, you are invited to develop a composite definition of effective teaching. You are encouraged to formulate your own definition and to take issue with the text as you develop your own vision of teaching effective-

"The process of mastery itself can be ecstatic, leading to delight that transcends mastery."—George Leonard.

ness. For now, you are left with a mountain to climb. Some educators hold that effective teaching is equivalent to mastery teaching—that is to say, if a teacher's goal is to teach you to drive a car so well that you score 100 percent on the state drivers' exam, then your mastery of the exam is evidence of excellence in teaching. Or if a teacher's purpose is to teach you to play *Moonlight Sonata* on the piano, and you play it flawlessly with the exact timing and technique which you were taught, then you will have achieved mastery and the teaching that brought this about is called effective. And if you are taught certain techniques of mountain climbing and you do them exactly as you were taught, then the teaching that resulted in your performance is said to be effective. But when you are in the midst of climbing that mountain, when you are thousands of feet up and out over the edge, the following quotation from George Leonard's *Education and Ecstasy* may be more relevant to your experience of the performance: "The process of mastery itself can be ecstatic, leading to delight that transcends mastery."[13]

■ *NOTES*

1. J. Kounin, *Discipline and Group Management in the Classroom* (New York: Holt, Rinehart & Winston, 1970).
2. Ibid.
3. Madeline Hunter, "Knowing Teaching and Supervising," in *Using What We Know About Teaching,* ed. Philip L. Hosford (Alexandria, VA: Association for Supervision and Curriculum Development, 1984), 169–170.
4. Arthur L. Costa, "A Reaction to Hunter's Knowing Teaching and Supervising" in *Using What We Know About Teaching,* ed. Philip L. Hosford (Alexandria, VA: Association for Supervision and Curriculum Development, 1984), 202.
5. Ibid., 198.
6. Ernest L. Boyer, *High School: A Report on Secondary Education in America* (New York: Harper & Row, 1983), 130.
7. Ibid., p. 150.
8. Ibid., p. 130.
9. Ibid., 151.
10. Ibid., 151.
11. Ibid., 152.
12. E. D. Hirsch, Jr., *Cultural Literacy: What Every American Needs to Know* (Boston: Houghton Mifflin, 1987), 32.
13. George Leonard, *Education and Ecstasy* (New York: Delacorte, 1968), 18.

CHAPTER 2

The High School Teacher Today: The Myth, The Reality, The Vision

Teacher lining up students.

*Teaching . . . is . . . honored and disdained, praised as "dedicated service,"
lampooned as "easy work" . . . Teaching from the inception in America has
occupied a special but shadowed social standing . . . Real regard shown for those
who taught has never been matched by professed regard.*

—Dan Lortie

Popular Views of Teaching

Between 1969 and 1981 the number of parents who said they would like their sons or daughters to become teachers dropped from 75 percent to 46 percent.[1] In the 1980 Nationwide Teacher Opinion Poll conducted by the National Education Association (NEA), 71 percent of the teachers said that the negative attitude of the public toward teachers had an adverse effect on their job satisfaction.[2]

The schools are attacked from many quarters—from "governors and state capitols, from dozens of state and local school boards, from hundreds of citizen task forces, from attention-getting reports of national agencies, from foundation-supported studies, and even from the Oval Office."[3] Each group has its own conception of excellence and how it is to be obtained. Meanwhile, the high school, in particular, is floundering and the teacher is blamed for much of what is wrong. Teachers are regarded by many as a passive, generally uninteresting group of people, who tend to "score below their peers in other programs on standardized academic achievement tests and to rank comparatively low in their high school graduating classes."[4] They are often viewed as drifters who become teachers because it is a convenient way station on the path to some other career. And to add insult to injury, many people hold the view that teachers have soft, undemanding jobs—that, after all, all they do is teach! As one parent put it: "I'm not sure what they have to complain about. After all, it's an easy life. The hours are good—nine to three—and you get the summer off."[5]

Realities of Teaching

The realities of teaching are quite different. The teacher has many responsibilities other than teaching. Let's note some of them.

In additions to teaching five to six classes per day, most American high school teachers do the following:

1. Review subject matter
2. Prepare lesson plans, some of which must be reviewed by an administrator
3. Correct and grade papers
4. Make out report cards
5. Counsel students
6. Sometimes perform menial tasks, supervise lunch rooms, police hallways, and chaperone students
7. Sometimes teach classes outside their specialty
8. Keep elaborate student attendance records

9. Make written reports to counselors
10. Call parents by telephone and send letters to parents
11. Keep current in their field of specialization
12. Strive to meet expected standards in three areas: content, methodology, and evaluation
13. Assess level of student ability and knowledge
14. Teach without textbooks
15. Have only 54 minutes of in-school preparation time
16. Teach in a context of physical violence—in the halls, parking lots, and even the classrooms
17. Often go unrewarded for creative ideas
18. Often work without recognition rewards
19. Work for salaries not comparable to starting salaries in other professions
20. Often resort to moonlighting to make ends meet—selling tickets, ice cream, babysitting, waiting tables
21. Engage in curriculum planning
22. Arrange for guest speakers
23. Collect money for various funds
24. Represent the school at community meetings
25. Sponsor plays, concerts, and assemblies
26. Hold parent conferences
27. Participate in PTA meetings
28. Chaperone students at dances
29. Work with the athletic program—selling tickets, supervising, and so on
30. Supervise safety regulations
31. Maintain standards of cleanliness and order in their classrooms
32. Report all cases of suspected child abuse to the proper authority

In some schools the teacher by contract does not have to perform menial tasks like hall and cafeteria duty; yet, having to do so is by no means an unusual condition. Most teachers work in a context involving some combination of these noninstructional expectations.

As Ernest Boyer reports in his book *High School,* many teachers receive so much disrespect in public that they often conceal the fact that they teach. Here are the statements of three teachers.

Teacher A:

I go places around town collecting items for my various courses and I'm almost embarrassed to say that I'm a teacher. It's people's view of teachers as goof-offs—that they get the summer off—that really hurts.

Teacher B:

I work as a meat cutter in the summer at one of the nearby butcher shops, and I don't usually tell them I'm a teacher. One butcher finally found out that I was a full-time teacher and his comment to me was, "Man, that's a dead-end job. You must be a real dummy."

Teachers often perform noninstructional and supervisory duties.

Teacher C:

Weekends I wait on tables at a sandwich shop to make extra money, but I don't tell anyone that I'm a teacher. They talk a lot about the school district and have only negative attitudes toward the schools. When I listen to them, it makes me feel really small to be a teacher.[6]

PROBE Make a list of judgments you have heard about the work of teachers. What was your reaction to those statements?

Academic Expectations

What do Americans think about the job high schools are performing? How would they grade the schools? A 1974 Gallup Poll showed that 18 percent of those polled gave the schools an A, and 6 percent gave them a D. In 1982, only 8 percent gave the schools an A and those giving a D grew from 6 to 14 percent.[7]

How accurate are these assessments? Scholastic Aptitude Tests are taken by one-third of all high school graduates. The Scholastic Aptitude Test, or SAT, as it is commonly called, is a multiple-choice test that was originally designed to predict students' ability to do college work. It is not designed to measure how much students have learned in high school; its purpose is to measure aptitude, not knowledge per se. Nevertheless, the SAT is now used as a yardstick for rating the effectiveness of high schools across America.[8]

The SAT results in recent years have been bad. Ernest Boyer reports that "between 1952 and 1982 the average score on the verbal section of the SAT fell 50 points, from 476 to 426."[9]

In 1975, an investigative panel identified some of the possible causes of the downswing of the SAT scores: (1) absenteeism, (2) automatic promotion, (3) reduced homework, (4) lowered textbook standards, (5) decreasing emphasis on writing, (6) changes in family structure, (7) television-viewing habits, and a host of other factors.[10]

Another major college entrance test is designed by the American College Testing Program (ACT). This test measures predictive ability in English, use of mathematics, the social sciences, and the natural sciences. High school students across the country have fared no better on ACT scores over the past decade than they have on the SAT. Mean scores for English, mathematics, social studies, and science all dropped significantly between 1970 and 1976. Between 1976 and 1982 the ACT scores on mathematics again dropped significantly.[11]

The National Assessment of Educational Programs (NAEP) surveyed student achievement in ten subject areas: art, career and occupational development, citizenship, literature, mathematics, music, reading, science, social studies, and writing. The results of the NAEP test show that simple computational skills in mathematics have slightly improved, but that inferential skills have been declining over a 10-year period.[12]

A similar pattern emerges in English, with the scores in reference skills—locating information—improving slightly, whereas the scores for comprehending the *implications* of textual material has dropped during the 10-year period.[13]

The United States did not fare well on comparative tests in a 12-nation study (1973–1977) comparing scores of 13- and 18-year-olds in seven subjects: mathematics, science, reading comprehension, literature, English and French as foreign languages, and civic education.[14] The U.S. high school students scored in the lowest one-third in reading comprehension. In mathematics, U.S. students scored lowest among the nations tested, while the Israeli, Japanese, German, and French students scored in the top one-third.[15]

Ernest Boyer says in *High School* that comparative interpretation of these scores is misleading since one is comparing a small number of students in Sweden and Germany, for example, with a large number of students in the United States. In Sweden 45–50 percent complete the *gymnasium* (grades 11 and 12), and in the Federal Republic of Germany only about 13 percent are enrolled in the *Oberprimarer,* the equivalent of our high school. In the United States about 75 percent of our youth complete high school.[16]

Torsten Husen of the University of Stockholm, Sweden, directed the leadership of the large-scale comparative tests. He points out that the top students in Europe and the U.S. vary little:

> The top 5 percent and 10 percent at the end of secondary education (i.e., the elite) tended to perform at nearly the same level in both comprehensive and selective systems of secondary education. Thus the elite among high school seniors did not differ considerably in their performance from their age-mates in France, England or Germany.[17]

But even if this is the case, should Americans take consolation in excellence for the elite? What has happened to the American ideal of equal opportunity and the possibility of excellence for all American youth? Paul Copperman, an educational analyst, has pointed out that "for the first time in the history of our country, the educational skills of one generation will not surpass, will not equal, will not even approach, those of their parents."[18] The sobering fact is that the average graduate of our schools and colleges today is "not as well-educated as the average graduate of 25 or 35 years ago, when a much smaller proportion of our population completed high school and college."[19]

Minimum Competency Movement

One attempt to stem this tide, remedy this situation, and ensure the maintenance of certain standards for high school graduates was the institution of minimum competency testing in the 1970s.

The minimum competency movement subscribes to the teaching and testing of basic skills so as to warrant that students who graduate from the public schools have learned those skills. This approach to education is not unique to this era. The 1920s also saw such a movement. At that time, "there was an intense concern with practical outcomes, with minimally essential and basic skills, and with testing."[20] In many school systems, " 'efficient' education came to be identified too closely with 'good' education and broader perspectives were "submerged in the concern with budgets and short-term 'results'."[21] Many would argue that a similar atmosphere exists in the back-to-basics movement of today. Indeed, Charles Cooper believes that high income and property taxes have caused middle-class property owners to insist that their current assessments should be sufficient and, rather than additional assessments, their educational tax dollars should be used more efficiently.[22]

The current minimum competency movement had its inception in the 1970s. At that time, the term accountability became popular and management-by-objectives–type programs were adopted.[23] The origins of the minimum competency/accountability movement are found in the industrial management approach, which emphasizes output and measures of output.[24] Thus the shift toward criterion-referenced testing began. An educational pattern was set in motion: "The pattern of instructional and program design became fixed: the definition of goals and objectives was followed by some form of treatment or program changes which were followed in turn by evaluation (testing)." In fact, "criterion-referenced, objective tests in the basic skills of reading, writing, and mathematics became the order of the day."[25]

During the 1970s, states such as Florida, Arizona, and New York mandated minimum competency testing for high school graduation. By the summer of 1984, "forty states were actively pursuing some form of minimum competency testing."[26]

The minimum competency movement has resulted in great abuse. To create the illusion that high percentages of students are meeting minimum standards, the standards themselves have been lowered to barely literate levels. Another abuse is the short-circuiting of the whole process by teaching *to* the test itself instead of the knowledge on which the test is based. The lowest possible common denominator is often selected as a standard.

In addition, there are measurement problems inherent in the very concept of minimal competency. What does minimum competency mean? As James Mecklenberger asks, is there "one kind for all, at minimum? Or is there a variety of educational experiences and outcomes that are acceptable?" He asks if there is "a minimum for every child or a minimum for all children?" And he asks the basic question, "What are competencies?"[27]

PROBE

1. How do you account for the recent decline in standards of high school students?

2. If you were setting standards for high school students, how would you decide what high school students should know or be able to do?

3. *American Heritage Dictionary* defines competence as "skill or ability."[28] Which skills or abilities would you include as standards for high school graduates? Why?

4. *Competent* is defined as "properly or well qualified; capable; adequate for the purpose; suitable, sufficient."[29] How does one decide the adequacy of the skill level for high school students? If competent is "adequate for the purpose," then what purpose?

The Dropout Problem

The graduation rate in large urban school districts is incredibly low:

> . . . in New York City, only 56.4 percent of the ninth graders go on to graduate; in Boston, 52.2 percent; in Chicago, 43.5 percent, in Detroit, 33.5 percent. To those who reply that a significant part of these figures represent transfers to other school districts, there is the question of why there is little similar evidence of transfers in the lower grades. It is clear that a significant proportion of these figures are made up of dropouts.[30]

For minorities the problem is even more severe. National reports indicate over 50 percent dropout rates for blacks and Hispanics. One report on urban high schools cited "a dropout rate of 80 percent for Puerto Rican and 85 percent among Native Americans."[31] Even more alarming are the data showing that not merely marginal students are dropping out; students who are dropping out perform at least as well as those who remain in school.

In her article, "Perspectives on Inequality: Voices from Urban Schools," Michelle Fine reports that in the fall of 1981 and the spring of 1982 a sample of students in alternative schools in the South Bronx completed a questionnaire including the factors of (1) attributions for success or failure, (2) levels of depression, (3) perceptions of inequality, and (4) willingness to challenge justice.[32] All students answering this questionnaire had either dropped out of a traditional high school or had been expelled at least once prior to 1981. Follow-up analyses were conducted in May of 1982 "to distinguish who graduated with a Graduate Equivalency Diploma, who dropped out of school, and who remained in school."[33] The results were surprising:

> The students who dropped out were, in the fall survey, most likely to name injustice in their social lives and at school, and most ready to correct it by challenging a teacher. Of all the students, those who dropped out were the least depressed and had attained academic levels equivalent to students who remained in school.
>
> Students who remained in school—who neither graduated nor dropped out—were most depressed, least likely to challenge an unjust act by a teacher, and most likely to provide socially desirable responses on their surveys.[34]

The paradox is that those students who recognize social and economic injustice and are ready to challenge them are most likely to leave school. Conversely, the students most hesitant to challenge inequities are likely to remain in school. Fine's study raises a critical question: To what extent do schools "nurture dependent, noncritical perspectives in students and punish more critical analyses and challenging behavior?"[35]

These dropouts no longer see high school as a "legitimate means to a legitimate end."[36] Are we losing critically astute students—students who can perform academically, yet choose not to do so because they see beyond the surface curriculum and demand more than they are getting? Are we educating only the sheep? How many potential leaders are we missing?

PROBES National reports like *A Nation at Risk* challenged the country to raise educational standards, such as increased graduation standards and increased use of competency testing. If standards in high school were made more rigorous, what effect would this have on the dropout problem? Would more marginal students drop out? Would bright students experience a greater challenge and remain in school? If so, what kind of curriculum would this require?

A Vision of Excellence

How can the standards of the schools be improved while at the same time increasing students' motivation and commitment to learning? Amid all the failure, how can we create a vision of excellence? And if we wish to make excellence more than a mere ideal, how can we set forth a viable plan to attain and sustain it?

Throughout the 1970s, Philip L. Hosford, a curriculum specialist, asked hundreds of teachers and administrators to select the top objectives from the following:

1. Wise use of leisure time
2. Knowledge of world problems
3. Skill in the use of the three Rs
4. Improved self-concept
5. Sense of patriotism
6. Preparation for college
7. Desire for learning
8. Physical and mental health
9. Respect for others
10. Preparation for employment
11. Mathematical understanding
12. Spiritual and moral values[37]

The four top priorities selected by the educators were: (1) desire for learning, (2) improved self-concept, (3) skill in use of three Rs, and (4) respect for others. Hosford refers to these priorities as the silent curriculum. Very little attention is given to articulating these as goals and almost no attention is given to measuring them. Yet, when they are not present, when teachers do not promote these goals, teaching breaks down, and the teacher is often terminated. Hosford points out that most teachers are terminated because of deficiencies in human relations skills, not lack of knowledge of subject matter, for which they are often well qualified.[38] Nevertheless, there is now an urgent demand for increasing subject matter requirements.

Chapter 1 cited the recommendation of Allan Bloom and E. D. Hirsch to restructure the curriculum of both high schools and universities, to return to a strong foundation in content, specifically in the liberal arts—history, literature, science, and mathematics. Their recommendations gain support from reports of several national groups: the Holmes Group, the National Council for Accreditation of Teacher Education (NCATE), the Carnegie Foundation, and the American Educational Studies Association.

The Holmes Group, made up of deans of research universities throughout the United States, calls for an increase in breadth and depth of the academic training of teachers, requiring content specialization in an academic discipline at the undergraduate level and a focus on professional courses at the Master's level.[39] NCATE mandates special training in the areas of biculturalism, the gifted, and early adolescent development.

In the Carnegie Foundation Report, *High School,* Ernest Boyer outlines recommendations for a complete restructuring of the American high school. Some of the recommendations follow.

Goals

Goals should be established and should be shared by teachers, administrators and parents.

Goals should focus on common learning, preparation for the world of work and community service.

Centrality of Language

Clear writing and clear thinking should be ensured by providing intensive summer terms for deficient students. Speech communication should be taught in schools; listening skills should be emphasized. The school has a special obligation to teach skills of written and oral use of English.

The Core Curriculum

All fluff courses should be eliminated. All students should take a common core of rigorous study. In addition to a study of usual traditional subjects such as history, mathematics and science, "emphasis should also be given to foreign language, the arts, civics, non-Western studies, technology, the meaning of work, and the importance of health." The arts are to be seen as central, not as electives or enrichment courses.

Transitions

The high school should establish connections "with learning places beyond the schools—such as libraries, museums, art galleries, colleges and industrial laboratories."

Service

"All high school students will complete a service requirement in a new Carnegie unit"—which would be based on volunteer work in the community. This requirement would be fulfilled in the students' free time—weekends, summer vacation, evenings.

Teacher Renewal

The work condition of teachers must be improved including reduced loads and increased preparation time. Small seminars and directed studies should be options for providing individualized growth of students.

Teachers should be exempt from noninstructional duties such as monitoring of halls and lunchrooms.

National salaries of teachers should be increased by 25 percent beyond the rate of inflation.

Teachers should be given merit awards and sabbaticals.

Teacher Education

After completing a solid academic major, teachers will complete a fifth year in the following courses: Schooling in America, Learning Theory and Research, The Teaching of Writing, and Technology and Its Uses, Classroom Observation and Teaching Experience, small group seminars on the Relationship of Special Fields to Contemporary Political and Social Themes.

A travel fund should be established for teachers to attend conferences in their specialty.

The outstanding high school students should be given scholarships to enter the teaching profession.

Skilled professional persons in business and industry should be recruited into teaching on a part-time basis.

Schools should enter into partnerships with business and industry. Teachers and business and industry employees should trade jobs for a two-year period.

Instruction

Teachers should use a variety of teaching styles; clear standards should be stated and students should be accountable for their work.

Teachers should have a strong voice in designing and selecting curriculum material.

Technology

Schools should purchase computers or other expensive hardware on the basis of educational objectives; cable channels should be used districtwide.

All students should study technology, but not just how to operate computers, and also the impact of technology on modern life.

Flexibility

Small high schools should expand their offerings by using the services of mobile classrooms and part-time professionals to supplement their offerings.

Large high schools should organize into smaller units.

All high schools should develop special arrangements for the gifted.

Connections

The high school should be connected with the university. Advanced students should be encouraged to take parallel college credit.

The high school should be connected with the business community. Businesses should offer cash awards for outstanding teachers, enrichment programs in science and mathematics for gifted students, corporate grants to outstanding principals, and sponsorships of science laboratories.

Public Commitment

The schools do not exist in isolation. Everyone is responsible for their effectiveness—"citizens, local school boards, state agencies and legislatures, and federal government. A network of community coalitions—Citizens for Public Schools should be formed across the nation to give leadership in . . . public education."[40]

PROBE Review the above recommendations. How do these recommendations differ from those you have heard from parents, teachers, friends or business associates? With which recommendations do you agree? Disagree? Why?

The American Educational Studies sums up its recommendation for educational change in *Pride and Excellence: Schools of Excellence for All the People.* We have in this document a challenge for excellence in the context of democracy. The problem is vast. It is a challenge to our professed ideals of both democracy and excellence. As John Gardner asked in his book *Excellence,* can we have excellence and equality too? Here is the challenge:

American public schools can be regarded as excellent to the extent that they promote learning and foster communication in which students find incentives for intellectual labor. Without toughmindedness education is a joke; without humaneness, it is inert. A third requisite originates within our national traditions. Educational excellence in our country also demands that schools be inclusive in intent and in availability.[41]

What do you think the schools should become? And what are you willing to become to make it happen? Together, we shall explore some possibilities toward these ends.

■ *SUMMARY*

Schools are attacked from many quarters—government and national agencies, citizen task forces, and even the Oval Office. Public opinion of teachers varies from giving lip service to the stereotypical "dedicated teacher" to a view of teachers as "drifters" holding undemanding jobs.

The realities of teaching are quite different. Teachers must engage in countless hours of preparation outside the classroom and communicate with parents, counselors, administrators, and students in a variety of contexts. To be effective they must keep current with their field of content as well as with recent developments in methodology and evaluation. In addition, they are in many cases responsible for menial tasks such as monitoring halls and lunchrooms. They are not often rewarded for creative ideas or performances, and they are, as a group, compensated less than other professionals.

The scores on Scholastic Aptitude Tests (SAT) and the American College Testing Program (ACT) show progressively significant decreases from the 1950s through the 1980s. Mean scores for English, mathematics, social studies, and science all dropped significantly between 1970 and 1976. The National Assessment of Education Program (NAEP) indicates a recent decline of inferential skills. Internationally, U.S. high school students compare poorly with students of other countries in most academic disciplines. These scores may be misleading, however, when one considers that in the United States 75 percent of youths complete high school, while in Sweden, for example, only 45–50 percent do. In the Federal Republic of Germany only 13 percent are enrolled in the *Oberprimarer,* the equivalent of our high school.

Minimal competency testing, instituted in the 1970s to ensure high school standards, has resulted in great abuse, such as teaching geared to the test itself. Another problem with minimum competency testing is that educators cannot agree on what constitutes a competency and what constitutes a minimum.

Meanwhile, the dropout problem has become paramount, with the rate being as high as 50 percent for blacks and even higher for Hispanics and Native Americans. Even more alarming, many who drop out can perform as well as those who remain.

Educators like Hosford argue that to promote excellence we must address a broader base than content alone—we must address the hidden curriculum: desire for learning, improved self-concept, and respect for others. Hosford includes the three Rs, but feels that content is consciously recognized and valued. The other factors are not consciously addressed. We only hope they will improve, and they don't.

Writers like E. D. Hirsch and Allan Bloom call for stronger liberal arts requirements in the schools. The Holmes Group, the National Council for Accreditation of Teacher Education (NCATE), the Carnegie Foundation, and the American Educational Studies Association call for improvements in the high school curriculum and university curriculum. Some recommended changes are a four-year liberal arts degree in a content field for all teachers, with professional training of teachers carried out at the graduate level. The teacher would have special training in teaching the gifted and talented, in multicultural education, and in early adolescent development. The role of work and its relation to school would be emphasized both in the preparation of teachers and in high school. More integration between business and industry and the school would be built into the curriculum. The value of service would be stressed.

■ *NOTES*

1. Ernest L. Boyer, *High School* (New York: Harper & Row, 1983), 134.
2. Ibid.
3. Mary Anne Raywid, Charles A. Tesconi, Jr., and Donald R. Warren, *Pride and Promise: Schools of Excellence for All the People* (Burlington, VT: American Educational Studies Association, 1985), iv.
4. Ibid., 29.

5. Ernest L. Boyer, *High School* (New York: Harper & Row, 1983), 155.
6. Ibid., 163.
7. Ibid., 22.
8. Ibid., 24–26.
9. Ibid., 22.
10. Ibid., 24.
11. Ibid.
12. Ibid., 26.
13. Ibid.
14. Ibid., 23.
15. Ibid.
16. Ibid.
17. Torsten Husen, "Are Standards in U.S. Schools Really Lagging Behind Those in Other Countries?" *Phi Delta Kappan,* March 1983, 456.
18. Paul Copperman, in *A Nation at Risk,* 11.
19. Ibid.
20. Charles R. Cooper, "Competency Testing: Issues and Overview," in *Nature and Measurement of Competency in English,* ed. Charles R. Cooper (Urbana: NCTE, 1981), 10.
21. Ibid., 10.
22. Ibid.
23. Beverly Anderson and Chris Pipho, "State-Mandated Testing and the Fate of Local Control," *Phi Delta Kappan* 66(1984):210.
24. Cooper, 2.
25. Anderson and Pipho, 210.
26. Ibid.
27. "Bad Penny Again," *Phi Delta Kappan* 59(1978):698.
28. *American Heritage Dictionary* (Boston: Houghton Mifflin, 1969), p. 271.
29. Ibid.
30. Edward Simpkins and Dennis L. Gibson, Jr., "The High School Dropout Problem: Strategies for Reduction; a Report of the High School Dropout Prevention Network of Southeast Michigan" (Detroit: The High School Dropout Prevention Network of Southeastern Michigan, 1985), 6.
31. Ibid.
32. Michele Fine, "Perspectives on Inequity: Voices from Urban Schools" in *Applied Social Psychology Annual,* ed. Leonard Beckman (London: Sage Publications, 1983), 221–222.
33. Ibid., 221
34. Ibid., 222.
35. Ibid.
36. Ibid.
37. Philip L. Hosford, "The Art of Applying the Science of Education," in *Using What We Know About Teaching* (Alexandria, VA: Association for Supervision and Curriculum Development, 1984), 146–147.

38. Ibid., p. 147.
39. Ibid.
40. Judith Lanier, *Tomorrow's Teachers: A Report of the Holmes Group* (East Lansing, MI: The Holmes Group, Inc., 1986), 15.
41. Raywid, Tesconi, and Warren, *Pride and Promise: Schools of Excellence for All the People,* 29.

PART TWO

Planning

Planning I: Defining Educational Values, Purposes, Goals, and Objectives

Earth seen from the moon.

"Cheshire Puss," she began . . . "Would you tell me, please, which way I ought to go from here?"

"That depends a good deal on where you want to get to," said the Cat.

"I don't much care where—," said Alice.

"Then it doesn't matter which way you go," said the Cat.

"—so long as I get somewhere," *Alice added as an explanation.*

"Oh, you're sure to do that," said the Cat, "if you only walk long enough."

—Lewis Carroll

Purposes and Objectives*

Just as Alice is not particularly concerned with precisely where she wants to go, so, too, many teachers do not have clearly defined objectives for teaching their subject. They do not know precisely where they are going and yet, like Alice, feel compelled to go somewhere. And, as the Cheshire Cat states it, they are sure to get somewhere if they travel far enough.

Doing most anything will get one somewhere, but often it is not a very desirable place. In their explorations, teachers meet many "mad hatters" en route from one place to another, and they may wonder how it is that they keep running into them.

If you were to set out from Detroit to travel westward, you could start by traveling to Chicago. But it is still possible to travel farther westward. You could travel from Chicago to Nevada, from Nevada to California. But even then you would not have exhausted the possibility of traveling westward. From California you can travel to Hawaii, and from Hawaii you can continue to travel around the world, always heading westward. Your purpose is to travel westward, and it is the nature of purposes that you never run out of things to do to stay on track of them. Purposes are inexhaustible. Broad educational purposes are also inexhaustible (see Figure 3.1). If you set out to have your students follow the directions of one of the Seven Cardinal Principles of Secondary Education, they would never run out of possible things to do. Here is the principle:

> *Health.* Good health habits need to be taught and encouraged by the school. The community and the school should cooperate in fulfilling the health needs of all youngsters and adults.[1]

How many practices and attitudes can you think of that would constitute "good health habits"? Is your list complete? What if you compared it with the list of another person? Would all medical doctors agree on what constitutes good health practices? The point is that a principle or a purpose is abstract and therefore can be used as a basis for generating many objectives. Also, no standard of verification is stated. How do we know when the principle has been satisfied?

---

*The distinction between purposes and objectives is drawn from the work of Werner Erhard, founder of the est Training and The Forum. The example above is an educational adaptation of this distinction.

Figure 3.1 "Would you tell me please which way I ought to go from here?"

An objective, in contrast to a purpose, is stated in quantifiable terms. It is measurable and subject to verification. It is finite. It can be completed. Let us assume that in traveling westward we set our objective to go from Detroit to Chicago by automobile. Furthermore, we want to do this in one day and make not more than three stops. We can specify all aspects of our performance, thereby providing a basis for verification. We can verify the number of stops, the time of arrival in Chicago, and the basic fact that we are traveling by automobile. If we were in a contest and had specified these behaviors, we would know exactly what to train for and perhaps make several trial runs before the day of the contest.

This analogy will hold true for the principle we were considering—health. We can specify the following: The student will complete at least one physical examination every two years for the duration of his academic career. The examination will be carried out by a licensed medical doctor and will include a chest X ray, a test of blood profile, a blood-pressure check, and the weight of the student at the time of the examination.

Here we know and the student knows precisely what must be done to satisfy the objective. Verifiable standards have been set.

Note that just as one can add specifications to the example of traveling westward (e.g., one can fly there or one can continue to travel westward by going on to Nevada or Hawaii), so too can the teacher add more specifiable behaviors that support the principle of maintaining good health. We can specify the characteristics of exercise, diet, and reduction of stress.

What, then, are the relationships between general principles and purposes of education and specific instructional objectives? From our examples, one can infer that principles and purposes point to a direction or demarcate a desirable area of concern. In following principles and purposes or attempting to fulfill them we discover that they are inexhaustible. Purposes and principles provide a range of possibilities from which specific objectives can be generated. Their power is in their generality, their openness to possibility. It is the power of suggestion, the power of abstraction.

Objectives, on the other hand, provide checkpoints on any given purpose line. Being measurable, they provide a way of verifying that we are on purpose, and to what degree we are on purpose. We need purposes to avoid getting lost in triviality; we need specifiable objectives to avoid getting lost in vagueness. Purposes without objectives are empty; objectives without purposes are blind.

■ *Educational Purposes as Values*

We have been considering such terms as *values, purposes,* and *objectives.* There are other words that are often classified with those terms, such as *aims, guidelines, principles,* and *goals.* These words are in common use and most people probably think they know what they mean when they use them. Can you draw distinctions between them? Should they be used interchangeably? After you try your hand at this, turn to page 38 and examine the dictionary definitions of these terms.

Following are some educational aims recommended by the President's Commission on Higher Education (1947):

1. To understand the ideas of others and to express one's own effectively.
2. To acquire and use the skills and habits involved in critical and constructive thinking.
3. To acquire the knowledge (and attitude) basic to satisfying family life.[2]

Do you notice anything that these objectives have in common? Perhaps your attention is drawn to the fact that each is stated in infinitive form. The verbals "to understand" and "to acquire" state some constitution of acts—acts of a general nature. Moreover, we are presented with recommendations that students should subscribe to certain values or choices.

In a free society, one is not likely to find educational purposes recommending slavery or repression of ideas. And in a society modeled on the ideal of technological productivity, one is not likely to find educational purposes recommending an antiwork ethic, nor in a society espousing free enterprise, is one likely to find educational aims recommending the equal distribution of wealth. In short, one is not likely to find educational purposes counter to the social values in which they were written.

What values were recommended by the Commission on Higher Education in 1947? Let us examine the aims listed above. Each statement is a recommendation, a statement of desirability. We find that it is desirable to understand the ideas of others, to do constructive thinking, and to satisfy family life. These statements are like general maps of areas selected as worthwhile. For this reason, educational purposes are sometimes called normative objectives. They point to norms of social standards or values. Therefore, it is a good idea to think of general abstract recommendations of national committees, as well as nonmeasurable objectives in curriculum guides, as educational purposes—even though writers sometimes call them objectives. Just remember that objectives can be measured while purposes cannot— and a purpose by another name is still a purpose.

From time to time, various groups of educators from commissions interpret and recommend broad educational aims for the nation as a whole. The President's Commission on Higher Education is a case in point, and the American Council on Educational Studies is another. In "A Design for General Education," the American Council set forth the following educational aims:

1. To communicate through his own language in writing and speaking at the level of expression adequate to the needs of educational goals.
2. To think through the problems and to gain the basic orientation that will better enable [the student] to make a satisfactory family and marital adjustment.
3. To act in the light of an understanding of the natural phenomena in his environment in its implication for human society and human welfare, to use scientific methods in the solution of his problems, and to employ useful nonverbal methods of thought and communication.[3]

The American Council further translated these statements into over 200 instructional objectives.[4] Here are some of them:

1. [Knowledge and understanding] of reliable sources of information on health.
2. [The ability] to read significant writings with critical comprehension.
3. The ability to apply techniques to new situations.
4. The ability to recognize form and patterns in literary works as a means of understanding their meaning.
5. The ability to identify and appraise judgment and values that are involved in the choice of a course of action.

The broad normative objective becomes useful, then, in providing a framework for generating many more specific objectives. Try your hand at writing other specific objectives using the same grammatical forms: "knowledge of . . ."; "to . . . (infinitive form); and "the ability to . . . (infinitive). After you have written five such objectives, turn to page 39 and see if you stated any objectives comparable to those listed there.

DEFINITIONS OF TERMS
Purpose   Something that one sets before himself as an object to be attained; an end to be kept in view in any plan, measure, exertion, operation. Synonym: intention.
Goal   The end toward which effort is directed. A condition or state to be brought about through a course of action.
Objective   Something toward which effort is directed; goal or object; boundary, limit.
Principle   A general and fundamental law, doctrine, or assumption on which others are based or from which others are derived; any generalization that provides a basis for reasoning or a guide for conduct or procedure.
Aim   To intend; to determine a course; purpose, intention, plan.
Value   The quality or fact of being excellent, useful or desirable; worth in a thing.
SOURCE: Webster's Third International Dictionary

Educators strongly influenced by behaviorism will argue that the statements listed on page 39 are not specific enough to qualify as instructional objectives. It is true that it would be difficult, if not impossible, to verify that they had been completed. Nevertheless, we are beginning to see a trend toward greater specificity—a movement toward stating many specific normative objectives in support of very broad aims. This trend will continue as we go through the history of educational purposes and objectives. At the same time, we will show how shifting social values are reflected in our educational expectations.

The Seven Cardinal Principles of Secondary Education

One of the most prestigious sets of educational aims was recommended by the Commission on the Reorganization of Secondary Education. This commission called these arms the Seven Cardinal Principles of Secondary Education. Following is a summarized version:

1. *Health.* Good health habits need to be taught and encouraged by the school. The community and school should cooperate in fulfilling the health needs of all youngsters and adults.
2. *Command of fundamental processes.* The secondary school should accept responsibility for continuing to teach and polish the basic tools of learning—such as arithmetical computation, reading, and writing—that were begun in the elementary school.

LIST OF OBJECTIVES

1. [Knowledge] of community organizations and services for health maintenance and improvement.
2. [Knowledge] of acceptable usage in articulation, pronunciation, capitalization, grammar, and spelling as a means of effective presentation.
3. The ability to listen to important oral statements with concentration and judgment.
4. [Knowledge] of the criteria of normal and neurotic adjustments.
5. [Knowledge] of the trends in American society affecting the structure and functions of the family and the role of women and children in our society.
6. The ability to read graphs, diagrams, and blueprints.
7. [Knowledge] of the techniques and methods used by scientists in seeking to answer questions about the world, and of the proper functions of scientific theory and experiments.
8. The ability to reorganize artistic quality in contemporary works of music and art.
9. The ability to formulate explicitly and systematically a pattern of values as a basis of individual and social action.
10. The ability to evaluate popular health benefits critically.

SOURCE: *Cardinal Principles of Education,* U.S. Bureau of Education, Bulletin No. 35 (1918), pp. 5–10.

---

3. *Worthy home membership.* Students' understanding of family interrelationships, in order for the give-and-take to be a healthy, happy affair, should be advocated by the school. Proper adjustment as a family member will lead to proper acceptance of responsibility as a family leader in later life.
4. *Vocation.* The secondary school should develop an attitude in students that will lead to an appreciation for all vocations. The basic skills of a variety of vocations should be made available to students who have the need and desire for them.
5. *Citizenship.* A basic commitment for proper citizenship on the part of students needs to be fostered and strengthened during adolescent years. The secondary school needs to assume their responsibility not only in the social sciences, where one would ordinarily assume it would be handled, but in all subjects.
6. *Proper use of leisure time.* The student should be provided opportunities while in secondary school to expand the available possibilities for leisure time. The commission felt that leisure time properly used would enrich the total personality.

7. *Ethical character.* The secondary school should organize its activities and personal relationships to reflect good ethical character, both to serve as an exemplar and to involve the student in a series of activities that will provide opportunities to make ethically correct decisions.[5]

It is not too difficult to identify some of the values recommended: teaching the basics, interpreted as arithmetical computations, reading, and writing; acceptance of responsibility as a family member; an appreciation of all vocations; commitment to proper citizenship; leisure time properly used; reflecting good ethical character; and making ethically correct decisions. That these values change over a period of time will become apparent when we examine recommendations made by later commissions.

The Educational Policies Commission

Vocational preparation became a priority in 1937 when the country was experiencing the Great Depression. In 1938, the Educational Policies Commission recommended four major divisions of educational purposes: (1) self-realization, (2) human relationships, (3) economic efficiency, and (4) civic responsibility. Specific objectives were spelled out under each of those broad purposes. By 1947, the "Imperative Needs of Youth"[6] reiterated the Seven Cardinal Principles, but shifted the emphasis from "command of fundamental processes (focus of the three R's) to a focus on "rationality, clear expression of thought and reading and listening with understanding."

In his report on the Woods Hole Conference in September 1959, in the wake of the Sputnik launching in 1957, Jerome Bruner, a cognitive psychologist at Harvard, made the following statement:

What may be emerging as a mark of our generation is a widespread renewal or concern for the quality and intellectual aims of education . . . accentuated by what is almost certain to be a long-range crisis in national security.[7]

Following the Woods Hole Conference the National Science Foundation provided funds for teams of scholars to develop intellectually rigorous science curricula. The Physical Science Study Committee (PSSC) was established in 1960. When the PSSC physics course proved to be too content-oriented to interest students, Harvard Project Physics was created to add an affective dimension to the curriculum.[8]

In each case, the national need was interpreted by a committee, which then recommended certain normative directives for the youth of the nation. Harry S. Broudy provides a forceful if somewhat exaggerated and humorous version of how educational purposes change with the changing priorities of the times:

. . . Given a new war, . . . given a new source of energy or a new ice age; given a surplus of the aged and a shortage of babies, given a drug that induces learning on demand or a neuro-surgical procedure that eliminates whatever stands in the way of loving school and study, improvements will be launched to change the schools. Whatever their nature, one can be sure that there will be conferences to assess their strengths and weaknesses, to encourage the loyalists, and to confound their detractors.[9]

Sources of Educational Purposes	We have already identified some major sources of educational purposes—from the Seven Cardinal Principles of Education (1918), to the 1947 Imperative Needs for Youth, to Bruner's Woods Hole recommendations following Sputnik in 1959.

Each commission reflected the social values of its time. Other common features of the educational purposes or normative objectives is that they are inexhaustible and nonverifiable. Their usefulness lies in their power of suggestion and abstraction. From these broad normative objectives, more specific instructional objectives can be generated.

Other sources of educational purposes are to be found in curriculum guides, both local and regional. Also, resource units list possible topics and values in various subject areas that can be used to generate objectives. Department heads and curriculum specialists sometimes create statements of educational purposes. Textbooks, by including some topics and excluding others, implicitly recommend certain values or emphasis. One can interview parents and students to determine interest. One can pretest students to determine the appropriate level of knowledge. Another strategy is for the teacher to become sensitive to the signs of the times. For example: What are the educational implications of recent legislation on mainstreaming? What are the educational implications of research in multiple intelligence? What are people doing with their leisure time? Their work time? What are current attitudes and values respecting knowledge, skills, and practical and theoretical pursuits? What are strong lobbyists demanding? In short, what are the signs of the times?

The importance of purpose in curriculum planning is registered in the work of Ralph Tyler, who in his *Basic Principles of Curriculum and Instruction* asks these salient questions:

1. What educational purposes should the school seek to attain?
2. What educational experiences can be provided that are likely to attain these purposes?
3. How can these educational experiences be effectively organized?
4. How can we determine whether these purposes are being attained?[10]

But where do we go to explore the nature of purpose? The beginning teacher is encouraged to develop a philosophy of education, a consistent set of assumptions, deductions, and ways of processing evidence about educational matters.

There will be times when no formula will give you the correct decision regarding educational purposes. You will often make decisions and act in the context of conflicting forces. For these situations you will need a philosophy that is integrated, both rationally and personally. Janet Bobby, master teacher at Redford High School in Detroit, puts it this way: "The effective teacher must sort through all the many purposes, aims and objectives that are recommended by various groups and make personal decisions guided by a personal philosophy of education, knowledge of educational research and personal style."[11]

Once purposes are decided upon and the journey begins, we are still not guaranteed that a Mad Hatter or two will not show up. The difference is that we will have planned alternate routes. And even when we have selected the direction for our journey, we must still translate value statements (purposes, principles, and normative objectives) into a useful number of measurable objectives. How to prepare such objectives will be examined in Chapter 4.

PROBES

1. How would you distinguish between purposes and objectives? Give two examples of each.
2. What are some possible grammatical forms of normative objectives?
3. Comment on the value of the Seven Cardinal Principles of Secondary Education as guides to modern education.
4. Comment on the value of the recommendations made by the Educational Policies Commission as guides to modern education.
5. List five sources of educational purposes. How would you evaluate each source from the standpoint of your educational philosophy?

■ *SUMMARY*

Educational purposes are abstract, inexhaustible, and unmeasurable. Their power lies in the suggestion of educational possibilities that can be stated in specific form. The teacher has access to many sources of educational purposes: from national committees such as the Educational Policies Commission to the Woods Hole Conference following Sputnik; from curriculum guides; from department head recommendations; from the stated needs and interests of students; and from reading the signs of the times.

Once teachers have identified the educational purposes they will use for planning, they must then translate these purposes into instructional objectives. The objectives should be written in such a way that they can be verified upon completion. Instructional objectives are measurable, even if not necessarily observable.

■ *NOTES*

1. *Cardinal Principles of Education,* U.S. Bureau of Education, Bulletin No. 35 (1918), 5–10.
2. The President's Commission on Higher Education, *Higher Education for American Democracy,* Volume I: *Establishing the Goals,* U.S. Government Printing Office, Washington, DC, December 1947.
3. American Council on Educational Studies, "A Design for General Education," American Council on Education, Washington DC, June 1944, 14.
4. Ibid., 31–44.

5. *Cardinal Principles of Education,* 5–10.
6. "The Imperative Needs of Youth of Secondary School Age," National Research Association of Secondary School Principals, Bulletin No. 31 (March 1947).
7. Jerome Bruner, *The Process of Education* (Cambridge, MA: Harvard University Press, 1960), 1.
8. Daniel Tanner, *Secondary Education: Perspectives and Prospects,* (New York: Macmillan, 1972), 205–206.
9. Harry S. Broudy, "Strengths and Weaknesses of Competency-Based Education," presented at the Second Annual National Conference on Competency-Based Education at Wayne State University, May 1975.
10. The basic tenets of Tyler's view of curriculum development are explicated in his *Basic Principles of Curriculum and Instruction* (Chicago: University of Chicago Press, 1950).
11. Interview with Janet Bobby, January 1987. Written statement submitted with permission to use in this text.

Planning II: Creating Effective Instructional Objectives/Cognitive Domain

Teacher explaining the mechanism of basic chemical reactions.

"Come, we shall have some fun now!" thought Alice. "I'm glad that we've begun asking the riddles—I believe I can guess that," she added aloud.

"Do you mean that you think you can find out the answer to it?" said the March Hare.

"Exactly so," said Alice.

"Then you should say what you mean," the March Hare went on.

"I do," Alice hastily replied; "at least—at least I mean what I say—that's the same thing, you know."

"Not the same thing a bit!" said the Hatter. "Why, you might just as well say that 'I see what I eat' is the same thing as 'I eat what I see!' "

"You might just as well say," added the March Hare, that 'I like what I get' is the same thing as 'I get what I like!' "

"You might as well say," added the Dormouse, . . . "That 'I breathe when I sleep' is the same thing as 'I sleep when I breathe!' "

—Lewis Carroll

Planning as Decision Making

Madeline Hunter says that teaching is decision making. Given the problems of decision making presented in the preceding chapter—choosing a source of value, reading the signs of the times, choosing broad educational principles and purposes in planning, selecting appropriate instructional objectives—it at least appears that the initial problem is, in fact, decision making.

But Madeline Hunter's claim is much stronger than this. The teacher, she says, does not make a number of decisions at the outset of teaching and stop there. She defines teaching as

> . . . a constant stream of professional decisions made before, during and after interaction with the student; and decisions which, when implemented, increase the probability of learning.[1]

Decision making can be clarified if the teacher focuses on three categories that are the "essence of the process of teaching."[2] One must decide (1) what to teach, (2) what the student will do to demonstrate learning, and (3) what the teacher will do to facilitate learning. One may also infer that it makes good sense to make these decisions in the order listed. How, indeed, would it be possible to decide how one will support student learning until the learning is defined? How does one define the learning without deciding in advance what the student will learn? And yet it is not uncommon for teachers to confuse student learning with student activities and even with teacher behavior.

How, then, are the first two decisions to be made? Another approach is to ask how we are to state instructional objectives.

PROBES

1. How would you go about clarifying the decision-making process in teaching?
2. How would you distinguish student activities from student learning?
3. Can you think of cases where objectives can become counterproductive?

Stating Objectives

In Chapter 3 we examined some of the useful sources in selecting objectives. We now want to turn to the task of stating objectives. How shall we state objectives so that they say everything we wish them to say, but do not say (or imply) things we do not intend? If the objective does not communicate everything you intend to say, then you have not taken the first step toward planning and ultimately teaching what you want to teach. Put another way, you have not taken the first step toward facilitating the final learning mastery you intend for your students. The second problem is that you can easily mislead your students. In attempting to decipher ambiguously stated objective, students can go off in all directions at once—or go in too few directions. This problem will be compounded when you begin to test and evaluate your students. If your students cannot interpret your objectives, how can you hold them accountable for what you intend them to learn? How can we say everything we want, and say it clearly?

■ *Scope and Precision as Criteria*

These two criteria—stating everything you intend in the objectives and stating it unambiguously—we shall refer to as scope and precision.[3] Other useful synonyms are comprehensiveness and rigor. Let us consider some sample objectives to see how these criteria operate. Consider the following objective written by student teacher A:

> By the end of the unit, the students will accurately know and thoroughly understand Hawthorne's novel, *The Scarlet Letter.*

What are the expressed intentions of the above objective? Probably few people, if any, would object to the general values expressed. "To know and understand" has been an ideal from the time of Socrates to the present. One can pursue knowing and understanding for practical purposes or just for the pleasure of knowing.[4]

The ideal or value of knowing, whether for practical purposes or for its intrinsic value, is not in question here. What we can question is the precision of the statement. Exactly what is being recommended? What kinds, specifically, of cognitive processes are being recommended?

What evidence must students have to be satisfied that they have completed the objective? Let us assume that most students interpret "know" in the above statement to mean recalling the names of characters and events in *The Scarlet Letter,* plus biographical information on Hawthorne that has been supplied by teacher A.

Suppose, further, that another, small group of students judges sheer memory of facts not to be very important. Instead, these students focus their attention on the task of identification and analysis of major themes in the novel. A third, even smaller group traces parallel situations in their own lives and *The Scarlet Letter.*

If we return now to our hypothetical student teacher and ask him what he intended his objective to communicate, it is likely that he or she would opt for meanings adopted by the second group, and yet this constitutes only a small percentage of the students. What are the expectations for the first, largest group and the third, smallest group? In this case we would say that the student teacher has written his or her objectives too broadly to express a more limited intent. The teacher's intent was for students to identify and analyze themes in *The Scarlet Letter.* But his or her objectives communicated information retrieval and the application of conceptual and experiential patterns, as well as the second group's interpretation: identification and analysis of major themes.

Suppose the student teacher we are discussing (teacher A) shares his or her objective with a fellow student teacher (teacher B) during lunch hour, and suppose teacher B interprets the instructional objectives to mean recalling specific information in the literature cited—the names of places and characters, and the author's background. Let us further assume that teacher B likes A's objective so much that he or she adopts it for use in class. Teacher B believes that it will be very desirable for the students to know literature in the sense of recalling factual information. The same students, however, interpret the objective to mean identification of major themes and finding parallels in their own lives.

Now we have a situation in which neither teacher A's nor teacher B's intentions are communicated to their respective students. Teachers have intentions, express them in symbols, and expect clear communication. But in this case the language used (symbols) is open to more interpretation than that intended by teachers A and B. The objective needs to be stated in narrower terms.

Is it possible to state an objective too narrowly? What of a case in which more is intended than that which is communicated?

Let us assume that teacher A finds out about the expectation of his or her students when giving the first examination and discovers that the students' poor performance is due to a misunderstanding. Teacher A then vows to state his or her objectives in unambiguous terms. The teacher devotes the next few weeks to the teaching of English grammar, with the objective of focusing on verbal and written recall. A sample objective follows:

> Students will recall and state in writing, the following definition: A complete sentence is a group of words expressing a complete thought. A sentence begins with a capital letter and ends with a period.

Following exhibition of this memory feat, teacher A assigns an impromptu essay, exhorting the students to be aware of and write complete sentences throughout their essays.

On going over the essays that same evening, teacher A is amazed to find innumerable sentence fragments and run-on sentences. The next morning, teacher A returns to admonish the students for not applying the knowledge they so clearly demonstrated the day before.

If we now inquire as to the intent of teacher A in having the students memorize the definitions of a sentence, we find that he or she intended that the students apply the concept of a sentence in written essay form. The teacher expected the students to interpret the objective in such a way that they would learn more complete skills than those stated in the objective. Here teacher A has written the objective too narrowly for the intent he or she wished to convey.

In writing objectives, then, the teacher can fail to express his intent by writing the objective too broadly or too narrowly. Let's summarize:

Broad: The teacher intends less than the objective states.

Narrow: The teacher intends more than the objective states.

Ideally, an objective must communicate one's full intent and do so unambiguously. We have returned to the problem of scope and precision. Let us first see if we can set criteria to ensure clarity in stating objectives. Then we can move on to the more difficult task of making sure that our objectives say everything we wish them to say. But how can we state all that we intend and still write an objective that is precise? (See Figure 4.1.)

Is it even possible to be precise about something like teaching? Is it not wise to ask just how precise we can expect to be before we launch an all-out effort toward rigor, only to find out that our project is unrealistic from the start? This same question was raised by Aristotle in respect to the study of ethics, a discipline that underpins much of the decision making in education. We can concede from the outset that

A. CONCEPTUAL OBJECTIVE:
students will understand quantum mechanics used in simple bonding configurations in previously selected molecules

B. BEHAVIORAL OBJECTIVE:
students, in groups of 2, will be able to construct, using molecular model kit, at least 4 of 6 given molecules.

Figure 4.1 It is effective to use a combination of conceptual and behavioral objectives.

analysis of educational problems is less precise than that of mechanics. As Aristotle states it:

> Our discussion will be adequate if it has as much clearness as the subject matter admits of, for precision is not to be sought for alike in all discussions, any more than in all the products of the crafts. Now fine and just actions, which political science investigates, admit of much variety and fluctuation of opinion, so that they may be thought to exist only by convention, and not by nature. And goods also give rise to similar fluctuation because they bring harm to many people, for before now men have been undone by reason of their wealth, and others by reason of their courage. We must be content, then, in speaking of such subjects and with such premises to indicate the truth roughly and in outline, and in speaking about things which are only for the most part true and with premises of the same kind to reach conclusions that are no better . . . for it is the mark of an educated man to look for the precision in each class of things just so far as the nature of the subject admits. . . .[5]

Education, though leaning heavily on the behavioral sciences for its descriptions and predictions, still operates, like ethics, as a normative discipline as well. Therefore, it will not be possible to express all educational statements with the same degree of precision as, say, statements in differential calculus. But it does not follow from this that we need abandon the quest for clarity altogether.

Robert F. Mager's *Preparing Instructional Objectives* is a tour de force in the art and technique of stating instructional objectives in precise terms.[6] Mager notes that there are many words open to a wide range of interpretation. Some examples of such "loaded" words follow:[7]

Words Open to Many Interpretations	*Words Open to Fewer Interpretations*
to know	to write
to understand	to recite
to *really* understand	to identify
to appreciate	to differentiate
to *fully* appreciate	to solve
to grasp the significance	to construct
to enjoy	to list
to believe	to compare
to have faith in	to contrast

You may recall in our example that teacher A's use of the word *know* led to a multitude of problems because of the ambiguity of the word. Mager, then, is suggesting that the ambiguous words be translated into precise language at the outset.

■ *Precise Objectives*

To ensure that instructional objectives are stated clearly, Mager recommended the following guidelines to the expression of instructional intentions:

First, identify the terminal behavior by name; you can specify the kind of behavior that will be accepted as evidence that the learner has achieved the objective.

Second, try to define the desired behavior further by describing important conditions under which the behavior will be expected to occur.

Third, specify the criteria of acceptable performance by describing how well the learner must perform to be considered acceptable.[8]

Mager does not think it necessary that all instructional objectives include all three steps. Rather, the object is "to write objectives that communicate." Sometimes all these steps will be necessary to achieve the desired clarity, and sometimes not.

As you examine Mager's guidelines, you will notice that the behavior of the student is specified. Learning is defined as "terminal behavior." Another way of saying this is that learning is indicated by observable actions that the student is expected to perform at the termination of instruction. This kind of instructional objective is often called a behavioral objective.

You will also notice that conditions of learning are specified in the guidelines. This information is usually stated in the form shown in the following specific examples:

Given a list of . . .

Given a matrix of intercorrelations . . .

Given a standard set of tools . . .[9]

Sometimes the preposition "with" (or "without") is used to state conditions:

Without the aid of references

Without the aid of tools[10]

The third guideline suggested by Mager is a criterion of acceptable performance. This feature is stated in terms of time limits, percentage of correct answers, minimum number of correct answers, ratios of correct to incorrect responses permitted, and other observable operations: for example, calculating a distance with an accuracy of not less than three decimal places.

Let us use Mager's guidelines in some sample instructional objectives. Following are some mixed behavioral objectives for different subjects and grade levels:

1. Given a series of developmental events in history, the tenth-grade students will be able to identify in writing the correct theory which subsumes these events.
2. Given a list of ten vocabulary words, the tenth-grade students will be able to correctly define in writing at least eight of them.
3. The twelfth-grade physics students will be able to recall and write all the appropriate laws covering a gravity experiment that has been demonstrated in the lab.
4. After having written a descriptive essay, the ninth-grade English student will be able to name orally five standards for judging the quality of descriptive essays.

5. After reviewing a short film clip, the education student will be able to recognize and state all the methods the teacher in the film was using in her instruction.
6. When shown a monthly series of graphs depicting changes in the economy, the senior economics student will be able to identify all the influences affecting price changes.[11]

In these examples, not all the objectives are criterion-referenced—that is, no standard of acceptable performance is given. Note also that conditions are sometimes stated in other forms than "Given" and "Without the aid of." You may be able to think of many other ways to state conditions. Notice, too, that some of the objectives require the student to perform tasks beyond simple recall of information. It is this latter point that we shall now explore, for it takes us into the second part of our initial problem—stating *everything* we intend as a learning outcome.

■ *Comprehensive Objectives*

In recent years, behavioral objectives have come under attack for focusing too much on lower levels of cognition—specifically, the recall of information. The argument is that it is very easy to state cognitive objectives for the recall of facts, but it is not so easy to state objectives for writing a complete essay, for analyzing a sonnet, or for evaluating competing experiments in a science class. If this is the case, then clarity is gained at the expense of sacrificing comprehensiveness. Let us now consider some of these arguments.

Samuel Stone, a language arts scholar, in a monograph comparing cognitive and behavioral instructional objectives, argues that behavioral objectives are supported by a position that focuses "so narrowly on data that it loses sight of hypotheses."[12] Teachers, says Stone, should observe student behavior, but they can interpret it as significant "only in relation to skills, facts, concepts, and principles that they want their students to learn."[13] Such principles and concepts involve mental functions like knowing and understanding.

Here we have returned to the flip side of behavior, the purpose which underlies it, for "knowing means the mental ability to behave accurately and purposefully," and only human beings behave purposefully. Computers and gauges can perform accurately; human beings also have the capacity to understand.

As John Dewey put it, all "routine and extremely dictated activity fail to develop the ability to understand, even though they promote skill in external doing."[14] And the focus of behaviorism is external doing. In behaviorism there is the tendency to treat knowing, understanding, and purpose as though they do not exist; hence, the behaviorist avoids these words. Karl Popper describes the behaviorist's strategy as the thesis that one day we shall abolish cats or elephants by ceasing to talk about them.

The danger of behavioral objectives, when used exclusively, is that they promote a narrow range of human performance. Problems in mathematics are solved by monkey-see–monkey-do steps. In English, students are taught that a paragraph always has three sentences. The first sentence is a topic sentence, the second sentence provides an example for the topic sentence, and the third sentence is a clincher.

The danger is all too apparent. What happens when the student is confronted with a living context and these formulas do not fit? Teaching to formulas such as the regional test questions makes a parody of education and paralyzes human purpose. It reduces education to a form of animal training.

In *The Educational Imagination,* Elliot Eisner points out that the behavioral objective reflects the means-ends model of thinking characteristic of Western technology. There is in this thinking an inherent assumption that the prespecification of goals is the proper way to proceed in curriculum planning. But as Eisner points out, we do not always adopt such a deliberate approach to learning. When we read a novel or go to a play or movie, we do not specify in advance what we will learn, nor do we define a problem to solve. And yet the learning outcome is often richer than we can imagine. Should this kind of learning be discounted? It should not, according to Eisner. He calls examples of this kind of learning "expressive outcomes." Expressive objectives describe the conditions of a rich learning environment, but they do not specify what behaviors are expected.[15]

Peter Kline, a consultant on the Lozanov method of using suggestion in teaching, says that it is useful to distinguish *expectation* from *expectancy.* Expectation specifies learning outcomes in advance; expectancy invites one to remain open to emergent possibilities.[16] It may be that specifying everything in advance gains clarity and security at the expense of discovery.

Bloom's Taxonomy of Educational Objectives

An early attempt to circumvent the narrowing of learning toward simple recall was the classification system, or taxonomy, developed by Benjamin Bloom and his associates.[17] One of the major purposes of this theoretical model of educational objectives is stated by Bloom as follows:

. . . Use of the taxonomy can also help one gain a perspective on the emphasis given to certain behaviors by a particular set of educational plans. Thus, a teacher, in classifying the goals of a teaching unit, may find that they all fall within the taxonomy category of recalling or remembering knowledge. Looking at the taxonomy categories may suggest to him that, for example, he could include some goals dealing with the application of this knowledge and with the analysis of the situations in which the knowledge is used.[18]

The plan of the taxonomy was to provide descriptions of levels of cognitive complexity, from the simple recall through analysis to evaluation. These levels of complexity do not necessarily correspond to psychological fact. They are, rather, logical levels of complexity. Nor is there an implication that content must be mastered sequentially from its lowest level of complexity to the higher levels of analysis and synthesis. Further, the taxonomy of Bloom is not a pure taxonomy of the kind used in the biological sciences. Bloom did not classify existent artifacts; he classified possible intended behavior of students according to varying levels of cognitive complexity—that is, knowledge, comprehension, application, analysis, synthesis and evaluation. An adapted set of descriptions from Bloom's cognitive domain follows:

1. *Knowledge*

   Knowledge, as defined here, involves the recall of specifics and universals, the recall of methods and processes, or the recall of a pattern, structure, or setting. For measurement purposes, the recall situation involves little more than bringing to mind the appropriate material. Although some alteration of the material may be required, this is a relatively minor part of the task. The knowledge objectives emphasize most the psychological processes of remembering. The process of relating is also involved in that a knowledge test situation requires the organization and reorganization of a problem so that it will furnish the appropriate signals and cures for the information and knowledge the individual possesses. To use an analogy, if one thinks of the mind as a file, the problem in a knowledge test situation is that of finding in the problem or task the appropriate signals, cues, and clues that will most effectively bring out whatever knowledge is filed or stored.

2. *Comprehension*

   This represents the lowest level of understanding. It refers to a style of understanding or apprehension such that the individual knows what is being communicated without necessarily relating it to other material or seeing its fullest implications.

3. *Application*

   This involves the use of abstractions in particular and concrete situations. The abstractions may be in the form of general ideas, rules of procedures, or generalized methods. The abstractions may also be technical principles, ideas, and theories that must be remembered and applied.

4. *Analysis*

   This is the breakdown of a communication into its constituent elements or parts so that the relative hierarchy of ideas is made clear and/or the relations between the ideas expressed are made explicit. Such analyses are intended to clarify the communication, so as to indicate how the communication is organized and the way in which it manages to convey its effects, as well as its basis and arrangement.

5. *Synthesis*

   This is the putting together of elements and parts so as to form a whole. It involves the process of working with pieces, parts, elements, etc., and arranging and combining them in such a way as to constitute a pattern or structure not clearly there before.

6. *Evaluation*

This requires judgments on the value of material and methods for given purposes, as well as quantitative and qualitative judgments on the extent to which material and methods satisfy criteria. It involves use of a standard of appraisal. The criteria may be those determined by the student or those given to him.[20]

Use of the Taxonomy

The teacher can use the taxonomy to get an idea of the possibilities for objectives. Perhaps a useful question for the teacher in this respect is, How can I open my students to the full range of their intellectual capacities? In this respect, the taxonomy provides some direction, though it does not dictate which objectives will be chosen, nor does it mandate a Heinz 57 Varieties approach to education. There is no implicit directive that all skill levels should be covered all of the time. To attempt such a feat would probably be counterproductive. What is important to master is the kind of language appropriate for each level of cognition. For example, "know" is translated into words like define, name, describe, match, and select, while "understand" is translated into words like convert, paraphrase, predict, and summarize. For the reader's convenience, "Instrumentation of the Taxonomy of Educational Objectives: Cognitive Domain" by Mitfessel, Michael, and Kirsner is provided in Appendix C. This chart includes the cognitive levels of description, showing appropriate key words for each level.

The taxonomies certainly increase our range of choice in stating our educational intentions, and they provide safeguards for ensuring clarity. Nevertheless, many educators think that behavioral objectives of the sort recommended by Mager are still too narrow, particularly for subjects like the humanities. This becomes even more of an issue when judgment, values, and emotions are recognized as part of the learning process. How to address some of these concerns is the subject of our next chapter.

PROBES

1. How would you distinguish an objective stated too narrowly from one stated too broadly? Give two examples of each.
2. Write five behavioral objectives, two of them criterion-referenced.
3. How do behavioral objectives differ from normative objectives?
4. What are two advantages of behavioral objectives?
5. What are two disadvantages of behavioral objectives?
6. How can a teacher use Bloom's *Taxonomy of Educational Objectives: Cognitive Domain?*
7. Using Appendix C, write two behavioral objectives representing different cognitive levels.

■ *SUMMARY*

Madeline Hunter says that teaching is decision making. One must decide what to teach, what the student will do to demonstrate learning, and what the teacher will do to facilitate learning.

In stating objectives one can err in two ways—by stating objectives too broadly or too narrowly. In a broad statement of objectives the teacher intends less than the objective states. In a narrow statement of objectives the teacher intends more than the objective states. Ideally, an objective must communicate one's full intent and do so unambiguously.

Robert F. Mager in his *Preparing Instructional Objectives* distinguishes between words open to many interpretations (words like "to know" and "to understand") and words open to fewer interpretations (words like "to identify" "to solve"). Mager recommends that objectives specify the "kind of behavior that will be accepted as evidence that the learner has achieved the objective"[21] and that one define the condition under which the behavior will be expected to occur. If one so desires, criteria of acceptable performance may also be added.

The danger of behavioral objectives, when used exclusively, is that they promote a narrow range of human performance. Bloom's *Taxonomy of Educational Objectives* can be used by the teacher to ensure clarity, distinguish levels of cognition, and increase the range of choice in human performance.

■ *NOTES*

1. Madeline Hunter, *Mastery Teaching: Increasing Instructional Effectiveness in Secondary Schools, Colleges and Universities* (El Segundo, CA: TIP Publications, 1982), 3.
2. Ibid.
3. Stephen Pepper, *World Hypotheses* (Los Angeles: University of California Press, 1942), 74–77.
4. Bertrand Russell expressed the ideal of knowing for pleasure as distinct from knowing for a purpose. In a statement to Alfred North Whitehead, Bertrand Russell said simply, "Isn't it nice to *know* things?"
5. Aristotle, *Nicomachaean Ethics,* trans. W. P. Ross (Oxford: Clarendon Press, 1925), Bk. I, chap. 3, p. 1094b. By permission.
6. Robert F. Mager, *Preparing Instructional Objectives* (Palo Alto, CA: Fearon Publishers, 1962).
7. Ibid., 11.
8. Ibid., 12.
9. Ibid., 26.
10. Ibid.
11. William J. Kryspin and John F. Fieldhusen, *Writing Behavioral Objectives: A Guide to Planning Instruction* (Minneapolis, MN: Burgess, 1974), 61–62.
12. Samuel Stone, Instructional Objectives, Cognitive Versus Behavioral, unpub-

lished monograph, Wayne State University, p. 1. Provided by permission of the author.

13. Ibid.

14. John Dewey, *How We Think* (Lexington, MA: Heath, 1933), 147.

15. Elliot W. Eisner, *The Educational Imagination: On the Design and Evaluation of School Programs* (New York: Macmillan, 1979), 99–103.

16. Peter Kline, Super Accelerated Learning Workshop, Wayne State University, May 1987.

17. Benjamin Bloom et al., *Taxonomy of Educational Objectives: Cognitive Domain* (New York: Longmans, Green, 1956).

18. Ibid., 2.

19. Ibid., 12.

20. Robert J. Kibler, *Behavioral Objectives and Instruction* (Boston: Allyn and Bacon, 1970), 47–55. A more complete set of descriptors is provided in Appendix C of this text.

21. Robert F. Mager, *Preparing Instructional Objectives,* 12.

Planning III:
Creating Effective Instructional Objectives/Affective Psychomotor Domains

Finding your inner clown—to be genuinely expressive and incredibly creative.

Lovers and madmen have such seething brains,
Such shaping fantasies, that apprehend
More than cool reason ever comprehends.
The lunatic, the lover and the poet
Are of imagination all compact.
　　　　　　　—William Shakespeare, *A Midsummer Night's Dream*

A genuine enthusiasm is an attitude that operates as an intellectual force. A teacher who arouses such an enthusiasm in his pupils has done something that no amount of formalized method, no matter how correct, can accomplish.
　　　　　　　—John Dewey, *How We think*

In almost any subject, your passion for the subject will save you. If you only care enough for a result, you will most certainly attain it.
　　　　　　　—William James

Feelings and Values in Learning

If Bill becomes ill or utters angry epithets every time English literature is mentioned, and if Bill is frequently absent from English classes, the teacher may rightfully infer that Bill has a barrier to approaching this discipline.

At the other extreme is Sally, who not only completes all English assignments on time, but actively seeks out ways to increase her participation in this subject. She writes poetry on her own, reads biographies of the English poets, and belongs to a writing group that meets after school.

In considering these two examples, we have entered the domain of feelings, values, and attitudes—the affective domain. We shall want to consider some basic questions regarding this domain.

Should affective behavior be evaluated? And if so, how? Should affective behavior be changed? And if so, how? And just what is affective behavior? Can we pin it down?

Mager characterizes affective behavior in terms of avoidance and approach responses.[1] Bill—Mager would say—has an avoidance response to English literature; that is, he moves away from it as much as possible and expresses hostility when coerced into performing in this discipline. Sally, on the other hand, finds every occasion to increase her participation in this subject. She has an approach tendency toward English literature. The challenge for the teacher seems obvious—increase approach tendencies and decrease avoidance tendencies. But with Bill and Sally we are looking at extreme cases. In any given class there are many more subtle manifestations of approach and avoidance behaviors. The beginning teacher needs training in *what* to look for as well as in techniques for converting avoidance behaviors to approach behaviors.

> *Affective Domain of Bloom's Taxonomy*

We need a different kind of classification system other than the cognitive domain for making fine distinctions between different affective behaviors. To assist the teacher in classifying affective response, Krathwohl, Bloom, and Masia developed *Taxonomy of Educational Objectives, Handbook II: Affective Domain.* [2] In this taxonomy, interests, attitudes, values and appreciation are plotted on a continuum that ranges from mere passive awareness at the lowest level of internalization to being characterized by certain values and attitudes. At the characterization stage, one's personality comes to be taken as equivalent to certain values. The person is those values, those attitudes. What values do you equate with John F. Kennedy? With Hitler? How would you characterize their values on education? On politics? On freedom of religion? How would you describe each person's character?

As we move from the most rudimentary affective level to the highest level, that of characterization, each level in between expresses a tendency toward character formation.

By examining the distinctions between levels by learning to recognize them, we can determine approximately where the student is in respect to developing a consistent value system. We can raise questions such as the following: Is the student passively or actively attending? Does the student merely acquiesce in responding or does the student show satisfaction in responding? Does the student merely acknowledge a value or defend that value? Does the student seek out those same values in interpersonal relationships? Krathwohl, Bloom, and Masia address these concerns and others by providing in their taxonomy a range of distinctions based on the degree of internalization of values. Following is a shortened version of this taxonomy.[3]

1.0 *Receiving (Attending)*
The learner is attending to what the teacher is presenting, but only passively. The responsibility of capturing student attention rests with the teacher.

1.1 *Awareness*
Awareness is distinct from cognitive level 1.0 (receiving [attending]) in that the student is not expected to recall facts, only to be aware of them. The student does not discriminate causes of the stimulus, but is aware of symbolic representation of people, things, and situations.

1.2 *Willingness to Receive*
There is a willingness to attend, but a suspension of judgment in regard to what is attended. This willingness may range from a toleration of stimulation to a willingness to take notice of the phenomenon.

1.3 *Controlled or Selected Attention*
At this stage the learner controls his or her attention and willingly selects the stimulus among competing stimuli.

2.0 *Responding*
This is the stage of active attending and goes beyond a mere willingness to attend. The student at this stage begins to participate with the stimulus phenomenon. This is the level of engagement corresponding to most teacher's "interest" objectives.

2.1 *Acquiescence in Responding*
Students are compliant with the stimulus to behave in a particular way—for example, they comply with health regulations.

2.2 *Willingness to Respond*
Here enters a voluntary dimension of response. Free choice is present.

2.3 *Satisfaction in Response*
The behavior is not only voluntary, but is accompanied by a feeling of satisfaction or pleasure. At this stage the student may find pleasure in solving math problems or in reading about national political affairs.

3.0 *Valuing*
A set of specified ideals or values are internalized. The learner may display this value consistently.

3.1 *Acceptance of a Value*
Consistency of response to the class of objects and phenomena with which the belief or attitude is identified. Others perceive one as holding a particular value.

3.2 *Preference for a Value*
Here the student not only accepts the value, but makes a commitment to it. The student takes a stand, puts himself on line. Loyalty, certainty, and a tendency to convert others to the values one holds characterizes this level of internalization.

4.0 *Organization*
Values are organized into a system. The value system functions to guide judgments relevant to a variety of situations.

4.1 *Conceptualization of a Value*
At this stage the value is conceptualized. The symbolic import of the value enables the student to relate it to other values.

4.2 *Organization of a Value System*
Disparate values are brought into a coherent relationship.

5.0 *Characterization by a Value or a Value Complex*
Values are organized into a world view. Stimulation of the value complex does not arouse strong emotion except when the individual is threatened or challenged.

5.1 *Generalized Set*
Internal consistency is added to the value complex. The value complex is seen as a consistent response to a family of situations.

5.2 *Characterization*
One becomes a living emblem of the values espoused.[4]

Identifying Feelings and Values

How, then, does the teacher identify the stage of value internalization for each student? And once identified, how does the teacher increase approach tendencies toward any given subject?

It will be useful to translate Krathwohl, Bloom, and Masia's taxonomy into operational terms. In doing so, we can get a handle on what behavior to look for. We can ask, quite directly, What do various stages of affective development look like in the classroom? Following are examples:

1.1 *Awareness*
Recognition that there may be more than one acceptable point of view. Sensitivity to social situations. Consciousness of color, form, and arrangement.

PROBE Imagine three classroom examples of 1.1

1.2 *Willingness to Receive*
Develops a tolerance for a variety of types of music. Sensitivity to social problems.

PROBE Recall a time when you experienced level 1.2

1.3 *Controlled or Selected Attention*
Listens for rhythm in poetry or prose. Reads aloud, showing preference for newspaper readings.

2.1 *Acquiescence in Responding*
Willingness to comply with health regulations. Reads the assigned literature.

PROBE How can you distinguish 1.3 from 2.1?

2.2 *Willingness to Respond*
Voluntarily looks for informative books dealing with hobbies or interests. Engages on his or her own in a variety of hobbies and recreational activities.

PROBE How can you distinguish 2.1 from 2.2 behavior?

2.3 *Satisfaction in Response*
Derives satisfaction in singing for others. Listens with pleasure to music.

PROBE Recall a time when you were satisfied with completing a task.

3.1 *Acceptance of a Value*
Seeks to obtain optimum health. Listens to and participates in public discussion.

PROBE How can you distinguish values from facts? Give two examples.

3.2 *Preference for a Value*
Deliberately examines a variety of viewpoints in controversial issues with a view to forming opinions about them. Preference for artistically appropriate choice.

PROBE Are values reflected in one's choices? If students do not engage in controversial issues, what does this say about their values?

3.3 *Commitment*
Loyalty to the various groups in which one holds membership. Takes a stand on human rights.

PROBE How can you tell if one breaks a commitment?

4.1 *Conceptualization of a Value*
Relates his or her own ethical standards and personal goals through the reading of biography.

PROBE Can you conceptualize your values?

4.2 *Organization of a Value System*
Begins to form judgments as to the major direction in which American society should move. Develops techniques for controlling aggression in culturally acceptable patterns.

PROBE Cite instances of 4.2 from your observations of children, adolescents and adults.

5.1 *Generalized Set*
Readiness to revise judgments and to change behavior in the light of evidence. Judges problems in terms of situation, issues, purposes, and consequences involved rather than in terms of fixed dogmatic precepts or emotionally wishful thinking.

PROBE Recall a time when you revised your judgment in the light of evidence.

5.2 *Characterization*
Develops a consistent philosophy of life and a conscience.

PROBE What would be evidence that one had developed a consistent philosophy of life?

Resistance to Affective Teaching

Though it may be acknowledged that feelings, values, attitudes, and interests are of great importance, there has been considerable resistance to the inclusion of affective goals in American education. There are many reasons for this resistance. There is, for example, the conviction that one's values are private and, as such, should not be made public in the way cognitive performance is made public.

Evaluation is another concern. To what extent, if at all, should a student's attitudes toward a course count as a grade? And if attitude does count, how can the teacher minimize the possibility that some students will fake affective behavior in order to receive a high grade? And if one is going to claim to measure affective response as relevant to evaluation of learning, then how does one measure it? What is useful and what is fair?

Some teachers may feel that if they include affective goals they may be setting themselves up for emotionally laden dialogue in the class—disputes, perhaps, that are difficult to resolve. Some teachers may fear that their teaching of values will be perceived by students as being soft.

Some teachers may opt for the ease of teaching to the lower-level cognitive objectives. By using a lecture format one can teach to factual recall. Tests are purposely designed to emphasize recall of facts so that there will be minimum ambiguity and minimum debate about what constitutes a correct answer. And, finally, a whole school system may in fact, if not in design, eliminate affective objectives as well as the higher-level cognitive objectives. Affective objectives may require difficult planning and data gathering over a period of years. If we want to know how certain values are being carried into adult life and the work world, we will need to conduct costly longitudinal studies. The expense may be prohibitive.

Relationships Between Domains

Prior to the research of the 1960s it was commonly assumed that if the teacher did an outstanding job teaching the cognitive aspects of a course, the students would, as a consequence, develop an interest in the course and continue to participate on their own, which would eventually lead the students to practical application. If students mastered the intellectual content, it was assumed they were "prepared for life."[5] Work skills and creative applications in the form of projects and further investigation would just naturally unfold. Unfortunately, the scenario was not so grandiose. Many students succumbed to boredom before reaching the stage of application and research.

Joseph E. Bogen, who pioneered some of the split-brain research, has called attention to the excessive dominance of cognitive objectives in the American school and recommended methods of offsetting this bias.[6] Carl Sagan, in his *Dragons of Eden,* provides a similar argument.[7] The most significant contribution to the fields

Student-designed book covers provide a way of connecting valuing with learning.

of law, ethics, music, science, and technology, he says, are the products springing from the combination of the affective and cognitive processes.

Leonard Kaplan, in his *Developing Objectives in the Affective Domain,* argues that the use of affective objectives creates the possibility of exploring higher-level cognitive objectives.[8]

Thomas B. Roberts builds his meditative teaching techniques, called "centering,"[9] on the transpersonal psychology of Abraham Maslow.[10] Georgi Lozanov's suggestopedic processes make use of imaging, body awareness, rhythm, and music—all processes requiring the use of affective objectives.[11]

And, yet, these practitioners all claim that their methods expand human effectiveness both cognitively and affectively. The affect actually increases intellectual power—a view that echoes Dewey's assertion that "enthusiasm is an attitude that operates as an intellectual force."[12]

In the 1960s much was made of teaching for relevance, which was often interpreted as teaching to the students' interest. The affective domain came to be equated with the "me generation" philosophy. This truncated version of approaching affect was a distortion of Dewey's views on education and experience. Of *interests* Dewey said:

> Interests in reality are but attitudes toward possible experiences; they are not achievements. . . . To take the phenomena presented at a given age as in any way self-explanatory or self-contained is inevitably to result in indulgence or spoiling.[13]

Interests, said Dewey, should be connected with cognitive learning to generate what he called "working power." The teacher can assume more responsibility for creating interests in subjects and in connecting that interest with long-range cognitive objectives, giving the learning working power.

There are many possible patterns effectively used by teachers in which affective and cognitive objectives are mixed. Can you imagine some ways in which they can be combined?

Stating Affective Objectives

There are a number of ways to state affective objectives. In writing affective objectives you may find it useful to keep certain questions in mind. How can one focus on attitudes and values in a way that will maximize learning and increase the probability that the student will continue to learn on his own? Here are some examples:

1. Shows a commitment to the safety and well-being of the chemistry class by encouraging class members to abide by the safety rules of the lab.
2. Indicates an interest in learning about the physical properties of the heavy metals by bringing to class current articles on the subject.

Notice that the first part of the objective—"shows a commitment to . . ." and "indicates an interest in learning about . . ."—states the affect, and that the part of the objective following the prepositional phrase provides public evidence of the affect.[14]

PROBES In respect to Krathwohl's taxonomy, which levels of the affective domain are represented in the above example? Using the format above write two affective objectives in your field.

The Fusion of Affect and Cognition

Alfred North Whitehead claims that affect is present in all subject matter. Every scientific treatise, he says, is shot through and through with emotion. The attempt to avoid affect may be an artificial pursuit masked by the pretense of objectivity. Moreover, when we move away from the hard sciences and consider history, social studies, literature, and physical education, it is not only difficult to avoid affect but probably counterproductive to do so. What would these subjects be if we stripped them of emotional content and value? Lists of dates and facts to be memorized? Canned arguments and interpretations provided by the text or teacher to be parroted by the student?

The way that we interpret facts and the beliefs we hold about a subject may actually shape our feelings toward that subject. The view adopted here is that as human beings we are physical, mental, emotional, and valuing beings. In this respect, the cognitive, affective, and psychomotor domains are artificial constructs designed to give us an intellectual handle on human qualities that emerge in concert. The affect and the physical response are present with the cognitive and vice versa. Teachers have the privilege of enhancing this interplay.

The Psychomotor Domain

The purpose of the psychomotor domain is to classify human movements on a continuum ranging from the simple to the complex. The basic movements of human beings—movements that do not require being taught—are running, jumping, climbing, lifting, carrying, hanging, and throwing. These movements are basic in another way. According to Anita Harrow, they represent "the need of the organism to stay active." Included in this taxonomy is "all observable voluntary human motion."[15] Following is a shortened version of Harrow's psychomotor domain:

1. Reflex Movements
   a. Segmental Reflexes
   b. Intersegmental Reflexes
   c. Suprasegmental Reflexes
2. Basic-Fundamental Movements
   a. Locomotor Movements
   b. Nonlocomotor Movements
   c. Manipulative Movements
3. Perceptual Abilities
   a. Kinesthetic Discrimination
   b. Visual Discrimination
   c. Auditory Discrimination
   d. Tactile Discrimination
   e. Coordinated Abilities
4. Physical Abilities
   a. Endurance
   b. Strength
   c. Flexibility
   d. Agility
5. Skilled Movements
   a. Simple Adaptive Skill
   b. Compound Adaptive Skill
   c. Complex Adaptive Skill

6. Nondiscursive Communication
   a. Expressive Movement
   b. Interpretive Movement

For years after Bloom and Krathwohl published their taxonomies of cognitive and affective domains the psychomotor taxonomy was seen as a promise, a taxonomy that would be useful to physical education teachers and for little else. But the psychomotor domain cuts across all disciplines and all human activity. The use of "other-hand writing" in an English class stimulates the organism in ways that often elicit novel forms of writing.[16] And, yet, physical stimuli is primary in this technique. The processing of information occurs in three basic ways—through vision, through hearing, and through psychomotor and kinesthetic activity.

Some students need physical engagement to achieve maximum performance. In giving a writing lesson on the descriptive qualities of a thunderstorm a teacher may inject, as part of the process, the physical creation of the sound of the rain—perhaps by having the students simulate the downpour with quick, repetitive slaps on their own legs. Handwriting, some visual responses, and even gesture used in speeches are all kinds of physical movement.

PROBES

1. How does affect differ from cognition? Give examples of each from your own experience.
2. Can you think of specific cases wherein cognition and affect would blend so that it would be difficult to distinguish the two?
3. It is commonly assumed that affective objectives are more difficult to write than cognitive objectives. Do you agree? Why?
4. Give six reasons teachers may avoid using affective objectives.
5. What are two basic uses of Krathwohl's taxonomy of the affective domain?
6. Write five affective objectives in your subject and state how you would use them if you were teaching.
7. How does the instructional use of affective objectives differ from teaching to student interest?
8. What are two research claims for using affective objectives in instruction?
9. Do you agree that teachers need training in discriminating degrees of affective behavior? See Leonard Kaplan's *How to Write Objectives in the Affective Domain* for a taxonomy specifically designed for observation of instruction.
10. Define psychomotor. How is this domain distinguished from the cognitive and affective domain?

■ SUMMARY

Students may tend toward a subject or withdraw from it. The determinants of this behavior—feelings, values, and attitudes—can be classified in a hierarchy developed by Krathwohl, Bloom, and Masia, published in *Taxonomy of Educational Objectives: Affective Domain.*

The simplest level of affect is receiving or passively attending; the highest level is characterization. At this stage the student has internalized a value system to a degree that he or she becomes a living embodiment of that value system.

The taxonomy provides a basis for observing stages of affective development in students as well as a guide to planning objectives for feelings, values, and attitudes. The taxonomy may also provide a systematic means of cutting through the resistance that has traditionally surrounded the inclusion of feeling and values in instruction.

There are many reasons for the traditional resistance to affective teaching. Among those reasons are the following:

1. The belief that one's values are private and as such should not be made part of public learning
2. The fear that the introduction of values will be construed as indoctrination.
3. The difficulty of agreeing on which values, attitudes, and feelings are important
4. The fear of being perceived by the student as a soft teacher—one tending toward sentiment rather than hard facts.
5. The difficulty of writing clear affective objectives
6. The ease of writing low-level cognitive objectives conducive to a fact-giving lecture format
7. The difficulty of evaluating the affective behavior
8. The assumption that cognitive content will automatically stimulate affective growth
9. The expense of longitudinal studies to test the effectiveness of long-range affective objectives
10. The fear of opening up heated dialogue that one is not trained to handle.

Building positive attitudes through affective teaching can actually increase cognitive learning. In this respect, it is counterproductive to eliminate affect—counterproductive even to the mastery of content. By using Krathwohl's taxonomy, teachers can systematically plan the enrichment of content by incorporating values and feelings, ranging from the simple to the complex, in their teaching.

The psychomotor domain is useful in describing human movement. Movements may range from simple reflex movements to highly skilled movements of the sort witnessed in gymnastics. At the highest level the body is precisely controlled without a support system. Examples of this would include a pass receiver twisting his body in midair at the precise moment to catch a pass or a Mary Lou Retton exhibiting a powerful but aesthetically precise Tsukahara on the vault. Yet, the psychomotor domain is not restricted to physical education and athletics. Typing skills, painting and drawing, and physics, as well as shop, all require dexterity and precision of movement. The humanities, in particular, can be enriched by the inclusion of psychomotor processes.

■ *NOTES*

1. Robert F. Mager, *Developing Attitude Toward Learning or Smats "n" Smuts* (Belmont, CA: Pitman Management and Training, 1984), 17–25.
2. David R. Krathwohl, Benjamin S. Bloom, and Bertram B. Masia, *Taxonomy of Educational Objectives, Handbook II: Affective Domain* (New York: McKay, 1964), 176–185.
3. Ibid.
4. Ibid.
5. Ibid., 85–91.
6. Joseph E. Bogen, "The Other Side of the Brain. VII: Some Educational Aspects of Hemispheric Specialization," *UCLA Educator* 17 (1975): 24–32.
7. Carl Sagan, *The Dragons of Eden* (New York: Random House, 1977).
8. Leonard Kaplan, *Developing Objectives in the Affective Domain* (Columbus, OH: Collegiate Publishing, Inc., 1978), 62 and 65.
9. Thomas B. Roberts, *The Second Century Book* (Englewood Cliffs, NJ: Prentice-Hall, 1977).
10. Abraham Maslow, *Toward a Psychology of Being* (New York: Van Nostrand, 1968).
11. Georgi Lozanov, *Suggestology and the Outlines of Suggestopedy* (New York: Gordon and Breach, 1979).
12. John Dewey, *How We Think* (Massachusetts: Heath, 1933), 32.
13. John Dewey, *The Child and the Curriculum* (Chicago: University of Chicago Press, 1902), 15–16.
14. Michael A. Lorber and Walter D. Pierce, *Objectives, Methods and Evaluation for Secondary Teaching* (Englewood Cliffs, NJ: Prentice-Hall, 1983), 39–50.
15. Anita J. Harrow, *A Taxonomy of the Psychomotor Domain: A Guide for Developing Behavioral Objectives* (New York: McKay, 1972), 31.
16. Marilee Zdenek, *The Right Brain Experience: An Intimate Program to Free the Powers of Your Imagination* (New York: McGraw-Hill, 1983), 34–35.

Planning IV: Designing Effective Lesson Plans

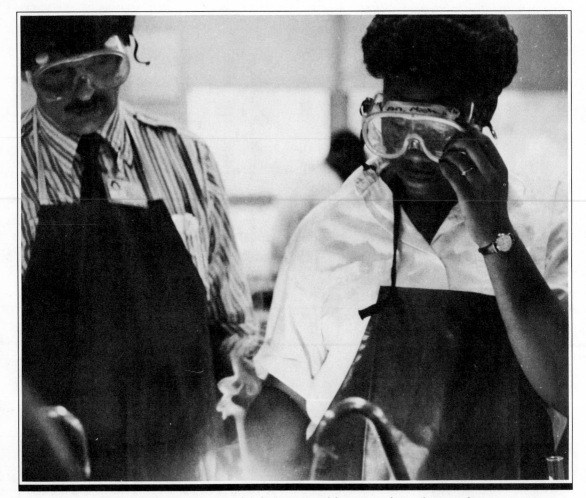

Burning magnesium: Planning includes practicing appropriate safety procedures.

Every educational system has a moral good that it triest to attain and that informs its curriculum. It wants to produce a cartoon kind of human being. This intention is more or less explicit, more or less a result of reflection; but even the neutral subjects, like reading and writing and arithmetic, take their place in a vision of the educated person.

—Allan Bloom

One way to get a handle on the kind of teacher you are becoming is to raise the question that Allan Bloom raises: What kind of human being do you wish to produce? Responses such as "I'm just teaching my subject; I'm neutral in regard to values" will not get you off the hook. Do you want the student to passively accept all your statements regarding the content you are teaching? Do you want the student to observe or enter into dialogue with others? Do you want the student to focus on lower-level cognition or to analyze and evaluate? Do you expect or allow emotional response? If you write an honest lesson plan, whatever you say about these matters, will be reflected in your plan. The very format of a lesson plan is an indication of your educational philosophy. Let's consider a basic format and then look at some alternative forms (see Figure 6.1).

Lesson Plan Format

Following is a lesson plan format that can be used in conjunction with the chapters in this text on instructional purposes and the writing of clear objectives in the cognitive, affective, and psychomotor domains.[1]

DAILY PLAN
    I. Type of Lesson
    II. Grade Level
       Time Allotment
    III. Objectives
       A. Conceptual Objectives
          (Sample terms: Know, understand, appreciate, grasp, enjoy, believe)
       B. Performance Objectives
          (Students will be able to write, recite, present, identify, differentiate, solve, construct, list, compare, contrast, etc.)
    IV. Instructional Strategies
       (Lecture, discussion, demonstration, workshop, silent reading, guided fantasy, etc.)
    V. Procedures
       A. Motivational Activity
          (How will the teacher stimulate interest)
       B. Developmental Activities
          1. The teacher will . . .
          2. The students will . . .

Figure 6.1 Select a lesson plan format that expresses your instructional purposes.

    VI. Materials
        (Books, pictures, movies, pencils, paper, etc.)
    VII. Summary/Evaluation

How will the teacher determine what was learned? Conceptual objectives (normative objectives) are open-ended. One can always continue to understand, to know to appreciate, to grasp, to enjoy, and to believe. This is the big picture. There may be thousands of manifestations of these norms. Select some of these manifestations and state them as performance objectives (III.B).

Now ask yourself how you are going to accomplish III.A and B. What instructional processes (lecture, discussion, demonstration, workshop, silent reading, guided fantasy, etc.) will you use? Selecting a method is all well and good, and there is evidence for the workability of most methods, but you should ask if the method is suitable for your instructional purposes and objectives. If so, how will you initially engage the students and hold their interest? This phase is often referred to as mood set or psychological set. In one case, a teacher may have appropriate music playing as students enter class; in another, a teacher may tell a personal anecdote. Part V.B of the lesson plan format calls for making a distinction between what you will do as the teacher and what the students will do. Some teachers find it convenient to split part of the page in half, showing teacher activities on the left and student activities on the right. If you later videotape your lesson, you can use a split screen to determine how accurately you have projected the relationship between student behavior and teacher behavior. In part VI you will list any materials needed. This is a checklist. You could compare it with preparing for a short trip. What will you need? Also, if you were traveling, you would probably check your equipment beforehand to make sure it works. You should do the same for teaching. Check everything in advance to make sure it works properly. Then put a check beside your items on the lesson plan.

Teacher Behavior	*Student Behavior*
1. Plays a cassette tape of Bach's *Brandenburg Concerto #1.*	1. Listens to the music.
2. Gives a reading with music (Bach), using a teacher-created story about proofreading.	2. Listens to the reading and, using colored crayons, writes a word mind map of the experience of the reading.
3. Gives students directions on creating a mind map of their experience of listening.	3. Using crayons, draws a picture mind map from the word mind map.

In the summary/evaluation section you will want to have the class re-create the lesson in some way so that it is complete and the students have a sense of ownership. This can take the form of asking key questions that promote synthesis. It can be done verbally through a short written test that the students score themselves or through reaction to images of the lesson projected on a screen.

The Same Format/Different Content

The same format can be used to organize instruction for different content areas. As you study these representative samples, ask yourself if you would change anything and why.

■ *Daily Plan: An Introduction to Decimals*

I. Type of Lesson: Mathematics—An Introduction to Decimals
II. Grade Level: Eighth
   Time Allotment: 55 min.
III. Objectives
   A. Conceptual Objectives
      The students will understand the basic concepts of the decimal system. They will know the correct names of the fractional places to the right of the decimal point.

B. Performance Objective

When given a written numeral, the students will be able to correctly identify a digit in a specific place in the place value system to the right and left of the decimal point. They will be able to read aloud decimal numbers using the correct terminology. The student will also be able to write the standard numeral when given the numeral in written or spoken form.

IV. Instructional Strategies

Lecture, discussion, demonstration, and workshop

V. Procedures

A. Motivational Activity

The teacher will write various dollar amounts on the chalkboard in decimal notation (i.e., $4.89, $15.99, $325.06) and begin a class discussion on the meaning of that notation. For example, .25 means twenty-five cents or twenty-five hundredths.

B. Developmental Activities

1. The teacher will review the place value system of digits to the left of a decimal point:

   2, 5 6 4, 3 2 8, 2 1 0

2. The teacher will then explain the concept of decimal fractions as being between whole numbers:

   2.45 is between 2 and 3

3. The teacher will then write a number on the board with digits to the right of the decimal point and explain the corresponding values:

   3 . 6 8 0 5 3 2

4. The teacher will then explain to the students how to read a decimal fraction.

   a. Read the part to the right of the decimal point as you would read a whole number.

   b. Then read the value of the last place to the right:

      6 . 8 7 9

      six and eight hundred seventy-nine thousandths

5. The students will then be given a worksheet to be completed in class. The students may work individually or in small groups.

6. After approximately 15 minutes, the teacher will correct the first part of the worksheet with the students answering aloud.

7. The teacher will ask for volunteers to write their answers onto the second part of the worksheet on the board.

8. The teacher will then lead a class discussion of each problem, explaining why or why not the answers on the board are correct.
9. The students will then have the opportunity to correct their own worksheets and will be asked to keep them for their personal reference.
10. The students will be given a homework assignment to be completed by the next class meeting. This assignment will be collected and graded by the teacher.

VI. Materials

Chalkboard, chalk, paper, pencils, ditto, textbook

VII. Summary/Evaluation

Through lectures the introductory concepts of decimal fractions will be introduced. Afterwards, the students will be given a worksheet that deals specifically with the concepts introduced. After student completion of the worksheet, the teacher will lead a class discussion of the worksheet problems. Through student participation and the answers to the questions, the teacher will have an idea of the students' level of understanding. The students will also be given a homework assignment, due at the next class meeting, to be handed in and corrected by the teacher.

■ **Worksheet on Decimals**

Part One: Read aloud:

1. 8.90
2. 48.006
3. 876.9876
4. 0.987
5. 12.08709
6. 5.098
7. 54.076543
8. 32.9876533
9. 1.234568
10. 3.000001

For 873.098431, give the digit that is in the

1. hundreds place _____
2. hundredths place _____
3. tenths place _____
4. millionths place _____
5. hundred thousandths place _____
6. ones place _____
7. ten thousandths place _____
8. thousandths place _____

Part Two: Write the standard numeral:

1. six and five tenths _____

2. forty-six and two hundredths _____

3. ninety-five thousandths _____

4. two hundred sixty-six and seven hundred fifty-two thousandths

   _____

5. three and five thousand seven hundred forty-nine ten thousandths

   _____

6. fifty-eight and three hundred ninety-two thousand six hundred fifty-four millionths _____

■ **Homework Assignment**
Page 21, Problems 1–8, 21–26

■ *Daily Plan: Basic Techniques of Badminton*

I. Type of Lesson: Physical Education
II. Grade Level: Eleventh
III. Objectives
   A. Conceptual Objective
      For eleventh-grade individual sports students to grasp the basic technique for underhand and overhead clears, to understand the importance of cooperative practice, and to know the desired flight pathway of the shuttle for the underhand and overhead clears.
   B. Performance Objective
      By the end of the class period, students will be able to alternate between overhead clear and underhand clear for at least six consecutive hits while in partnership practice formation.
      Upon completion of the unit, the students will be able to properly diagram the desired pathway for the underhand and overhead clears when given a side-view diagram of a badminton court.
IV. Instructional Strategies
   Lecture, demonstration, and workshop
V. Procedures
   A. Motivational Activity
      Initial demonstration of the skill will serve as motivation for students as well as the anticipation of acquiring the skills necessary to engage in game play.

B. Developmental Activities
   1. Students will obtain proper equipment (1 racquet and 1 shuttle each).
   2. Teacher will lead class in warm-up activities.
   3. Teacher will call group in and introduce the underhand clear.
   4. Teacher and student will demonstrate underhand clear.
   5. Teacher will analyze underhand clear in terms of component parts.
   6. Teacher will repeat demonstration and ask for questions.
   7. Students will practice underhand clear motion individually against the wall.
   8. Teacher will circulate, providing students with help and feedback.
   9. Teacher will stop group and instruct students to partner-up and practice across the net as in the previous demonstration.
   10. Teacher will circulate to help keep students on task and provide assistance.
   11. Teacher will call students in. *Repeat* steps 3–10 with overhead clear.
   12. Students will practice with partner using both underhand and overhead clears, trying for maximum consecutive hits.

VI. Materials
   25 racquets
   25 shuttles or yarn balls
   4 standards
   3 nets
   Shuttle pathway cards
   Lecture note cards

VII. Summary/Evaluation
   The knowledge components will be evaluated at the completion of the unit on a written examination. The application of the knowledge and students' abilities to practice cooperatively will be evaluated through behavioral observation of skill technique and students' ability to stay on task. More specifically, skill acquisition will be determined by the students' ability to consecutively strike a shuttle across the net and will be reflected by the maximum number in one sequence reached by each partnership.

■ *Daily Plan: Quantum Mechanics Used in Simple Bonding*

  I. Type of Lesson: Chemistry
     Time Allotment: 50 min.
  II. Grade Level: Eleventh
  III. Objectives
    A. Conceptual Objective
      The students will understand quantum mechanics used in simple bonding configurations of previously selected molecules and be able to visualize these patterns.
    B. Performance Objective
      Using molecular model kits, the students, in groups of two, will be able to construct at least four of six given molecules. The students will also be able to exhibit the same proficiency drawing the quantum mechanical models.
  IV. Instructional Strategies
    A. Motivational Activities
      The teacher will explain how model making can be an asset in chemistry, and if properly learned, how today's lesson will save them countless hours of boring memorization.
    B. Developmental Activities
      1. Before class the teacher will draw a Lewis dot, a stick, and a quantum-mechanical model of the same molecule on the chalkboard.
      2. The teacher will start the class with a discussion of model making and how to save time studying by learning today's lesson.
      3. The teacher will introduce the content of the lesson by comparing the three drawings.
      4. The teacher will then add 3-D to the lesson by demonstrating how to build a molecular model.
      5. Any confusion or unclarity will be discussed.
      6. The students will then be given a list of six molecules and molecular model kits to be shared by two students each.*
      7. The students will build the models to be observed by the teacher as they work.
      8. The students will be given homework, in which they must draw the quantum mechanical models of the six molecules.

*A typical list of six molecules includes: HCl, HNO_3, CH_3COOH, H_3PO_4, NaOH, and NH_4OH. For extra credit, CO_2 could be added.

VI. Materials
Chalkboard, chalk, 15 molecular model kits, and the following questions:
1. How many of you have ever built a model?
2. Did you know that model building is a very important talent to a chemist?
3. How many of you would rather go to Friday night's basketball game than study chemistry?

VII. Evaluation
The teacher will gain a general knowledge of the students' capabilities through observation during class to help those who need it. The homework will be collected the following day and will be graded according to the number of correct structures.

■ *Daily Plan: The Logic of Soviet-American International Relations*

I. Type of Lesson: Political Science
II. Grade Level: Twelfth
Time Allotment: 50 min.
III. Objectives
A. Purposes
The students will comprehend the concepts and nature of Soviet-American relations as they are defined by the logic of international relations. They will understand the concepts of mutual deterrence, amoral doctrine (realpolitik), and the prisoner's dilemma theory. The students will have a working knowledge of the complexity of foreign policy and international relations as applied to decision-making strategies.
B. Evaluation Statement
The students will be able to differentiate between the moral doctrine and the amoral doctrine. Likewise, they will be able to offer a conceptual analysis of Soviet-American relations and apply three out of four factors in the success of the mutual deterrence strategy of the last 28 years between the two superpowers. Finally, they will be able to identify the dangers of playing the deterrence strategy. This will be done through in-class observation and homework to be handed in at the next session.
IV. Instructional Strategies
Lecture, game, discussion, homework

V. Procedures
  A. Motivational Activity
     As students walk into class, they will be assigned to a group identified with numbers 1 through 4. There will also be an announcement to the students that they will be participating in the international community game.
  B. Learning Activity
     1. The teacher begins class by outlining the major concepts with which the class will be dealing:
        a. moral doctrine vs. amoral doctrine
        b. logic of conflict in international relations
        c. mutual deterrence
     2. The teacher introduces the game:
        a. each group to represent an individual community
        b. rules
           i. absolute secrecy between communities
           ii. each community allowed one vote of yes or no
           iii. if there is a unanimous vote of yes among all the communities, each group gets 15 points
           iv. if there are yes and no votes cast, yes = 3 points and no = 10 points
           v. if there is a unanimous vote of no among all the communities, each community receives 10 points
     3. Teacher conducts game:
        a. four ballots taken
        b. first three cast with absolute secrecy
        c. fourth ballot taken after delegates from each community meet
     4. Discuss outcome by answering the following questions:
        a. what happened
        b. were those groups casting negative votes immoral or amoral
        c. was this just a game
        d. when or at what level does it stop being a game
        e. what happened on the fourth ballot
        f. were there cheaters on the last ballot
     5. Discuss criteria affecting the outcome of the prisoner's dilemma:
        a. information and communication
        b. the existence of lags

          c. dynamics of the rivalry
            i. are they continuous?
            ii. are they one-shot affairs?
          d. dynamics of the payoff structure
      6. Assign homework sheet

VI. Materials
    Chalkboard/chalk, paper, pencils, homework sheet

VII. Summary/Evaluation
    Evaluation will take place in three ways. The first and most immediate feedback will come from in-class observation and informal evaluation through the discussion segments of the lesson. The second form of evaluation will occur in the homework assignment, while the final evaluation will take place in the examination at the end of the unit.

HOMEWORK ASSIGNMENT

1. From class discussion, what are three of the four factors discussed as affecting the outcome of any prisoner's dilemma scenario? (List them below.)

   a. _____
      _____

   b. _____
      _____

   c. _____
      _____

2. Using the three factors above, explain in your own words why the United States and the Soviet Union have not yet gone to war. In other words, do they possess qualities that alleviate the tension of guessing what the other is doing? (Use a separate piece of paper.)

3. Using your knowledge of the amoral doctrine or Bismark's realpolitik, and your knowledge of the moral doctrine and how immorality can be linked to these, try to categorize the following events, giving a short explanation for each answer. (Use a separate piece of paper.)
   a. The continued U.S. sanctions against Cuba, specifically the economic sanctions
   b. The U.S. boycott of the 1980 Summer Olympic games
   c. The Soviet boycott of the 1984 Summer Olympics
   d. The bombing of the U.S. Marines' headquarters in Lebanon
   e. The U.S. invasion of the Grenada Islands.

■ *Daily Plan: Creative Writing*

I. Type of Lesson: English Composition
II. Grade Level: Eighth
   Time Allotment: 30 min.
III. Objectives
   A. Conceptual Objectives
      To develop students' ability to use a variety of descriptive words and phrases in their writing.
   B. Performance Objectives
      Students will be able to look at a person or object and list five or more words that describe that person or object.
IV. Instructional Strategy
   Lecture and group discussion
V. Procedure
   Motivational Activities: The teacher will ask the students if they have ever tried to describe something that they really liked or enjoyed or were very excited about, and allow the students to give examples.
   Developmental Activities
   1. The teacher will show the students a picture and ask them for words that describe what is in the picture.
   2. After students have had some practice in generating descriptive terms the teacher will pass out an exercise that asks them individually to list descriptive words for a picture.
   3. After the students have compiled a list of descriptive words, the teacher will ask them to write a short paragraph that incorporates what they think are the best descriptive words from their list.
   4. The teacher will collect the papers at the end of the lesson.
VI. Materials
   Pictures, printed exercise, pencils
VII. Evaluation
   Students should be able to write a short paragraph using not less than four of the descriptive words from the lists that they have generated.

■ *Daily Plan: Uses of the Metric System*

I. Type of Lesson: Math
II. Grade Level: Eighth
   Time Allotment: 55 Min.

III. Objectives
   A. Conceptual Objectives
      For eighth-grade students to develop an understanding of the metric system—its vocabulary and uses—and become familiar with measuring weight (mass) in the metric system.
   B. Performance Objectives
      Students will be able to complete a word puzzle on metric vocabulary, to estimate the mass or weight of objects in metric units, to verify their estimates using a metric scale, and to complete a metric worksheet for homework.
IV. Instructional Strategies
   Lecture, group discussion, individual worksheet exercises, class worksheet exercise, measuring and weighing workshop.
V. Procedure
   Motivational Activities: The teacher will display various posters and discuss examples of how the metric system is already used in the United States. The class will discuss these and other examples. What are some of the advantages of the metric system? What are some of the disadvantages of the metric system?
   Developmental Activities
   1. The teacher will display a chart and introduce the three commonly used units of measure in the metric system—meter, liter, and gram. The teacher will show an example of each unit.
   2. The teacher will explain the meanings of the metric prefixes and display a chart of the prefixes.
   3. The teacher will use flash cards to explain the basic metric vocabulary and their abbreviations.
   4. Each student will be given a metric vocabulary worksheet to be done together in class.
   5. Each student will be given a metric vocabulary word puzzle to complete in class. The first student to complete the puzzle will be the winner.
   6. The teacher will discuss the commonly used metric units of mass, the gram and kilogram, and provide examples of objects weighing one gram (a paper clip) and one kilogram (1000 paper clips).
   7. Each student will be given a chart for estimating weight in the metric system. Each student will record on the sheet the estimated weight in kilograms of each student in the group. Then each student will be weighed on a metric scale, and the actual weights will be recorded on the chart. The difference between the estimated and actual

weights of each student will be determined, and the differences for the entire class will be totaled. The student with the smallest difference between the estimated and actual weights of the group will be the winner.

8. A metric unit worksheet will be assigned for homework.

VI. Materials

Worksheets, pencils, flash cards, metric scale, paper clips, posters, charts, metric measuring cup

VII. Summary/Evaluation

The worksheet given for homework will review the metric units presented during the lesson and will contain simple word problems involving metrics. The students' ability to complete these worksheets will reflect their understanding of the metric units of measure. The teacher will also explain that tomorrow's lesson will involve activities that deal with measuring length in metric units.

It is worth noting that each lesson plan presented here is in a different discipline, yet the same format is used throughout. This format is highly flexible. The format forces one to spell out relationships between conceptual objectives and performance objectives. In doing so, one must state the big picture *and* specific manifestations of that picture in the form of observable behavior.

The very format of a lesson plan, then, reveals the thinking of the person designing or using it. One could, for example, focus only on behavioral objectives or only on conceptual objectives.

PROBE What other pedagogical assumptions are revealed in the above format? Can you think of alternative formats for IV (unstructured strategies) and V (procedures)?

Some Alternative Formats for Lesson Planning

Following are models of lesson plans representing three of the most popular educational movements: the Hunter model, the behavioral model, and the SALT model.

■ *The Hunter Lesson Format*

Madeline Hunter identifies seven elements in a basic lesson plan. She calls her format "a basic white sauce for teaching." Seldom does a creative cook use a plain white sauce.

The techniques used in making a basic sauce are also used in culinary masterpieces. In like manner, teachers expand basic techniques. By noting the development of the seven basic elements of planning, a teacher has a way of identifying what is needed in the event a lesson is not effective. Here are Hunter's seven basic elements:

1. *Anticipation Set.* This is the development of a mental set that supports the student in learning what is to be learned. This can take the form of a directive, a question, or both: "Look at the picture of these flowers and tell me which ones you prefer."
2. *Objective and Purpose.* Students learn more effectively when they know what they should be learning *and* teachers teach more effectively if they have explicitly stated their purpose: "People often say flowers are beautiful, but they rarely say on what basis they prefer one type of flower over another. Today we get to discover something about the way we rank our preferences for flowers."
3. *Input.* The teacher will have "task analyzed" the final objective to determine the knowledge that is required. Information is necessary to any lesson, whether that information comes from discovery, discussion, reading, listening, or observing.
4. *Modeling.* The student should see how the skill looks. If the information is factual, then a demonstration of its use will accelerate learning. Several models should be used to suggest creative expansion and application of the basic information.
5. *Checking for Understanding.* This can be done verbally or by a show of hands. It can be done with the entire class or via spot-checking. The teacher will be checking for necessary minimal skills before moving to complex material.
6. *Guided Practice.* This is done under direct supervision. The teacher wants to make sure a skill is learned correctly, not incorrectly. This is the feedback portion of the lesson.
7. *Independent Practice.* This is assigned only after the teacher is assured the students will not make serious errors.[2]

PROBE Compare the Hunter model with the model given on page 66. What differences do you note? What inferences would you make about the philosophic differences in these two models? Do you think you could detect any differences in teaching based on the two formats?

▪ *Behavioral Format*

Recall that educators tending toward behaviorism will state instructional objectives in terms of student behavior. Quantitative minimum standards are often given (e.g.: List at least six characteristics of romanticism), and the manner in which the behavior is to be manifested is explicitly stated (in writing or verbally). Consider the lesson plan that follows.

I. Class: Elementary Computer Science   Unit: I/O Devices
   Date: 10/3
II. Objective: The student will describe, in one paragraph each, the ways in which at least four devices can be used to feed information into a computer. (Comprehension)

III. Content: Input devices and modes include at least the following:
1. *Punch cards.* Metal brushes or photoelectric cells detect holes.
2. *Paper tape.* Analogous to punch cards.
3. *Magnetic tape.* Spots are magnetized or demagnetized on a strip of plastic tape coated with a ferromagnetic substance, and their state is "read" by the computer.
4. *Terminals.* Typewriterlike devices used to code data directly or indirectly into a computer.
5. *Consoles.* Analogous to terminals but usually linked directly to the central processing unit (CPU).
6. *Electron pens.* Penlike devices that "write" with a stream of electrons. Used with cathode ray tube (CRT) displays and electronic tables.
7. *Magnetic ink.* Character configurations written in magnetic ink are matched against precoded configurations. Used on most checks.
8. *Optical scanners.* Uses light reflected from pencil marks made at specific locations on a sheet of paper to "read" data.
9. *Profile scanners.* Still experimental but will use a TV-like device to convey images to a CPU for comparison with precoded images.

IV. Teaching-Learning Activities
1. Begin by engaging students in a discussion of how information can be fed into a computer. List points on the overhead projector (5 min.). Possible questions:
   a. What are those strange figures at the bottom of most checks? (Numbers written in magnetic ink.)
   b. What happens to machine-scored tests after you finish coding in your answers? (They are run through a device that senses—via a beam of reflected light—exactly where your marks are, and these data are then fed into a computer via electrical impulses.)
2. Presentation of the remaining points, using the overhead projector (15 min.).
3. Turn off the projector and review the main points via questions and answers (10 min.).
4. Hand out paper and have students attempt the objective (10 min.).
5. Collect the papers and go over two or three (at random) to provide feedback to students (5 min.).

V. Materials: Overhead projector

VI. Evaluation: The papers will be checked by the teacher. (The teacher adds comments about the effectiveness of the lesson.)[3]

PROBE   How do you know this lesson plan is skewed toward behaviorism? Is there anything in the language of the plan that reveals this orientation? If so, what specifically? Could you reorganize this plan to create a Hunter-like model? Or the eclectic-type plan given on page 81?

■ *Suggestive Accelerative Learning Techniques (SALT) Plan*
   The purpose of the SALT plan is to tap the deep reserves of consciousness. Here is such a plan.[4]

Day of Week: _____ Date: _____
I will achieve *joy, unity,* and *suggestive linkage* by:

	Minutes
Physical exercises	
Bend overs	
Whole body tension	
Waves of tension	
Diagonal stretching	
Side bends	_____
For mind calming I am going to use	
Early pleasant learning restimulation	
Imagery example	
Tape no. ? from Lupin set	_____
Suggestions I will use	
Enjoy learning	
I have learned much	
Relaxing is easiest	_____
Preview of information unit	
Where does this fit into the course?	_____
Active presentation	
Background music	
Baroque or classical	_____
Practice activity	
Worksheet	
Game	
Work alone or in groups?	_____
Passive concert	
Summary outline	
Metronome (60 hz)	
Baroque largo	_____
Self-assessment	
To collect or not to collect?	_____
Review of information unit	
Did it fit into the course?	_____

PROBES

1. How many features can you list that make this plan different from the others we have considered?
2. What assumptions about learning would be held by a person committed to this type of plan? How do those assumptions differ from the assumptions of a behaviorist? A teacher adopting the Hunter model?
3. Do you notice any similar features between the four plans? If so, what are they?
4. Can you use these similar features as a basis for designing your own plan? What other features would you add, if any? Why?
5. What does your decision to add or not add features say about your assumptions regarding learning and teaching?

Design Your Own Plan

The foregoing models are designed to obtain specific results. As such, they are highly workable. But what results do you want? You may wish to create results that are hybrids of all four. You may wish to create a format that is startlingly different—unique in every respect.

Find a plan that is congruent with you—that you believe in and from which you can do your best teaching. *And* try some experimentation. From time to time stretch yourself by trying an alternative format, and then take note of both your experience and that of your students, of student learning *and* your learning. Notice your assumptions about learning and teaching. And remember—nowhere is it written that if you find a better way, you cannot change those assumptions.

A Teacher's View of Planning

The following discussion is based on the author's interview of a highly successful teacher, Doug Smith.

I was having lunch with Doug Smith, a chemistry teacher in an inner-city school of Detroit. Doug, honorary chairman of chemistry in his department, is an outstanding chemistry teacher, not just by peer rating and administrative consensus, but by the consistent testimony and productivity of his students. He teaches chemistry through laboratory experiments. Each experiment is selected far in advance, prior to the beginning of the term. And each experiment is selected for a particular purpose—to illustrate a law or concept in chemistry. Each experiment "fits" the material selected, the concept level of the students, and the practical use of chemistry in the home and in industry. In short, Doug's courses are highly structured, highly organized. And, yet, he is very spontaneous before the class. Moreover, his students are *"on* purpose." They know clearly step by step what to look for in an experiment. They are engaged, alert, and spontaneous. There is a minimum of "going through the motions" in Doug's class.

Having observed Doug's instruction over a period of six or seven years, I decided to ask him how he achieved his acknowledged effectiveness. I knew that he planned thoroughly, so I started with some questions about planning.

"Some teachers," I began, "both beginners and ones with years of experience, resist developing lesson plans. Do you have any idea why this is so?"

"I think some teachers have the idea that an explicit lesson plan will restrict them," he said. The waiter came over and we both ordered salads. Doug continued. "A lesson plan can actually give you more freedom," he said.[5]

"You mean you can build in flexibility? Build in options?"

"You can do that—but what I mean is that the plan itself frees you. You see, planning allows you to focus your energy on class management instead of on 'What will I do next?' "

"In many methods courses," I said, "a single format is often required of the students. Perhaps this accounts for some notions of rigidity?"

"It may also be the result of an administrative directive," he said, "—a directive requiring teachers to submit plans that adhere to a particular, and sometimes rigid, form. Many teachers doubt the utility of these requirements."

"If, then," I interjected, "lesson plans are actually freeing and empowering, how can teachers get past the feeling that they are being restricted?"

"I think it's useful to personalize the plan—to think of the lesson plan as one's personal script. A useful lesson plan is a script for daily teaching. During your class sessions a well-developed script will act as your 'cue cards' and help you stay on track."

"An interesting way of looking at it," I commented. "This actually personalizes the plan, makes it your own."

"It is your own," said Doug.

"Like notes to yourself," I said.

"Exactly," said Doug.

It was getting late and we had finished our salads. We got up to leave and Doug promised to show me a computerized system he and his son had developed—a system for organizing one's grade book. "More personal organization," I thought.

"Show it to me next time," I said.

And we were off.

Later, I recalled what Doug had said about planning, about the need for a plan, the need to personalize it, and the power and freedom a good plan can bring to one's instruction. I also recalled some of the beliefs that can stop one from planning—that it is a rigid external form, imposed from without and that it is consequently destructive to creativity and to spontaneity in teaching.

PROBES

1. How do you feel about planning instruction?
2. Do you think planning lessons can be a barrier to creative teaching? Why? Why not?
3. Do you see any relationships between planning instruction and time management? (See Chapter 3.)

4. How does planning for a lesson compare with planning for a speech? What are similarities? What are differences?

| Myths About Lesson Plans | There are some deeply entrenched myths about lesson plans that we must confront at the outset. Some of these are common to student teachers; others persist after years of teaching and reemerge in the teachers' lounge from time to time. |

Myth #1

There is one right way to write a lesson plan (i.e., there is *a* correct format).

Response

The format of a lesson plan is determined largely by one's purposes. In some cases you may wish to focus on criterion-referenced objectives; in others you may wish to stress conceptual objectives. It is not a matter of one format being correct and the other being incorrect. It is a matter of appropriateness to your purposes. Sometimes you may wish to focus on your own behavior and sometimes you may wish to show a relationship between your behavior and the students' response. In each case your purposes and assumptions about instruction determine format. Format is not something that falls from the sky, divinely decreed.

Myth #2

Lesson plans are rigid; they allow no flexibility.

Response

Perhaps they can be rigid if they are followed as a mere formula. You must take the responsibility of personalizing them. How can a given format empower your instruction? How can you build in options?

Myth #3

I don't need a plan. I can remember what I want to do and say.

Response

Probably not. Some experienced teachers appear to be teaching without a plan, but their plan is mental and is largely an accumulation of many plans now bordering on habit. Experienced teachers will still profit from writing out a plan in advance. The very process can open up new ways of seeing old patterns. For beginning teachers, the probability of straying off purpose, of getting lost, is too great to risk teaching without a written plan.

Myth #4

I will create a plan as I go. This will result in more creative teaching.

Response

Most of the studies on creativity do not support this belief. There are definitive stages to creation and a major one is descriptive organization. True, after putting oneself through the paces of research and organization, creative ideas may come to one—and insight may come to one at any time in any place—while driving on the freeway, soaking in a hot tub, or listening to a symphony—or even during a teaching episode. But one should not count on insight or inspiration as a substitute for planning. Moreover, note that in terms of stages of development, creation usually follows discipline.

Sources for the Lesson Plan

Doug Smith was testing electronic equipment in his lab. It was his prep period, so I dropped by to chat.

"Setting up for next period?" I queried.

"No, as a matter of fact, this equipment will not be used until midsemester. But it's in the master plan and I want to make sure it works properly."

"You do more planning ahead than many of your colleagues, Doug. How did you become so turned on to planning?"

"As a beginning teacher in 1968, I felt insecure about my mastery of the subject material I was teaching. I quickly discovered, however, that my real concern needed to be that of classroom management. I also discovered that my best tool for solving management problems was a well-prepared set of lesson plans."

I picked up a piece of chalk and drew a time line on the board (see Fig. 6.1).

"I like the way you can move forward and backward in time," I said. "You know exactly what you are going to teach months in advance. And you make everything fit together."

Doug picked up some chalk and proceeded to divide my time line into sections.

"A teacher needs long-range (one year), medium-range (one semester), and short-range (daily and weekly) plans to give focus and direction for student behavior."

"Many students," I said, "complain that they don't know which objectives to include in their day-to-day planning. There is a strong tendency to use the textbook as a guide to planning."

"The textbook is one source that I use," said Doug. "But if I used the text exclusively I would include too much. I would fall into the trap of making the aim of teaching equivalent with *coverage of material.*"

"And this doesn't square with the concept of unit planning, does it?" I said.

"No. The emphasis for a unit is a theme—a group of related concepts, skills, and facts. This is what you should be teaching—concepts, skills, and related facts—all centered around a theme."

"Then would you say that the daily plans are determined by the more global aim of the unit?"

"Exactly. And if you organize this way, textbook chapters may be part of a unit. But you can use other sources, too. And your daily lesson plans will be determined by the objective of your unit."

"And where do you get the themes for your units?" I asked.

"I create them," said Doug, and he handed me one of his creations. It was a course syllabus on college prep chemistry.[5]

COURSE SYLLABUS

College Prep Chemistry

Mr. Douglas E. Smith, B.S., M.E.
Murray-Wright High School

Course Description: College prep chemistry is an advanced science course designed for the college-bound student. The course content emphasizes basic chemical knowledge, problem solving, use of formulas, and the ability to relate specific facts to general chemical theory.

Required Textbook: Modern Chemistry or *Chemistry: A Modern Approach.*

Supplementary Materials: The Detroit Free Press or *The Detroit News,* a dictionary, and a college-level encyclopedia, such as the *Encyclopedia Britannica.*

Credit: 5 credit hours per semester.

Attendance: Students are expected to attend class each day and to be on time. Parents are expected to monitor their son's or daughter's attendance and to provide the teacher with a written note explaining each absence. A parent conference will be required if absences become excessive.

Grading: 20% class and home assignments
50% tests and final exam
20% lab reports
10% class participation
100% final grade

Homework: Each student is expected to study the textbook and review the notes every night. Written home assignments will be collected each week. Students are expected to make up missing assignments within one week of returning to school.

Expectations for students: Students are expected to attend class each day, to be respectful of the learning process, and to complete all required assignments.

Subject area topics and goals: A complete outline of core objectives for chemistry is available from the Science Division of the Detroit Public Schools. First semester chemistry covers chemical properties, elements, atomic theory, and the gas laws. Second semester chemistry covers orbital theory, chemical bonding, and advanced equation solving.

■ *First Semester Text Assignments: Modern Chemistry,* 1986 edition

Chapter 1: "Measurements in Chemistry"
1. Organization
2. Matter
3. Energy
4. Metric measurements
5. Physical properties
6. Problem solving

Chapter 2: "Matter and Its Changes"
1. Mixtures, elements, and compounds
2. Metals and nonmetals
3. Periodic Table
4. Classification of elements and compounds
5. Symbols and formulas
6. Formation of compounds
7. Energy changes during chemical reactions

Chapter 3: "Atomic Structure"
1. Evidence for the existence of atoms
2. Atomic theory
3. Atomic particles
4. Atomic number, mass, and weight
5. Avogadro number, mole, and gram-atomic-weight
6. Problem solving

LABORATORY ASSIGNMENTS

Lab–1 Solution formation and energy changes
Lab–2 Solvent, solutes, and supersaturated solutions
Lab–3 The filtration process
Lab–4 Analysis of a mixture with paper chromatography
Lab–5 The formation of crystals
Lab–6 The properties of water
Lab–7 Glass—an amorphous solid
Lab–8 The properties of the nonmetal sulfur

HOME ASSIGNMENT

Chapter 12: "Liquids-Solids-Water"

Chapter 13: "Solutions"

Chapter 10: "The Gas Laws"
1. The properties and measurements of gases
2. Kinetic molecular theory and entropy

3. Solving gas law problems
4. Using calculators to solve chemistry problems

HOME ASSIGNMENT

Chapter 11: "Molecular Composition of Gases"
1. Law of combining volumes of gases
2. Diatomic gases
3. Problems

NONLECTURE CHAPTERS (ASSIGNMENTS GIVEN IN ADVANCE)

Due on the ninth week of the semester:

Chapter 14: "Ionization"

Chapter 15: "Acids, Bases, and Salts"

Due on the nineteenth week of the semester:

Chapter 10: "The Gas Laws"

Chapter 11: "Molecular Composition of Gases"

EXTRA CREDIT CHAPTERS

Chapter 17: "Carbon and Its Oxides"

Chapter 18: "Hydrocarbons"

CHEMISTRY PAPER (FIVE PAGES, HANDWRITTEN, IN INK)

Topic:
1. A chemical element
2. A chemical process
3. A chemical in the environment
4. Your science-fair research paper

■ **Second Semester Text Assignments: Modern Chemistry, 1986 edition**

Chapter 4: "Arrangement of Electrons in Atoms"
1. The discovery of electric charge
2. Magnetism and electric charge
3. Electromagnetic radiation and the spectrum
4. The role of the spectroscope in chemistry
5. The wave mechanical model of atomic electrons
6. The radiation and absorption of energy
7. The electron configuration of atoms
8. Quantum numbers

Chapter 5: "The Periodic Law"
1. The Periodic Table of Elements
2. The atomic number and chemical property
3. Electron configuration and chemical property
4. Ionization energy and metallic property
5. Electron affinity and nonmetallic property
6. Noble gas chemistry

Chapter 6: "Chemical Bonds"
1. Valence theory
2. Ionization, the formation of (+) and (−) ions
3. Ionic bonds
4. Covalent bonding
5. Polar bonds and molecules, the dipole moment
6. Electronegativity

LABORATORY ASSIGNMENTS

Lab–1 A freezing point determination
Lab–2 A boiling point curve
Lab–3 Identification of chemical changes
Lab–4 Hydrogen replacement activity of eight metals
Lab–5 The activity of metals as a function of voltage
Lab–6 The preparation and properties of carbon dioxide
Lab–7 The preparation and properties of oxygen
Lab–8 The preparation and properties of hydrogen

Chapter 9: "Two Important Gases: Oxygen and Hydrogen"

Chapter 22: "Oxidation-Reduction Reactions"

Chapter 7: "Chemical Composition"
1. Chemical symbols and formulas
2. Chemical nomenclature
3. Writing formulas and naming compounds
4. Molecular and empirical formulas
5. Molecular and formula weights
6. The mole and the gram-formula-weight
7. Problem solving

NONLECTURE CHAPTERS (ASSIGNED IN ADVANCE)

Due on the ninth week of the semester:

Chapter 24: "The Metals of Group I"

Chapter 25: "The Metals of Group II"

Due on the nineteenth week of the semester:

Chapter 26: "The Transition Metals"

Chapter 31: "Radioactivity"

EXTRA CREDIT

Chapter 29: "Sulfur and Its Compounds"

Chapter 30: "The Halogen Family"

THE CHEMISTRY PAPER (FIVE PAGES, HANDWRITTEN, IN INK)

Topics:
1. How chemistry will help my career
2. Chemistry in the kitchen
3. The chemistry of clean
4. Chemistry and cars
5. Chemistry and cosmetics
6. The chemistry of good health
7. The chemistry of drug action

STUDENT LEARNING CONTRACT
COLLEGE PREP CHEMISTRY

I, _____ pledge to successfully fulfill the requirements of the above-mentioned course at Murray-Wright High School by continually working toward the specific goals outlined in the course syllabus.

Student's Signature: _____

Parent's Signature: _____

Teacher's Signature: _____

Date: _____

Please secure appropriate signatures and return to the chemistry teacher.

■ **Mr. Douglas E. Smith,** *College Prep Chemistry,* **Murray-Wright High School,** *Modern Chemistry,* **1986 edition**

WEEKLY LESSON PLANS FOR 9/28/87 TO 10/2/87 (WEEK TWO)

MONDAY 9/28/87
    II. The Scientific Method
        A. Science is unique because it uses experiments to solve problems.
        B. All science information is obtained from empirical data.

    C. Facts are repeatable observations.

    D. Laws describe conditions that always lead to the same result.

    E. Models are simulations of real objects or events.

    F. Theories are used to predict new facts.

Demonstration. Discuss the development of the Law of Gravity and the theory of gravitational force. Use two different diameter plastic spheres to illustrate that acceleration due to gravity is independent of mass.

TUESDAY 9/30/87

  III. Observations and Assumptions

    A. Discuss the following quotations:

      1. "Genius is 1 percent inspiration and 99 percent perspiration."

      2. "Chance favors the prepared mind."

      3. "If you want to know how science works, look at what a scientist does."

    B. An assumption is a guess about the identity or cause of a substance or event.

    C. An observation is an exact record of a substance or event that you have seen.

Demonstration. Students are to observe and record their observations of the reaction conducted by the teacher. The reaction consists of adding glycerol to a small crucible mounted in a wire triangle. The crucible contains potassium permanganate.

WEDNESDAY 9/30/87

  IV. The Experiment (Part 1)

    A. A sequence of observations carried out under controlled conditions.

    B. An experiment consists of a problem, a procedure, a control, and an analysis of the results.

    C. The control allows the tested condition to be compared to the normal result.

Demonstration. A burning candle is mounted in a small bowl supported by a tripod. Water is added to the bowl and a 500-ml florence flask is converted and placed over the candle. The students are to record their observations of the changes that take place.

Assignment. The student is to write up a suggestion for an experiment that will help to answer this question: Why does the candle flame go out when covered by the flask? The write-up must include a procedure, a list of required equipment, and a description of the control that would be used in the experiment. NOTE: The student is to come up with an experiment, not an answer to the question.

THURSDAY 10/1/87
- V. The Experiment (Part 2)
  - A. Ask for experimental ideas from the class.
  - B. Try out as many ideas as possible.
  - C. Experimentally eliminate all factors.
  - D. Verify class observations that the exclusion of air is responsible for extinguishing the flame.
  - E. By experimentation demonstrate that the flame requires oxygen.

FRIDAY 10/2/87 (QUIZ DAY)
1. Ten essay questions covering class notes I–V and pages 1–6 in Chapter 1, *Modern Chemistry*
2. Students must write the questions and put their answers in complete sentences.
3. The quiz is due five minutes before the end of the period.

LESSON PLAN FOR THURSDAY 10/1/87

Objective
At the conclusion of the lesson the student will be able to cite the experimental procedure and evidence that establishes the requirements of open-air combustion.

Board Notes
An outline of today's experimental approach to the question, Why does the candle flame go out when covered by the flask?

Time Activity

1	The students are to copy the procedure outline on
2	the chalk board. Describe today's activity.
3	
4	Complete taking attendance. Make announcements
5	about ID cards and the Code of Student Conduct.
6	Complete signing absence excuses and other forms.
7	
8	Query students about the principles of the
9	experimental method discussed yesterday.

10	1. A unique method of solving problems.
11	2. Controlled conditions.
12	3. The tested condition.
13	4. The purpose of the control.
14	
15	Remind the students of the requirements of the
16	assignment due today.
17	1. A description of an experimental
	procedure
18	2. A list of needed equipment.
19	3. A description of the control.
20	
21	Solicit and test various student suggestions for
22	determining why the flame goes out when covered by
23	the flask.
24	1. With and without water in the bowl.
25	2. Different size and shape flasks.
26	3. Use a glass plate instead of a bowl.
27	4. Mount a candle in the bottom of a large
28	beaker and demonstrate that the flame
29	continues until the top of the beaker is
30	covered.
31	Ask students to summarize their observations.
32	"The flame goes out when air is excluded."
33	
34	Discuss the composition of air.
35	1. 78 percent nitrogen
36	2. 21 percent oxygen
37	3. 1 percent other gases (CO_2, H_2O, Ar, etc.)
38	
39	Ask students: Which gas is responsible for the
40	flame? How can we be certain?
41	
42	Demonstrate the collection of nitrogen and oxygen
43	gas by water displacement from stock cylinders.
44	1. Demonstrate the flame test for nitrogen.
45	It does not support combustion.
46	2. Demonstrate the glowing splint test for
47	oxygen. It does support combustion.
48	

49   Fill a prepared flask with a mixture of 21 percent oxygen
50   and 78 percent nitrogen gas; invert it over a burning
      candle mounted in a bowl of water to demonstrate
      that it produces the same effect as a flask of
      air.
      Ask students to summarize their observations.
      Collect the assignment and remind the students
      about Friday's quiz.[6]

■ SUMMARY

Lesson plans reflect the values one wishes to impart in the teaching process. The format of the lesson plan indicates the instructor's intention. The instructor must decide the cognitive and affective level of the lesson and the degree of interaction of the student.

There are a number of specialized formats designed to deliver a particular method of teaching: the Hunter lesson format, the behavioral format, and the SALT format. Effective teachers will experiment with alternative formats depending on their purposes.

■ NOTES

1. James Boyer, Models of Student Lesson Plans, edited compilation of submitted student lesson plans. Unpublished. Wayne State University, 1987. Included by permission of editor-compiler.
2. Madeline Hunter, "Knowing, Teaching and Supervising," in *Using What We Know About Teaching,* ed. Philip L. Hosford (Alexandria, VA: ASCD, 1984), 175–176.
3. Michael Lorber and Walter D. Pierce, *Objectives, Methods, and Evaluations for Secondary Teaching* (Englewood Cliffs, NJ: Prentice-Hall, 1983), 190.
4. Donald H. Schuster and Charles E. Gritton, *Suggestive Accelerative Learning Techniques* (New York: Gordon and Breach Science Publishers, 1986), 144.
5. Dialogue with Doug Smith is based on verbal and written interviews, March–October 1987 and on his monograph, "A Strategy for Effective Teaching," copyright 1987. The material is reprinted here by permission of author.
6. Douglas Smith, Course Syllabus: College Prep Chemistry, unpublished monograph, copyright 1987. Reprinted by permission of author.

Creating Units and Courses

Units show relationships between short-term and long-term objectives.

When I heard the learn'd astronomer,
When the proofs, the figures, were ranged in columns before me,
When I was shown the charts and diagrams, to add, divide, and measure them,
When I sitting heard the astronomer where he lectured with much applause in the
    lecture-room,
How soon unaccountable I became tired and sick,
Till rising and gliding out I wander'd off by myself,
In the mystical moist night-air, and from time to time,
Look'd up in perfect silence at the stars.

—Walt Whitman;
from "When I Heard the Learn'd Astronomer"
in *Leaves of Grass*

A word of warning. Beefing up traditional academic courses, while essential,
is not sufficient. When students are required to take another course in language
or science or history, they may be introduced to a slice of these specialties with
little thought given as to how the separate subjects are connected or how collec-
tively they relate to the larger world.

—Ernest Boyer

The Unit as Relationship

Can you recall a motion picture—perhaps a Disney film you saw as a child—in which an image of the earth gradually took shape out of a sea of stars and blackness? The camera then zoomed in to lead your eyes on a very fast journey across mountains and farmland. Your final destination was a farm somewhere in Iowa where you suddenly found yourself looking in on a family having breakfast. The technique is called globalization. When applied to teaching, globalization is articulated by the unit and course design. The unit and course design show thematic and structured relationships between the big picture and the little picture.

■ *Purpose and Rationale*

Usually, a teacher will start the development of a unit with a broad purpose. In a unit on genetics, "Patterns of Heredity," for example, the purpose may be stated as follows: "This unit of study will introduce students to the fundamental principles of inheritance. Emphasis will be placed on the genetic continuity of life. The social, moral, and ethical implication of contemporary genetic technologies will also be addressed."

The purpose gives the teacher and the student a sense of direction. This sense of direction is supported by a rationale designed to answer the question, Why are we doing this? A rationale consists of one or more generalizations, which may be descriptive or normative or a combination of the two. The rationale for the genetics unit, for example, may be stated as follows:

The fundamental principles of inheritance provide an excellent example of the experimental approach and the process of scientific inquiry . . . the genetic laws as defined by Mendel function in every human being. The study of genetics is relevant to an understanding of current issues in biomedical technology that affect or will affect all American citizens. A basic knowledge of inheritance patterns will provide students with the background needed to make intelligent, ethical decisions concerning the future welfare of the human population.

■ *Concept Development*

In Chapter 3 we define purposes as inexhaustible. There may be a multiplicity of actions, concept masteries, and processes that support a purpose. The unit makes a connection between the big picture, the global purpose, and the specific concepts that will enable the student to realize those purposes. In the genetic unit cited above for example, the following concepts and principles may be included:

CONTENT
    I. Mendelian Genetics
        A. Experiments of Mendel
        B. Principle of Dominance
            1. Dominant trait
            2. Recessive trait
            3. Homozygous
            4. Heterozygous
        C. Principle of Segregation
        D. Principle of Independent Assortment
    II. Genetic Expression
        A. Allele
        B. Genotype
        C. Phenotype
   III. Genetic Crosses
        A. Monohybrid
        B. Dihybrid
        C. Punnett Squares
        D. Probable Ratios
    IV. Human Heredity
        A. Inherited Characteristics
        B. Genetic Disorders
        C. Pedigrees
    V. Genetic Technologies
        A. Amniocentesis
        B. Genetic Counseling

Many beginning teachers make the mistake of launching into the teaching of specific concepts without providing the student with the big picture and without showing relationships between global and specific perspectives. The effective teacher is able to shuttle back and forth between perspectives as the students' need to understand requires. Think of the unit and course design as a master map of a large city. If you were to specifically describe a subway in New York City, but did not explain how to get to it and how to use it, it would be stored at best as isolated information—what Whitehead calls inert knowledge. Some teachers treat subject matter this way. They throw out chunks of information randomly selected, perhaps on the basis of textbook organization or personal preference, forgetting that they are aware of the relationship between this information and its global values, but that the student may not be so aware. Global values and purposes must be spelled out. To learn effectively, students must internalize these larger gestalts, these big pictures, and see the relationships between the large and the small. A well-written unit supports the teacher in doing this. Following is an outline of the major elements for unit development:

    I. Purposes
   II. Rationale
  III. Content (concepts and principles)
  IV. Procedures (including instructional objectives)
    V. Materials
  VI. Culminating Activity
 VII. Evaluation

Thus far we have examined elements I through III for a typical unit on genetics. The continued development of this unit is given in its entirety to show how the unit is designed.

SCIENCE SAMPLE UNIT

Patterns of Heredity

IV. Procedures
    A. *Monday:* Begin unit by showing filmstrip "Understanding Mendel's Crosses."
      1. Distribute handout of questions for discussion after filmstrip (Attachment A). 20 minutes
      2. Lead discussion of Mendelian genetics using handout as a guide.
      3. *Assignment:* Students will read sections 10.7–10.11 from their text and make a list of questions they have concerning the material.
    B. *Tuesday:* Discuss student questions from homework assignment.
      1. *Lecture:* Explain difference between genotype and phenotype using examples from the experiments of Mendel and human traits.
      2. Using the overhead projector, introduce the use of Punnett squares to visualize genetic crosses and determine probable genotypic and phenotypic ratios of offspring for monohybrid and dihybrid crosses.

3. Work sample problems of crosses on overhead and have students supply answers.

4. *Assignment:* Work Punnett square problems (Attachment B). Read the following sections from the text: 13.1, 13.4, 13.9–13.-11.

C. *Wednesday:* Student volunteers will work homework problems on the blackboard and explain their answers to the class. Collect homework.

1. *Laboratory:* Begin the study of human heredity with Investigation 13: Human Inheritance (Attachment C).

2. Announce group activity for Friday. Divide class into groups of four and distribute appropriate articles to each group to be read for homework.

D. *Thursday:* Lead follow-up discussion on Wednesday's laboratory investigation. Collect lab reports.

1. *Lecture:* Pedigree analysis, human genetic disorders and detection techniques (amniocentesis). During lecture, show slides of examples of genetic disorders and human pedigrees.

2. Small group discussions during the last 20 minutes of class in preparation for Friday's presentations.

E. *Friday:* Group presentations.

V. Materials

A. Basic

1. Text: *Biology* (Harcourt Brace Jovanovich); chalkboard, chalk, pens, pencils, paper

B. Supplementary

1. *Monday:* Filmstrip "Understanding Mendel's Crosses" (part 4 of the series *The Path to Genetics: Mendel's Laws*); filmstrip projector, handouts (Attachment A).

2. *Tuesday:* Overhead projector, transparencies, grease pencils, handouts (Attachment B), projection screen.

3. *Wednesday:* Handouts (Attachment C), articles from *BSCS Biomedical Technology—Innovations: The Social Consequences of Science and Technology Program* (see VI. Culminating Activity).

4. *Thursday:* Slide projector, slides of the following: pedigree of Huntington's disease and cystic fibrosis, Down's syndrome, Turner syndrome, and Klinefelter's syndrome; projection screen.

VI. Culminating Activity (Attachment D)
Genetic Screening and Confidentiality Group

PRESENTATIONS

The class will be divided into groups of four (total of six groups). Four of the groups will receive a Case Study Worksheet and a Decision-making Worksheet, and the other two groups will receive articles concerning the legal and social aspects of genetic screening, as well as the Decision-making Worksheet. Each group will elect a group leader, secretary, and two presenters. The group leader will monitor the small group discussion; the secretary will prepare a written summary of the group's position to be turned in for evaluation; the two presenters will each make a 3-minute oral presentation on their group's article or case study. Each group must summarize their article or case study and present their reactions and decisions. The class and teacher will have the opportunity to question and challenge each group.

VII. Evaluation

The success of this unit will be determined by:

1. Homework assignment on Punnett squares to be collected and graded
2. Laboratory report to be collected
3. Group presentation summary report to be collected and graded
4. Class participation

■ Attachments: Mendelian Genetics

Answer the following questions as you view the filmstrip, "Understanding Mendel's Crosses." Your responses will help you during our discussion after the film.

1. Why was Mendel's selection of pea plants so important to the success of his investigations?
2. How is the Principle of Segregation different from the Principle of Independent Assortment?
3. Define the following and give an example of each from Mendel's experiments:
   a. Dominant trait
   b. Recessive trait
   c. Allele
4. T = tall and t = short. How would you write the homozygous dominant condition, the homozygous recessive condition, and the heterozygous condition?

Name: _____

PUNNETT SQUARES

Show all your work for the following problems.

1. In the guinea pig, black fur (B) is dominant over white fur (b). A homozygous black guinea pig is crossed with a heterozygous black guinea pig. Construct a Punnett square showing this cross. What are the possible phenotypes of the offspring?
2. Construct a Punnett square showing a cross between two heterozygous black guinea pigs. What is the probable ratio for phenotypes of offspring produced in this cross? Genotypes?
3. In pea plants, green pods (G) are dominant over yellow pods (g) and smooth seeds (S) are dominant over wrinkled seeds (s). Construct a Punnett square showing a cross between two pea plants that are both heterozygous for pod color and seed texture. What phenotypes will be expressed in the offspring? What is the probable ratio of genotypes of these offspring?

Name: _____

INVESTIGATION 13: HUMAN INHERITANCE

The purpose of this investigation is to observe the occurrence of certain traits in humans.

Materials
1. mirror
2. calculator

Procedure
1. Record all of your data in the table below:

Trait	Phenotype class	%	Phenotype class	%
Finger hair	H		h	
Tongue rolling	R		r	
Earlobes	F		f	
Shape of hairline	V		v	
Dimples	D		d	
Cleft chin	CM		cm	
Freckles	MO		m	
Blood type	O		A	
Blood type	B		AB	

2. Examine the second or middle joint of each finger for hair. If hair is present, circle the letter H in the Phenotype column in the data table. If no hair is present, circle the letter h.
3. Stick out your tongue and try to roll it up at the edges. Look in the mirror to examine the results. If it can be rolled, circle the letter R. If it cannot be rolled, circle the letter r.
4. Use the mirror to examine your earlobes. Are they attached directly to your head? If they are attached, circle the letter f. If they hang free, circle the letter F.
5. Examine the hairline at the front of your head. If it comes to a point and seems to form a V, circle the letter V. If it is straight across or curved, circle the letter v.
6. Once again, look in the mirror. Do you have dimples? A cleft chin? If you have dimples, circle the letter D. If not, circle the letter d. If you have a cleft chin, circle C. If not, circle c.
7. Do you have freckles? If so, circle M. If not, circle m.
8. If you know your blood type, circle the appropriate type in the data table.
9. Transfer the data about yourself from your data table to the chalkboard, where the instructor has prepared a chart to collect this information.
10. Place the total class numbers for each of the traits in the appropriate column in your data table.
11. Calculate the percentages of each of the contrasting genes for the class.

Discussion
1. What was the ratio of the calculated percentages for each of the traits?
2. What advantages, if any, are there in collecting data from more than one person or class?
3. What conclusions can you make from the results of this investigation?
4. How have inherited traits helped certain organisms to survive?

PROBES
1. If you were teaching from this unit, how would you show a relationship between purposes, concepts, and activities? What is the point of including the text in the list of materials needed? How is the text to be used in conjunction with the filmstrip, handout, slides, and the unit itself?
2. Try your hand at writing more explicit instructional objectives for the daily lesson plans given here. Mix up your objectives, writing some conceptual, some behavioral examples. Why is a culminating activity needed? Can you

think of an alternative culminating activity? Can you think of an alternative approach to evaluation? In the next section, you are invited to apply these questions to a unit in the humanities.

The Unit and the Course

Units have a time span of anywhere from a week to eight weeks, with most units having a time length of two to six weeks.

For simplicity, the unit provided at the beginning of this chapter is to be completed in one school week. But there are longer units. Moreover, units may be strung together to form courses. For example, in a physics course a unit on electricity and a unit on magnetism would go hand in hand. It is the same with the humanities. The effective teacher considers related themes and builds connections between these themes. In Colleen Carol Topous's *A One-Semester Course on Supernatural Literature,* for example, she divides the course into several units, entitled Something Eerie, *A Christmas Carol,* and *The Crucible.* Here is her breakdown of the general structure and content of the entire course:

TABLE OF CONTENTS

Chapter	*Page*
I. Introduction and Endnotes	1
II. Something Eerie	17
Teach Yourself Astrology	18
The Detroit News: "UFO's Showing up in Missouri"	24
The Detroit News: "Photo of UFO or Just 'Lens Flare'"	34
The Magic Paw	40
Scope Magazine: "Superstitions and the Facts"	50
"The Raven"	58
Scope Magazine: "The Shadow"	62
Rationale	78
Objectives	80
Opening Activity	82
What is Astrology?	83
"UFO's Showing Up in Miss"	87
The Magic Paw	93
"The Raven"	97
"The Shadow"	100
Culminating Activity	104
III. *A Christmas Carol:* Introduction	105
A Christmas Carol, script	107
Objectives	129

Introductory Activity 130
Crossword Puzzle 131
Study Questions, Act I 133
Word Exercise, Act II 135
Study Questions, Act II 136
Word Exercise, Act III 138
Study Questions, Act III 140
Word Search Puzzle, Act IV 141
Study Questions, Act IV 142
Word Attack Exercise, Act V 146
Study Questions, Act V 148
Culminating Activity 149
IV. *The Crucible:* Introduction 150
Summary of Play 151
Teaching Technique Used 152
Note on Vocabulary, Word Attack, Comprehension Exercises 153
Creative Activities and Composition Topics 154
Objectives 157
Introductory Activity 158
Crossword Puzzle, Act I 160
Word Attack and Comprehension Exercises 162
Basic Understandings, Act I 165
Study Guide, Act I 166
Vocabulary Exercise, Act II 170
Word Attack and Comprehension Exercises, Act II 171
Basic Understandings, Act II 174
Study Guide, Act II 175
Vocabulary Exercise, Act III 177
Word Attack and Comprehension Exercises, Act III–IV 179
Basic Understandings, Act III–IV 185
Study Guide, Act III–IV 186
Culminating Activity 189
Final Test 190
Bibliography 192

Each unit has its own theme and purpose. The individual units are tied together by an overriding theme of exploring the supernatural.

Colleen Carol Topous is a master teacher in a large inner-city high school of Detroit. Let's examine her rationale for developing a course on supernatural literature. Notice, in particular, how she builds motivation and then builds connections between the units of the course. Notice also how she layers learning activities in progressively more challenging steps:

Many of the books provided for our classrooms do not offer the action and enjoyment needed to help our students enjoy English. In addition, many of the books are written on a reading level far above our students' levels. Thus, many teachers have been faced with the task of rewriting materials as well as formulating word attack and comprehension exercises that are appropriate for the high school student who is behind in his reading ability.

If a teacher observes high school students closely enough she may notice that many of them wear jewelry and clothing depicting their astrological signs. Others even go so far as to wear symbols used in witchcraft and Satanism. . . .

If you have ever checked on their social life you may find that movies such as *The Exorcist* never fail to fascinate students. Likewise, Halloween time brings mobs of adolescents and teens to the J. C. Haunted Houses that are created all over Detroit and the suburban areas.

The Supernatural Literature course that will be presented on the following pages has been prepared primarily for a group of inner-city high school students. The school they attend is located in a ghetto area of Detroit. A majority of the students who attend this school come from middle-lower to lower-lower class homes surrounding the school. A small percentage, perhaps 10%, of the student body is composed of Southern White and Spanish-speaking students. The other 90% is Black.[2]

After an overall rationale and purpose have been developed, the rationale for each unit is developed.

SOMETHING EERIE

"Something Eerie" is a thematic unit consisting of an opening activity, four learning activities, and a culminating activity. This unit comes first in the course so that it may serve as an introduction to the whole idea of the Supernatural. In the introductory exercise the students start immediately to think about the word "supernatural" by giving their own definition of the term. With each of the four learning activities that follow, they are led into thinking about astrology, superstitions, UFOs and the possibility of life on other planets. They are also introduced to the works of Edgar Allan Poe, who is a master of macabre and morbid writing. Poe's fears about death as well as the settings he used in his stories and poems make his works perfect in a course of this type. The unit culminates with an activity in which the students are again given an opportunity to pool their ideas concerning their own meaning of the term "supernatural" and present their information to their classmates. . . .

A CHRISTMAS CAROL

A Christmas Carol is a story which is on the lighter side of the supernatural. The plot revolves around Scrooge and his supernatural ghostly visitors of Christmases Past, Present, and Future. In this unit the students are provoked into thinking about life and death as well by these preternatural beings.

The unit also consists of reading comprehension, word attack skills, and vocabulary exercises which are prepared specifically for the poor reader. They precede each act of the play. These exercises can easily be changed or rearranged to meet varying student needs. However, the fact remains that reading exercises are a very important part of a unit including a longer piece of literature. Such exercises help to assure complete understanding of the material as well as to continually help the student to improve his overall reading ability.

The questioning prepared for the unit is teacher directed. The reading of each act is followed by a list of these questions. The main purpose for including teacher-directed questions in this unit is to add variety to the overall course of study. In the unit which follows *A Christmas Carol,* the class will work on independent study guides which involve a more thought-provoking activity. The teacher-directed questions for *A Christmas Carol* can help to prepare the students for the independent activity which follows. . . .

THE CRUCIBLE

The Crucible by Arthur Miller . . . has been reserved for the end of the course, mainly because of its difficulty and complexity. It ties in with the idea of supernatural because of the fact that witches and all of their preternatural powers are mentioned. This unit is also very effective because it allows the student to see that the imagination is very powerful. When one allows it to wander as did the three young girls in the play, it can cause great harm to oneself as well as others. It has been emphasized throughout the entire unit that supernatural happenings can exist in anyone's imagination if he so desires. It can also be erased from the mind in the same manner.[3]

HUMANITIES SAMPLE UNIT
The Crucible

The unit on Arthur Miller's *The Crucible* is given here in its entirety.

PROBES Go back to the questions given on page 109 and apply them to your reading of the following unit. What similarities and differences do you notice in organization of the unit on genetics and this unit? Can you think of some themes in your field that could be useful in developing units?

■ *The Crucible:* **Introduction**

Everyone knows at least one witch. Could it be the old lady who lives by herself in the old, spooky house down the road? Or could it be the girl next door who never has a date because she is skinny and ugly? Everyone has his own concept of a witch just as did those three young girls in *The Crucible* by Arthur Miller.

The Crucible is not only a story about witches and witchcraft; it goes a little deeper into human nature and how weak man actually is. It gives the students a chance to think about certain weaknesses man possesses and how cruel he can be to his fellow man.

■ Summary of *The Crucible*

The Crucible opens in Salem, Massachusetts in 1692. The main characters are all of Puritan origin. Thus they live by strict ethical morals. These rules are observed by everyone for fear of receiving harsh punishment. This atmosphere lends itself very easily to the hysteria that starts early in the play.

Three young girls—Betty, Abigail, and Mary Warren—cause a great disruption in the town after Betty becomes sick and loses consciousness. Rumors circulate throughout the town that the girls were seen in the woods dancing naked and practicing witchcraft with a black servant named Tituba. All of the blame is placed on Tituba, and she is accused of being a witch and trying to corrupt the three girls.

As the play progresses, many of the townspeople begin to believe that witchcraft does exist. The three girls begin to accuse many women of being witches.

The first woman who was accused by Abigail of being a witch was Elizabeth Proctor. John Proctor, her husband, had been trying prior to this accusation to stay as uninvolved as possible. His reason for this is dramatically motivated by his past adulterous actions with Abigail Williams.

As the play draws to a close, we hear about the witch trials and the many innocent women who are accused of being witches.

■ Teaching Technique Used

Study guides are often a very helpful way of causing students to draw the correct conclusions from a story or a book. In formulating these study guides the teacher must first decide upon the understandings that she wants to get across in a particular guide. These understandings must be passed on to the student as he completes the study guide. The purpose of each study guide is to assist the student in learning; thus it is best to make him aware of the fact that he will not be graded on the work itself. Grading should come with the compositions, vocabulary exercises, and the like.

After the student has had sufficient time to thoroughly answer the questions, he is placed in a group of three or four students. These groups are to discuss the various possible answers to the study guide questions. Thus, the students will be able to see many views of the same idea and be able to draw their own conclusions.

The format of the study guides is set up in the following way. There is one question presented that calls for a listing of some of the facts in the book. It is followed by a question asking the student to consider these facts and come to some conclusion. For each understanding listed at the beginning of the guide you will find at least one fact-type and one opinion-type question. All of the questions are of the true-false, multiple-choice, and fill-in-the-blank types so as to allow the student to have more than one opinion for each question. Sample study guides for each act of *The Crucible* follow.

■ **Note on the Vocabulary, Word Attack, and Comprehension Exercises**

There is a comprehension, a word attack, and a vocabulary exercise at the beginning of each act of the play. Each should be completed before the students begin to read that act.

All of the vocabulary for the crossword puzzle and word games was taken from the act. It is hoped that in doing the puzzles and word games the student will at the same time be able to memorize the words' spelling, pronunciation, and definition. Each student will be required to know all of these vocabulary words for the test at the end of the unit.

The writer has also added a word attack and a comprehension exercise for each act. Most of the sentences for these exercises were taken right from the act or based on information contained in the specific act. Each exercise was prepared exclusively for use in helping the student gain some of the skills necessary in becoming a better reader.

The exercises are composed in such a way that they can be used in conjunction with or separate from the play. However, the writer feels that they would be more effective if used with the play.

■ **Creative Activities and Topics for Each Act (to be used in the event that students tire of study guides)**

ACT I

Creative Activities
1. Act out the final scene in this act, starting from where the three girls accuse Tituba of making them act and dance in the woods.
2. Draw a picture of one of the scenes from Act I.
3. Find a modern work of art that seems to show the fierceness and hysteria that becomes part of the last scene in Act I.

Composition Topics
1. Can Tituba be compared with any modern-day Black woman? Explain.
2. Is Reverend Parris the kind of person you would like to have as minister of your church? Explain fully.
3. How would you feel if you had to live and grow up in the same atmosphere as the three young girls in the play? Explain completely.

ACT II

Creative Activities
1. Dramatize the scene when Cheever enters the Proctor home and accuses Elizabeth of being a witch.
2. Do some research work on the history of the voodoo doll and tell how this is connected with the poppet given Elizabeth by Mary Warren. Then present the information in a panel discussion.
3. Make a poppet similar to the one in the play for display in a cabinet or on a table in the classroom.

Composition Topics
1. Put yourself in the place of Elizabeth Proctor, who is unjustly accused of being a witch. Give your feelings.
2. Mary Warren resists the authority of the Proctors in this scene. Have you ever had the desire to resist authority and talk back to your elders? Explain the situation and compare it to Mary's.
3. Compare and contrast Reverend Hale in Act II with Rev. Parris in Act I.

ACT III

Creative Activities
1. Do some research on the Salem witch trials and present the information in the form of an oral report for the class.
2. Write a poem about what a heroic person John Proctor is.

Composition Topics
1. Compare and contrast the court described in Act III with today's courts.
2. Create a collage titled "Injustice in Our Lives Today" and compare it to the Salem witch trials.

Composition Topics
1. Describe how John Proctor's character changes in Act III and how he decides that he must help his friends.
2. Describe the complete change in Reverend Hale by the end of Act III.

Creative Activities
1. Draw up a copy of the confession that the judges prepared for the accused to sign. Create an enlarged copy that could be posted on a bulletin board.
2. Prepare a bulletin board titled "John Proctor, the Hero."
3. Elizabeth Proctor had a child before she died. Assume that this child has reached the age of 22, and he realizes the injustice dealt to his parents. Imagine that he is attempting to clear his parents' name and that he is known all over the United States for his work. Supposing that Phil Dona-

hue has asked him to appear on his talk show, prepare a script including Mr. Donahue's questions and Proctor's comments.
4. Write to "You Asked for It" and request that they show the actual courthouse in Massachusetts where these Salem witch trials took place.

Composition Topics
1. Compare the trials in *The Crucible* with the Watergate trials.
2. Describe the real John Proctor.

Objectives
1. Students will listen to the recording on witchcraft narrated by Vincent Price.
2. By listening to the witchcraft recording students will begin to realize that witches have been in existence for many years and still exist today.
3. By listening to the witchcraft recording students will see how the concept of witchcraft has changed over the centuries.
4. Students will complete all vocabulary exercises that accompany each act of *The Crucible.*
5. By completing these vocabulary exercises students will improve their own vocabulary.
6. Students will complete all of the word attack and comprehension exercises that accompany *The Crucible.*
7. By completing the word attack and comprehension exercises the students will improve their own vocabulary.
8. Students will complete each study guide that accompanies each act of *The Crucible.*
9. By completing the study guides the students will attain the understandings listed before each guide.
10. The students will write the culminating essay.
11. By writing the culminating essay the students will realize that evil exists only in the minds of those who allow it to stay there.
12. Students will show what they have learned in *The Crucible* by passing the final test with a score of 70 percent or better.

■ *The Crucible:* **Introductory Activity**
The entire class will listen to a recording on witchcraft narrated by Vincent Price. In this recording Mr. Price talks about the history of witchcraft, the tortures administered to those who were accused of being witches, and the utensils and materials used by present-day witches in casting their spells. There are also step-by-step recipes for potions that are guaranteed to bring satisfaction.

After listening to the recording, the class will informally discuss some of the ideas brought out in the recording. The teacher will point out the fact that witches still exist today and that they practice many of the same rituals used by the earlier cults. It will be emphasized, however, that the witches of today can practice their rituals openly and feel assured that they will not be punished for their beliefs. Today, everyone sees witchcraft as more of a religion than anything else.

■ Additional Introductory Activity

In a one-page paper, an artistic design, or in a poem, each student should describe his own concept of a witch. After all of the students have finished their pictures, compositions, or poems, they will be examined and compared with one anothers. Each will be posted around the room during the time that the play is being studied. This assignment should help the students realize that a witch is only something that exists in the human imagination. They should notice that each drawing, poem, or composition depicts a figure that is truly unique in many ways.

Directions: Use the following clues to help fill in the correct answers to the crossword puzzle.

ACROSS

1. Uncontrollable fear or other strong emotion
2. Seeming almost uncivilized
3. A woman who practices sorcery or is believed to have dealings with the Devil
4. A preference or partiality
5. A town in Massachusetts where many men and women were tried and found guilty of practicing witchcraft
6. A statement of the essential articles of a religious belief
7. A true statement that seems contradictory or absurd
8. A severe test of endurance or character
9. The fortified part of a city
10. To wander in search of; plunder

DOWN

4. To harass and oppress; particularly because of differences in religion
7. A person who is extremely strict in his life and morals
11. Referring to the paternal leader of a city or a tribe
12. Injury done to retaliate for injury received
13. Without power to move, act, or resist

■ **Word Attack Exercise for Act I**

WHAT IS THE ROOT WORD?

Directions: Read each sentence and look at the *italicized* word. In the first blank at the right put the root word from which the italicized word was formed. In the second blank put the ending that was added to the root. The first is done for you.

1. Through its *leaded* panes the morning sunlight streams.
         _____lead_____ __ed__

2. The room gives off an air of clean *sparseness.*
sparseness _____ _____

3–4. The roof rafters are *exposed,* and the wood colors are raw and *unmellowed.*
exposed _____ _____
unmellowed _____ _____

5–6. Reverend Parris is *discovered* kneeling beside the bed, *evidently* in prayer.
discovered _____ _____
evidently _____ _____

7. They were *dedicated* folk by and large.
dedicated _____ _____

8. Parris brought her with him from Barbados, where he spent some years as a merchant before *entering* the ministry.
entering _____ _____

9. "The parlor's *packed* with people, sir."
packed _____ _____

10. Abigail, *quavering,* as she sits . . .
quavering _____ _____

■ **Comprehension Exercise for Act I**

Act I of *The Crucible* is very dramatic. It could have been written up by a newspaper reporter. How do you think the story would look in the newspaper?

Before you can answer that question you must know something about newspaper style.

The first item in a news story is the *headline.* As you know, this gives the main idea of the story.

The first paragraph after the headline is called the *lead* (pronounced leed). The lead tries to answer the questions What (happened?), Who (did it?), Where (did it happen?), and When (did it happen?). It may also answer Why (did it happen?) and How (did it happen?).

These questions are known as the five W's and H. The paragraph following the lead will add the facts that have been left out of the lead. (You may not be able to fit in all the five W's and the H.) Or they may give details about the facts. *Remember:* The most important details and facts come first.

1. Below is an example of a good lead taken from a high school newspaper:

   The tenth-grade students from Benjamin Franklin High School viewed a performance of *Julius Caesar* at the American Shakespeare Festival at Stratford, Connecticut, on June 20.

   Answer the following questions:
   Who: _____
   What: _____
   Where: _____
   When: _____

2. Now that you have read the lead, make up a short second paragraph for the above story. This second paragraph should answer the questions Why (did the students attend?) and How (did they get to Stratford?).

   _____
   _____
   _____
   _____
   _____
   _____

3. Try to write Act I of *The Crucible* as a news story, following the outline below. This outline is set up so that you give the most important facts first. Refer to the text of the play to help you remember the facts.

   A. Headline (main idea)
   B. Lead (brief summary)
   C. 2nd Paragraph (major details)
   D. 3rd Paragraph (less important details)

■ **Basic Understanding of Act I**
   1. The townspeople of Salem, Massachusetts, are living under very strict conditions. They are mentally uneasy, and the atmosphere lends itself easily to the hysteria that is to follow.

2. Reverend Parris is a very unhappy, greedy man who does not care about anything except his position as minister of his church. He has no regard for his family or friends.

3. Tituba is a very unfortunate, frightened black slave who becomes the scapegoat for Reverend Parris and the three young girls, and the victim of society.

4. Abigail Williams is a very promiscuous, heartless young girl who would do anything to become the wife of the already married John Proctor.

■ Study Guide for Act I

I. When *The Crucible* opens, we find ourselves in Salem, Massachusetts, in the year 1692. Below is a list of sentences describing the setting and tone of the story. Place a check mark next to the statement(s) you feel to be true.

_____ The townspeople were very religious and morally strict.

_____ The atmosphere throughout the town was jovial, and it would be lots of fun living there.

_____ There is a general feeling of insecurity among the townspeople.

_____ The townspeople often have fun at parties, picnics, and dances.

_____ The young people of the town enjoy themselves while growing up.

_____ Everyone is very happy.

_____ Everyone is very unhappy.

_____ The atmosphere in the town lends itself very easily to the beginning of witchcraft.

_____ Other _____

_____

_____

II. The personalities of many of the main characters become evident in the first act. Reverend Parris is one such person described in the act. Below is a list of statements. Place a check mark next to those that you feel best describe Reverend Parris.

_____ He is a minister.

_____ He is a very warmhearted man.

_____ He is so kind and very interested in his family and community.

_____ He is a pitiful man.

_____ He is selfish.

_____ He has only one interest, which is to secure his position as minister of the town.

_____ He is a greedy man.

_____ He is a generous man.

_____ He is a strict Puritan concerned with keeping order in the town.

_____ He has a pleasing personality.

_____ Other _____

_____

_____

III. You also met Abigail Williams in Act I. Using the text of the play, describe her personality and character. Be as complete as possible.

IV. Briefly review your statements above. Then place a check mark next to the following statement(s) that you feel to be true of Abigail Williams

_____ She is a kindhearted young girl.

_____ She is a very promiscuous young girl.

_____ She wants to marry John Proctor.

_____ She wants to date nice young men of her own age.

_____ She does not care if people talk about her.

_____ She is a sinful person.

_____ Other _____

_____

_____

V. Finally, you met Tituba in Act I. Make separate lists of her characteristics, her reactions toward Parris, and her fears.

VI. Briefly review your statements above. Then place a check mark next to the statement(s) that you feel to be true of Tituba.

_____ She is a frightened black slave.

_____ She is a victim of society.

_____ She realizes her knowledge of black magic could cause harm to herself and others.

_____ She was very unknowing and innocent when she showed the magical practices to the young girls.

_____ She loves Reverend Parris.

_____ She dislikes Reverend Parris very much.

_____ Everything she does is what she wants to do.

_____ She does what everyone else tells her to do.

_____ Other _____

_____

_____

VII. Briefly review your answers for questions I–VI above. Check the statement(s) below that would seem to be true about Salem, Massachusetts, and its townspeople during the spring of 1692.

_____ There is a general feeling of unrest among the townspeople.

_____ Many of the people of Salem, Massachusetts, in 1692 are very insecure.

_____ The strict Puritan ethics are becoming so harsh and difficult to contend with that many of the townspeople have started to rebel in their own way.

_____ Many of the people of Salem are afraid for their own welfare while these witch trials are taking place.

_____ Everyone is happy and wants the town to continue as usual.

_____ All of the townspeople are like saints, loving one another all the time.

_____ The town will remain peaceful throughout the entire play.

_____ Other _____

_____

_____

■ Vocabulary Exercise for Act II

The class will be divided into five groups. Each group will be assigned to work on only one of the following words: _fraud, suspicion, magistrate, shuddery, noose._

Each group will do the following with their word.

1. They will find the word in the second act and write down the entire sentence.
2. The group is to review the sentence and try to decide what the word means in context.
3. After the group has decided upon its own definition of the word, it is to check the dictionary definition to make sure that the group's decision is correct.

After all five groups are finished, one spokesperson from each group will share the group's information with the rest of the class.

■ **Word Attack Exercise for Act II**

WHICH SOUND IS IT?

The consonant letters *c, g,* or *s* may stand for more than one sound.

The letter *c* may stand for the *k* sound as in *cat* or the *s* sound as in *city.* Write k or s below the *c* in each of the following words to show what sound the letter *c* stands for.

common	face	indicating
–	–	–
curtain	fireplace	corner
–	–	–
carrying	proceeds	care
–	–	–

The letter *g* may stand for the *g* sound as in *gun* or for the *j* sound as in *gentle.* Write j or g under each of the following these words to show what sound the letter *g* stands for.

brings	grin	governor
–	–	–
indicating	gently	good
–	–	–
green	magistrate	great
–	–	–

The letter *s* may stand for the *s* sound as in *sad* or the *z* sound as in *runs.* Write s or z under the *s* in each of the following words to show what sound the letter *s* stands for.

girls	rising	sits
–	–	–
silly	starts	magistrate
–	–	–
stubbornly	smile	sick
–	–	–

■ **Comprehension Exercise for Act II**

Magicians frequently amaze audiences by seeming to pick an article from air.

It is very easy to do a magic trick if you just follow these simple directions step by step.

Tie one end of a black thread to a small silk handkerchief and tie the other end of the thread to a button on your shirt. Be sure that you wear a dark-colored shirt. Then roll up your shirt sleeve above the elbow and conceal the handkerchief by stuffing it under your left sleeve. You are now ready to appear before your friends.

Stand in a dimly lighted corner of the room, far enough away from your audience so that the thread will not be seen. Then announce that you intend to pick a handkerchief from the air.

After you have started talking, catch the thread between the thumb and first finger of each hand. Next stretch out your right arm quickly. The thread caught on the right thumb will jerk the handkerchief from the sleeve, carrying it through your left hand and to your right hand.

The silk handkerchief will move so suddenly that your audience will think it was actually produced from the air.

Directions: Number the steps below in the order in which you are told to do them in performing the trick.

_____ Hide the handkerchief under your shirt sleeve.

_____ Tie a black thread to a corner of a handkerchief.

_____ Roll up your sleeve.

_____ Catch the thread between the thumb and first finger of each hand.

_____ Tell your audience what you are going to do.

_____ Tie one end of the black thread to a button on your shirt.

_____ Stand in a corner of the room that is only dimly lighted.

_____ Stretch out your right arm.

■ **Basic Understandings for Act II**

1. There is havoc in the once-peaceful Proctor home because of the witch hunt.
2. John Proctor suffers from his past mistake in having an affair with Abigail Williams.
3. Proctor must learn to accept his own responsibility and judge himself.
4. People are first "somewhat mentioned" as being witches, then they are condemned.

5. Proctor is possibly functioning as the absolute individual who creates his own private world apart from the larger realm of society.

6. Reverend Hale's Puritan doctrine has also taught him that the Devil is attacking everywhere and everyone. He can therefore readily accept the fact that many seemingly innocent people have been deceived by the powers of the Devil.

7. John Proctor can be compared with Pontius Pilate in that he, too, wants to wipe his hands of all involvement in condemning innocent people unjustly.

■ **Study Guide for Act II**

I. The events listed below are in scrambled order. Rearrange the events in the order in which they actually occur in Act II. You may do this by placing the number one (1) next to the first event, the number two (2) next to the second event, and so forth.

_____ John scolds Mary Warren for leaving the house all day.

_____ Elizabeth meets John at the door and asks him why he is so late getting home.

_____ Mary Warren resists John's authority and they argue.

_____ Mary gives Elizabeth the poppet that she had made that day.

_____ Elizabeth and John start to argue about his going to Salem to see Abigail.

_____ Mary Warren enters the Proctor home and tells where she had been all day.

_____ Elizabeth prepares dinner for John, and he eats it.

II. Examine the sequence of events in the first question by paying particular attention to what is happening in the Proctor home. Then decide which of the statements below seem justified. Place a check mark next to your choice(s).

_____ The Proctor home remains as peaceful as ever.

_____ The Proctor home is not as peaceful as before.

_____ There is considerable havoc in the Proctor home.

_____ Everyone is suspicious of one another in the Proctor home.

_____ No one loves one another in the Proctor home.

_____ There is no trust in the Proctor home.

_____ Other _____

_____

III. John Proctor has many personal problems to face. Using your book, list as many of those problems as you can find or infer. Then, list John's attempts to correct each of his problems.

IV. In Act II you have met a new character, Reverend Hale. He has a unique character. Using the text of the play, list some of his character traits.

_____

_____

_____

_____

_____

V. Briefly review your statements in questions 3 and 4. Some might say that Reverend Hale and John Proctor are similar to Pontius Pilate. Why would this be true? List some of both men's characteristics that would make this statement true.

■ **Vocabulary Exercise for Act III**

Directions: Each of the following sentences has been taken from *The Crucible,* Act III. Using your knowledge of defining words through context clues, define each of the following underlined words. If you cannot decide on your own meaning, you may use the dictionary as a last resort.

1. The room is <u>solemn</u>, even forbidding.

_____

_____

2. Now, Martha Corey, there is <u>abundant</u> evidence in our hands to show that you have given yourself to the reading of fortunes.

_____

_____

3. Judge Hawthorne enters. He is in his sixties. A bitter, <u>remorseless</u>, Salem judge.

_____

_____

4. Then, let him <u>submit</u> his evidence in proper <u>affidavit</u>.

_____

_____

_____

_____

5. We build a hot fire here; it melts down all <u>concealment</u>.

_____

_____

Directions: All of the words you have defined previously are in this word search puzzle. See if you can find them. Circle each word as you find it.

```
A  X  Z  B  D  E  S  F  N  C  R  N  O  U  S
K  A  D  I  S  P  O  S  I  T  I  O  N  A  R
P  A  D  E  I  A  L  C  Q  S  W  A  R  Z  X
C  F  R  A  D  E  E  G  H  I  U  W  E  E  R
T  F  U  S  U  B  M  I  T  I  O  P  M  A  S
D  I  F  G  H  J  N  K  L  Z  X  C  O  V  B
N  D  M  Q  W  E  R  T  Y  U  I  O  R  P  A
A  A  B  U  N  D  A  N  T  S  D  F  S  G  H
J  B  B  N  M  Q  W  E  R  T  Y  U  E  I  O
P  I  A  S  D  F  G  H  J  K  L  Z  L  X  C
V  T  B  N  M  Q  W  E  R  T  Y  U  E  I  O
P  I  A  S  D  F  G  H  J  K  L  Z  L  X  C
V  T  B  N  M  Q  W  E  R  T  Y  U  E  I  O
C  P  A  S  D  F  G  H  J  K  L  Z  S  X  R
C  O  N  C  E  A  L  M  E  N  T  A  S  E  L
Q  W  E  R  T  Y  U  I  O  P  A  S  D  F  G
H  J  K  L  Z  X  C  V  B  N  M  Q  W  E  R
```

■ **Word Attack Exercise for Act III**

Directions: One word is underlined in each of the following sentences. First of all, look at the six words in the three boxes. Also, look at the underlined word in the sentence. In the blank space below the sentence place one of the words from the boxes with the vowel sound that is most nearly the same as in the underlined word. The first is done for you.

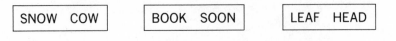

| SNOW COW | BOOK SOON | LEAF HEAD |

1. The vestry <u>room</u> of the Salem meeting house, now serving as the anteroom of the General Court

   soon

2. As the curtain rises, the room is empty, but for sunlight pouring through two high <u>windows</u> in the back wall.

   _____

3. <u>Heavy beams</u> jut out, boards of random widths make up the walls.

   _____

   _____

4. At the left another <u>door leads</u> outside.

   _____

   _____

5. Voices of <u>townspeople</u> rise in excitement.

   _____

6. Thomas Putnam is <u>reaching out</u> for land.

   _____

   _____

7. <u>Looking</u> directly at Giles: "Who is this man?"

   _____

■ **Comprehension Exercises for Act III**

WHEN DID IT HAPPEN?

Directions: As you read each sentence below, you will see two things happening. Sometimes one thing happens after the other, write the number 1 over the part that happens first and the number 2 over the part that happens after it.

If the two things happen at the same time, do not mark the sentence. The first one is done for you.

	1	2

1. Eric checked the front and the back tires before he got on his bike.
2. Mrs. Fielding got ready for bed after she put away her knitting.
3. As the lanky batter stood up, the chanting crowd became quiet.
4. While her mother sorted laundry, Elizabeth cleaned her dresser drawer.
5. After he wrote the letter, Mr. Smith put it in an envelope.
6. Mrs. Swift sang to herself as she did her household tasks.
7. Before they reached the city, the boys saw the distant capitol dome.
8. While the mischievous kitten played with the spool, Polly tried to write an essay.
9. Before Eve went to the party, she took her dog for a walk.
10. The customer got out after the taxicab got stuck in the ditch.
11. The composer listened attentively as the band played his march.
12. After Jacob paid his fare, he boarded the train for Detroit.
13. Before he enlisted in the Marines, Dave worked for a baker.
14. As the toboggan zigzagged downhill, I tried to keep my balance.
15. After the baby tottered across the room, she slumped to the floor.
16. Mr. Tucker looked for his umbrella before he went to vote.
17. Before Mrs. Black served refreshments, the guests posed for a picture.

■ Word Attack Exercise for Act IV

THINK ABOUT THE MEANINGS

Read the first four words at the left and then the two sentences at the right. In each blank write the word that fits the meaning of the sentence. Continue with the other groups of words and sentences.

1. appears
   reappears
   appeared
   appearing

   It _____ empty.

   Betty _____ in the doorway of John's room.

2. announce
   announcement
   announcer
   unannounced

   Abigail's first arrival in the Proctor home was _____ .

   Eventually John made the _____ that he had committed adultery.

3. remove
movers
movement
removal

The purpose of the witch trials was to

_____ all of the witches from Salem.

The three judges were in charge of the

_____ .

4. pay
repay
unpaid
payment

Death was the _____ given to each of
the women who would not confess to being a witch.
The question remains, Who will _____
the families of these innocent women who were
accused and killed unjustly?

5. perfect
imperfect
perfectness
perfectly

Even though everyone in Salem was a Puritan, it
didn't mean that they were _____ .
John Proctor was _____ correct in
saying that his wife was unjustly accused.

■ **Comprehension Exercise for Act IV**

WHAT'S THE BEST WAY TO READ STORIES, PLAYS, AND POEMS?

Stories, plays, and poems are meant to be enjoyed. In order to fully understand them and to get the most pleasure from them, you should read them at
whatever speed is most comfortable for you.

As you read, try to put yourself in the situation you're reading about. Put
yourself in the place of the characters and try to understand them. Try to know
the characters well enough to guess what they're going to do next. Think of
experiences that you've had that are similar to those in the story.

If you really take part in a story, play, or poem, if you feel it, it will become
so real to you that studying it will not be necessary.

Directions: Read each of the following story parts. Afterward, answer the questions at the top of each.

a. How did the author feel at the beginning?

_____

_____

b. What can you tell or guess about Jake from the way he looked?

_____

_____

1. One September day, I was tired and depressed and thought I would get away from it all. I hopped a Greyhound for Chicago. I got into the city at ten that evening and sat around the lobby, watching people. This is where I noticed Jake. I watched him for several minutes before he noticed me.

   I think it was his appearance that made me keep looking at him. His ears were rather large, and almost hidden by his brown, shaggy hair. His face was covered with freckles. He had brown eyes that looked completely lifeless—not a glint, shine, or anything. I thought this strange for a boy who looked only nine or ten years old. He had on a pair of bib overalls with an old gray-white T-shirt underneath. He wore no shoes.

   a. What can you tell about the person telling the story?

   _____

   _____

   b. How would the person feel if his three friends decided they didn't like him anymore?

   _____

   _____

   c. What information in the story leads you to believe that?

   _____

   _____

2. I liked Alec and Tony and Mike. I was proud to be part of that crowd. Let's face it. I'd have been glad to be part of any crowd. Somehow I was always the one who was left out. I don't know why. There's nothing wrong with me. I mean I look all right. I dress about the same as the rest of them. But it has always been hard for me to make friends. It meant a lot for me to go around with Mike and Tony and Alec.

   I liked the way someone would say, "Steve, tell Tony I want to see him." I liked people to know that I belonged to Tony's crowd.

■ **Basic Understandings for Acts III and IV**
1. People who criticize the court are considered witches. The court hearings are a combination of outright lying and suppression.
2. No matter what one believes in he must be able to defend his beliefs. John Proctor defends his beliefs by defending his friends.
3. Hale wants justice, but Danforth does not.
4. Hale finally becomes a man of reason in this third act. He finally sees that the children are irresponsible fanatics. Thus, he denounces the court and leaves.

■ **Study Guide for Acts III and IV**

I. Now that you have read act three, read the following multiple-choice questions. Decide which answers seem most correct and circle them.

At the beginning of the act Giles Corey claimed that he had
a. evidence that Putnam was reaching out for land
b. evidence that Proctor was guilty of lechery
c. become a warlock after his wife Elizabeth was convicted of being a witch

Giles's second plea was that
a. he was not guilty
b. his wife was being lied about
c. he wanted Putnam killed

The final outcome for Giles's plea was that
a. he was dragged from the courtroom
b. he left the courtroom voluntarily
c. he must obtain evidence in proper affidavit if he is to be believed by the judges
d. he was sentenced to hang

When Francis Nurse entered the room with his plea of not guilty, Danforth and Hawthorn
a. kept him from telling the whole truth by instilling fear into him
b. listened with open minds to his testimony
c. paid no attention at all to his words

II. John Proctor also entered the courtroom and stated his feelings. Read the characteristics below and place a check mark next to those which best describe Proctor in this act.

_____ John's main interest was in freeing his innocent wife.

_____ Proctor did not want his wife freed, for he wanted to marry Abigail.

_____ Proctor brought Mary Warren with him to help prove that the young girls' pat testimony was pretense.

_____ Proctor knew that the young girls were frauds.

_____ Proctor was truly an honest man.

_____ Proctor had a rough time dealing with the two judges because they were not after the truth.

_____ Proctor repented for all of his sins.

_____ Other _____

_____

_____

III. Briefly review your selections for exercises I and II. Then, decide which of the following statements seem most correct. Place a check mark next to your choice(s).

_____ Both Danforth and Hawthorn were completely honest.

_____ Both Danforth and Hawthorn were very just men.

_____ Both judges always tried to listen to all sides of the stories.

_____ Both of the judges were one-sided. They believed that everyone who was accused was guilty.

_____ The judges were trying to frighten the defendants into answering the questions to their approval.

_____ The judges wanted all of the defendants to follow their words or die.

_____ The judges wanted witchcraft to exist in the town.

_____ The judges were trying to gain complete control of the courtroom by instilling fear in all of the people.

_____ Other _____

_____

_____

IV. Two men were very outstanding in the courtroom, because they lived up to their beliefs even though it was very difficult for them to do so. These two men were Hale and Proctor. List their beliefs and why each of their beliefs was in conflict with the feelings of the court and judges.

■ **Culminating Activity**

The students will listen to a taped Kung Fu television show that was shown last October. In this show Cain goes to a small town in which all of the people fear one particular man because they feel he has supernatural powers that may destroy them.

As the show progresses, Cain convinces the people that this man's power exists only because they allow it to exist in their own minds. Without their cooperation this man would be powerless. Cain convinces the townspeople that they can use their own minds to destroy all of the powers which this man possesses.

This program does an excellent job of getting the fact across that evil can exist only in the minds of men.

For their final activity the students will be required to compare the powers of the character in the Kung Fu show with the powers of the three young girls in *The Crucible.* They will talk about how both towns were harshly affected because of the evil that existed in the minds of these people.

■ **Final Test for the Book**

I. **Matching:** Match the following definitions with the correct word by placing the numbers of the definition next to the correct word.

_____ fraud
_____ solemn
_____ abundant
_____ affidavit
_____ vengeance
_____ crucible
_____ hysteria
_____ remorseless
_____ noose
_____ magistrate

1. Love for one's neighbor
2. A loop formed by running a knot in a rope
3. A swindle; trick
4. Merciless
5. Severe test of endurance or character
6. Gloomy; somber
7. Civil officer with power to administer the law
8. A written declaration made under oath
9. Plentiful
10. Uncontrollable fear or other strong emotion
11. Retaliation for wrong or injury

II. **Identification:** In two or three sentences tell why the term or character is important in the play. Be specific.

1. John Proctor _____
2. Rev. Hale _____
3. Abigail _____
4. Tituba _____
5. Francis Nurse _____
6. Danforth _____
7. Goody Proctor _____
8. Parris _____
9. 1692 _____
10. Salem Witch Trials _____

III. **Short Essay:** Choose any two of the following and answer each in three to four paragraphs. Be complete. Both of these essays should be written on your own lined paper.

a. Describe the town of Salem, Massachusetts, during the witch trials, emphasizing the conditions that made the blooming of witchcraft completely possible.

b. The system of justice in Salem, Massachusetts, at the time of the witch trials was very corrupt. Explain why by listing certain situations involved in this form of justice as seen in characters such as the two judges and the young girls who started the craze of witch-hunting in the town.

c. In Act III Hale is compared to Pontius Pilate. Explain the reasoning behind this by showing the comparisons between these two men. Likewise, Hale has gone through a great change of heart in Act III. What is this change? Explain it completely.

d. Trace Proctor's change from a sinful man in Act II to a loving martyr in Act III.

e. This question may be answered only if you have seen *The Exorcist* at the movies or have read the novel. Are there any similarities or differences that you can draw between *The Exorcist* and *The Crucible?* List and explain at least five similarities, differences, or both.[4]

■ *SUMMARY*

In this chapter we have examined how study units provide an instructional design, showing relationships between the global objectives and the supporting objectives. The standard format of the unit was outlined: purposes, rationale, content (concepts and principles), procedures, materials, culminating activity, and evaluation. Two units were provided for in-depth study, one from science and one from the humanities. It is useful to compare the formats of these model units to note similarities and differences.

■ *NOTES*

1. Geralyn Narkiewicz, "Unit of Study: Patterns of Heredity," unpublished manuscript, 1987. Used with permission of the author.
2. Colleen Carol Topous, A One Semester Course on the Supernatural, Master of Arts in Reading thesis, Wayne State University (directed by Dr. Jacqueline Tilles, 1974), 9–11. Used with permission of the author.
3. Ibid., 12–14.
4. Ibid., 150–191.

PART THREE

Instruction and Evaluation

Teaching Styles and Strategies

The use of puppets in teaching can enhance spontaneous communication.

A master teaches essence. When the essence is perceived, he teaches what is necessary to expand the perception. The Wu Li Master does not speak of gravity until the student stands in wonder at the flower petal falling to the ground. He does not speak of laws until the student, of his own, says, "How strange! I drop two stones simultaneously, one heavy and one light, and both of them reach the earth at the same moment!" . . . In this way, the Wu Li Master dances with his student . . . The Wu Li Master always begins at the center, at the heart of the matter.

—G. Zukav

Whatever you can do, or dream you can, begin it. Boldness has genius, power and magic in it.

—Goethe

We will either find a way or make one.

—Hannibal

A method is a way. It is a way of sensing, thinking, acting, feeling, and being. It is not a dry formula or recipe; rather, it is a design, embodied in action. It is intention made manifest. Methods are grounded in disciplines that guide the shape of action. If the method works, it will create access for students to think, to feel, to sense, to act, and to be in ways that formerly appeared closed to them.

In Chapters 1 through 7 we examined the present milieu of teaching, ways of formulating objectives, and ways of translating objectives into lesson plans, units, and courses. You should be able to state objectives for what you wish to accomplish instructionally and to provide a rationale for these objectives. In the process you will have the opportunity to create or adopt a specific physical form in which to express your objectives. What will the action in the classroom look like? And what are the advantages and disadvantages of any given mode of action? In short, what are your methods?

In this chapter we will examine both traditional and nontraditional methods. With each method you should note the central purpose, its strong and weak points in producing results. Never should methods be taken as mere arbitrary ways of acting in the classroom. There is an intentionality about each method that directs its power. Without this intentionality, the method becomes a dead ritual.

Traditional Methods

■ *The Lecture*

In recent years the lecture has been disregarded and maligned by some educators. Much empirical research has been amassed to show shortcomings of the lecture as an instructional vehicle. Some common arguments are that students have too short an attention span to focus on a lecture for more than 10–15 minutes at a time. Without correct feedback it is easy to misunderstand what has been said. NLP (Neurolinguistic Programming) operators say that only 7 percent of what we receive as a message is carried by the words one uses in speech. The speaker's tonality carries 38 percent of the message and his body posture carries 55 percent of the message.[1] Most teachers are not specifically trained in oratorical skills. There is the conjoint problem of teachers tending to focus on subject matter, forgetting *how* they are communicating, and lapsing into a monotone delivery—the deadliest form of lecture. There is, moreover, the tendency of the lecturing high school teacher to imitate the lecture format, the style of delivery, and the technical vocabulary of the college professor. After all, they still have those neat notes and everything is packaged so logically!

All of the foregoing objections are valid criticisms. High school teachers can, however, lecture effectively. The lecture is not intrinsically evil; indeed, for a quick overview, for summation, and for describing logical relationships it is sometimes indispensable. It must, however, be adapted to its audience. If a few basic skills are mastered, the lecture can become one of the teacher's stable methods.

Your lectures will be more powerful if you use visual images, analogies, and graphic representations. For example, in explaining the concept of resistance in electricity, you can use the students' familiarity with water flowing through a pipe, noting how the water pressure rises as the pipe narrows. In like manner, the flow of electrons is resisted by certain metals, creating a kind of pressure called voltage. You can use a seesaw to represent algebraic equations. If you are teaching students classification skills, start them off with familiar objects in the room, such as the chairs they are sitting in, rather than immediately introduce technical vocabulary, such as the Latin names of species, genus, and phylum, or the system of nomenclature in chemistry.

Begin your lecture with a question. This supports the student in following your main points. Repeat the question throughout the lecture to keep the students engaged. Invite the student to search for solutions to the questions you raise. When students do not offer solutions, you need to be prepared to play two roles—the person posing the question and the one attempting to answer the question. This is most effective when the teacher dramatizes the interplay between question and response, building toward a conclusion or a more penetrating examination of the question and revealing different aspects of the search layer by layer.

Avoid speaking in a monotone. Match your expression with your intent by varying pitch, stress, and juncture accordingly. Sometimes it is useful to vary the loudness or softness of your speech. Many beginning teachers think that if they speak louder students will listen more attentively. The converse is more often the case. Try dropping almost to a whisper and notice how students will begin to listen very carefully. Then you can just as unexpectedly change to a louder, more emphatic speech pattern. This challenges the students to adjust their listening. It also adds an air of mystery to the delivery—since the students will not know beforehand when you will change speech patterns. The element of mystery and surprise is just as important in learning as recurrence and expected patterning.

Beginning teachers sometimes unconsciously pace the floor, moving from one side of the room to another. The observing students' heads move as though they are watching a tennis match. To avoid this, think out where you want to be standing as you develop different parts of your lecture. You can divide the room into quadrants and intentionally move into each quadrant at different stages of your lecture. For example, after introducing the question "Why do we need to communicate?" the teacher may move to the left side of the room, give some information on communicating in pantomime, provide a quick pantomime, then move to the right side of the room to discuss ways we designate things, illustrate by pointing to objects, and then ask a related question, "How is pointing and acting things out like using words?" The teacher may then walk to the back of the room and ask even more pointed questions: "What would happen if we did not have words? What would it be like if words were not available right now?"

The shift in position in the room corresponds to the development of the lecture, providing a spatial metaphor for organization. As the teacher walks back to the front of the room to sum up, the very return to the front of the room, to the beginning point, suggests a completion, a completed square, circle, or other shape. These movements are intentional. They can be planned in advance or they can be used spontaneously. Either way, they are intentional—not random pacing.

Ivan Barzakov, founder of the Barzak Educational Institute in San Rafael, California recommends that teachers practice pantomime and variation in voice intonation and rhythm to increase significantly the power of communication in their classes. When body movements are coordinated with verbal statements, the use of imagery

Ivan Barzakov trains teachers to use effective movements and voice to empower their style.

and appropriate analogy, humor or music, the lecture is transformed from a mere rendering of information to an art form that can engage students on many levels.* The teacher can further invite student participation by having students en masse stand up or raise their hands to vote on key statements made throughout a lecture.

Much has been written on the value of eye contact. For the new teacher, initial discomfort can be overcome by focusing on the students' foreheads. Another tactic is to move eye contact quickly from one student to another. Learning to relax while lecturing can be assisted by breathing deeply between statements and by using visual imagery. For example, to calm the jitters, imagine that you are a tree solidly rooted in the earth.

Many beginning teachers have a tendency to rush their speaking. An optimal rate of delivery is about 110–130 words per minute. Key statements and key questions throughout will be more effective if the teacher allows for "hang" time; that is, give students time to process the statements and questions.

The use of an overhead projector expands the possibilities of a lecture. In place of an outline hidden from the students, which is time-consuming and distracting to read during the lecture, a projected outline or mind map provides a common frame of reference. Transparencies can be planned in advance to accentuate key points, and information can be built up in layers. For example, in presenting various systems of the human body, a transparency can visually present the skeletal system, with an overlay for the organs, another for the nervous system, and still another for the muscular system. A final overlay may show the layers of human skin. This setup provides the student with a visual schematic of general relationships between biological systems.

Diagrams can be worked out in advance. Cause-and-effect relationships can be depicted with arrows and with flowcharts. Drawings, symbols, mnemonic devices, images, and metaphors can be artistically incorporated into the transparencies, adding rich whole-brain stimuli to the language of the lecture.

The lecture is useful as a way of reviewing, particularly when the student is encouraged to verbally participate in the lecture. A fill-in-the-blank format can be inserted throughout the lecture, inviting the student to supply answers. This is a way of bridging the lecture with recitation.

■ *Recitation*

In the 1940s and 1950s, recitation was thought to be a way of "disciplining" the student's mind. It was often done in a stiff, formal manner by having the student stand or come to the front of the class and pour forth memorized facts on any subject from the life of Shakespeare to the reproductive cycle of tadpoles. In the 1960s, recitation came to be thought of as a meaningless exercise based on a false theory of learning.

*In the Optimalearning programs for teachers and trainers at Barzak Educational Institute, a special emphasis is placed on this type of training. "The lecture," says Ivan Barzakov, "becomes an invaluable tool for fast delivery of large amounts of information—while engaging a multiplicity of senses—to be cemented in the long-term memory."

If we look at this process, however, in terms of Bloom's taxonomy, we can see that what is lacking is not so much the rendering of knowledge, but the restriction to a first level of cognition.

Recitation can be made exciting by having students bring their own perceptions, values, and ideas to bear on the content being studied. Teachers can ask students to summarize the key ideas in the material presented. It is important that students state this information in their own words. The very process of restating information in their own words challenges the students to personally process the information. Students can also be encouraged to give examples of the new information operating in their environment and to state how they feel about practical and ethical implications. It is one thing to have students recite definitions of cloning as a process for producing a group of genetically identical cells descended from a single common ancestor or a group of organisms descended asexually from a single common ancestor; it is quite another to engage the student in a quest for values in respect to genetic cloning. How do they feel about cloning? What are the ethical implications of cloning human beings in a democratic society? When recitation is opened up in this way, it can lead naturally into one-on-one sharing and research projects for individuals or groups.

■ One-on-One Sharing

Many times, students will not know what they think about a problem you present in lecture format. Ideas may come too rapidly for them to follow, and they may need a framework in which to think through the new ideas to sort out their feelings about them. One-on-one sharing provides the framework. Safe, nonjudgmental sharing is the primary thrust of this process (see Figure 8.1). The teacher has the student turn to the student in the next seat to choose an A or a B. When the teacher says go, each side will have an uninterrupted five minutes of sharing, during which the student listening responds nonverbally through eye contact, gesture, facial expression, and body movement. After five minutes the roles reverse. If B listened, B now talks.

This technique can be done with or without a structured format. If done in an unstructured format, the student may speak on any topic that comes to mind. At first, students may have difficulty speaking continuously for five minutes. If so, the roles do not reverse. The students may remain silent for a few minutes, but it is the students' time for being listened to if and when they choose to speak.

Often in one-on-one sharing students experience a breakthrough in the development of their ideas and values. Since they have been given a chance to sort out ideas and feelings, they may also have a new sense of confidence and will be more willing to share with a larger group. In this respect, one-on-one sharing is a natural lead-in to small group sharing or open class sharing.

■ Group Work

Groups of four to six students work best. In larger groups it is too easy for students to hide, and in groups of two or three students the possibility of interaction is not optimal.

Group work should give each student an opportunity to assume different roles.

Figure 8.1 One-on-one sharing provides a framework in which the student can build trust and freedom of expression.

Groups need a moderator and a recorder. The remaining students provide oral summaries of what went on. The recorder checks what they say against the notes, providing corrective feedback and making note changes where necessary. The moderator ensures that each student participates in the ongoing inquiry by using a round robin procedure, by encouraging students who hold back, or by preventing one or more students from dominating the group. Maximum participation of all students and development of role skills are key elements in group process. As a vehicle for teaching content, there is more flexibility provided. Some students learn content best in a leadership role, some through organizing notes, and some through the give-and-take of the round robin procedure. For follow-up and presentations to the class, each additional role can be assigned. For example, some students can present the information in skit or pantomime form. Others can draw pictures, doodles, or mind maps—schematic and pictorial representations of idea flow. Still others can give oral summaries, sometimes varied with readings of dramatic scripts.

■ *Brainstorming*

Brainstorming is used to generate the flow of ideas in a class. All answers, no matter how wrong they may seem to the teacher or other students, are accepted as *possible* solutions. Brainstorming can provide the groundwork for creating a workable hypothesis, but at the brainstorming stage correctness and workability are not used as criteria. The teacher or another student records all statements on the board or on flip charts. Later, the flip charts can be torn off and taped up about the room, giving the sense of shared creation.

Brainstorming has the mood of a delightful quest, a playful search. Sometimes a play-like question can be brainstormed and then converted to a content question. An example is, How many things can be done with a tree? Students list countless possibilities, from practical replies such as "make wood" to aesthetic responses such as "enjoy its beauty and form" to humorous answers such as "to get my parachute caught in." No answer is excluded. A parallel question may then be raised by substituting the word "poem" for "tree," and the same procedure is followed.

■ *The Project Method*

To be effective, projects should organically evolve from an already-engaged-in question. Projects are artificial, inert, antilearning constructs when they are merely assigned to students without any prior processing. Projects can evolve from group work, one-on-one sharing and particularly from brainstorming sessions. When the project evolves from brainstorming, the teacher must sense the brainstorming quest is complete before shifting to a feasibility search. In this process each possibility generated in brainstorming is reexamined on the basis of feasibility. Items can be eliminated, modified, put on hold, or selected out for the planning phase of the project. The group searches for resources to carry out the possibilities. The focus is on what will work. Lists are made, and strategies are explored. When this process is complete, the teacher can then raise the question of *who will do what by when.* All the prior explorations are necessary to build a solid foundation for a project. Beginning teachers sometimes try to start with the question of who will do what by when and later wonder why the project failed. The project must evolve as a creation. When it is merely assigned, the students will be unlikely to make any sense of it or have any investment in its purposes.[2]

■ *Role Playing*

The presentation given above leads naturally into the use of role playing as a technique. Role playing expands the students' sense of personal power. The use of the technique need not be restricted to the humanities; it can be equally useful in the sciences.

For example, students can assume the identity of Thomas Edison and his assistants or Alexander Graham Bell and his assistants and reenact the invention of the electric light and the telephone. They can be Pythagoras or Euclid as they explore mathematical concepts, and they can be Madame Curie or Michael Faraday in chemistry class. Teachers can enhance this fantasy by addressing the students by their adopted names and by having name tags made up for the students to wear. In science class, important discoveries and experiments can be dramatized; in literature, scenes from plays and short stories as well as events in the lives of authors can be acted out (see Figure 8.2). In social studies, courtroom dramatization of legal-ethical conflicts, both actual and hypothetical, is a time-honored and effective means of creating student participation and learning.

Dramatization and role playing increase affective and kinesthetic learning. They provide a rich fantasy in which to re-create facts and concepts, thereby enhancing long-term memory. They also create a safe space in which students can explore concepts, feelings, and values. Because the space is free, the student will often act

Figure 8.2 Role playing expands the student's sense of personal power.

out of an identity that is larger than the habitually restricted self and reach levels of performance that surprise the student. Gradually, the limiting self-concepts tend to drop away, and a new confidence and belief system of personal performance emerges.

Nonverbal Methods

Aldous Huxley distinguishes between knowledge and understanding—the distinctions between the world of concepts and the world of experience, between the world of words and the world of nonverbal awareness. We are humanized, Huxley says, through our use of language, but we must free ourselves from the tyranny of words, conditioned reflexes, and social conventions in order to understand:

> Knowledge is acquired when we succeed in fitting a new experience into the system of concepts based upon our old experiences. Understanding comes when we liberate ourselves from the old and so make possible a direct, unmediated contact with the new, the mystery, moment by moment of our existence.[3]

We have already seen a partially nonverbal technique in one-on-one sharing. The person remaining silent often reports having as much insight and reorganization of thought as the person speaking. Moreover, the person remaining silent must *learn* to remain silent. In a culture that competes for every microsecond of verbal space, this requires great discipline. The tendency is to interrupt, to modify, to finish the sentences, to counter, or to help one struggle through communication barriers. But no—one must remain silent. In silence one can discover a different dimension of knowing and experiencing. Consider the mandala, for example.

■ *The Mandala*

The mandala is a geometric pattern designed in such a way that the right hemisphere of the brain is brought into play. The right brain becomes fascinated with exploring the spatial configurations of the mandala (see Figure 8.3). With the right brain dominant, habits of incessant chattering and figuring out associated with the left brain are temporarily suspended.[4] When questions arise about what one is observing, the student is simply instructed to return to gazing at the center of the mandala. What, then, is the instructional value of the experience?

The value of the mandala is that the right hemisphere of the brain is brought into play. Students have a direct experience of processing information in radically different ways. Individual differences become readily apparent as the teacher asks students to share. Each student has a different experience to share with great conviction. And yet all of them were observing the same mandala. Some report movement. Some report different geometric patterns forming and dissolving before their eyes. Some report a need to analyze what is going on. The teacher can point out the variety of interpretations and draw out parallel approaches to interpreting movies, novels, and political events. The process is also useful as a prewriting exercise, opening the student to possibilities outside the literal direction of a writing assignment. The student's subjective powers are brought forth as a creative resource. Instead of writing a dry plot outline of *The Color Purple* as a book report, the student may be more inclined, after experiencing the mandala, to use personal expression to enrich the reading of the book.

Figure 8.3 The mandala is a visual pattern designed to elicit right-brain functioning. (From *The Right Brain Experience* by Marilee Zdeneck. Copyright © 1983 by Marilee Zdeneck. Drawing by Hal Fletcher, Jr. Used by permission of the author and McGraw-Hill Book Company.)

■ *Other-Hand Writing*

Writing with one's nondominant hand is a way of eliciting the function of the right brain.[5] Writing itself is nonverbal in the sense that one is not speaking audibly. One may, however, be speaking inaudibly or subvocally. By writing with the nondominant hand one is likely to get a more spontaneous flow of association, often sprinkled with imagery. Again, this process is useful as a lead-in to writing and as a way to elicit creative output. It can be used as a prelude to brainstorming. The student is instructed to list items related to a concept as rapidly as possible with the nondominant hand. The process is particularly useful in assisting the student to break through barriers that limit self-concept. The process is but an adaptation and facilitation of free association, a technique common in psychoanalytic therapy. Here, however, the motive is to bring forth the reserve consciousness, to elicit past associations to be used in interpreting content, not to resolve neuroses.

■ *Transitional Objects*

Transitional objects are physical entities like autographed baseballs or old photographs that reelicit past memories.[6] They are particularly useful in recalling past incidents, including past successful learning experiences (see Figure 8.4). Teachers use these objects effectively by having students recall and write specific descriptions of experiences from the past.

Figure 8.4 Transitional objects are physical entities like autographed baseballs or old photographs that reelicit past memories.

■ *Dreams as Methods*

Freud said dreams were the "royal road to the unconscious." Dreams contain action, character, setting, dialogue—all the elements for good story telling. With minor revision students create skits from their dreaming. In an Atlanta high school one English teacher has students working in groups, sharing what they wish from their dream diary. They use whatever dreams they wish in putting together a skit, refashioning one dream or perhaps a combination of several. They write a script for a video production, edit the script, film it, and then write critical reviews of each other group's productions. Patricia Garfield's *Creative Dreaming* and Marilee Zdenek's *The Right-Brain Experience* are useful sources for planning lessons using dream work.

■ *Sensory Stimulation*

Sensory stimulation can be entirely self-created as when one supplies both stimulus and response, or it can be elicited by the teacher. In this instance, the process is verbal to the extent that the teacher may supply images in words, but the words are used to elicit nonverbal images for the student. The teacher says, "When I give an image, just allow yourself to experience whatever comes up; if nothing happens for you, allow the word to pass." Then the teacher gives a series of words as a stimulus:

1. freshly mowed lawn
2. fresh strawberries
3. rainfall on a summer evening
4. walking on newly fallen snow
5. a beginning sunburn

The students then report their sensations and associations. The process supports the student in making sharp sensory discrimination.

■ *Humor as Method*

In Appendix A, "Teaching to the Whole Brain," the value of humor is explained in respect to brain function and learning. In Chapter 18, humor is recommended to break up fixed states, particularly *fixed states of anger.*

In teaching any subject, humor can be injected to increase rapport. Even so-called boring subjects can be made interesting and enjoyable through the use of humor. Consider the teaching of punctuation—not a favorite topic of many people, teachers and students alike. But then look at the fun that Lewis Thomas has in *The Medusa and the Snail* when he casts punctuation in a humorous light:

> There are no precise rules about punctuation (Fowler lays out some general advice (as best he can under the complex circumstances of English prose (he points out, for example, that we possess only four stops (the comma, the semicolon, the colon and the period (the question mark and exclamation point are not, strictly speaking, stops; they are indicators of tone (oddly enough, the Greeks employed the semicolon for their question mark (it produces a strange sensation

Visualization can take the form of student-made book cover designs used as bulletin boards.

to read a Greek sentence which is a straightforward question: Why weepest thou; (and, of course, there are parentheses (which are surely a kind of punctuation making this whole matter much more complicated by having to count up the left-handed parentheses in order to be sure of closing with the right number (but if the parentheses were left out, with nothing to work with but the stops, we would have considerably more flexibility in the deploying of layers of meaning than if we tried to separate all the clauses by physical barriers (and in the latter case, while we might have more precision and exactitude for our meaning, we would lose the essential flavor of language, which is its wonderful ambiguity)))))))))))).

. . .

I have grown fond of semicolons in recent years. The semicolon tells you that there is still some question about the preceding full sentence; something needs to be added; it reminds you sometimes of the Greek usage. It is almost always a greater pleasure to come across a semicolon than a period. the period tells you that that is that; if you didn't get all the meaning you wanted or expected, anyway you got all the writer intended to parcel out and now you have to move along. But with a semicolon there you get a pleasant little feeling of expectancy; there is more to come; to read on; it will get clearer.[7]

■ *Mind Maps*

Mind maps have been used throughout this text to assist you in processing the concepts in this book. The technique is also very effective in assisting students to process any discipline. The teacher provides a stimulus—a video presentation, a Bach concerto, a poem, a silent reading. The student is then instructed to draw a circle in the center of the page and to put a word or short phrase in the circle that represents the summation of the experience. He then draws lines away from the circle, writing associative words and phrases on the lines. Subconcepts are placed on lines branching from the original lines. Ideas related to the central concept are represented by new lines drawn from the center.

The mind map is an intermediate step between the verbal and the nonverbal (see Figure 8.5). The student can shuttle between image and concept. Visualizations can be increased by having students translate their words into images—or the teacher can have students start with images by having them draw pictures or symbols for each branch of the mind map. The process can be shifted toward the verbal simply by having the student translate the mind map to a fellow student, a group, or the entire class.

See Tony Buzan's book, *Use Both Sides of Your Brain* for a more complete explanation of mind mapping.[8] The instructional value of the technique has long been recognized by Evelyn Wood Reading Dynamics, an organization that teaches the technique as a tool to recall and to reconstruct material read at a rapid rate. Evelyn Wood refers to the mind map as a recall pattern.[9] Gabrielle Rico uses a similar technique called clustering in her book *Writing the Natural Way*—a self-instructional text designed to teach writing skills through the elicitation and restructuring of imaging, association, use of metaphor and awareness of organic relationships.[10]

■ *Visualization*

Visualization plays a part in many of the foregoing techniques. It is one of the primary modes of information processing, recognized by both NLP (Neurolinguistic Programming) practitioners and Lozanov trainers.* The process can be used to engage the student in any discipline, including the sciences. The student can be taught to visualize molecules, the circulatory system, the muscles of the human body. Excellent sources for visualization are Adelaide Bry's *Visualization: Directing the Movies of Your Mind,* and Gay Hendricks and Thomas B. Roberts's *Second Centering*

*According to Ivan Barzakov this applies only to those instructors and trainers who are using adaptations of Suggestopedia in the West. Dr. Lozanov himself is thoroughly opposed to the very notion of using guided visualization as a carrier of information. As a matter of fact, Barzakov reports that at his summer training in 1987 in Bulgaria, Lozanov clearly stated that he has authorized no Westerner to represent his work or train teachers on his behalf.

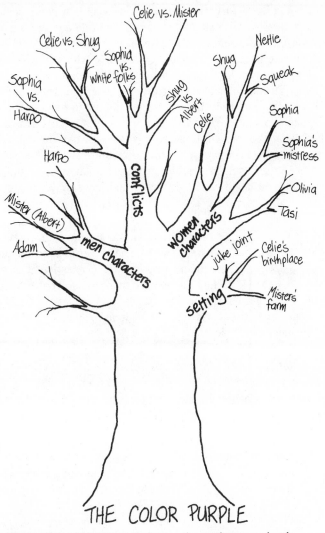

Figure 8.5 Using the mind map, the student can shuttle between image and concept.

Book, and the late Beverly-Colleene Galyean's *Mind Sight: Learning Through Imaging.* Consider this simple use of visualization to teach the concept of classification. Visualize yourself walking at dusk through a beautiful garden that is filled with colorful plants, flowers, and trees. As you walk you can hear the rush of the waves from the nearby beach. Begin to notice the *similarity* of the trees and the plants, and recall all the *similar* trees, plants, and flowers you have seen in the past. Notice the *details* of the plants and the *various parts* of the flowers and think of *all* the flowers and plants that have *those parts.* And just allow yourself to begin to *group* those plants and to notice any *similarity* and *differences* as you continue to walk through the garden. Listen to the rush and rhythm of the tide and gradually visualize the classroom you are sitting in. Gradually open your eyes and come back into the room.

The above process is specifically designed with embedded images of classification. The italicized key words provide a lead-in for exploring concepts of class formation. The students are directed to focus on similarities and dissimilarities of the plants, flowers, and trees, to note the details and to reflect on how they would group the details. This process is a natural lead into a science lesson on taxonomy.

Following the visualization process, the teacher can ask: What did you notice about the trees, the flowers? Were there similarities? If so, what were they? Have you noticed these similarities in your observation of trees and flowers in the past? How would you begin to classify trees and flowers? What are some examples?

Questions as Method

From the time of Socrates questions have been recognized in Western tradition as powerful instruments of teaching. There are many ways in which questions can be used in teaching. They can be used to assess student knowledge, to focus attention, to aid in the organization and recall of information, to direct study and research, and to frame an entire world view—a Weltanschauung (world view) that provides the basis for independent learning.

■ *Questions and Bloom's Taxonomy*

Instructional questions are often derived from the levels of cognition in *Bloom's Taxonomy* (see Chapter 5). Hence typical cognitive questions may be written in the following form:

1. Knowledge	What is the chemical symbol for sodium?
2. Comprehension	What is meant by debit and credit?
3. Application	If $5x = 250$, then what is the value of x?
4. Analysis	What are the uses of symbolism in William Blake's poem, *The Tyger?*
5. Evaluation	Which Van Gogh painting is best and why?

■ *Questions and the Teaching of Precision*

Questions can be used to probe for progressively more precise answers. Students often respond to questions by using vague or overgeneralized language. To cut through the fluff, teachers can develop a repertory of responses to vague language.

Anthony Robbins, an NLP practitioner, outlines some specific suggestions. In response to the judgments "too much, too many," the teacher can counter, "Compared to what?" If the student says "they" or "it" caused it, the teacher can respond, "Who or what specifically?" If a student says, "I can't do the assignment," the teacher can respond, "What would happen if you did?" or "What causes or prevents you from doing it?" When a student says, "The character in the novel acts weird," the teacher can respond, "How, specifically?" requesting the student to qualify the stated action. Finally, when a student uses universals indiscriminately, words like "all, every, never," the teacher can simply convert these words to questions: "All? Every? Never?"[11]

The idea is to notice these signals of overgeneralized language when the student uses them and redirect them to more specific usage. By using these techniques one can confront vague language *and* remain in rapport with the student.[12]

■ *Questions as Embedded World Views*

Questions can be designed to contain key words that imply a world view. The key words can be played upon, extended, and elaborated until the world view becomes articulated. Two examples are given.

1. What is the basis for classifying books, plant and animal life, numbers, and literary periods?

This question promotes a search for structures underlying classification. It points, perhaps, to the generation of a theory of classes.

2. What is the basis for cause and effect in human action, response to the arts, and physical change?

The question assumes cause and effect as a given and prompts one to search for a theory justifying cause and effect, thereby directing one toward a mechanistic explanation of the world.

Convergent questions can be used to channel a student's thoughts toward a specific response, and *divergent questions* can be used to expand the student's thought to related concepts. Convergent questions are arranged in a series that progressively move toward a conclusion. For example, if you want students to draw the conclusion that salt intake should be reduced in order to reduce water retention, you could begin by asking how sodium affects water retention and then ask which foods are high in sodium.

Divergent questions work in the opposite way—to broaden the students' associations. Examples are "How is a poem like a flower?" or "In what way is a beehive like a democracy? Like a monarchy?" Ideally, the teacher should use a balance of divergent and convergent questions.

| *Critical Thinking as a Method* |

According to Harun-Ur Rashid of the philosophy department at Wayne State University, "Critical thinking may be described as a sceptical reflective attitude toward things and events relating to life and the universe." Harun-Ur Rashid points out that critical thinking not only helps us to assess the truth or falsehood of informative statements (i.e., formal and factual statements); it may also be used as method (or technique or strategy) of evaluating the validity of deductive arguments (arguments in which the premises provide conclusive support for the conclusion) as well as the strength of inductive arguments (arguments in which the premises provide partial support for the conclusion).

In order to determine the validity of a deductive argument we may use various strategies. One of these strategies is to use the method of deduction that involves the use of rules of inferences. Let us suppose that P and Q (shorthand symbols) are variables which stand for any arbitrary statements that may have either true or false truth values. Given these two logical variables, arguments involving the following logical structures are valid.

If P then Q

P

———————

Q

The technical name for this rule of inference is *modus ponens* (or *affirming the consequent*).

Let us take a concrete example of an argument which has the above logical structure.

If it rains then the ground is wet.

It rains.

———————————————————

The ground is wet.

Any argument of this structure must be valid no matter what the contents of the variables are.

Rule of *modus tollens* (or *denying the consequent*):

If P then Q

Not Q

———————

Not P

Let us take a concrete example of this form of argument.

If the moon is made of green cheese, then the earth moves around the sun.

The earth does not move around the sun.

———————————————————

The moon is not made of green cheese.

Consider an argument that looks valid but not really so.

If you work hard, you'll get an A in the course.

You do not work hard.

———————————————————

You won't get an A in the course.

The above argument is fallacious (the technical name of the fallacy is *denying the antecedent*). In the above argument, the antecedent of the first premise "You work hard" is a sufficient condition for the consequent "You will get an A." While the presence of the sufficient condition guarantees the presence of the consequent, the absence (or negation) of the antecedent does not necessarily imply the absence or negation of the consequent. That is why given that both the premises are true, the conclusion could be false, and the argument invalid.

Take another example. Here is an argument which seems to be valid but in fact it is not.

You will get an A only if you work hard.

You work hard.

_____

You will get an A.

This argument may be considered as inductively strong, but it is deductively invalid. The validity of a deductive argument depends on the very structure of the argument, not on its contents. Given that both the premises of the argument are true, the conclusion could be false and hence the argument is invalid. The technical name of this fallacious structure of argument is called *affirming the consequent.*

Consider the following structure:

If you know what you're talking about then you are Socratic.

If you are Socratic then you should pursue death.

Should you pursue death, you're not human. (since humans don't want to die)

_____

If you know what you are talking about then you are not human.

The conclusion sounds counterintuitive, but the argument is perfectly valid. In other words, given that all the premises are true, it is logically impossible for the conclusion to be false. The technical name of the above argument is hypothetical syllogism.

There are other deductively valid forms of arguments. Some of them are given under.

Disjunctive Syllogism

Either the Pistons lose or the Celtics win.

The Pistons don't lose.

_____

The Celtics win.

[Note that "or" is being used here in the inclusive sense]

Rule of Simplification:

Shawn is buttering the toast and Shawn is in the kitchen.

_____

Shawn is buttering the toast.

Rule of Conjunction

Bill is drunk.

Bill is sober.

Bill is drunk and Bill is sober.

Rule of Addition

The earth is floating on water (Thales)

Either the earth is floating on water or George is a wimp.

This is a valid argument although the second disjunct of the conclusion looks quite irrelevant to the first disjunct. From the commonsense point of view the argument is not a good one but logically it is valid.

There are many other valid rules of inferences. These rules are useful insofar as we are concerned with the determination of the validity of arguments.

Harun-Ur Rashid states the case for critical thinking:

> In this country people nowadays think that students are being indoctrinated in their classrooms. These students are said to have closed minds. They are blamed for dogmatically taking things to be true or false without investigating the rationale or justification for those beliefs. They don't make a distinction between opinions and knowledge. Critical or reflective attitude helps people to have an open mind—a nondogmatic rational behavior. Critical thinking helps people to realize that they should not accept anything and everything they hear or they learn from whatever sources of information they might have. It helps us to understand what it is for something to be justified and what criterion we should adopt in order to justify our beliefs and/or convictions.

Critical thinking not only improves our education; it may be said that it is a requirement that is absolutely necessary for education. It not only helps us to diagnose a problem or recognize a problem to be a problem; it also helps us to suspend our unsupported dogmatic beliefs. It also teaches us how to internalize methods of analysis, synthesis, and evaluation.

Self-Instructional Packages

Students do not master skills uniformly. Some students drop behind because they are absent for long periods. To assist students to progress at their own rate, the self-instructional kit is useful. The kit usually contains a set of objectives, a preassessment test, and directions to the student on how to proceed. The kit may direct the student to read certain articles, to view videos or slide presentations, or to work with a peer tutor. When the student has completed the directions and reviewed the materials in the kit, he is directed to take an examination, which may be given by the instructor or managed by a test lab. This process often fills a specific student need, but is not intended as a replacement for human interaction.

| *Games and Puzzles as Method* | Games and puzzles can be used to open students to new possibilities of thinking and experiencing. Some games such as charades and twenty questions can be used to teach specific skills such as classification. Crossword puzzles can be used to |

build language skills (see the study unit on *The Crucible* in Chapter 7), and verbal and mathematical puzzles can open students to alternative modes of conceptualization.

A. SPIDER/FLY PROBLEM

Assume that the room you are in is 30 ft long and that it is 12 ft high and 12 ft wide. A spider on one 12-by-12-ft wall is located 1 ft from the ceiling and 6 ft from either side. A fly on the opposite 12-by-12-ft wall is located 1 ft from the floor and 6 ft from either side. *Question:* What is the shortest route that the spider can crawl to devour the fly? The shortest possible distance is not 42 ft, the commonsense answer obtained by adding the length of the room, 30 ft, plus 11 ft for one wall, plus 1 ft for another wall. This answer assumes the spider must crawl parallel to the sides of the room. But what if one steps outside this assumption? What possibilities open up?

B. SPACE DESIGN PROBLEM

On the board the instructor draws three figures: a circle, a square, and a cross. Then he tells the class to assume that these figures are empty—to imagine that these configurations are openings in a wooden block (see Figure 8.6). The task is to imagine a solid figure that can be passed through these openings and *fit perfectly* as it is passed through. Students can be given styrofoam and cutting instruments to experiment with various configurations.

SOLUTION A: The room can be flattened out. Then the shortest possible line is drawn between the spider and the fly. The Pythagorean theorem can be used to determine the length of the hypotenuse—the line on which the spider crawls. When the room is closed up again, the spider uses the sides of the walls in its journey toward the fly (see Figure 8.7).

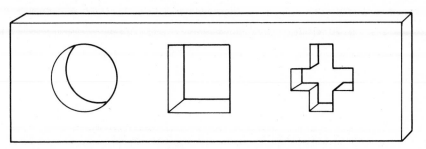

Figure 8.6 Imagine a solid figure that can be passed through the above openings and fit perfectly in each opening as it is passed through them.

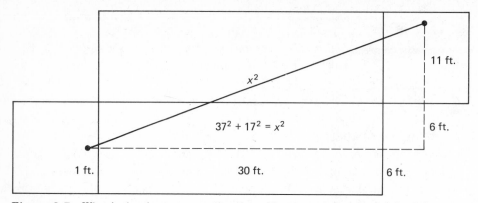

Figure 8.7 What is the shortest route that the spider can crawl to devour the fly?

SOLUTION B: The circle and the square are fused into one figure, forming a cross pattern where they intersect. The thickness of the styrofoam or wood must equal the width of the arms of the cross. When this figure is inserted into the empty cross, it creates an exact fit. Turn it on another side and it fits the square; at another angle it fits the circle (see Figure 8.8).

These puzzles can be presented along with some sketches by M. C. Escher. The effect, after perhaps some enjoyable confusion, is to open the student to the possibility of multiple perspectives—to the teaching of a kind of critical pluralism. Such techniques, then, provide analogical ways of introducing a student to competing scientific theories and competing interpretations of poetry or art. There is no assent to randomness here. Each judgment is responsible, even rigorous—yet different. I can analyze a poem in terms of the canons of Aristotle's *Poetics,* and I can analyze the same poem in terms of the canons of romantic criticism, using Coleridge's *Biographia Literaria* as my yardstick. Both can be rigorous—and different. If I am a scientist I can (following Heisenberg's quantum mechanics) subscribe to a probabilistic view of the universe *or* I can follow Einstein and say, "God does not play dice with the universe"—that there must be universal laws even if I cannot know what they are. Both views are rigorous, but in different ways. How can we teach our students to explore alternative possibilities, to search for new perspectives, to press through to the next paradigm shift—and at the same time teach them to maintain a high degree of rigor? The methods in this text are designed in part to do this. They are a beginning. But what others can you create?

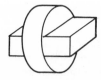

Figure 8.8 The circle and square are fused into one figure, which, when turned at different angles, fits perfectly in each opening in Figure 8.6.

PROBE Interview two teachers and ask them to describe the methods they typically use. Analyze their methods in terms of verbal and nonverbal characteristics. Expand these methods by incorporating techniques from this chapter.

Integrative Approaches

There are a number of methods that produce integration of the verbal and the nonverbal, build synthetic connections between various disciplines and encourage the student to explore relationships between knowledge, application, and the nature of reality. Through these methods the student is invited to become the artist, the scientist, and the philosopher. Many of these methods promote a childlike playfulness, a sense of permission to engage in "what if" thinking.

■ *Imagery as Language*

Werner Erhard speaks of learning as a function of "dwelling in the language of a discipline."[13] In teaching mathematical concepts like pi, for example, he has the student play at being a geometer, invent a language useful in describing characteristics of circles, and from this language derive pi.[14] Peter Kline takes a similar tack to the same problem, promoting the development of a syntax useful for mathematical thinking. Note his use of imagery in this method:

> If the formula "$C = \pi d$" caused a similar picturing process to occur in the brain, then one could move from that picture back to the formula gain. Let us now construct a picturing process that might occur. If we imagine a large circle on the ground on which kerosene has been poured, and this circle has been set on fire, and we then imagine a long rope which has the capacity to smother the fire to be placed at the diameter of this same circle, we can imagine lifting the rope, placing it on the circumference to smother as much of the fire as possible, and then observing how many more times we must place it in order that all the fire may be put out. After we have placed it on the circumference three times, we have only a very little bit of the fire left, so we know that the number of times needed for extinguishing the fire with the rope is a little over three.[15]

This method encourages the development of transformation within the specialized language of mathematics. In natural languages we can readily see how this works. In the sentence "Mr. Jones persuaded Mr. Smith to learn to play golf," we know the meaning represented by the words used, but we also understand many things that are implied by the sentence. In fact, we cannot be said to understand the sentence without understanding its implications.

Let us consider some of the statements that are true (or probably true) by implication, based on this sentence.

1. Mr. Jones and Mr. Smith are not the same person.
2. Mr. Smith did not at first wish to learn to play golf.

Relativity, *by M. C. Escher.*

3. Mr. Smith did not at first know how to play golf.
4. Mr. Jones thought it would be a good thing for Mr. Smith to know how to play golf.
5. Mr. Smith and Mr. Jones are men of sufficient leisure and of a cultural orientation to value the playing of golf.
6. Mr. Smith and Mr. Jones have a relationship that extends at least to the playing of golf.
7. Mr. Smith and Mr. Jones are men and they are of some dignity and formality, since they are not referred to here by their first names.[16]

Now, when we apply the same transformational principles to the above formula, $C = \pi d$, we can, according to Kline, derive many true statements. It ought to be true that the formula $C = \pi d$ leads to a fairly rich deep structure as well. Let us

Waterfall, *by M. C. Escher.*

see how many statements we can make out of our experience of the circle and the diameter:

1. The diameter extends from one side of the circle to the other at the widest section.

2. The lines above and below the diameter which make up the circumference are curved lines, while the diameter is a straight line.
3. It is possible to imagine the diameter being changed from a straight line to a curved line in order to compare the lengths of the two lines.
4. If the diameter were longer, the circle would be larger, and the circumference would be longer, and if the diameter were shorter, the circle would be smaller, and the circumference would be shorter.
5. All circles look alike except for size.
6. The relationship between the diameter and the circumference is unvarying throughout the universe.
7. The way around is longer than the way through.
8. Half the circumference is not twice as long as the diameter.[17]

■ Puppets and As-If Thinking

Ordinarily puppets are associated with primary grades, but students of all ages, even adults, respond positively to them. The author regularly uses two puppets in his graduate classes. One is a colorful parrot named Charlie. The other, the delightful creation of a local artist, is a little guy with a black body, long red arms and legs, and a sad hound-dog face; his name is Dork. If you can visualize a mirror image of an eighth note, you will have a picture of Dork's shape. After the class is well under way, the author introduces Charlie and interviews him before the class. Since the author is not a ventriloquist, Charlie whispers his answers in the author's ear to be relayed to the class. Charlie asks questions about the course that have come up in past classes or that students want to but are reluctant to ask. Charlie asks these questions for them.

Midway in the class the author introduces Dork. By this point students are willing to play—to accept Dork on a pretend basis. Students are individually invited to share with Dork some concept they have learned and anything that puzzles them. It is amazing how they open up to Dork. By the end of the class period the students' review is proceeding nonstop. One graduate student explained to Dork, in detail, just how she planned to apply her newfound knowledge when she taught the following term. In the midst of her animated planning she exclaimed, "Dork, I'm just like you!"

Lynn Dhority, author of *Acquisition Through Creative Teaching,* regularly uses puppets to teach his classes in German: "Onkel Fritz is a balding 70-year-old Bavarian adventurer who loves Schnapps and females and is convinced he is as young (at heart) as anyone. In Dhority's class students practice their German by speaking and writing letters to Onkel Fritz, "giving him a range of advice from motherly reprimands . . . to brotherly alliance."[18]

■ Science Fiction as Integration of Learning

In *Broca's Brain,* Carl Sagan recommends using science fiction as a method to inspire creative thought about science and mathematics. "One of the great benefits of science fiction," says Sagan, "is that it can convey bits and pieces, hints and phrases, of knowledge unknown or inaccessible to the reader."[19] Good science fiction, says Sagan, can introduce a student to mathematical and scientific concepts in delightful and understandable terms: "Heinlein's 'And He Built a Crooked House' was for many readers probably the first introduction they had ever encountered to four-dimensional mathematics that held any promise of being comprehensible."[20]

Science fiction can be used in conjunction with expert opinion in many fields to develop possible future scenarios. Not only the sciences, but the humanities as well—music, literature, art—can be recontextualized by considering their manifestations in possible futures. This is true of normative disciplines like ethics also, for one must learn to make new value choices in new contexts.[21] What, for example, are some ethical implications of genetic cloning? Of transplants? Legal and moral questions are being raised for which we have no history of cases. The student is invited to explore not only what is possible, but what is desirable and permissible.

■ *Music as Integration of Learning*

We all know the dramatic power of music to set a mood, to underscore an idea or a theme. We have only to recall some of our favorite movies or TV ads. Music can be used in similar ways in teaching. In fact, there are at least five distinct ways music can be used in teaching: (1) to anchor a desired response "an anchor is any stimulus that evokes a consistent response pattern from a person."[22] Just as a well-designed TV ad will recall a set of images and ideas through qualified theme music, so too the teacher can provide music that is specifically associated with peak learning states and specific content mastery: (2) to promote relaxation and (3) to establish a mood. You may wish to teach a lesson on a story set in a Mexican village. You can set the mood by playing appropriate music as the students enter class: (4) to stimulate the imagination and promote fantasy, and (5) to give access to long-term memory.

Ivan Barzakov, former master teacher in the Lozanov* Schools in Sofia, Bulgaria, and founder of Optimalearning and Barzak Educational Institute in San Rafael, California, describes his technique of reading with music (Reading w/Music™) as

> a type of reading (or talking) with music whereby you *read (talk) aloud* and your vocal rhythm and inflections reflect the rhythm and change of mood expressed in the music.
>
> Imagine a surfer and a wave. Your voice is like a surfer and music is your wave. You are clearly reading, not singing; however, your voice is like a new instrument added to the orchestra and serves as a *counterpoint* to the music.
>
> Read at a comfortable pace, don't rush. Make small pauses to listen to how the music is changing. When the tempo or mood of the music changes, reflect these changes in your tone of voice, e.g., more or less emphatic, wistful, tender or strong. Vary the voice to avoid monotony. It is best to familiarize yourself with the music beforehand.[23]

The content that is read with music does not matter. It can be a passage from any subject—mathematics, physics, economics, or accounting, as well as art history, poetry, philosophy, or any other humanities subject. It is only important that it be

---

*The BBC filmed Barzakov's teaching as a model Lozanov class.

read *with* instrumental music. The music is not to be regarded as background and should be used sparingly and selectively to evoke the desired learning state. The volume of the music is slightly lower than the voice. One speaks *through* the music. But why all these specifications? Are they arbitrary or idiosyncratic? In short, what does this technique produce? Ivan Barzakov explains the multiple effects of "Reading with Music" (sometimes called a "concert reading") as follows:*

> Now what happens in [this type of] reading? First when you read with music, the left hemisphere, which normally processes the sequential, logical material of the text, is required to follow the musical phrase, to note how the music is changing, to enter and pause with the music. So the left hemisphere is linked both ways. [On the other hand,] wide open to music, the "intuitive" [right] hemisphere sees the text and meaning as a whole. So the two hemispheres of the brain, in a cross-link, are processing the same material. . . . [But the brain consists of more than the neo-cortex. Along with the limbic system (of the paleomammalian layer) there is the reptile brain which governs our basic instincts of preservation. These lower levels of the brain generate] reactions we experience as anxiety or joy, elevated heartbeats and blood pressure, and other physical reactions which affect learning negatively or positively.
>
> So we are talking of a *global activation* which inhibits counterproductive tensions and excites the emotional/cognitive structures which encode and refine information and knowledge. We are using the conscious and unconscious, the whole brain. We are not using just left and right hemispheres, [the subcortical structures, and the limbic system in particular, are activated along with the neo-cortex, *at the same time*. The result is a burst of creative energy and increased motivation with self-assuredness.]
>
> What is more, the specific state of inhibition-excitement evoked through the directed light stimuli you receive is so pleasant that you want more. So the more pleasant and relaxed you are, the more energized you feel and the more information signals you want. So the more you learn, the better you feel; and the better you feel, [even more you learn. At the same time, the more you learn, the more creative you become and the more creative you become—the more you learn and the better you feel . . . an endless upward spiral!][24]

In reading with music, special varieties of Baroque music are used to support the learning of terminology, facts and figures, technical data and language vocabulary. Both the fast and slow movements are used. Romantic, Classical, and some Baroque music are recommended for working with fantasy, storytelling and stimulating the imagination. The sequencing of the appropriate composers, compositions, tempos, and key pitch requires many months and years of extensive experimentation and research. The following is a sample of Baroque selections which comprise one of the six Optimalearning music cassettes for memory concentration, delivery of information, storytelling, parenting, relaxation, problem solving, and more. [There are also specialized cassettes for driving, imagination and creativity, guided visualizations, mood uplifting, contemplation and artistic inspiration.]

*Words in brackets within the following Barzakov citations reflect updating and clarifying revisions made by Barzakov since his article was first printed.

Pachelbel—*Canon in D Major* (7:15)

Pachelbel—Excerpt from *Partita no. VI in B-flat Major* (3:40)

Handel—Andante from *Concerto in B Minor* (3:10)

Corelli—Pastorale from *Christmas Concerto no. 8* (3:53)

Manfredini—Largo from *Concerto Grosso no. 12* (1:58)

Scarlatti—*Pastorale* (2:57)

Locatelli—*Sonata in G Major no. 4* (9:23)

Antonio Vivaldi (1678–1741), Jean-Pierre Rampal, flute—Four concerti for flute and orchestra, op. 10, no. 1 in F-Major (7:07); no. 2 in G-Minor (9:08); no. 4 in G-Major (6:56); no. 5 in F-Major (8:17)[25]

The use of music does not stand alone. The use of music is planned to work synergistically with many other elements—story telling, interaction games, [lectures and guided visualizations.]* (see Figure 8.9). Renata M. Nummela and Tennes M. Rosengren describe Barzakov's Optimalearning as a kind of symphonic expansion, a layering of experiences that continues to build beyond limit:

> The teacher begins with what Barzakov calls "pre-exposure" to the subject. The Optimalearning pre-exposure acts as introduction and primary motivator. . . . The pre-exposure could be a story, an experience, a guided imagery or Reading w/Music™ (a practiced reading to baroque or other classical music). Using careful transitions, the teacher then moves on to the "exposure." The exposure introduces the subject more clearly, usually through a multidimensional experience, which is then further developed in the third phase, the "expansion." The final "re-creation" creates experiences that allow students to express and use what they have learned, and subtly introduces the next lesson. Teaching moves like a symphony, with its major theme repeated numerous times, always in a slightly different context. Material is repeated in a variety of ways, leading to long-term storage and bypassing rote memorization or "forced" instruction. Additionally, the teacher uses all methods that aid in the experiential acquisition of material, including a broad incorporation of the arts.
>
> [The Optimalearning] teaching model calls for the teacher to orchestrate complex, "real-world" teaching environments. What may appear to be a spontaneous learning environment is, in fact, the result of precise planning. Such planning focuses almost entirely on how the classroom can create "here and now" experiences for the student, rather than on expected outcomes. The expected outcomes are goals that guide the lesson from pre-exposure to re-creation, but they are not the focus of planning. This is important because it virtually eliminates the threat

---

*Optimalearning instructors and trainers also use guided visualization with both instructional and self-instructional technology. There is, however, one essential conceptual difference. While suggesting visualization of a "favorite place in nature," Barzakov is *not* recommending delivery of new information *during* the guided visualization, but rather *immediately following it,* in the so-called "intermediate state." "This way," says Barzakov, "a possible strain in the brain processes is avoided. Also avoided is a possible arousal of 'blocks' as a result of previous negative learning experiences."

Figure 8.9 Suggestopedia uses music synergistically with other elements—story telling, visual imagery, instructive games, and lectures.

of meeting specified outcomes, and it allows what Barzakov calls "educative feedback to guide learning." Both student and teacher look upon learning as an expansion of knowledge . . . and not as the accomplishment of goals to be evaluated and rewarded.[26]

Specialized Format for Language Teaching. If a foreign language is being taught, then a second reading is used, a reading in which the meaning of whatever is read determines the way it is read. Students do not take notes or follow the reading with their texts. Instead, they "close their eyes and experience the easy flow of words and music."[27]

In the teaching of all other subjects, only the first reading (reading guided by the music) is used. Only in the teaching of a foreign language are two specialized readings used. (See Appendix A for a more comprehensive presentation of whole-brain learning and Appendix B for further ideas on using music as a method of teaching.)

■ *Love as Integration of Learning*

Barzakov speaks of the ultimate purpose of Optimalearning, "to guide, to direct, to empower individuals to achieve optimal freedom." He speaks of the gifts of love and freedom. Ocie Woodyear, a foreign language teacher at Lozanov Learning Institute, Silver Spring, Maryland, describes relationships between authority, love, and learning in a suggestopedic classroom:

The person in a suggestopedic classroom is treated with love, and this is the feeling which the students have for the teacher. On beginning a language class the teacher enters after the students are already seated in the classroom. She goes around the class shaking each person's hand and saying hello. Continually throughout the class the student knows by the teacher's manner and facial expressions that he is loved. The student feels very secure in the classroom, because the teacher acts as the authority, letting the student know by this that he will be

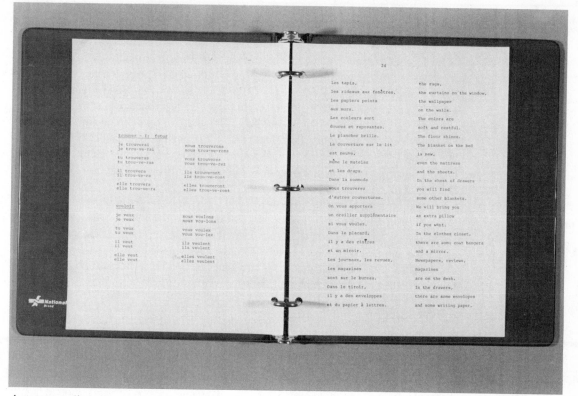

A suggestopedic language text.

able to learn, because he is in the hands of an expert who loves him. Didactically each unit of work is very large. This suggests to the student that he can learn great amounts of material. Both the global and the particular are taught at the same time.[28]

What, then, are the results of this kind of teaching? Does it really make a difference in learning capacity? Let's consider some research.

In 1984 Dhority compared the language acquisition rates of a regular German class taught by the audio-lingual drill approach and a pilot group taught by accelerative learning methods. The regular German class received 360 hours of instruction versus 108 hours of instruction for the pilot group. "Of regular program students, only 26% achieved the first level one in mastery in reading. In contrast 73% of the pilot program students taught experimentally, achieved a 1 or better on the listening test and 64% a 1 or better in reading."[29]

Ramirez (1982) in a controlled classroom study, taught English vocabulary to Spanish-dominant Chicano third-grade children. "Children taught vocabulary with Suggestopedia learned significantly more words (19.78) than did the children taught conventionally in the control group (12.79)."[30]

Vannan (1981) compared experimental and control groups of university students in a science course. "The control group was comprised of teachers and their scores in all sessions in 1975 and the experimental group was teachers in 1976 taking the same course for the whole year."[31] Students taught suggestopedically "received 78% A grades vs. 11% A grades for those taught traditionally. The high achievement trend has continued through 1980 with a 76% A grade for the experimental years of 1976–80 inclusively."[32] In general, studies show suggestopedia to increase learning at a faster rate than conventional methods. The method tends to decline in effectiveness, however, when some of its elements are not used (e.g., imagery or relaxation).

At the 1987 SALT (Society for Accelerative Learning and Teaching) conference in Ames, Iowa, the focus of research shifted by declaration toward how well learning is integrated rather than how much one learns.

It will be interesting to note in the coming years the kinds of research studies that will be conducted on whole-brain methods. Research that focuses on qualitative features such as integration will probably differ markedly from traditional quantitative studies. We are in a cumulative movement toward what Aldous Huxley called "integrate education," an education that stresses discovering relationships between all things in one's experience and all things in one's world.[33]

■ SUMMARY

A method is a way of sensing thinking, acting, feeling, and being. If the method works, it will create access for students to think, to feel, to sense, to act, and to be in ways that formerly appeared closed to them.

In this chapter, traditional methods—the lecture and recitation, for example—are expanded to include whole-brain processes. Using variations of expression in speaking, intentional but natural movements, and verbal imagery can transform a lecture that focuses on information alone. An overhead projector adds yet another dimension to the lecture, the voice being supported by visual images of graphs, flowcharts, drawings, and so forth.

Recitation is a useful method when it includes a range of cognitive levels and the student is encouraged to interpret the content.

Groups of four to six students work best. Groups should be designed to give each person in the group an opportunity to assume different roles. Role playing and dramatization can expand self-concept and the performance levels of the student. Whole-brain techniques such as the mandala, other-hand writing, transitional objects, dreams, mind maps, and visualization activate the left and right hemispheres and the limbic system, increasing both motivation and long-term memory. (See Appendix A for more detailed explanations of whole-brain learning.)

Questioning techniques are used to explore various cognitive levels, increase the rigor of student response, provide alternate world views, focus a predetermined answer, or expand associations. Games and puzzles can be used convergently to increase informational skills in certain areas, and also to open students to new possibilities of thinking and experiencing.

Integrative approaches to teaching promote exploratory relationships between the verbal and the nonverbal, between various disciplines, and between knowledge and the nature of reality. Music can be used in a variety of ways to promote the joy of learning, as an anchor, as a mood set, as a relaxing agent, as a stimulus to long-term memory.

Research in comparing suggestopedia with conventional teaching has shown superior results using quantitative measurements of learning rates. The effectiveness of whole-brain techniques drops off proportionately when key elements are dropped out—visualization, relaxation, use of music, and so forth. By declaration, future research in whole-brain learning will focus on the integrative effectiveness of the method rather than the amount learned or rapidity of learning. What these studies will show remains to be seen.

■ *NOTES*

1. Anthony Robbins, *Skills of Power Seminar,* Robbins Research Institute, Inc., Detroit, May 1987. This seminar explores NLP strategies, particularly in respect to business and education.
2. Werner Erhard and Associates, *The Communication Course,* Detroit, August 1987. This course explores communication as a function of effective project planning.
3. Aldous Huxley, "Knowledge and Understanding," in *Adonis and the Alphabet* (London: Chatto & Windus, 1956), 39.
4. Marilee Zdenek, *The Right Brain Experience* (New York: McGraw-Hill, 1983), 130, 155, 170, 190, 209, 224.
5. Ibid., 34–35, 160–161, 179–180, 196–199, 213–214, 230–231.
6. Ibid., 45, 66–67, 75, 82, 105.
7. Lewis Thomas, *The Medusa and the Snail: More Notes of a Biology Watcher* (New York: Bantam Books, 1979), 103–104.
8. Tony Buzan, *Use Both Sides of Your Brain* (New York: Dutton, 1974). Techniques for studying, reading, and remembering, including the use of mind maps.
9. Evelyn Wood Reading Dynamics, © 1969 by Diversified Education and Publishing Corporation, pp. 44–58. There are Evelyn Wood institutes in principal cities throughout the world.
10. Gabrielle L. Rico, *Writing the Natural Way: Using Right-Brain Techniques to Release Your Experience Powers* (Los Angeles: J. P. Tarcher, 1983).
11. Anthony Robbins, *Unlimited Power: The New Science of Personal Achievement* (New York: Simon & Schuster, 1986). See chapter 12, "The Power of Precision," 196–206.
12. Ibid., 201.
13. The Education Network, *Leadership for Education: The Future by Design,* a seminar presented by Werner Erhard, Chicago, Ill, October 18, 1987.
14. Ibid.
15. Peter Kline, "Transformation, Analogies, and the Deep Structure of Learning," presented at the Super Accelerated Learning Workshop, Wayne State University, Detroit, October 1987.

16. Ibid.

17. Ibid.

18. Lynn Dhority, *Acquisition Through Creative Teaching: The Artful Use of Suggestion in Foreign Language Instruction* (Sharon, MA: Center for Continuing Development, 1984), 10–2, 10–3.

19. Carl Sagan, *Broca's Brain: Reflections on the Romance of Science* (New York: Random House, 1978), 141.

20. Ibid.

21. James Quina and M. Jean Greenlaw, "Science Fiction as a Mode of Interdisciplinary Education," *Journal of Reading,* Nov. 1975, 105–111.

22. Lynn Dhority, *Acquisition Through Creative Teaching,* 6–11.

23. Ivan Barzakov, Instructional Card: Specialized Optimalearning Baroque Cassettes Music, Barzak Educational Institute, Inc., San Rafael, CA, 1987.

24. Ivan Barzakov, "The Singing School: Means of Suggestion in Suggestology and in Optimalearning," *Journal of the Society for Accelerative Learning and Teaching* 7(2): 181–182 (1982).

25. Ivan Barzakov, Instructional Card.

26. Renate M. Nummela and Tennes M. Rosengren, "What's Happening in Students' Brains May Redefine Teaching," *Educational Leadership,* May 1986, 51–52.

27. Lynn Dhority, *Acquisition Through Creative Teaching,* 9–5.

28. Ocie Posener Woodyear, "Suggestopedy," *The Journal of the Mexican Association of Teachers of English to Speakers of Other Languages,* 6(1): 24 (1982).

29. D. H. Schuster and C. E. Gritton, *Suggestive Accelerative Learning Techniques* (New York: Gordon and Breach Science Publishers, 1986), 43.

30. Ibid., 40.

31. Ibid., 53.

32. Ibid., 53–54.

33. Aldous Huxley, "Integrate Education," in *The Human Situation: Lectures at Santa Barbara* (New York: Harper & Row, 1977).

The Teacher and Technology

JOHN W. CHILDS

Every teacher is responsible for mastering those technology skills that will allow effective professional performance.

The potential of technology is to free teachers from the rigidity of the syllabus and tap the imaginations of both teacher and student to an extent that has never been possible before. Today, teachers and school librarians can capture instructional materials—films, videocassettes, computer programs—and fit them appropriately into the curriculum. Such programs can help students study on their own.

In the long run, electronic teachers may provide exchanges of information, ideas, and experiences more effectively (certainly differently) than the traditional classroom or the teacher. The promise of the new technologies is to enrich the study of literature, science, mathematics, and the arts through words, pictures, and auditory messages. To achieve this goal, technology must be linked to school objectives.

—Ernest Boyer

This chapter should help you become more familiar with the following:

1. The history of instructional technology
2. The current use of instructional technology in the school
3. Ideas about the future application of instructional technology

While the chapter's main sections are arranged in the author's preferred order, you may want to read the chapter sections in a different order. Each section was written with the intent that it could stand by itself.

■ *Author's Perspective*

The author sees instructional technology as a process involving the teacher, the student, the school environment, communications media, and specific products of technology such as the microcomputer. The critical characteristic of technology in the school is the use to which it is applied. Two instructional technology products—direct face-to-face instruction and the printed text—can be the most sophisticated technologies known to the teaching profession. At times they are misapplied. At times they are applied appropriately. The reader should examine all instructional technology products critically, keeping in mind the *application,* the *student,* and particularly the desired *learning outcome.* The author's views regarding the appropriate application of instructional technology to schooling are embedded in the ideas expressed throughout the chapter. You should consider the positions expressed in the context in which they appear. Think about suggested applications in the context to which you, the reader, will need to make application.

■ *The Anticipated Readers' Perspective*

The author has anticipated that the reader will be a preservice teacher in training. You may be reading this chapter as an assignment, or you may have arrived at this chapter through your own search for information on technology and the school. In writing this chapter, the author has assumed that you have some general knowledge of technology in school settings. Your knowledge may have been obtained by experience (as a student) and/or by specific instruction. The chapter does not provide detailed descriptions of particular instructional technologies, nor does it provide comprehensive reviews of current practices. It is assumed that you will search for added depth where you have the most urgent need. The references and the probe questions may help you in your search.

■ *Organization*

This chapter is organized into several main sections with appropriate headings. Any main heading may be read as an independent component. The content of these sections is complete to the level of specificity intended for the beginning investigation of the main idea and point of view.

■ *Chapter Outcomes*

The field of instructional technology has long stressed the importance of precisely stated outcome objectives as a part of effective instructional material. Therefore, upon completion of study of this chapter the user will:

1. State the two critical issues facing schools and teachers in the application of instructional technology.
2. Name three applied examples of instructional technology.
3. Identify six items of hardware used as a part of the application of instructional technology in schools.

> *Instructional Technology Application: In a Place Called School*

The focus of this section is the school and what teachers and students do in the school setting. Schools are special places in our society. Your reading of this text should indicate to you the unique characteristics of schools, the different views people have of what schooling is about, and some of the alternate, conflicting points of view about schools.

The discussion of instructional technology needs to be guided by your knowledge of at least three different ways in which the term *technology* is used in this chapter: as process, as product, and as object.

1. *Technology as Process*

   The opening quotation for this chapter asserts a technical definition of instructional technology as the process by which one prepares and delivers instructional acts. This definition is preferred by those who design instruction using a systematic instructional design, development, and implementation model. Using this definition, the book as an instructional component is perhaps today the most highly developed technology available to teachers. The process of designing, developing, and implementing instruction with a book is widely known, frequently used, and generally thought to be quite efficient and effective. In counterpoint, the instructional interactive videodisc is seen as the current best example of a high-technology system for the design, development, and implementation of instruction.

2. *Technology as Product*

The definition of technology as product comes from identifying the use of complex electronic tools to create an instructional delivery system to achieve a particular instructional outcome. An example, in conventional terms, would be the use of a televised teacher to reach a mass audience. An alternate example would be the selection of existing textbooks to meet the instructional outcomes judged to be appropriate to the course or subject area. Here the book is the product of the printing technology.

3. *Technology as Object*

The definition of technology as an object comes from our everyday experience perception of technology. We look at a videotape recorder, a digital watch, or a programmable coffee maker as technology. This is the common definition. It is useful shorthand in conversation. However, within the discussion of instructional technology this usage can be misleading. The author prefers to use the expression "technological device" in reference to the object. In schools, an interchangeable term for this definition may be "media." You will also see the expression "media and technology" used on occasion in reference to instructional activities in the school. Here, two objects are being referenced: the device being used and the software (print, film, tape, computer program, etc.) being used with the device. Remember that in these uses of technology, the objects themselves are the products of the application of technological processes.

■ *Audiovisual History*

The introduction of the concept of instructional technology cannot be satisfactorily completed without a small historical account. Most of what is now considered instructional technology had its origin under the name of audiovisual education. The movement to use more than the teacher, chalkboard, and text in the school arose early in the twentieth century. The discovery of still photography, motion pictures, sound recording, and radio broadcasting stimulated some people, usually nonteachers, to urge an educational application.

From 1900 to 1930 little substantive application occurred in the typical school classroom. Technology in the classroom primarily involved the use of products, such as the lantern slide, the phonograph recording, and the motion picture, which were distributed from central sources in large school districts. Maps, globes, books, and the chalkboard were the dominant products seen in the typical school classroom.

During World War II the motion picture film, the viewgraph (overhead projector), and the self-instructional booklet became highly developed for rapid training purposes. At the close of the 1940s many individuals who had experience in wartime training techniques returned to the schools and universities. They brought the notion of applying systematically developed instructional materials in the school environment.

Producers of film and slide materials sought to market their production capacity and products to schools. Many teachers and administrators, seeking methods to enhance the instruction of increasing numbers of students, jumped on the bandwagon of audiovisual instruction. The net result was the development of substantial applications of the motion picture film. Large research efforts were conducted to study the effect of the motion picture film on students in classroom instruction. The basic rules for effective application of technology products emerged from classroom experience and research results. They could be summarized as follows:

1. Select appropriate materials for the student, the subject, the desired instructional outcomes, and the school environment.
2. Prepare the student group for the use of the material.
3. Use equipment and a facility that work and are suitable for the students.
4. Follow up the usage with direct instruction that is related to the desired instructional outcomes, . . . e.g., review.
5. Re-use the instructional material for reinforcement, discussion, review.
6. Test for achievement of the desired instructional outcomes.

Similarities to the 1950s through 1970s. Technology use in today's school is very similar to that of 10, 20, or 30 years ago. Some devices are new. The teacher-use patterns are alike. The challenge to you, the reader, is to become a skilled user of technology as process, product, and object.

Impact of Microcomputing Capacity on School Practice. The microcomputer has the greatest impact of any current technology. Its impact on teachers and schools has been significantly different from that of other technologies introduced in the last three decades. Teachers have accepted the microcomputer and microcomputing at a faster rate and in larger numbers. Teachers believe that computing offers more diverse opportunities for application to schooling than prior technologies. You will need to develop computing skills as they relate to applications that you can use to enhance your instructional actions. You will need computing as a personal tool, as an instructional delivery system, and as an object of instruction.

■ *Teacher and Technology*

The teacher's role with regard to technology is an instructional role. The teacher must serve as a role model in the use of technology under all three definitions. You will find yourself teaching within the content areas using technology as product, applying technology as process to solve substantive problems, and using technology as object of instruction. Throughout your teaching career an increasing percentage of your instructional activity will be assisted by computing technology. From lesson design, content selection, information access, and communications to lesson delivery, student learning management, and student assignment guidance, computing will be a major aspect of your teaching activity.

■ *Student and Technology*

Students' use and application of technology to their learning experiences is broad based. It will become even more pervasive during the next decade. Students will study technology as an object, create and use technological processes, and acquire and use technology products as objects. Video communication, computing, and the use of information utilities at school and in the home will be common. Students will expect the teacher to be technologically literate, to be good at applying technology to instruction, and to understand how to assist students in the use of technology.

■ *Current Schooling Challenges*

Educators have been challenged by many different issues in the 1980s. The nature of schooling has been questioned, the need for specific subject matter requirements has been asserted, and the demand for quality instruction has been made by spokespersons for many groups. The profession has responded with study groups—national, state, and local. Many curricular modifications have been implemented, asserting that the modification would effect change in one or more of the above areas. The real challenge to teachers in schools is to educate all students. The use of technology (all definitions) may provide part of the means to meet this challenge. There is adequate research to support differences among learners in learning rate, style, and subject matter. Technology provides the teacher with opportunities to adjust instruction to these learner differences.

■ *Current Teacher Practices*

Teachers use technology differently. Different applications provide variety within the school for the diverse student population. Teaching with technology is often a matter of the individual teacher's experience and interest. Each teacher must identify that technology which they can manage effectively. Current practice tends to focus application on the individual teacher. Increasingly, teachers are working together to design, develop, and implement instruction using technology.

Current Teaching Problems.   Teaching with technology is a logistical problem for teachers in most schools today. Materials must be ordered from several days to weeks in advance; projectors, monitors, VCRs, computers must be scheduled. When it is time to use a technological delivery system, the hardware and software must be moved by the teacher and/or students to the classroom and set up for use. The ideal applications setting would place the necessary equipment and materials in the teaching environment on a more permanent basis. The school media center often serves as the focus of technology use in the school. If the school has a full-time media professional, then teachers may find the time and energy required to use technology effectively at their own teaching station.

Apart from the physical problems of technology use, the teacher must plan effectively for the integration of media in the flow of instruction. This must necessarily involve selection of materials, development of student activities, pre- and post-use assessment, and follow-up instruction. Use of technology-based instruction may require consultation with other teachers, the principal, and, at times, parents. As computing and communications technology provide access between home and school to information, exercises, drills, homework helps, and other functions, the teacher will need to be prepared to work with parents.

■ *Expectations for Tomorrow's Technology*

Parents, administrators, teachers, and students all have considerable expectations of future technology in the school environment. The public particularly expects computing to resolve many long-standing issues. The promise of computing and communications technology is perceived as substantive and certain to improve teaching and learning. If these expectations are to be fulfilled, we will need to change the way schools, teachers, administrators and students put technology to use. First, we will need to carefully analyze which functions technology can perform effectively, and second, we will need to plan and implement the uses in the context of the school structure—including economic reality. You as an individual teacher will need to know how to use a broad range of devices: video, computing, computing graphics, telecommunications, interactive videodisc, data-retrieval systems, and others. Later in this chapter several technological delivery systems will be described. An individual teacher will find several ideas for application in any given subject area.

Preservice Future Teachers. If you are in the process of preparing to teach, your interest in this chapter must focus on the existing and future technology of teaching. Your knowledge base should be formed by the use of communications media to deliver instructional messages to groups of students at one site, a group with its members located at different sites, and to individual learners. You need to develop implementation skills in order to use technology to perform your instructional role effectively.

Specifically, the preservice teacher must have knowledge and skill in the following areas:

1. Using technological processes to create instruction (technology as process)
2. Selecting media to communicate instructional messages (technology as product)
3. Selecting instructional delivery systems (technology as product)
4. Creating instruction about technology (technology as object)
5. Evaluating the results of technology based instructional delivery (technology as process)

The preservice teacher and the in-service teacher can increase their own skills in applying technology to instruction. Formal classes, individual study, and actual trial experiences offer opportunities to increase your skills. Actual experience may contribute the maximum immediate and longest-lasting growth.

The Future Student.   Persons now entering the K–12 schools will be graduating in the twenty-first century. Basic skills, reading, writing, speaking, listening, and computing will continue to be the essential underlying elements of schooling. Changes will occur in the environment for using reading, writing, speaking, listening, and computing. These students will come to the school with thousands of hours of experience in electronically assisted communications. These students will begin their adult lives in a local, national, and world environment that has extended electronic computing systems into every dimension of living. The work environment will be a highly complex electronic communications environment. The knowledge to use technology processes and products effectively will have become a new critical basic skill. The student will be writing, reading, listening, speaking, and computing with tools and techniques unknown to teachers during their initial training. Your teaching will need to use the maximum application of technology in all three definitions to achieve command of the basic skills by *all* students. Use of technology by an economic, social, or other "elite" group of students will be unsatisfactory.

The teacher in the school in 2001 will find students more aware of technology and its positive and negative benefits. Students will often be—in fact, are today— skilled in the use of technology. Nearly all students in 2001 will have mastered the

In the future, students will be writing, reading, listening, speaking, and computing with tools and techniques unknown to teachers during their initial training.

application of electronic computing to reading, writing, listening, speaking, and computing. The absence of these skills from the school, from the teacher's methods, will inhibit effective instruction.

Current and Future Teaching Technology

The electronic communications revolution has expanded the variety and extent of basic teaching devices. Historically, the principal tools were the blackboard, the display, the book, and perhaps the worksheet. Today the list of potential teaching devices is expanded by mechanical and electronic devices—television, film projector, computer, transparency projector, and so forth. In this section you will find discussion of some of the technology products that teachers and students may use to achieve instructional objectives.

■ *Communications Hardware*

Each of the devices and associated media discussed here may be used to capture the message of either the teacher or the student. Each is usually used by a teacher to meet specific student needs. The most important consideration is the careful planning of the teacher's intended use. If messages embodied within the media and transmitted through the use of communications hardware are simply displayed to students, no known objective is achieved. The maker of a mediated message may have a specific objective for students, but the using teacher may not accept or recognize the objective. The uncritical selection and display of communications media is the most frequent misuse of technology in the school. Such uses waste valuable learning time. The teacher should consider carefully the value (objective) of a given presentation. Those that do not advance the learner toward defined objectives should be omitted from the instructional plan. There is no place for "time fillers" in the curriculum today or tomorrow.

■ *Current School Communication Media*

The following discussion considers the display device along with the medium used to create and effect the display of images and audio information.

Projected Media. The uses of motion pictures or videotapes, projection or monitor, slides, or computer generated images with groups of students require appropriate preparations. The general guidelines for the use of projected images and sound with groups are:

1. Select only objective related material.
2. Preview and prepare your presentation strategy.
3. Prepare the presentation environment:
   a. control room lighting
   b. assure working projection/display devices
   c. arrange good viewing of the projection surface

4. Prepare students for the presentation:
   a. state the objective
   b. provide context
   c. give instructional directions
5. Control the presentation.
6. Follow up the presentation:
   a. student activities
   b. inclusion in ongoing work
   c. if appropriate, review repeat presentation
   d. prepare students to move to new instruction

While these guidelines are relevant to the use of these media with individual learners, some modifications by the teacher are necessary. First, the projection environment is likely to be a small-screen environment, a video monitor, a rear projection screen, or a small computer monitor. Such a viewing situation changes the message particularly in the affective dimension. The impact of the instruction may be shifted. Detail may be either enhanced or lost, dependent upon the structure and/or format of the message. The attention of the learner may be increased or decreased. The mastery of the objectives may be increased or decreased. Second, the teacher, in using the technology of individualized instruction, must recognize the essential communication elements in the media chosen. The image and/or audio presentation must be adapted to individual use. Third, the guidance in interpreting the message, which might be supplied directly by the teacher in group instruction, must now be contained in the presentation. Many materials claiming multisituation use fail in the individualized environment for lack of carefully constructed instructional directions.

Nonprojected Media.   The use of other delivery devices such as the on-demand audiotape, the display, the exhibit, the bulletin board, and the still picture require modified planning procedures. These image and audio devices tend to be used over longer display times. Their complexity demands that learners have several opportunities to acquire the message being presented. Typically, students make a number of alternative interpretations of the message. Teacher guidance through the use of directions, discussion, and direct presentation is needed to obtain an instructional effect. The message transmission alone will not generate an instructional outcome. The teacher needs to assure adequate display time, good directions for study, probe or guide questioning, synthesis of the learner observations, and timely removal or replacement of the display items. Materials that are simply interesting or attractive certainly may be used within the classroom. However, space and learner time should be more effectively used by selecting material to meet known instructional objectives.

In today's world we often believe that instructional messages must be either audio and visual or print. Many excellent uses are evident in classrooms for audio alone. The audiotape, the radio or satellite broadcast, or the prearranged telephone conference call can be used to bring instructional content to the classroom or individual learner. The guidelines for the use of projected media can be adapted here to provide guidance for effective use. In addition, the preparation should include the selection of excellent sound reproduction devices. The inexpensive audiotape recorder/player is useful for one-on-one recording and playback. It is unsuitable for group use. Good-quality industrial and educational audiotape recorder/players are needed for the classroom. When telephone communications are to be presented to groups, special-purpose amplification is necessary to maximize intelligibility of the message.

■ *Media as Object of Instruction*

We have been examining the use of media as a tool for the teacher to deliver instruction or as a tool for the student to obtain an instructional message. Technology as an object of instruction may be an essential area of outcome objectives. Skill with the pencil and pen was a critical element of basic skills a half century ago. Then along came the typewriter, and typing gradually become a basic skill. Today, using a word processor in a general computing environment is becoming an essential skill. Other media use and knowledge skills are emerging from the increased use of computing. Computer-based drawing, painting, data retrieval, and information analysis appear to be fundamental future skills. Communicating through video- and audiotape, telephone networks, and computer systems is already very common. Effective use of these tools will require the school to teach specific skills. As we examine the means we use to transact social and business communication, we focus on technology as object.

■ *Computing Technology*

Throughout the short history of using computing in instruction, there is a duality of focus and direction. Teachers have focused on computing itself, and on the application of computing to the act of individual instruction. Some educators have been interested in the role of digital computing since its invention. Early efforts to apply technology to teaching focused on textlike presentation. Initially, computing was applied to data-processing functions such as payroll, attendance and other records, and limited drill activities. As interactive computing became possible, greater efforts were made to use the "logic" of computing to guide individual learning sequences. These applications were termed computer-assisted instruction (CAI). Among the earliest and still continuing applications of computing to direct instruction is the PLATO effort at the University of Illinois. PLATO stands for Programmed Logic for Automated Teaching Operations.

Several perspectives are available today on the use of computing technology in schools. Certainly, teachers and other school personnel will use computers to process data, keep and retrieve records, contact information utilities (libraries, information data bases, etc.) and perform computational tasks. Increasingly, teachers are using the computer to provide direct delivery of instruction. This development is a result of the creation of small personal computers with a large computing capacity.

Direct Instruction Using Computing. Today, over 400 different instructional authoring systems are marketed to allow instructors to design and present instructional interactions to individual computer users. The programs produced usually can be described as fitting one of the following categories:

1. Drill/practice
2. Tutorial
3. Game/simulation
4. Tutored problem solving
5. Combination

Research on the use of computer-based instruction has provided mixed results. This author views the results as positive. Educational outcomes can be achieved, but teachers need to learn a great deal about the creation of effective lessons. When selecting existing marketed lessons, you must be extremely cautious. The availability of quality lessons is limited in many areas of instruction. The commercial lesson may or may not operate on your computing hardware, may or may not help learners achieve specific learning outcomes, and may or may not be cost effective.

The use of your time to create your own computer-based lessons for a single class is very inefficient. The average high-quality, effective lesson of about one-hour duration requires 100 to 200 hours of development time. Few teachers can afford this investment of time for the benefit of a single group of students. In the future, most useful computer-based lessons will be prepared commercially or by a teacher team carrying out the design, development, and production as a special assignment.

■ Computing Hardware

The advent of computing for educational purposes in the 1960s exposed the educator to an exciting new technology. At its inception, school computing required a physically large electronic machine. Its operating environment required air-conditioning and a large supply of electric power. Most early educational computing was done in collaboration with a university computing service through time-shared access. The most common device for connection to the central computer was a teletype machine.

Today, computing hardware is compact, either desktop or portable; it requires very little electric power (no more than a 150-watt light bulb) and only ordinary home or office heating and cooling. The personal computer based on a microchip has reduced the price of a computer unit a thousandfold, from $1 million in the 1950s to $1000 in the 1980s.

This change has increased the area of educational applications immensely. We can now consider every teaching station and every learner station as a potential site to be served by computing in the 1990s. The issue now becomes a teaching issue rather than a computing hardware issue. What will teachers and students do with computing hardware? Certainly, most teachers and students will use computing to perform preprogrammed tasks. In addition, students will have some instruction delivered by computing hardware. Students and teachers will continue to study computing hardware. The primary concern of the teacher will be the effective use of the computing hardware to achieve planned educational outcomes. To achieve this, appropriate computing software will need to be invented for and by teachers.

■ *Computing Software*

Computing software for instruction falls into three logical groupings—direct instructional delivery, indirect instructional support, and computing tools. Students and teachers now use all three classes of instructional computing software. A short discussion of each class will help the reader conceptualize the variety of computing software being applied to schooling.

Direct Instructional Delivery.　Earlier in this chapter we presented the option of using computing to deliver instruction directly to the student. Software commercially produced or generated by the teacher for direct instruction of the student may be categorized as listed on page 184. Each of these types of direct instruction typically is intended to serve one student at one work station. This type of instruction requires flexibility. Each student will spend a different amount of time on each lesson presented. Teacher management of this kind of delivery system appears to be most satisfactory if the instructional setting is arranged as a learning station environment.

The various types of direct instructional software occur in all subject areas—math, social science, language arts, and so forth. The bulk of existing commercial lessons are variations on the drill and practice or tutorial types. These types are useful in augmenting regular classroom instruction and may be used to replace classroom instruction in special cases. Students needing a slower or faster pace than that of the entire class may benefit from tutorial lessons. Students needing additional practice benefit most from the drill and practice type. No direct instruction software should be purchased without carefully considering its relationship to the curriculum and its effectiveness in achieving particular objectives. The prescription of a particular lesson for a given student should be carefully matched to the student's immediate needs.

Indirect Instructional Support.　The operation of the total instructional environment can be enhanced through the use of computing software. The teacher can use appropriate instructional software that is commercially available to facilitate the following functions:

1. Student records
   a. Testing and grading
   b. Objectives achieved/not achieved
   c. Instructional materials used
   d. Current/future assignment
   e. Past performance using given materials
2. Instructional plans (daily, weekly, semester)
3. Student/parent reporting

4. Instructional materials development
   a. Text (word processor)
   b. Graphics (worksheet, transparency)
   c. Direct instructional lesson (authoring)
5. Administrative tasks (principal, committees)

This list is only a brief example of the types of things teachers are accomplishing through increasing use of computing. The future will present new opportunities to use computing for group presentation, accessing remote information, teleconferencing, and exploring new learning methods by the application of artificial intelligence.

Computing Tools.   Teachers will individually make use of a variety of general-purpose computing tools ranging from computer languages to special-purpose instructional design and development support work stations. Recent developments in computing make it possible for individual teachers to have a special-purpose computing environment tailored to the creation and production of their own instructional materials. Such a system provides for conception and development of instructional content, organization of an instructional program, development of instructional materials, and the production of print materials used by both the instructor and student. In addition, masters for visuals and computer-based instruction can be generated.

During the late 1980s and early 1990s, teachers will increasingly find themselves using computing tools for routine tasks. Initially, most teachers will use word processing. As computer-based presentation systems become generally available, most teachers will make use of information presentations generated and controlled by computing software.

■ *Computing Instruction*

Throughout the prior discussion, computing has been examined from the perspective of teacher or student use to accomplish instructional purposes in a specific subject-matter area, such as English. Computing has become an area of specific instruction throughout the K–12 curriculum. We now turn our attention to computing as a subject of instruction. Early efforts to bring computing instruction into the school curriculum have concentrated on either generalized computing literacy or on programming skill. Now most schools have moved beyond simple computing machinery identification skills and are concentrating their computing literacy efforts on the use of computing for particular applications—word processing, data base, and the like.

The Great Literacy Debate.   Teachers, administrators, and the public have been involved in a widespread effort to bring knowledge of computing to students during the 1980s. Many persons have felt that *computer literacy* means skill in programming a computer to perform a range of tasks. Others have considered computer literacy to mean knowledge and skill in using general-purpose computing software. This has led to instruction in using computing to accomplish particular tasks, such as solving a math equation, preparing an essay, or retrieving and interpreting social statistics such as the U.S. Census.

Formal teaching of computer science as a discipline is now well established in the high school. College entrance requirements increasingly anticipate that persons pursuing a career in creating, inventing, and constructing computing machines and software will have initial knowledge and skill upon admission. With the high school assuming the responsibility for initial knowledge in computer science, the balance of the K–12 program has the responsibility to ensure the acquisition of computing skills in all other subject areas. The use of computing with specific existing software can begin in the first years of schooling. Preschool children can, and do, apply computing to perform tasks at their level. Teachers must examine their own subject areas for opportunities to apply computing technology to the learning processes of the student.

All students should have access to, and ability to use, computing to advance their learning. In most cases this means they will need to know what programs are available and how to use them to meet instructional and learning needs. To accomplish this goal, the teachers must master the use of computing within their areas of instruction. If that area is creative writing, for example, the teacher must be familiar with the use of such tools as word-processing, spelling and grammar checking, and thesaurus software.

Computer Science.   The high school is basically responsible for the formal initial instruction in computer science. This instruction should begin where student knowledge and skill form the basis for beginning instruction. If we have implemented computer literacy throughout the curriculum, then the basic use of a computer will already be a part of student skills.

Formal computer science instruction will need to begin with analysis of computing equipment and software. Programming instruction needs to begin with known concepts and proceed to unknown concepts. Students can be taught sound programming ideas by examining well-written programs, testing them, learning what makes them function, learning to read source codes, and then moving on to simple program modifications.

Historically, programming instruction has begun with commands and syntax followed by logic and simple program construction. The author recommends quite the reverse. Begin with a working program. Run it. Analyze the program. Teach the reading of the program. Encourage simple alterations followed by more complex modifications. Only after students are completely capable of using and modifying existing programs should they be taught to create a program.

The development of high school computer science programs during the 1990s will follow a different trend from that of the 1980s. This will be caused by the widespread availability of computing outside the school. However, the school program itself will stimulate new development in high school computer science programs. Most of what is now contained in high school programs will need to be replaced by newer, more advanced work. Students will enter the high school program with sophisticated computing skills. The high school program will need to build on the skills acquired in grade school and outside the school program. The high school program of the 1990s will be driven by complex computing applications development tools rather than current programming languages. Students will reach beyond the computing equipment of their own school to use supercomputers located thousands of miles from their school. The National Science Foundation has announced the development of a worldwide network to make supercomputing available to qualified projects at any university and educational institution.

PROBE Why do teachers choose to use instructional technology? Is their choice—pro or con—rational? Research based? Can the learner (K–12 setting) with technology available be "taught" without any teacher intervention whatsoever? Can you be an effective teacher in the 1990s without applying computing technology? What applications of computing technology will improve learner performance in your subject-matter area? Can current applications of computing technology within the school program remain static? Who is responsible for the effective application of technology in schools?

■ SUMMARY

This chapter has attempted to share with the reader a few key concepts for teaching with technology. The available types of technology are constantly becoming more varied. The knowledge to use technology in all three definitions—as process, as product, and as object—is crucial to effective teaching and effective schools.

Every teacher is responsible for mastering those technology skills that will allow effective professional performance. Constant renewal and individual study will be necessary throughout your teaching career. Many current text resources exist to assist individual study. The use of information data-retrieval systems can help the individual teacher know what technology is developing and how to obtain application skills. University and school district in-service programs will help you adapt to changing technology.

The emerging dominate position of computing in our world requires all educators to master the application of computing technology. Effective schools demand the application of the best technology possible.

CHAPTER 10

Multicultural Education for an Urban Society

WRITTEN WITH RODOLFO MARTINEZ AND RICARDO MARIN IBAÑEZ

A View of Toledo, *by El Greco*

A democratic society requires that we work together to understand each other's worlds and develop a shared perspective that will enable us to learn from each other and govern ourselves while preserving a pluralistic reality.

—Bruce Joyce and Marsha Weil

Values and Education

Because we live in an age of skepticism and annihilation of values, it is necessary to define the role of values in the enterprise we call education. Each age imprints its own way of socializing the person into the fabric of the community. Each sector of society controlling the educational enterprise insists on mandating its own brand of objectives, ideals, and educational strategies. These different values enable us to characterize and typify each system and each institution according to those values it represents. The importance of this process is that the values learned are for the individual and for society; values are multiple and are imposed by the various sectors of society that control education.

Another concept closely linked to values in education is the role of *culture*. The educational system transmits the prevailing culture in the most effective and efficient manner, selecting those characteristics that have the most value according to the imposed dictates of the society. Thus, to educate is to culturally elevate the student and integrate him or her into society.

The Meaning of Culture

The term *culture* can be interpreted from several perspectives. When we speak of a cultured person, for example, we assume that the person is optimally educated. Likewise, when an individual's behavior is socially acceptable and urbane, the person is thought of as being cultured.

When using the term in this sense, it rests principally on the cognitive plane; that is, the cultured person possesses a vast amount of information, superior to the norm of the group. However, this "encyclopediaism" is not sufficient to label a person cultured. We are not referring to the accumulation of data. In fact, modern communications media such as radio, television, and newspapers transmit enormous quantities of information from the various cultural sectors, and not infrequently we encounter persons who are on familiar terms with public figures and even repeat the same varieties of information in their social communication. Yet we do not value these persons as cultured. We demand of them that they explain, cite, and understand profoundly the mosaic created by the flood of information that the media produces. We demand that the cultured person possess a precise, exact, and systematic comprehension of the world about him, and that he be capable of interpreting this information in the context of its origin. Thus, the richness and precision of concepts, theories, and laws, as well as the articulation and systematization of knowledge, and the capacity not only to receive, but also to pass judgment on the various elements

Photographs depicting alternative cultures are useful in the instructional process.

that make up culture—all require a conscious effort to search for truth. This makes up a cultured person, and the process by which this culture is acquired is clearly an educational process.

Culture has another objective: to preserve all of the products of humankind. What encompasses culture is intentionally created by the human being while searching for truth and the good life.

The origin of the term culture (from the Latin, *colera*) clearly suggests an intentional quest to satisfy a particular need. This is seen in the derivation of the term agriculture (the culture of the farm). While nature produced the elements necessary for cultivation, it was man who perfected and improved the growth of crops. Likewise, this can be seen in the development of art, sculpture, architecture, dance, and music, as well as mythology and religion. These were created early on as a response to the spiritual necessity of mankind.

■ *Lower and Higher Culture*

The distinction between *lower* and *higher* culture has its origin in the classical period. For the Greeks, *paideia* was the training of the ideal person, who was to be eloquent, learned, and ready to defend his ideas in the public forum. The ideal person was well versed in literature, philosophy, and the art of government. On the other hand, utilitarian work involving manual arts was considered improper for the free and cultured individual; it ranked below his station.

Higher culture was identified in certain periods of history as representing that of the dominant groups as well as the cultures of imperial colonizers.

Thus, the norms of behavior, symbols of the historical period, institutions, values, and preferences of each dominant group constituted its culture. This is true not only of the culture of the society at large, but also of marginal subgroups that function within the main framework of the national social structure.

Culture is made by humans. It is *subjective* when the individual acquires from it the knowledge and systematic theories, concepts, and laws that describe the social framework within which he or she exists. Culture is *objective* when it contains all of the acts, institutions, values, and the like that have been produced by present and past generations, each with the seal and stamp of approval by those who made or make up the society.

The Challenge of Unity Versus Cultural Pluralism

We are faced with a serious conflict that will be sharpened in the years to come. That is the risk and, at the same time, the hope that there will be a developing closeness between the cultures of the world, as well as an approximation of similar values, which may produce an impoverishing uniformity that will undoubtedly reduce the richness produced by cultural diversity. The risk of losing an individual identity has produced reactions against this trend. Movements to preserve the past and to go back to one's roots have surfaced, giving rise to the preservation of language, customs, folklore, and all of those elements that portray a culture. Humanity is faced with the pendular movement of unity to multiplicity, from a simplistic equality to a complex diversity. Today this tendency is more radical than ever before.

Globalization of Culture

The most relevant and visible tendency in the contemporary world is the *globalization* of all dimensions of culture. For example, the smallest military conflict has repercussions that transcend national boundaries. An economic crisis can affect all parts of the globe with the slightest ease. Political concepts are easily diffused throughout the world. The slogans of the "flower children" of the 1960s spread from San Francisco to Rome, Berlin, London, and Madrid.

Throughout the universe, for example, young people wear the same blue jeans and dance to the same rhythmic beat of rock music. The jet age has produced similar airplanes and transistor radios. The manuals for the teaching of English and mathematics or science go out beyond the East and West or North and South of the United States. The messages of computers or airlines are in English. And all news is instantly transmitted throughout the world by way of a well-established mass-media communications system.

Further evidence of this globalization is maintained by the United Nations Education, Scientific, and Cultural Organization (UNESCO), which similarly suggests that human endeavor in all areas of exchanges and relations demonstrates a growing interdependence among nations. The growth of agencies of cooperation among nations mandates that all problems of the world, no matter how small, require global problem-solving actions that will take into consideration the interests of the various nations, whether they are industrialized or underdeveloped.

It can be argued that the cause and effect of the rise of these international organizations is the globalization of culture. Born as the result of World War II, today the United Nations (UN) serves as the umbrella organization for many international agencies that claim the membership of nearly all of the nations of the world.

Significant acts and declarations of these international organizations have served to globalize culture: the Universal Declaration of Human Rights (UN, 1948); the Declaration of the Principles of International Cultural Cooperation (UNESCO, 1966); the proposals for a New World Economic Order (UN, 1974); and the Declaration for a New World Information Service (UNESCO, 1980).

From another perspective, we see the same move toward a globalization of culture. Every year more than 2 million scientists attend international conferences and symposiums. And thanks to international satellite communications, it is technically possible to instantaneously transmit from any corner of the world.

The globalization of culture has another consequence—that is, all humanity may move toward a uniformity of culture in which the differences and the richness of diversity may give way to a leveling of culture by a technological civilization. Today, radio emissions can be heard all over the world by way of shortwave radio, and the same movies and television series are shown in all countries.

In addition, more than 60 percent of scientific communication is in English, while more than two-thirds of all publications are published in only five languages: English, Russian, Spanish, German, and French.

This unifying tendency has dramatic consequences, the first of which is the equalizing of ideals and aspirations. For example, a television commercial, simultaneously vying for the attention of millions of children in order to sell a particular toy or of a multitude of homemakers in order to make the sales pitch, creates a trend toward uniformity of aspirations and values. This uniformity of ideals and aspirations is also demonstrated in areas other than economic. While this unifying trend may seem ideal, there are other consequences of the globalization of culture that affect the world adversely. The inequities that abound in the field of education, for example, suggest that educational attainment is not solely based on social and economic position, but that who gets educated depends on the sex of that person. Females are not afforded the educational opportunities worldwide that males have; nor do they expect to enjoy the benefits the educational system provides. Tinker and Bramsen (1975) maintain that cultural attitudes inhibit the female's participation in institutions of higher education and that those who do enter the university are confronted with a curriculum that is irrelevant to their needs in order to become a full contributing member of the society.[1]

A more effective approach would be to establish a teaching philosophy in those curricular areas that foster a feeling of self-respect and human dignity in all children so that they can direct their energies toward full participation in the educational system.

Multicultural Methods

Education is ultimately a highly personal learning activity. Methods that promote such learning must humanistically focus on the individual. Ideally, the learning should be balanced, self-sufficient, free, and responsible and, at the same time, should promote participation in a society and culture to which the student claims allegiance.

Learning can be systematic in its approach, working within available resources to accomplish established goals and objectives. Thus, educational activities can be programmed in the classroom so that the student will naturally interact with values and concepts representing cultural diversity.

Encounter Teaching

In *Joy: Expanding Human Awareness,* William Schutz maintains that there are four types of development necessary to realize one's full potential: bodily functioning, personal functioning, interpersonal development, and relating to one's social institutions and culture. Interpersonal development and relating to social institutions and culture can be taught through encounter methods, an interpersonal training based

Malaga's Seminar of the Concilar Diosisana overlooks the Mediterranean Sea.

on "openness and honesty, self-awareness, responsibility, awareness of the body, attention to feelings and an emphasis on the here-and-now." Encounter teaching is usually done in groups. Its aim is to "remove blocks to better functioning . . . to create conditions leading to more satisfying use of personal capacities."[2]

Inclusion, control, and affection are for Schutz the three basic needs of all relationships. Each person must come to terms with these basic needs. People without inclusion problems are comfortable whether alone or with others. People who have resolved control problems are comfortable giving and taking orders. And people who have resolved their need for affection believe that affection is based on relationship. Dislike is not a function of being unlovable. Healthy affection is characterized by being comfortable in both close and distant relationships. Healthy relationships, Schutz believes, can be taught through encounter strategies.[3] Let's examine some encounters to see how they operate. The following encounter provides a framework for exploring one's comfort zones in regard to physical proximity:

> All members of the group are asked to gather close together, either sitting on the floor (which is preferable) or sitting in chairs. Then they are asked to close their eyes and stretch out their hands, "feel their space"—all space in front of them, over their heads, behind their backs, below them—and then be aware of their contact with others as they overlap and begin to touch each other. This procedure is allowed to continue for about five minutes.
>
> Usually there are a variety of clear reactions. Some people prefer to stay in their own space and resent as an intrusion anyone coming into it. Others feel very chary about introducing themselves into another's space for fear that they are not wanted. Still others seek out people and enjoy the touch contact. Where one person is inviting, another may be forbidding and simply touch and run. Discussion following this activity is usually very valuable in opening up the whole area of feelings about aloneness and contact.[4]

According to Bruce Joyce and Marsha Weil, the encounter group is "really a social encounter that is all-dependent on the social climate generated—a willingness to explore oneself; a sense of responsibility in assisting others to explore themselves; an openness to interact over issues, however intimate they may turn out to be; a consideration of one's own need for growth and others' need for growth, and above all, a recognition of the shared need for people to work together to improve their possibilities as individuals and groups."[5]

As one begins to explore alternate cultures, the elements of relationships become more apparent. Consider the feelings of being included or excluded from a group. If you do not speak the language of a group or dress like them, you may feel varying degrees of exclusion, particularly if the group does not perceive you or give you reasonable attention. Consider the following scenario:

> "I want you to form a circle." Mr. Homulka's request is aimed at a group of six junior high school students standing in the middle of the classroom. The desks have been pushed aside to make an open space. The boys and girls join hands. "Now, Tommy and Marion, try to get inside the circle, and the rest of you try

to keep them out. You have to keep your hands joined, and the idea is for you to keep a chain strong enough that they can't get in."

Everyone looks a little puzzled.

"OK, now," he says to Tommy and Marion, "let's start."

Tommy and Marion begin tentatively. They get on opposite sides of the ring and begin to push at the other students. When the ring stays strong they begin to push more firmly. As they meet with resistance, they push even stronger, and they succeed in bending the chain back upon itself, but the students in the circle hold firm and crowd in toward one another so that there is actually no place on the inside. Tommy tries to duck under their arms, but there is no place to go in the crowd at the center. The struggle goes on for a couple of minutes. Then Mr. Homulka calls time.

Tommy and Marion have expressions of anger on their faces, and the other students look a little puzzled but very determined.

"Let's begin with some of the observers," Mr. Homulka suggests. "What did you see?"

"Well, of course, we saw them try to get in," volunteers one.

"It began gently at first, but they were all really pushing at the end."

"Toward the end everybody looked mad or at least determined."

"How did you feel?" asks one of the students in the circle.

"How did *you* feel, Jane?" Mr. Homulka directs this question at one of the girls in the circle.

"Well, at first I thought it was kind of silly, but then I began to push harder and I really didn't want them to get inside. I thought it was none of their business to get inside this group."

Marion agrees. "That's what I thought you felt. We've been friends all through school and I couldn't understand why you wanted to keep me out."

"Neither could I," Sally says, shaking her head. "It was kind of as we did this the feelings came along with it."

"That's what I felt," nods Tommy. "At first I thought it was just silly and then I couldn't understand why you wanted to keep me out. I still feel mad about that."[6]

This encounter could be expanded by showing films of persons traveling in foreign cultures, paying particular attention to the subtitles of inclusion and exclusion. The sensuously beautiful film, *A Passage to India,* is a case in point. At points in the film the British feel excluded; at other points the Indians feel excluded. The same is true of the film *Gandhi.* And in Ralph Ellison's novel *The Invisible Man* the feeling of exclusion becomes objectified: The protagonist, no longer attended to, becomes invisible. Documentaries of civil rights history will also expand the theme of inclusion/exclusion.

| *Fantasy and Cultural Exploration* | Films and encounter methods can be combined with fantasy episodes that provide rich experiences of alternate cultures. |

Films and encounter methods can be combined with fantasy episodes that provide rich experiences of alternate cultures.

The teacher can propose a scenario that includes scenery, dialogue, images of dress, architecture, customs, beliefs, and the language of an alternate culture. Consider the following fantasy journey designed to dramatize the story Maria Concepcion:

LESSON PLAN
A Fantasy of Culture
Based on Katherine Anne Porter's *Maria Concepcion*

I. Type of Lesson: Multicultural

II. Class Description: Eleventh-grade bilingual Hispanic students

III. Objectives: Students will develop knowledge and appreciation of the setting and cultural background of the characters in Katherine Anne Porter's short story, *Maria Concepcion.* Students will identify the indigenous, Spanish, and North American elements related in this story.

IV. Summary of Story: *Maria Concepcion* is the story of three Mexican Indians caught in a triangular relationship nursed by love, jealousy, and revenge. Maria Concepcion, the independent protagonist, who is married to Juan Villegas, is pregnant. She discovers that her husband is making love to Maria Rosa just before Juan and his mistress run off to war together. Maria Concepcion becomes stolid, refusing even to cry when her child is born and dies. When Juan and Maria Rosa return, Maria Rosa delivers a healthy child, but before the day is out, she has been fatally knifed by Maria Concepcion. Everybody knows the wife's motives for vengeance, but when the police investigate, both Juan and the other villagers protect her. She takes Maria Rosa's baby for her own and goes home with husband, child, and sanity restored.

V. Content
  A. First day
     1. Brief overview of Mexican history and mythology
     2. Introduction to Aztec poetry
     3. Suggestopedic technique
     4. Discussion
     5. Reading assignment, *Maria Concepcion*
  B. Second day
     1. Discussion of reading assignment
     2. Questions concerning setting
     3. Draw picture of stage set
     4. Give list of character qualities as take-home assignment
  C. Third day
     1. Discuss characters. Discuss characters in different settings
     2. Discuss how characters differ from one another
     3. Ask students to relate the character to the setting. Have students draw character with setting
     4. Discuss Mexican mythology—ask how setting, characters, and plot relate to myth
VI. Procedure: Procedure will be outlined on the following pages.

VII. Materials
1. E. Kissam. *Poems of the Aztec Peoples.* Ypsilanti, MI: Bilingual Press/Editorial Bilingue. 1983.
2. *Maria Concepcion* by Katherine Anne Porter
3. Women's clothing that reflects indigenous Mexican life
4. Record selections: *Canto por la Raza* by Gabino Palomares; *The Rite of Spring* by Igor Stravinski
5. Jasmine incense
6. Mexican serape
7. Clay pottery
8. Cactus plant
9. Map of Mexico
10. Chalk and chalkboard

VIII. Evaluation: Students will identify at least one image of indigenous Mexican culture, one image of Spanish influence, and one image of U.S. influence in Mexico found in the story *Maria Concepcion.*

■ Centering Script

Students, already familiar with centering processes, will be asked to sit back and relax. A picture of a Mexican woman dressed in rebozo and native dress will be taped to the chalkboard. In addition, a number of Mexican objects—a serape, cactus plants, clay pottery, and the like—will be placed at the front of the room. The centering script is as follows:

Relax your eyes upon the picture at the front of the room.

Feel yourself become less tense and more relaxed.

Concentrate on your breathing.

Let all tensions flow from your body.

Close your eyes.

Let thoughts flow from your mind as easily as they enter.

Concentrate on your breathing.

Imagine you are walking in a remote area.

The view is beautiful.

The sun, the colors, the fresh air, . . .

You are walking down a dirt path—past cacti and tropical plants.

You come across a field of flowers.

Stop and smell and touch these flowers.

(The teacher will light the jasmine incense at this point.)

In the distance you see the outline of a small village.

Approach this village. Enter the village.

Look at the people busy in the marketplace.

Notice the sounds and the smells. Notice all the sounds and all the smells.

Now look upon the woman who sells live fowl—chickens, turkeys, and ducks.

Listen to her call out to her customers: "Compren un pollo. Los pollos a diez pesos."

Now turn your attention away from the woman and the marketplace. Down the road, at the center of town, is a church.

Enter through the big wooden doors. Walk slowly up the aisle toward the altar.

Look around you. It is dark and smells of incense and musk.

Feel the emptiness of this cool place.

Focus upon the woman kneeling in front of the altar.

Notice this woman. She is praying somewhat aloud—"Santa Maria ruega por nosotros—Ave Maria, Santa Maria."

Now slowly exit the church.

Adjust your inner eyes to the bright sunlight of the outdoors.

Listen to the sounds of the village—children laughing, yelling, and playing.

Feel the sun on your shoulders and the dust at your feet.

Take in the smells.

Look around this village one last time.

Now slowly let your attention come back to the people around you. Open your eyes.

After the process has been completed, a discussion as to what the students experienced will take place. To guide this discussion, some of the following questions can be asked. Students should feel that they are not pressured to participate.

1. Would anyone like to share an experience with the class?
2. How did you feel in the countryside, the marketplace, and the church?
3. What did the village look like?
4. What was the woman in the marketplace like? How about the woman in the church?

■ **Second Day**

After students have read the story, follow up with a general discussion of the story. This general discussion will be followed by a detailed study of the setting and the characters in the story.

1. Who are the main characters in the story?
2. Describe what happens in the story.
3. Did you like this story? Why or why not?

Ask the students to define the following vocabulary words. After the definition is clear, have students find the word in the context of the story. Then ask each student to create a sentence containing the word.

maguey	jackal
fowl	trench
rebozo	bravado
jasmine	to placate
infidelities	to condescend

After the main points of the story are clear to the student, continue with a discussion of setting. The questions concerning setting follow.

■ Setting

The following questions are to be asked after the students have read the short story *Maria Concepcion* by Katherine Anne Porter.

1. When and where did the story happen?
2. Could the story have happened somewhere else? At another time?
3. How long a period of time is encompassed by the events in the story?
4. Would it have changed the story any if the author had shortened or lengthened the time period?
5. Does the author follow one time line from beginning to end or jump back and forth in time (flashbacks)?
6. Is the setting important to the story? Why or why not?
7. Does the setting influence the plot or the characters in any way?

Continue the study of setting by posing the following problem: You have been asked to design a stage set for a one-act play based upon the story *Maria Concepcion.* You cannot change the scene because that would take too much time and money. Draw a picture of the stage set you would design. Then explain how the action of the story would take place in that set.

■ Character

The following exercise is to be given as individual homework. Students are to check the words that are most appropriate for the protagonist, Maria Concepcion. A similar exercise will be done in class tomorrow, with the students divided into groups. Each group will describe one of the secondary characters.

Qualities of a Character

Mental Qualities

intelligent	unintelligent		
educated	unschooled		
smart	dumb		
wise	ignorant		
gifted	simple		
clever	puerile		
ingenious	obtuse		
learned	narrow-minded		
scholarly	shallow		
competent	incompetent		
sensible	unreasonable		
talented	incapable		
rational	irrational		

Moral Qualities

moral	immoral
kind	cruel
considerate	inconsiderate
idealistic	unprincipled
innocent	corrupt
righteous	vile
truthful	lying
honest	unscrupulous
honorable	dishonorable
loyal	untrustworthy
helpful	self-centered
polite	insulting
respectable	unrespectable

Physical Qualities

strong	weak
healthy	sickly
handsome	hideous
beautiful	ugly
pretty	graceless
robust	clumsy
hardy	awkward
charming	coarse

Social Qualities

cooperative	contentious
hospitable	inhospitable
congenial	impolite
cheerful	sullen
supportive	antagonistic
worldly	provincial
elegant	unpolished
tactful	crude
cordial	crabby
encouraging	critical
merry	grumpy

Aztec mythology is directly related to the story *Maria Concepcion*. The teacher will tell of these myths using a story-telling technique. This could also be another centering process. When students are comfortable with this myth, ask them to associate the myth with the story. Possible questions may include:

1. How is the setting important to the story?
2. Give similarities between Quetzalcoatl and Juan. In which ways are they alike? Are they different in any ways? What about Xochipilli and Maria Rosa? Xochipilli and Maria Concepcion?
3. How does the murder of Maria Rosa relate to ancient Mexican mythology?
4. Why do you think the people of the village protected Maria Concepcion? Why did Juan protect her?[7]

A similar fantasy journey takes us into the ghetto of Brewster Project:

LESSON PLAN

A Fantasy of Culture

Based on Gloria Naylor's *The Women of Brewster Place*

Place two pictures of buildings on the chalkboard. Ask students if anyone has ever lived in a housing project or moved from one city to another. Wait for responses. Introduce the lesson as follows:

"Today, students, we are going to meet characters from Brewster Place and the pictures on the board are examples of what Brewster Place might look like. The first character we are going to meet is Mattie Michael. I will give a brief description of Mattie's background. I want you to recall different things that your parents have done for you. [Wait for responses.] Next we will meet Etta Mae Johnson [brief description]. Have any of your parents taught you survival techniques on how to make it on your own in the world after growing up? [Name a few.] Our third character is Kiswana Browne [brief description]. Have any of you ever protested or demonstrated against something in school? Who will share some of their experiences? Our next person is Lucielia Turner [brief description]. Our fifth character is Cora Lee. [Give brief description of Cora Lee.] Can someone tell me some things that you wanted for Christmas when you were younger? Our last two characters are Theresa and Lorraine [brief descriptions]. Has anyone ever been treated differently because of an idea, knowledge, or background?"

Students will be told how Brewster Place was developed in a busy district for returning war soldiers. The housing project was originally a main street toward the heart of the city. After a brick wall was put up to form a dead-end alley, the housing area began to lose its "upper-crust" residents and lower-income blacks began to move into the neighborhood. Knowing the background behind the creation of B.P., students will be able to contrast the neighborhood

The study of novels can expand the exploration of the inclusion/exclusion theme. Here are two Hucks and a Tom from Mark Twain's Huckleberry Finn.

of B.P. with their own individual neighborhoods. The students will answer the following questions:

1. What similarities are there between your neighborhood and B.P.?
2. Can you imagine or guess what type of people originally lived in B.P.?
3. Why would a brick wall change both the people and the attitudes of the people toward B.P.?
4. Do you think the lifestyles of the characters fit the living environment of B.P.
5. Do you think that a neighborhood reflects the people living there, or do the people reflect the environment of the neighborhood?
6. Could B.P. be changed to become a better place? If so, how?
7. Do you think or believe that the characters would have made a difference in B.P. if their situations had been different?[8]

PROBE Make a tape recording of the fantasy journeys beginning on page 198. Create the story of Maria Concepcion in your mind. Conform your voice to the reading pattern indicated on the page. Notice the separation of sentences, the longer pauses indicated by dots. Fill the imagery as you create the scenes for your imaginary students.

Now play back the tape and notice the effect your tape has on you as a listening participant. Does it produce the desired effect? What changes would you make? Exchange the tape with a fellow student and offer mutual supportive criticism.

Follow the same procedure for *The Women of Brewster Place.*

> ### *Music and Culture*

Music can be an entrance into culture, a way to comprehend in a felt sense the values of culturally divergent groups. Many high school teachers discover the power of relating to students through music: rock, jazz, and "new age." In Detroit, several teachers have created lessons using rap music appropriately and thematically. Music can communicate more than words alone. Teachers should use music purposefully. Music should not become mere background sound for a class. Doing this diminishes its impact. Instead, thematic music can be coupled with film and fantasy selected to match mood and meaning. Appendix B provides suggestions for use of thematic music.

■ *SUMMARY*

Each culture and each subculture transmits values. Culture implies a quest to create and preserve the products of the human societies. Various groups of people express their highest values in art, sculpture, language, architecture, dance, music, mythology, religion, and customs. These values tend to be perpetuated through education.

There is in contemporary society a tendency to globalize the dimensions of culture—to expand and diffuse cultures throughout the world. This has the effect of putting us in touch with an enormous range of cultures. It also has a leveling effect. There is a tendency toward homogenization. To preserve the richness of cultural diversity it is necessary to teach appreciation of the unique values each culture perpetuates. To do this, the methods of encounter are useful. Encounter increases one's awareness of relatedness to groups and individuals perceived as different. Encounter processes can effectively be coupled with nondirective exploration of feelings, the viewing of films depicting cross-cultural interaction, the use of fantasy journeys to explore cultures, and the use of thematic music.

■ *NOTES*

1. I. Tinker and B. M. Bramsen, "Proceedings of the Seminar on Women in Development," in *Women and World Development,* ed. I. Tinker and B. M. Bramsen (Washington, D.C.: American Association of Science, 1975), pp. 138–218.
2. William Schutz, *Elements of Encounter* (Big Sur, CA: Joy Press, 1973), 3.
3. Ibid.
4. Bruce Joyce and Marsha Weil, *Models of Teaching* (Englewood Cliffs, NJ: Prentice-Hall, 1986), 187–188.

5. William Schutz, *Joy: Expanding Human Awareness* (New York: Grove Press, 1967), 123.
6. Bruce Joyce and Marsha Weil, *Models of Teaching,* 193.
7. Ibid., 184–185.
8. Julie Brown, "Multicultural Lesson Plan: Maria Concepcion" Unpublished. Printed by permission of author.
9. Shielia Wiggins, "Multicultural Lesson Plan: The Women of Brewster Place?" Unpublished. Printed by permission of author.

CHAPTER 11

Identifying Special Learning Problems

PAULA C. WOOD

Handicapped graduating high school student with his teacher.

We walked down the path to the well-house attracted by the fragrance of honey-suckle with which it was covered. Someone was drawing water and my teacher placed my hand under the spout. As the cool stream gushed over one hand she spelled into the other the word water, first slowly, then rapidly. I stood still, my whole attention fixed upon the motion of her fingers. Suddenly I felt a misty consciousness as of something forgotten—a thrill of returning thought; and somehow the mystery of language was revealed to me. I knew then that "w-a-t-e-r" meant the wonderful cool something that was flowing over my hand. That living word awakened my soul, gave it light, hope, joy, set it free! There were barriers still, it is true, but barriers that could in time be swept away.

I left the well-house eager to learn. Everything had a name, and each name gave birth to a new thought. As we returned to the house every object which I touched seemed to quiver with life. That was because I saw everything with the strange, new sight that had come to me.

—Helen Keller

Moving handicapped students into regular classroom settings is of vital importance to the learning and socialization of both handicapped and nonhandicapped students. It is possible to do this effectively without extensive specialized knowledge and to use the special education resources available to enhance learning for all students in your classroom, not just for the handicapped students. Everything you do to enhance the learning of a handicapped student can have a positive effect on the learning of other marginal students or other students who will benefit from a different presentation style or who need a chance to rework information in a more effective manner. If you, as a teacher, understand this, you can see that obtaining information about how to work with handicapped students is in your own best interest and the best interest of your total classroom, not just in the interest of the handicapped student.

Historically, our society has not been sensitive to or effective in integrating people with handicaps into normal life or even in acknowledging the presence of these individuals in society. Only recently, since 1976, are schools mandated by federal law to serve all handicapped students. Prior to that, many students with handicaps were educated by private agencies or charitable institutions, or, most unfortunately, not educated at all. It is therefore unlikely that today's teachers ever had a handicapped student as a classmate or ever watched a teacher effectively working with a handicapped student alone or in a group with other nonhandicapped students. This lack of exposure brings with it discomfort, ignorance, and fear. Attitudes of adults in our society toward handicapped people are less than exemplary, mostly, the author feels, because of lack of exposure.

Coupled with this lack of previous experience are the extensive concepts and terminology that exist in the field of special education. Anyone looking for simple answers is quickly frustrated and frightened away by the complexity and specialized terminology that surrounds the study of handicapped students and how they learn. While the labeling and terms were developed to clarify and delineate specific information about procedures in special education, the nonexpert is more confused than enlightened by the overwhelming amount of information available. What are the differences among emotionally impaired, learning disabled, and mentally retarded students? What is mandated by state legislation, and what is mandated by federal legislation?

A third complicating factor is the jargon particular to special education that has grown out of the specific terminology used. A conversation heard recently between two special education teachers is a good example of how jargon has infiltrated the everyday language of special education: "Has the e.i. student you thought might have a.d.d. had his I.E.P.C. yet?" "Yes, but unfortunately the M.E.T. ruled that he was s.m.a. according to the new 198 provisions and so he is now ineligible." While this may be natural in any discipline with an abundance of very discrete terminology, it has the effect of distancing the nonspecialist from the area. Given the need for regular classroom teachers to participate actively in the education of handicapped students, the effect of such jargon is especially unfortunate.

You may begin to examine the significance of your role in the education of handicapped students by analyzing what brought about the move to educate handicapped students in the regular classroom. Simply explained, when long-term research was done on the effects of placing mildly handicapped students into special segregated programs, it was discovered that the isolation from normal peers and normal types of classroom activities did not have a positive effect on the learning and socialization of handicapped students.[1] Specialized techniques were needed to teach, but these were most effective when used in an environment of normal peers that was rich in stimulation and interaction. Unfortunately, appropriate social interaction did not occur spontaneously in these settings.[2] An appropriate setting for mildly and moderately handicapped students appears to be one that adapts to their special instructional needs, exposes them on a regular basis to interaction with their nonhandicapped peers, and provides special assistance for the socialization and actual integration of the handicapped students into learning and social activities. It is apparent that the teacher's attitude and abilities are critical for this to occur.[3] This chapter attempts to prepare the teacher who is not an expert in special education to effectively develop a classroom that accommodates all students and that provides for the learning and integration of students with varying ability levels and varying learning styles.

The best advice that can be given to a regular classroom teacher is not to be intimidated by the extensive terminology that exists in special education, along with the accompanying jargon. As a teacher, you have a right to know about any student in your classroom and to know what you can do to provide the best education possible for that student. If special terminology or jargon gets in your way, say so. If you don't understand something, ask for clarification. If clarification does not come, demand it. Do not allow yourself to be intimidated by your lack of any information. Ask your questions in terms of the students you are trying to serve and what you need to know to serve them better.

PROBE Try free associating for ten minutes, using the words "handicapped students" as a beginning stimulus. Write down everything that comes into your mind. Now write a paragraph or two summarizing your free associations in regard to handicapped students. As you read through the chapter, stay aware of your initial free associations.

Diagnostic Categories

Numerous discrete diagnostic categories have evolved in special education to describe specific disabilities. These specific categories were useful in the development of specialized educational interventions and in seeking funds and conducting research about handicapping conditions. For your purposes, however, the most important part of any diagnosis is *the impact a handicap has on a student's learning.* Adaptations to your teaching and the structure of your classroom evolve from your understanding of the impact of a condition on learning. For any handicapped student assigned to your classroom, the important question to ask is, What is the impact of this condition on the student's learning? The next step, then, is to plan adaptations and modifications to accommodate these students. The following sections offer descriptions of the most common handicapping conditions we see in school-aged students, along with information on the impact of the handicapping condition on learning. Some suggestions for adaptations are made, but these adaptations are offered only as suggestions. Appropriate adaptations vary from student to student. The ones listed here are not meant to be all-inclusive but, rather, to represent the variety of adaptations that are possible. References at the end of the chapter contain much more detailed and readily accessible information. When a student with a handicap is assigned to your classroom, you are urged to check out the resources included here for a more thorough listing of adaptations and considerations.

■ *Students with Physical Handicaps*

Physical handicaps include disorders of vision, hearing, the brain, bones, muscles, the nervous system, chronic illness, or orthopedic deficits, such as missing limbs. Each of these disabilities has a different effect on the learning of a student.

Visual handicaps include a range of disabilities from total blindness to limited vision that makes reading difficult when print is small or light is low. Other visually impaired students have a limited range of vision that allows them to see only telescopically and not peripherally. There are two major implications of the handicap on a student's learning: Visual tasks are obviously difficult for these students, and safety is an issue because the student may not see hazards or objects that pose a danger. Generally, concept formation, while at times a bit impaired because of lack of exposure to environmental events, is close to, at, or even above grade level. How, then, do you effectively plan for the instruction of a visually impaired student? Numerous books, many of them excellent, have been written about mainstreaming students with various handicapping conditions. Some particularly helpful books are found in the references for this chapter at the end of this book. These books contain extensive lists of possible adaptations. Software has also been developed to help a teacher adapt a classroom for a handicapped student.

For our purposes here, however, there are some generalizations that will be useful to you in formulating your own adaptations. You need to provide the students with all course information in a format that they can comprehend. This may mean large type, particularly dark type, adaptive equipment that enlarges type, tape-recorded books, braille lessons, or readers to assist the student. There should be a consultant who serves visually impaired students. This consultant can provide the special materials you may need or supply the equipment the student may need to "read" the material being used. If no consultant is directly available, contact the director of special education in your district and ask for the department's consultant, who can easily assist you in making your instructional materials more accessible to a visually impaired student. Logic, common sense, and consideration will supply the additional information and ideas you need, if you keep in mind the necessity for providing the material in a usable format. You need not do it all yourself—prerecorded books exist and you can have good readers record texts or supplementary books while reading them for their own purposes. Volunteers from other classes or service clubs can also read personally to the student. It is important to consider the format you will use ahead of time, so that the visually impaired student has access to the information. During lectures a visually impaired student can take braille notes, if necessary, or other students can take notes and have the notes transcribed into a format the visually impaired student can understand.

Safety is the other major consideration for a visually impaired student. You must keep doors and drawers closed, chairs under the tables or desks, and aisles and walkways clear of objects. Neatness is important for the teacher and for the other students when a visually impaired student is in the class. Alert the other students to this, and they can help monitor for safe conditions. If anyone drops something, it should be picked up immediately.

Auditory problems, like visual problems, vary in degree. A student with an auditory handicap can hear no sound or can have a more moderate hearing loss and still hear some sounds. The impact of an auditory handicap on a student's learning can be very serious and potentially more academically debilitating than a visual handicap. Information that is given orally—in some classrooms 90 percent of all information—will not necessarily be useful for a student with an auditory handicap. Even more seriously, students with auditory handicaps are almost always delayed in language development. The lack of auditory acuity is serious because *language* deficits make higher-order thinking and learning very difficult. The student may also appear to be noncompliant when, in fact, he or she might not have heard the directions.

Many student with auditory acuity problems wear amplification devices. These devices pick up and amplify all environmental sounds, not just speech. Students generally learn to use other cues for ascertaining meaning from a situation. They become very good imitators, so that they may appear to be doing an activity appropriately when they do not understand the task at all. Some students use alternative communication systems such as signing or letter spelling to communicate.

The teacher's role in teaching a student with a hearing impairment involves providing support and alternative means of input for all auditory activity and the development of monitoring of language skills and complexity. The student should be seated so that all speakers are easily viewed without having to look up too high or too far away. The light source should be behind the student so that speakers are illuminated, rather than having the student look into the light and miss some of the potential for lip-reading. Place the student away from distracting sounds like hallway noise and mechanical equipment. Other students can take notes for the student on specially treated paper that makes copies without carbon paper, so that the student will be able to watch the speaker and will not need to look down to write notes and miss any clues to what is being said. Before a lesson begins, ask yourself if the student with the auditory handicap will comfortably be able to see what is going on and if you have provided him or her with a means for note taking that will not interfere with watching the speaker. Clarity of speech is more important than loudness, but if you speak rapidly, slow down.

Social integration of the student is also critical. Hearing-impaired students have difficulty integrating into informal conversations and interactions that depend on oral language. You will need to create groups that are small and can include the student with an auditory impairment in social activities, such as planning for a class party. In addition, you will need to encourage your students with normal hearing to take the time to include the handicapped student in play or other in-school recreational activities. If classmates understand that including the student will be difficult at first, but that inclusion will be very important to the student with an auditory impairment, they will usually cooperate. You can also assign a volunteer buddy or assistant to the impaired student to help form bonds between the handicapped student and others in the classroom. These bonds extend into other social situations, thereby helping the student in those areas as well.

Students with cerebral palsy will have motor disabilities caused by damage to the immature brain. The muscles that produce speech are sometimes involved, and speech may be slurred or produced with great difficulty. Do not confuse this inability to produce speech sounds well with a language deficit. Receptive language, which is so critical to learning, may be intact for these students. Therefore, they can understand what is said and what is going on in your classroom, although their physical limitations may produce some deficits in experience that will have an impact on learning. The performance of activities or tasks will be slower for a student with this particular handicap and, because of the extra effort needed, may be more tiring for the student. Keep in mind that it is the understanding of ideas and concepts and not the output of written work that you want to stress for these students. Modify your requirements for written work if at all possible so that these students expend their energy to learn and not just to produce written work.

Spina bifida is another physical disorder seen in school-age students. It results in physical problems such as paralysis or numbness from the point at which the spine did not close completely during gestation. Some students with spina bifida are in wheelchairs or on crutches. Mobility is usually the primary problem along with possible bladder-control difficulties. The student should be able to manage these physical problems with a little consideration and assistance from you. For all students with physical handicaps, make self-care activities as easy and accessible as possible. The student should be able to get a drink or use the bathroom with ease and when they need to do so, without seeking special permission or assistance. Adaptations may be needed, such as nonskid treads on bathroom floors and adjustment of the height of work tables and other activity centers so that the student can reach the surface comfortably.

Students with chronic illnesses are also labeled physically handicapped. Illnesses seen in school-age students include juvenile diabetes, heart conditions, cystic fibrosis, asthma, seizure disorders, and sickle-cell anemia. For students with *any* of these or other health conditions, the teacher should *always* ascertain what signs or symptoms the student might exhibit that would indicate a health emergency and what action should be taken in case of such an emergency. The impact on learning for these students comes from two primary sources: fatiguing easily, not being able to complete work or pay attention for long periods of time, and, missing school frequently due to illness or hospitalization. With some planning, both of these concerns can be addressed. Have an area of your classroom or space within your building where the student can rest when necessary. Don't push the student to complete written tasks when fatigue is apparent. Make sure the student understands the concepts involved or let the student perform orally for you rather than complete a written assignment. Other students can be very helpful during an illness or absence from school by taking notes for the student, by keeping copies of the assignments they complete while the student is absent, and by keeping in touch with the student while he or she is out due to the physical condition. Communication devices are available for keeping a homebound or hospitalized student in constant touch with what is going on in the classroom. Again, your special-education consultant should be able to help you with these adaptations.

One very important consideration for physically handicapped students, including those with seizure disorders, is monitoring the student for any adverse effects of medications. The various medications may cause drowsiness, agitation, stomach upsets, bowel problems, dizziness and other complications. If you observe any of these, report it to the school nurse and the parents as soon as possible. Keep a written record of days and times these manifestations occur for the parent to take to the physician.

■ *Students with Cognitive Handicaps*

A student may have a cognitive/reasoning problem for a variety of reasons. Some students are retarded, meaning that there is a general lack of intelligence in all areas of the student's functioning. This lack of intelligence makes it more difficult for a student to understand information and ideas. Once something is learned, it is not forgotten any more readily by retarded students than it is by other students, but the initial learning is more difficult. Abstract concepts and higher-level thinking usually never develop in a retarded student. Most students who are retarded, however, grow up to marry and raise families, and some hold down regular jobs. These students benefit particularly from having their normal peers in class with them. The discussion and other oral learning that takes place, along with the modeling that can occur from good learning strategies, are probably the elements that have a very positive influence on retarded students.

The lack of intelligence of a retarded student also makes it likely that the reading level of the student will be low. Therefore, when reading is required, an alternative means of getting the information needs to be made available to the retarded student. Readings can be tape recorded in advance; someone can read to the student; students can read information in small groups, with the best readers reading to all the other students; or the teacher or other assistant can summarize the information for the student. Reading tests may also be difficult for retarded students. It is particularly helpful if all tests can be taken orally as well as in a written format, so that the test measures the information the student has and does not reflect just the low reading level of the student.

For the retarded student, socialization is also a major concern. Research on retarded students indicates that they tend to be socially isolated even in mainstream settings.[4] The author believes that this reflects our competitive culture and our basic nonacceptance of individual differences in society. As a teacher, you can be of great significance in forming attitudes by emphasizing the positive dimensions of individual differences and by allowing for individual differences calmly and willingly in your classroom. Students' attitudes develop from the way in which adults behave. If you deprecate or are impatient with or ignore the needs of a retarded student, the other students value that classmate less. Your positive and accepting attitude will have a long-lasting influence on the other students in your classroom.

Learning-disabled students are the other group who will have cognitive and learning problems. This is the most difficult handicap for nonexperts to understand because the intelligence level of these students is average or above, but the *processing* or production of information is faulty. The learning-disabled student may actually hear what is said, but may not be able to process the information to give meaning to it. Think of your own days as a student. Nearly everyone has had the experience of having a classmate who seemed intelligent and who, in some areas, may have actually excelled. Yet this classmate, even with real effort, never read well or never did well on examinations. The author has a close friend whom she has known since high school. They were in numerous classes together in high school, and we attended the same college, majoring in education. We frequently studied together and discussed and argued about the information we were learning in our classes. He was very intelligent, and the author was convinced that, in courses we took together, he knew all the information she did. Yet his grade was always one or two levels lower than the author's, even after they had studied together extensively. After entering the field of special education the author came to realize that he was probably learning-disabled and that his processing of the test he was reading was what produced his deficit performance. Writing, too, was difficult for John. Verbally he was a strong speaker and debater, but writing was agony for him. It was not until adulthood, where performance was measured by something other than an examination, that John began to be recognized for the intelligent man he is. This is typical of many learning-disabled students, who do not begin to achieve to their abilities until the constraints of formal schooling are exchanged for more flexible criteria. Thomas Edison, Albert Einstein, John F. Kennedy, and Nelson Rockefeller are all examples of people who were probably learning-disabled, but whose intelligence and other remarkable traits made them outstanding human beings.

Learning disabilities are manifested in a variety of ways. Some students will have difficulty with reading, others with spoken language. Auditory stimuli may be terribly distracting for some learning-disabled students; others may have an inability to pay attention for any length of time.

Your adaptations for any student with learning disabilities will vary. You will want to present information in whatever format is most readily understandable for the student. Processing in multiple channels—visual, auditory, and kinesthetic—can also be helpful. The student, his or her special education teacher, or the parents can be very helpful to you in planning for the learning-disabled student. Many of the adaptations mentioned above are appropriate because they allow the student maximum opportunity to learn and minimum penalties for low reading levels.

If a learning-disabled student has difficulty attending to a lesson, you will need to make particular efforts to engage the student's attention. Warn the student before you begin something and review frequently what has been said. Wait for the student to pay attention before you begin a lesson or an explanation. Learning partners or learning buddies can also be very helpful if done in a supportive rather than a punitive manner. These helpers can repeat directions and remind the students with attention problems where to focus their attention.

When you have a student with a cognitive problem in your classroom, try to plan lessons so that the deficit is minimized and the opportunity exists for the student to show you what he or she knows in ways other than traditional pencil and paper exams. These same techniques can be very useful for other students with low reading ability in your classroom.

■ Students with Emotional Handicaps

Students who are *emotionally disturbed* will vary in the types of problems they present as well as in the manner in which they present the problem. The approach by the effective teacher will likewise vary. The ultimate goal is to integrate the student into the classroom and to maintain control and consistency of management in the classroom while addressing each type of problem.

Simply stated, emotional problems manifested by high school students will fall into two broad categories: adjustment problems and behavioral problems. Adjustment problems are usually situationally induced and relatively amenable to intervention. They occur in response to a specific stress either in family or community life or from events such as death in the family or a change in living environment. Behavioral problems are well-ingrained maladaptive patterns. Other symptoms—withdrawal, inability to concentrate, lack of attention, inability to form relationships, fluctuating moods, anger, flatness of affect, and the like—will be observed in these students. Emotional problems affect the student's ability to learn. The student experiencing a situational adjustment problem is much less likely to be diagnosed as handicapped, but the issues of management of the students will be similar.

The first step to successful management of the behavior of a student with emotional problems is to realize that the student is not misbehaving or acting inappropriately on purpose. An emotionally disturbed student is behaving in the only way he or she knows how to behave or in response to inner conflicts or personal problems. It is not a personal attack on you, nor is it a reflection on your ability as a teacher. You would not reject a student because of a physical handicap; try to have the same attitude toward a student with an emotional handicap. It presents you with a challenge, not with a threat. *Do not personalize the student's behavior or attitude.* Your ability to remain calm and emotionally in control of yourself will be of great advantage for you.

Usually an emotionally disturbed student will have a behavioral management plan devised by a professional expert in consultation with a planning committee. The effective teacher will read the student's file to determine the plan of action best suited to the student.

The difficulty in the management of the emotionally disturbed student in the classroom derives from the fact that emotionally disturbed persons are unpredictable, resulting in behavior that may be difficult to control. This unpredictability is most often and most consistently seen in more severely disturbed students. It will be important for the effective teacher to be alert to the risks involved in managing these students. (It would be wise for *all* teachers to become familiar with the signs and symptoms of suicide and other violent behavior. Your school guidance counselor or school social worker or a local suicide prevention center can provide training in this area.)

When students are a danger to themselves or others, the emotionally disturbed students should be identified as mentally ill and in need of supervision beyond the control of the classroom. The first responsibility of a teacher is to be aware of this fact and to leave to other professionals the task of treating such students. In the case of a student at risk, you have an obligation to refer the case for evaluation and attention to a school administrator, mental health professional, guidance counselor, social worker, or the director of special education in your district. Referral procedures should be standardized within each district. If you are concerned about a student, follow these referral procedures. *Immediately* inform a mental health professional and/or an administrator if you suspect imminent danger. Make certain that the professional follows up.

It has been stated that the ultimate goal in working with the emotionally disturbed student is to integrate that student within a regular classroom. The effective teacher can contribute to this in a number of ways.

First, the rules set up for the classroom will apply to the handicapped student as well as all other students. Second, the effective teacher will become familiar with the management plan for the student. Suggestions on handling the student will be contained within that plan. It should include a means for discipline within a classroom. If no plan is available, seek direction from the special education professionals. A plan is written from least restrictive to most restrictive intervention. Least restrictive examples that would be suitable for a regular classroom include verbal interventions or possibly modeling suggestions or correction guidelines. Interventions of a more severe nature are reserved for teachers trained in special class placements.

Perhaps the most helpful intervention the teacher can contribute to the education of an emotionally disturbed student is observation. From observation, modification of the management plan can be made. As an observer of behavior and an implementer of a management plan, the effective teacher becomes a team member in the guidance of the emotionally handicapped student. Observations should include: precipitating event to the behavior, function of the behavior, time and place the behavior is occurring, and the like. The behavioral observation will contribute not only to the treatment program but also to the educational process. (Ask your mental health professionals or special education staff for observation guidelines.) It will suggest what motivates or reinforces the student and by what method or how a student learns.

PROBE Again, take 10 minutes to free associate your response to "handicapped student." Again write a paragraph summarizing your free associations. Compare your initial paragraph with your new summary. Are there changes? How many changes do you note? As you continue to read the chapter, keep both summaries in mind.

Your Role in the Special Education Process

Federal legislation, P.L. 94-142, mandates that appropriate educational services be provided to all students, regardless of handicap. This legislation contains very specific requirements for procedures relative to referrals, diagnostic procedures, determination of handicap and placement of handicapped students.

Special education services exist in a district to provide appropriate educational opportunities to handicapped students. If you have a handicapped student in your classroom, you should have access to the assistance of one or more special education professionals to plan for your interaction with the handicapped student. You may need to be assertive in finding and using the expertise that exists. Because you are not specially trained, you should be willing to ask for assistance where needed and to assert yourself in obtaining the assistance you need.

You also have the right to refer any student you suspect of having a handicap for evaluation. The principal in your building or the director of special education in your district should have appropriate forms and should be able to tell you where to send these forms to begin the process of referral. Some teachers report that they are intimidated by what is asked on these forms relating to the adaptations they have tried in their classroom to assist the students. This is important information for the diagnosticians. Just fill it out honestly.

Once a formal referral has been made by a teacher, other professional, or a parent, the parent must give written consent for the evaluation to proceed. After assessment is completed, an individual education planning committee will be convened. At this meeting, there will be an administrative representative, a representative of the evaluation team, and a teacher who has had the student in class or a teacher who works with the same level of students. The parents are also invited to attend. This committee will decide if the student is handicapped and, if so, what are the goals for the student while in special education and the type of setting in which the student will be placed. The guiding rule of placement is that the student should be placed in the *least restrictive environment* where he or she can function effectively. It is this stipulation that leads to *mainstreaming,* or the placement of handicapped students in regular classrooms with their nonhandicapped peers. Mainstreaming is not mandated for all handicapped students, but placement in the least restrictive environment *is* mandated. If a student is placed in your classroom and he or she does not seem to be able to do the work, even with adaptations and a reasonable amount of assistance, you have a right and an obligation to report this to the department of special education through a special education teacher or by beginning the referral process again.

General Classroom Adaptations and Procedures

There are a number of general classroom adaptations you can use that will be very useful to any handicapped students assigned to you that will also enhance the overall effectiveness of your classroom. These adaptations include attitudes, learning formats, special learning programs, and general effective teaching techniques.

■ *Attitudes*

The inclusion of handicapped students in your classroom will be much more successful if you continually convey the attitude that we all have individual differences and that your classroom will be a place where individual differences are tolerated and allowances made for these individual differences. All students are expected to work hard and to try their best, of course, but all students are not expected to have the same strengths and abilities. Students have the obligation to learn the material you want them to learn, and you have an obligation to present the information in a way they can comprehend. Many of the previously suggested adaptations are examples of putting this attitude into action. For nonreaders or poor readers this may mean providing information on tape or orally rather than just in a printed text. When you have acknowledged and adapted for the individual difference of these students, they can more appropriately be expected to learn to the best of their ability. This attitude has the added advantage of helping nonhandicapped students to accept their handicapped peers as *different* rather than view them as wrong or as inadequate. A classroom where individual differences are accepted is comfortable for all students and enhances the learning of all students. It is important that you maintain high expectations for all your students and that you frequently convey these expectations to them. The acknowledgement of individual differences allows the students to examine what they do best and how they learn best to achieve the learning that you expect. A student who does not read well should still feel obligated to learn, but if material is only presented in textbooks, the student may not learn and may not feel that he or she is expected to learn.

■ Learning Formats

Good instruction provides for a variety of learning formats. Many of these have been discussed previously. Formats that are particularly effective for handicapped students include alternative presentation of written material such as taped lessons, peer assistance, and small-group work, where students attempt to learn information together rather than competitively. Multiple channeling of information may also be effective.

■ Special Learning Programs

There are a number of special learning programs that are especially effective for handicapped learners. A relatively new, commonly used special learning format is cooperative learning.[5] This learning format takes special training; however, once understood, it is not difficult to use. It calls for developing learning through group processes and cooperation rather than through competition and individual work. Special training in this technique is available from many school districts, colleges and university schools of education, and from other agencies that provide in-service education to educators.

Peer tutoring and cross-age tutoring are other learning formats that can be helpful to all your students. Information on these techniques is available from your local education library. These techniques can usually be used without special training, although special training is helpful. You may need to initiate a request for this type of special training on the in-service days provided by your school district, or you may seek the special training through universities, colleges, and other support institutions.

■ General Effective Teaching Techniques

There are a number of teaching techniques that will enhance your students' learning. These include being an authoritative teacher, communicating high expectations to all students, monitoring of work and assignments, giving direct corrective feedback, and using nonintrusive techniques to manage behavior that occurs.

An authoritative teacher is calm and in control of the classroom. Expectations are communicated positively, clearly, and firmly. Students are put to work on learning activities immediately and kept on task with positive reminders and nonverbal cues.

The authoritative teacher is comfortable being in charge and willing to be calmly assertive to communicate to the students that they should be working. This is the most effective management style.

■ *Monitoring Work and Assignments*

Students only invest as much interest in an activity as you do. If you give work and then never check the work, the students assume it is not important work and cease to do it. If you give an assignment, check it and give the student feedback on the assignment. You need not grade everything they do, but you do need to check it to see that it is done correctly. The author has seen students as early as first grade cease doing worksheets and start misbehaving when they were supposed to be doing written assignments because the teacher never checked these assignments.

■ *Direct Corrective Feedback*

An effective teacher gives consistent messages about what is expected and how to do things correctly. Don't dwell on what students did incorrectly or on misbehavior. Tell the student(s) exactly what you want done or how to change their behavior to bring it into compliance with your expectations. If a student has done an assignment incorrectly, reexplain the directions and ask the student to complete the assignment again. If the student does not know how to do the assignment, take the time to explain it or ask one of the other students to explain and assist. Resist the temptation to rail at the student or to dwell on what the student did incorrectly. Your goal is to focus the students on appropriate learning activities, which is best done with positive directions and focusing on exactly what you expect the student to do.

■ *Nonintrusive Behavior Management*

Effective teachers tend to deal with misbehavior in ways that are nonintrusive and nondisruptive to whatever activities are in progress. Instead of distracting everyone in the classroom by stopping a lesson when a student misbehaves, you can plan to ignore the misbehavior or you can give the misbehaving student a look that communicates your attention is focused on him or her and you are not pleased with what is occurring. Sometimes this look is sufficient to bring the student back to the appropriate task. Proximity is also a nonintrusive intervention. Move near or directly beside the student who is off task, and the student may get back on task. These interventions should be attempted first because they do not take the focus off the appropriate activity. Such nonintrusive techniques do not always work, especially if a student is hostile or out of control or if the student is attempting to anger or upset you. Nonetheless, for many instances of mild misbehavior or off-task behavior these techniques are effective and efficient.

PROBE In two to three days after reading this chapter, again put yourself through the free association exercise. Again write a paragraph. Then go back to your first two paragraphs and note any changes. How do you feel about the changes that you note?

■ SUMMARY

Working effectively with handicapped students is a challenging but important task. The terminology and jargon inherent in the field of special education require that the effective teacher be assertive in seeking clarification from "experts." Most teachers have had limited previous experience with handicapped students, and frequently have inaccurate perceptions of these students' abilities and limitations.

The impact of a given handicap on a student's learning is critical information for a teacher. Once this is understood, a teacher can make appropriate adaptations with the assistance of special education consultants and other resources. Certain general adaptations and procedures, including appropriate teacher attitudes, varied learning formats, special learning programs, and the adoption of general effective teaching techniques, can promote better learning for all students, handicapped *and* nonhandicapped.

■ NOTES

1. L. M. Dunn, "Special Education for the Mildly Retarded: Is Much of It Justifiable?" *Exceptional Children 35* (1): 5–22 (1968).
2. R. L. Jones, "Student Views of Special Placement and Their Own Special Classes: A Clarification," *Exceptional Children* 41(1): September 1974, 22–29.
3. M. K. Garrett and W. D. Crump, "Peer Acceptance, Teacher Preference, and Self-Appraisal of Social Status of Learning Disabled Students," *Learning Disability Quarterly* 3(3): 42–48 (1980).
4. J. Gottlieb and Y. Leyser, "Facilitating the Social Mainstreaming of Retarded Children," *Exceptional Education Quarterly* 1 (4): 57–70 (1981).
5. D. W. Johnson and R. Johnson, *Learning Together and Alone: Cooperation, Competition, and Individualization* (Englewood Cliffs, NJ: Prentice-Hall, 1975).

CHAPTER 12

Metaphor as Method

William Blake's interpretation of Paradise Lost.

There are techniques that can help us name our dreams and dragons. They are designed to reopen the bridge between right and left to through traffic, to increase the left brain's awareness of the counterpart. Metaphor builds a bridge between the hemispheres, symbolically carrying knowledge from the mute right brain so that it may be recognized by the left as being like something already known.
—Marilyn Ferguson, *The Aquarian Conspiracy*

. . . part of the meaning of any experience is elusive, and it is the use of metaphor that formulates this elusive meaning and makes it available to us as an understandable figure of speech.
—Ronald S. Valle and Rolf von Eckartsberg, *The Metaphors of Consciousness*

When Carl Sagan was a boy he lived in the Bensonhurst section of Brooklyn, New York. Even at a young age he would look at the twinkling and remote stars and wonder what they were. When he asked adults what they were, they would reply, "They're lights in the sky, kid." Sagan says he could see that they were "lights in the sky. But what were they? Just small hovering lamps? What for?"

As soon as his parents gave him his first library card, Sagan began reading about the stars. He discovered, he says, something astonishing: "The book said something astonishing, a very big thought. It said that the stars were suns, only very far away. The [s]un was a star, but close up."[1]

The metaphors "the sun was a star" and "the stars were suns" provided an opening—an intellectual awakening for Sagan. He reasoned that if the stars were suns, "they had to be very far away—farther than 85th Street, farther away than Manhattan, farther away probably than New Jersey. The cosmos was much bigger than [he] had guessed."

Later Sagan read another "astonishing" fact: "The earth, which includes Brooklyn, is a planet and it goes around the sun. There are other planets. They also go around the sun."[2] Since the sun is a star, Sagan reasoned that the other stars must have planets, too, ones we have not yet detected. "Some of those other planets should have life (Why not?) a kind of life probably different from life as we know it—Life in Brooklyn. So I decided," says Sagan, "I would be an astronomer, learn a lot about the stars and planets and if I could, go and visit them."[3]

Metaphor as a Way of Knowing

What, exactly, is metaphor and how can one learn through metaphor? The *American Heritage Dictionary* defines metaphor as "a figure of speech in which a term is transferred from the object it ordinarily designates to an object it may designate only by implicit comparison or analogy. . . ." In the phrase "All flesh is grass," flesh is equated with grass, causing one to ask in what ways grass and flesh are related. It is the power to suggest possible relations between seemingly unrelated objects and concepts that makes metaphor useful as a learning instrument.

Sagan's discovering through metaphor is not unique among scientists. Harun-Ur Rashid of the philosophy department at Wayne State University contends that metaphor has been used throughout the history of science, philosophy, and technology to extend the development of concepts in these fields. Scientific and technological developments are extended by extending the uses of language. Heraclitus referred to time as "a child at play." Charles Darwin referred to natural selection as a "struggle for existence." The modern philosopher, Gilbert Ryle, in his *Concept of Mind,* refers to the belief that one has a separate body and mind as the "ghost in the machine" theory. If we are interested in teaching students to expand upon present knowledge, we cannot afford to ignore the teaching of metaphor as a way of knowing.

In *Metaphorical Way of Learning and Knowing,* William Gordon outlines his system of Synectics, a system of using metaphor as a vehicle for problem solving, fictional character development, exploration of language, investigation of culture, and personal insight.

Gordon uses metaphor to make the familiar strange and the strange familiar. For example, Gordon points out that William Harvey's discovery of blood circulation—from the heart to the lungs to the heart to the arteries to the veins and then back to the heart—was based on the use of a metaphor, "The heart is a pump," which came to Harvey when he was observing a fish's heart that was "still beating after the fish had been opened up.[4]

Harvey's metaphorical interpretation of his observation of the fish's heart enabled him to recontextualize how he viewed circulation and break with the accepted sixteenth-century interpretation—"that blood flowed from the heart to the body, surging in and out like tides of waves." Gordon described this function of metaphor as "making the familiar strange." It is using metaphor to discover new possibilities, to innovate, to create.

Gordon goes on to say that for the novice the same metaphor may be used in a converse sense: "making the strange familiar." Understanding a concept, Gordon says, requires bringing a strange concept into a familiar context. A professor of physiology may explain to a student that the heart acts like a pump and thereby remind the student of other connections:

> The student may be reminded of a swimming pool where dirty water is pumped through the filter and back into the pool. The student, of course, makes the obvious connection between the heart and the pump. But he develops other connections as well. He sees how lungs and the liver act as "filter" when they cleanse the blood. Thus, through an example from his own experience, the student creatively contributes to his own learning. He makes the STRANGE FAMILIAR to himself by means of a highly personal connection process.[5]

Diagramatically, the process is represented in Figure 12.1. The diagram shows how meaning can be recontextualized, can shift in two directions—from the familiar to the unfamiliar and vice versa. Another way of putting this is that two fields of

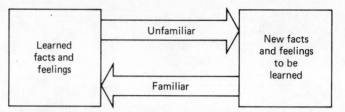

Figure 12.1 Meaning can shift in two directions—from the familiar to the unfamiliar and vice versa.

meaning can be altered by linking those fields of meaning through metaphor. Consider the woodcut by M. C. Escher entitled *Still Life and Street?* (page 225) It can be interpreted as a visual metaphor:

> The field of meaning associated with the street (commerce, conversation, washing, children at play) is conjoined with the field of meanings associated with an accidental grouping of books on a table (reading for relaxation, amusement, the comfort of a pipe) to create the world of the imagination to be found in vicarious travel of the armchair peripatetic. The effect of the metaphor is "to open up the world of reading."[6]

PROBE Try this quick process: Imaginatively, place yourself at the study table looking out toward the street. Note that experience. Now be one of the persons in the street and reflect on the world of reading about your immediate experience. Did you notice a shift in both fields of meaning?

■ *Basic Metaphors (Root Metaphors)*

Basic metaphors, called *root metaphors* by Stephen Pepper, are ways of organizing one's world. In *World Hypotheses,* Pepper says:

> A man desiring to understand the world looks about for a clue to its comprehension. He pitches upon some area of commonsense fact and tries [to see] if he cannot understand other areas in terms of this one. This original area becomes then his basic analogy or root metaphor. He describes as best he can the characteristics of this area, or if you will, discriminates its structure. A list of its structural characteristics becomes his basic concept of explanation and description. We call them a set of categories. In terms of these categories he proceeds to study all other areas of fact whether uncriticized or previously criticized. He undertakes to interpret all facts in terms of these categories. As a result of the impact of these facts upon his categories, he may qualify and readjust the categories, so that a set of categories commonly changes and develops.[7]

■ *Formism, Mechanism, Contextualism, and Organicism*

The four basic metaphors that Pepper identifies in Western thought are formism, mechanism, contextualism, and organicism. The root metaphor of formism is similarity, that of mechanism is the machine, that of contextualism is the changing

Still Life and Street, *by M. C. Escher. Escher's sketch can be interpreted as a visual metaphor. The actual street scene is conjoined with the world of imagination to be found in books.*

historical event, and that of organicism is integration or harmonious unity. Each root metaphor provides a different vision of the world. As this author has said elsewhere:

> To see the world formistically is to see the world in terms of similarity—the similarity of trees, the similarity of rectangles, the similarity of poems and of human types, the similarity of botanical specimen. It is to see the world in terms of identity and difference, as type and subtype, class and subclass. Mathematical, logical, and aesthetic forms lift off the face of the world as essential realities. There are two days, two fish, two persons, two songs—there are two . . . [see Figure 12.2]. To see the world mechanistically is to envision space, time, action and reaction, stimulus and response, to see quantities emerge, to ask the questions when, where, how much, how often; it is to see the world as a machine [see

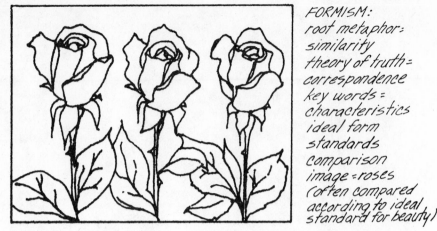

FORMISM:
root metaphor:
similarity
theory of truth=
correspondence
key words=
characteristics
ideal form
standards
comparison
image =roses
(often compared
according to ideal
standard for beauty)

Figure 12.2   The root metaphor of formism is similarity.

Figure 12.3]. To see the world contextually is to see it as a series of experiential moments, always coming to completion, only to begin again, opening into new textures, becoming new strands of experience. It is to see the world as a continual unfolding of experience, an encountering of new streams of experiencing and re-experiencing, of interpreting and reinterpreting [see Figure 12.4]. To see the world organically is to see it as integrated organism, as completed puzzle. It is to see that all the pieces in the puzzle must fit or else find a larger whole. All things are related, all things are integrated: poems are integrated, suns and moons are integrated, bodies are integrated, tapestries are finished and perfect. To see in this way is to see the whole in relation to its parts [see Figure 12.5].[8]

From these initial visions one proceeds to organize the world. One can apply the categories generated from each root metaphor to organize and comprehend any subject: astronomy, art, poetry, music, sculpture, and drama. Let's explore two broad instructional uses of root metaphor: the study of science and the study of literature.

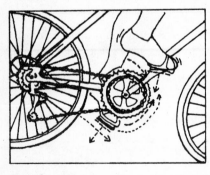

MECHANISM:
root metaphor=
machine
theory of truth=
casual-adjustment
key words=
cause
effect
stimulus
response
physical laws
sensations
space·time
association
image=bicycle gears or hammer
(with force of propulsion
depicted)

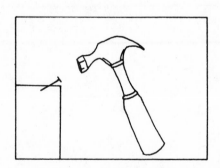

Figure 12.3   The root metaphor of mechanism is the machine.

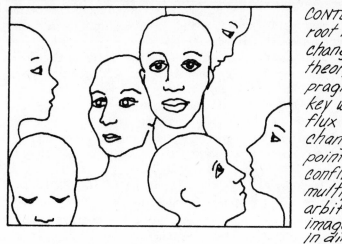

CONTEXTUALISM:
root metapor =
changing
theory of truth =
pragmatic
key words =
flux
change
point of view
conflict
multiple realities
arbitrary
image = focus looking
in different directions
(different points of view)

Figure 12.4   The root metaphor of contextualism is the experiential moment or point of view.

ORGANICISM:
root metaphor =
integration
theory of truth =
coherence
key words =
integration
nexus
unity
wholistic
complete
image = spider web
(with interconnected
continuous strands)

Figure 12.5   The root metaphor of organicism is integration of part and whole.

Root Metaphors in Science

In the literature of scientific investigations, root metaphors can be identified. These root metaphors shape the direction of scientific inquiry.

■ *Formism in Science (The World as Similarity)*

Lichtenberg, who discovered the shape dust took on a dielectric plate after it was charged, described the phenomenon in terms of correspondence between the configuration of the dust and other aspects of nature: "They are like small stars at certain points," he said. Intentionally, he sprinkled more dust on the plate and the stars became the "Milky Way and bigger suns." Again he said, they were like "crystals on a frozen window pane."[9]

The power of formistic metaphor is the discovery of similarity in seemingly dissimilar things. As Bronowski puts it: "The apple in the summer garden and the grave moon overhead . . . are surely as unlike in their movements as two things can be. [Yet] Newton traced in them two expressions of a single concept—gravitation."[10] Whitehead sees awareness of similarity as the basis of mathematical creation. "The first man," he says, "who noted the analogy between a group of seven fishes and a group of seven days made a notable advance in the history of thought."[11]

■ *Mechanism in Science (The World as Machine)*

Archimedes, in describing the principles of the lever, said, "Give me a place to stand, and I will move the earth," and Boyle, in exploring air pressure, thought that air under pressure must act like a number of coiled springs.[12] Boyle's contemporaries tried to counter him by arguing that if air had springs in it, one would feel them on one's skin. Here we see an instance of confusion arising from taking the metaphor too literally. Nevertheless, by adopting a mechanistic view of phenomena, both Archimedes and Boyle were able to explain many other related phenomena. The image of the universe as a machine was common to both.

■ *Contextualism in Science (The World as Historical Moment)*

The literature of scientific discovery is filled with contextual images—images of the scientist as a purposive agent—experimental, pragmatic, goal seeking. "Those sciences are vain," says Leonardo da Vinci, "which are not born of experience." "Invention," says Benjamin Thompson (Count Rumford), "seems to be peculiarly the province of the man of science . . . discovery his harvest, utility his reward."[13] The attitude of insistence that nature yield a harvest is perhaps best explained by Edison. What he said was, "There's a better way to do it . . . Find it." What he did was more astonishing. In pursuit of a breakthrough of the electric light bulb he accumulated 9,999 failures—each a potential breakthrough. Experiment 10,000 yielded the electric light.

■ *Organicism in Science (The World as Integrated Whole)*

A final metaphor, organicism, takes a highly visual form in the work of the German chemist Kekule, who not only postulated the theory of the carbon ring but also the concept of the double bond. Encouraged by his father to become an architect, Kekule instead applied his ability in spatial visualization to the three-dimensional structures of theoretical chemistry. He found the structure of benzene in 1866, and on the twenty-fifth anniversary of his discovery, he described the experience of his discovery, which originated in a dream:

> The atoms were gamboling before my eyes. I saw how frequently two smaller atoms united to form a pair, how a larger one embraced the smaller ones; how

still larger ones kept hold of three or four of the smaller, whilst the whole kept whirling in a giddy dance

And later:

> Again the atoms were gamboling before my eyes . . . My mental eye, rendered more acute by repeated vision of this kind, could now distinguish larger structures manifold conformation; long rows, sometimes more closely fitting together, all turning and twisting in snake-like motion. But look! What was that? One of the snakes had seized hold of his own tail, and the form whirled mockingly before my eyes.[14]

Kekule had immersed himself in a search for the structure of benzene. He knew the molecular formula of benzene was C_6H_6, but the valences didn't make sense in terms of a structural formula he could imagine. Carbon has a valence of 4, hydrogen a valence of 1. Any linear structure he could imagine would leave free radicals—an impossible situation given the chemical behavior of benzene. How, then, were the atoms integrated? How did they fit together?

The vision of the atoms linking together and turning into a serpent that bites its own tail gave Kekule a spatial metaphor that resulted in a powerful paradigm shift in the history of theoretical chemistry. Atoms did not have to be arranged in linear structure; they could be integrated as a ring structure. Hence the formula for benzene. From here it was only necessary to postulate alternating double and single bonds to satisfy the valence of carbon and hydrogen.

We have here a perfect organic metaphor suggesting integration of fragments. As we translate the spatial metaphor of the swirling serpents into intellectual terms, we are driven toward unity—all the parts of the structure must fit and there must be no unnecessary parts (see Figure 12.6). Everything is integrated. The coherence revealed in the dream is a kind of truth. Listen to Kekule: "Let us dream, gentlemen, and perhaps we shall know the truth." This was Kekule's recommendation to his

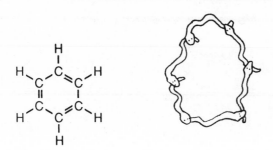

Figure 12.6 All parts of the structure must fit and there must be no unnecessary parts.

colleagues at the twenty-fifth anniversary of his discovery. Another way we can translate his statement is that we investigate nature through hypotheses, but what about the generation of hypotheses themselves? For Kekule, the dream was a bridge—a viable method of creation. Can we, then, take a cue from Kekule and teach students metaphoric creation through the dream?

PROBES

1. Identify the use of the root metaphors in descriptions of other scientific discoveries. Which metaphors tend to dominate these descriptions?
2. How many things can you say about a tree? Brainstorm this question. Write down everything you can think of, then go back and see if you can discover which root metaphors you were using all along.
3. Try the same exercise using a cake. How many things can you say about a cake? How many things can you do with a cake? In the process of exploring these probes you may discover many things about your own thinking, your own way of seeing the world.

One student, for example, created a poem as she worked with the cake exercise:

Creating

by Mary Banish

She's baking a cake.
Eggs and flour meet
in the bowl.
All of the ingredients
have been added.
She folds them in.
With a slow, sure movement,
she pours the mixture
into clean, white pans.
Confidently, she places them
into the oven, and waits
for a change.
Her eyes catch the spoon
and hold it
until the spoon becomes
a thick-petaled rose,
deep gold with a
deeper gold reverse,
just beginning to open.

The image freezes
at this stage,
and the room is filled
with a rich, heavy fragrance.
She feels it's time.
Carefully, she takes them
from the oven
and places them on the sill.
She lets them cool.
Beyond the sill,
a garden emerges—
a blend of colors
and textures.
When she knows
she has waited long enough,
she gently lifts the layers
from the pans
and joins them.
She will frost them now,
Smoothing over the cracks.
She stands back—
It is just a cake.

| *Root Metaphors in Literature* | In traditional Western literary criticism, root metaphors can be identified. These root metaphors shape the direction of critical inquiry. |

■ *Formism in Literature (The World as Similarity)*

In literature, formism shows up as classification. There are similar characteristics for each literary period—medieval, Renaissance, neoclassical, romantic. There are similarities of type character and definitive ways of classifying literary works by genre—the novel, the poem, the essay. Moreover, the structure of literature can be taught through the metaphor of similarity. For example, Herman Hesse's *Narcissus and Goldman* can be taught as an exploration of ideal types. Narcissus is representative of the Apollonian rational being, and Goldman, of the Dionysian, artistic being. Exploration of character in Lloyd Alexander's *Chronicles of Prydain* can serve as a rich background for a later study of the same generic types in Tolkien's stories and, on a more advanced level, for the study of character in Chaucer's and Mallory's works. In writing the *Chronicles of Prydain,* Lloyd Alexander says he dipped into the same vat for his characters as that used by Tolkien, Mallory, and Chaucer.

■ *Mechanism in Literature (The World as Machine)*

The vision of the universe as cause and effect, as stimulus and response can be suggested through images of a hammer striking a nail (Figure 12.3), a series of pendulum balls striking one another, or a simple seesaw.

Let's consider how stimulus and response can operate in a poem. As you read through John Tobias's "Reflections on a Gift of Watermelon Pickle," write down your exact experiences of the poem—any emotions, memories, thoughts, associations, notations of patterns, pleasurable and unpleasurable responses. Here is the poem:

During that summer
When unicorns were still possible;
When the purpose of knees
Was to be skinned;
When shiny horse chestnuts

(Hollowed out
Fitted with straws
Crammed with tobacco
Stolen from butts
In family ash trays)

Were puffed in green lizard silence
While straddling thick branches
Far above and away
From the suffering effects
of Civilization.

During that summer—
Which may never have been at all;
But which has become more real
Than the one that was—
Watermelons ruled.

Thick pink imperial slices
Melting frigidly on sun-parched tongues
Dribbling from chins;
Leaving the best part,
The black bullet seeds,
To be spit out in rapid fire
Against the wall
Against the wind
Against each other . . .[15]

Review what you have written down: the sensations, emotions, associations, and so forth. Now circle those specific lines of the poem that you think caused those sensations, emotions, and associations. When complete, you will have performed a mechanistic analysis of this poem. You will have hypothesized cause-and-effect (stimulus-and-response) relationships between the poem and your aesthetic response to it.

■ *Contextualism in Literature (The World as Historical Moment)*

Contextualism is suggested by the visual metaphor of multiple faces (see Figure 12.4), representing multiple viewpoints and change of perspective. There are other physical representations of change. For example, in Hawthorne's "Dr. Heidegger's Experiment," the doctor reverses the aging process to determine if and how one learns from experience.

In teaching this story contextualistically, Brian Kish, a suburban teacher, makes use of a number of props: a metronome, a burning candle, an hourglass, a diary, a boyhood baseball cap, a human skull, and a ball of string. As he unwinds the string he talks about his childhood and the process of growing older. Each prop is used as a physical analogy suggesting the passing of time. The students' personal reactions to the props are connected with parallel metaphors of change in the story (see Figure 12.7).

■ *Organicism in Literature (The World as Integrated Whole)*

Organicism is visually represented by the web. Other graphic representations are the jigsaw puzzle, the garden, the molecular model, and the universe as planetary relationships. On the human plane, the idea of personal relationships can be suggested through these images and others.

One teacher uses singing in rounds to embed the idea of human relationships. He shows up attired in cap, camp shirt, shorts, backpack, and whistle. He leisurely describes the joys of going camping as he simulates building a fire. (He actually does

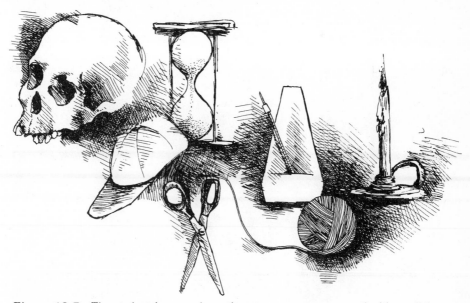

Figure 12.7 The students' personal reactions to props are connected with parallel metaphors in the story.

burn pine resin, creating the olfactory suggestion of being there.) Then he leads the class in singing rounds of camp songs. Relationships between various singing groups are underscored while he proceeds to comment on the good story he is reading. The story he is reading on the camping trip—yes, you guessed it—is *Bless the Beasts and Children*.

Before the mood of playing and surprise has subsided, the teacher swiftly draws out the analogy of the round (e.g., "Isn't it amazing how humans are able to integrate harmony, melody, rhythm and inflection at the drop of a hat?"). The teacher next moves the focus toward the center of the room by turning on a lantern or flashlight in the center of the room (where the other physical objects and pine cone embers have been located) while continuing to speak: "Humans are capable of doing that. Especially on an adventure, an expedition, a quest, a mission. Like Bilbo Baggins the Hobbit, or Odysseus on his voyage, or Huckleberry Finn and Jim (or other adventurers familiar to the students). And especially at night." Here the teacher shuts out the overhead lights, so the center of light moves to the lantern. The teacher then moves toward the tape recorders, one which has a tape of wave sounds, the other a tape of some acoustic guitar music, suggesting: "Especially in the moonlight, near the ocean, or near a lake or a river, or in the woods, in a forest, on a country road, (etc.) or maybe in a cabin."[16] [See Figure 12.8.]

Figure 12.8 Suggestopedic audio tapes provide alternative methods of delivery. See Chapter 13 for techniques of audio tape recording.

| *Teaching Root Metaphor Suggestopedically* | Root metaphor can be introduced to students through a delightful fantasy. Analysis of the concepts can be introduced *after* the students have imaginatively processed these metaphors. The following guided fantasy is best presented as a Reading w/Music™ (see Chapter 8), using either romantic or |

Baroque music. This type of music will enhance the fantasy.*

■ The Story of the Great Rock

Long, long ago there lived a tribe of people called the Old Ones. They lived in a remote village settled high in the mountains of a faraway land. It was said they could trace their ancestry back to the very beginning of civilized thought.

The Old Ones prided themselves on their knowledge of the world. They knew they were different from the nomadic tribes that roamed the valleys, and they knew they were always the same Old Ones—members of the same family of people.

The Old Ones believed that the way to know the world and the things in it was very simply to find out what a thing is. One did this by comparing things. Some things were similar, some dissimilar. They knew the animals and birds by their shape and form, and they classified animals, plants, and rocks. The world had order, and everything had its place. They knew good plants from poisonous ones by the design of their leaves, and they knew the stars by the patterns of light they made in the night sky. There was order in the world, and there was a right way of acting—a way which corresponded to the normal ways of the Old Ones.

The Old Ones did not travel very much. It is said they were the first to organize libraries and museums. Here they spent most of their time classifying knowledge.

One spring, however, they traveled west to a part of the mountain they had never seen. Here they discovered something they could hardly believe they were seeing. A gigantic rock of a different shape and texture from the mountain rock was embedded in the side of the mountain. "What is it?" they asked, and they began to compare it with things they already knew about. Its size was larger than their libraries and museums put together. Its surface was not like any material they had known, and its placement on the side of the mountain seemed strange to them. Rocks as they knew them did not have this pattern.

*For planning a reading of *The Story of the Great Rock* the following music selections are suggested:
1. The Old Ones: Albinoni (Giazotto) *Adagio in G Minor.*
2. The Hammerheads: J. S. Bach *Sinfonia* from *Cantata No. 29.*
3. The Surfers: Sibelius *Finlandia*
4. The Wise Webbed Ones: Pachelbel *Canon*

Many hundreds of years had passed when a new group of travelers discovered the Great Rock. They came down from the northern mountains, carrying with them instruments for measuring the world. They came to be known as the Nordic Conquerors, or more commonly as the Hammerheads. Out of the materials of the earth they fashioned instruments for measuring things. They measured the weight and shape of rocks and trees and the distances between things.

When the Hammerheads first saw the Great Rock, they asked: "What caused this? How did this happen?" They were an energetic tribe, and they set about discovering the cause of the Great Rock.

By day they worked long and hard. In the evening they built immense fires and stimulated themselves with lively conversation, good food and drink, and tales of valor—tales about their conquest of nature and of nomadic tribes.

Then from the South the Surfers came. They came on ships crafted for discovering new lands, new treasure, new adventures. They loved surfing over the waves and exploring the sheer novelty of unexplored territory, of seeing new landscapes, new reflections of sun and moon. They were eager to learn new languages, to experience unusual foods, to experiment with novel ways of dressing—even if occasionally it meant being uncomfortable.

The Surfers wanted to see the world through many eyes, to explore many directions and find practical outcomes. When they first discovered the Great Rock they exclaimed: "What can be done with this? What are the possibilities?" So they set about fashioning an entertainment center out of the area. They sculpted the land to make paths leading to the Great Rock even more interesting to the eye. Eventually they charged a fee for other groups (the Old Ones and the Hammerheads) to walk their sculpted paths. And for this fee these groups could find a prime spot to do what they thought important. The Old Ones continued to properly classify the Great Rock and the Hammerheads continued to explore the cause of the Great Rock—and to dance and sing long into the night.

After many years the Surfers were besieged by yet another tribe—a fourth tribe which came out of the East. The new group called themselves the Round Ones, but came to be known as the Wise-Webbed ones.

The Wise-Webbed ones thought that all things had to be connected like the connections in a Great Web—and complete like a circle. Everything was related—the plants and the earth, the moon and the tides, the azure sky and the eyes that beheld it.

To the Wise-Webbed ones the Great Rock was a natural part of the universe. It was silly to look for one cause of the Great Rock as the Hammerheads had done. There were many relationships that could be discovered. When you discovered those then you would have knowledge. You could then answer the question: How are things related? How are things integrated? This was like asking why are things the way they are. It was like gazing upon raindrops on flower petals and knowing that *everything* was appropriate if only one could apprehend all the connections.

The Wise-Webbed ones did not make very good customers for the Surfers. Though they were interested in the Great Rock, they were equally interested in all of nature, including the behavior of the Surfers, whom they constantly studied—along with their study of the Hammerheads and the Old Ones, and along with their study of color patterns of rainbows and the texture of linnet wings.

PROBE Which tribe do you like and why? How would each tribe approach a study of science, literature, art, commerce? What are the basic assumptions of each tribe? How would each group differ in their approach to morality and ethics? Cite evidence from the fantasy to support your views.

Rational Extension of Root Metaphors: World Hypotheses

Each root metaphor generates a set of categories that forms a hypothesis about how the world is constructed. Pepper calls these *world hypotheses.* They are unrestricted in scope—not tied to one field, such as physics or psychology—and they are rigorous—that is, they have explanatory power. Let us turn now to an example of that explanatory power: an application of the four root metaphors as a critical method. In the following section, Elizabeth Blaszczak, a suburban high school English teacher, shows how formism, mechanism, contextualism, and organicism can be applied to a study of John Knowles's *A Separate Peace.* The following section begins with a synopsis of *A Separate Peace* provided by *Masterplots.* [17]

LESSON PLAN
A Pluralistic Approach
Based on John Knowles's
A Separate Peace

The time is 1942, and the upperclassmen at Devon School have been taking extra physical training in order to prepare themselves for the draft into military service. One of their exercises, and one forbidden to the younger boys of the school, consists of climbing a tree beside a nearby river, inching one's way along a projecting branch, and then jumping into the water below. This thrill has been denied to boys of the lower forms because, if the jumper should fail to leap far enough out into the river, he would fall either on the bank or in shallow water and could possibly kill himself.

Not being one to be told that he cannot do something, Finny decides to jump from the tree, and he insists that Gene follow him. Gene, even more afraid of not following than of jumping, does so. This feat then becomes something of a ritual among their group.

One night, while Gene is trying to study, Finny coerces him into going to the tree and again making a jump. This leap is going to be even more daring than anything they have tried before because they will both jump at the same time. Finny is the first to crawl out on the limb. He then turns to wait for Gene, who purely on impulse, before he realizes what he is doing, gives a slight jar to the limb and causes Finny to fall and injure himself seriously.

Gene's act, it is plain, must be construed as a blind, impulsive attempt to get even. He had just realized, on the way to the tree, that much of what he had earlier decided about his relationship with Finny was false. He had thought that because he felt he was in competition with Finny, his roommate felt that way also. He had thought that Finny was constantly interrupting his studies to keep him from obtaining the top grades in the class, that Finny was supposedly going through the motions of being a true friend only to prove himself better in a different way. That night, while they were on their way to the tree, Gene realized that all he had believed was wrong. Finny had achieved his goals as an athlete without ever feeling that he must prove himself in any way, without ever suspecting Gene's jealousy and resentment. Finny himself was so well satisfied with the world that he unthinkingly assumed everyone else took the world for granted also, and he had never known that Gene needed to become the top man in his class in order to feel himself his friend's equal. Thus Gene, really in anger with himself, has caused Finny to fall.

In handling his theme, Mr. Knowles is careful to preserve something of the ambiguity of character and motive that makes life itself a battleground, for Gene's struggle is the ancient strife of the human spirit in its conflict with self. It is, as Gene discovers, a battle in which each man must be his own army; there are no allies. "My war ended before I ever put on a uniform," he says. "I was on active duty all my time at school. I killed my enemy there."

The accident is, of course, the end of the fine athlete, the end of his dreams of going to the Olympics, but not the end of a friendship. Gene tries several times to tell Finny what had really happened, but crippled Finny either will not listen or cannot understand. Refusing to acknowledge that Gene could have caused his fall, he subtly tries to make Gene take his place as a candidate for the Olympics. When he begins training his roommate, Gene gladly does whatever Finny says.

Gene's secret guilt and moral torment find release in a scene that relates his inner turmoil to the feverish background of the war for which the students of Devon School have been preparing themselves. Forced to accept the truth,

Finny suffers another accident and dies shortly afterward. Before his death, however, Gene makes him realize that the first accident had not really been an accident at all. Finny, knowing that his fall had been the result of a blind, impulsive act, bears no ill will. Being the true friend in the almost classic sense, he forgives all; it would have been impossible for him to believe that his friend could have planned and carried out such an attack on him.

Through his friend's death, Gene is able to come to terms with himself. Afterward he realizes that he was never in any danger of being overshadowed by his friend, and he is able to face up to the real situation: "I did not cry then or ever about Finny. I did not cry even when I stood watching him being lowered into his family's strait-laced burial ground outside of Boston. I could not escape a feeling that this was my own funeral, and you do not cry in that case." One part of him is now dead, his unconscious fear of himself and his own worth.

A Separate Peace is taut, unsentimental, unsparing in its account of the gap that every man must bridge between innocence and experience, youth and maturity.

This novel received the first award of the William Faulkner Foundation as the best first novel of 1960.

■ **A Suggestopedic Approach to *A Separate Peace*[18]**

Aims
1. An understanding of character motivation, specifically Gene.
2. Through this understanding a realization of theme.
3. To teach this (a) through experience with direct descriptive passages, the use of action, and dialogue; and (b) the employment of the world hypotheses used serially.
4. An understanding of the belief that one needs to have experienced a feeling to be able to truly grasp its meaning for another.

A Fantasy Script
1. Sit comfortably.
2. Close your eyes.
3. Take a good, deep breath.
4. Let your mind and body relax.
5. Let go of any tension.

Think about friendship. What do you look for in a friend? What do you think is *important* for a good *friendship?* Could you think of one characteristic that is more important to you than any others, possibly loyalty or sincerity? Is there one friend in particular that you now feel very close to or did in the past; a friend whom you've known for many years or one who has just recently become your friend; a friend whom you can trust or depend on. Picture that friend in your mind. Keeping that picture in front of you, answer as honestly as you can the following questions: How would you describe your friend? What adjectives would you use? Do you have a trusting relationship with this friend? Would you do almost anything for your friend if he were in trouble? Have you ever had a fight with this friend? Or maybe you made some *critical remarks* that hurt you both. Did your relationship suffer because of this? Afterward, were you ever able to feel the same about your friend? Have you ever felt that your friend was lying to you? Have you ever lied to your friend? Why? Was there an occasion when you felt jealous of your friend, possibly because of your friend's new house, car, good looks, money, or good grades? Did you ever wish you were more like your friend? Did you ever feel any rivalry with your friend? Did you ever compete with your friend? How did you feel about the competition? Were there any feelings that you tried to hide from your friend or even from yourself? Have you ever felt guilty because you thought or said something bad about your friend, possibly some gossip you should not have repeated? Did these feelings ever depress you? Did these feelings affect your relationship? How? If there was one thing you could do to improve your friendship, what would it be?

Allow the picture of your friend to fade. You are alone with your thoughts. Your mind begins to wander; you find yourself in a boy's room; allow yourself to enter the boy's mind. It is a *tormented mind.* You become one with the boy named Gene. (At the discretion of the teacher, passages from the novel, *A Separate Peace,* may now be read. This will build a strong connection between Gene's thinking in the novel and the fantasy. Suggested passages from *A Separate Peace* are found on pages 44, 45, and 46 of the 1979 Bantam edition.)

The room fades, and you find yourself standing on the high limb of a tree holding tightly to the trunk. Your mind reels with fear, but not because of the height. It is because your understanding of yourself is menaced. (At the teacher's discretion, another passage from *A Separate Peace* may be read at this point. A suggested passage is found on page 5 of the 1979 Bantam edition.)

You take a step toward your friend, then your knees bend, you jounce the limb. Finny (your friend) tumbles sideways and hits the bank below with a sickening, unnatural thud. You move out on the limb and jump into the river, every trace of your fear of this forgotten.

Breathe a sigh of relief. Allow all your images to fade. Gradually "return" to the classroom. Slowly open your eyes.

The students are now led through an examination of the novel based on the four world hypotheses. These approaches will be used serially, beginning with formism, mechanism, then contextualism, and finally organicism.

FORMISM

1. Compare the differences in character of Finny and Gene. List similarities and differences in their reactions to the first experience of jumping from the tree. Refer to differences in attitude toward war, friendship, and school.
2. Note the differences in how Gene, Finny, and Leper attempt to cope with reality (evil in world and man).
3. Read "Young Goodman Brown," by Nathaniel Hawthorne (a story about the inability of a man to recognize evil in the world); also read the poem "Out, Out," by Robert Frost (a poem about a boy who refuses to live with the reality of a lost hand). Compare the similarities and differences of themes with *A Separate Peace.*

MECHANISM

1. How did you feel when Gene jounced the limb?
2. Was your feeling intense? Of what duration?
3. Why did you feel that way?
4. What in the text (selections from that particular chapter) caused you to feel that way? Refer to specific passages.
5. Identify any appeals to the senses that had a recurring pattern. Were these pleasurable or not?
6. Write a passage of description (employing the five senses) that reveals your feelings at that time.

CONTEXTUALISM

1. How does your perception of Gene change as he is described in different contexts? Refer to the following chapters or scenes:

Chapter 1: The adolescent Gene describes the tree.

Chapter 2: Gene is saved from falling when Finny steadies him.

Chapter 3: As they fall asleep on the beach, Finny reveals that Gene is his "best pal," but Gene does not reply in kind, although he starts to do so.

Chapter 4: Gene decides that Finny has been purposely drawing him away from studies to keep him from being valedictorian.

Chapter 5: Gene tells Finny the cause of the accident, but Finny refuses to believe him.

Chapter 6: Gene reveals that he wants to "become a part of Phineas."

Chapter 8: Gene discovers Finny's need for him, and his attitude toward the war changes.

Chapter 12: Gene compares his action and the result to the many acts of hate and their more horrible results in the war.

Chapter 13: The adult Gene explains the change that Finny's death has caused in him.

2. Using your series of perceptions into Gene's character, answer the following questions:
   a. If Gene realizes that the jealousy, selfishness, and rivalry exist only in himself (Finny has revealed that he believed Gene excelled in class as effortlessly as he, Finny, excelled in sports), then *why* does he jounce the limb?
   b. Immediately after Finny falls, Gene jumps with "every trace of his fear of this forgotten." *Why* is his fear gone?
   c. The fall is the turning point in the novel because it introduces Gene to a new problem. *What* is it?
   d. ". . . there was always something deadly lurking in anything I wanted, anything I loved. And if it wasn't there, as for example with Phineas, then I put it there myself. ". . . it was this liberation we had torn from the grey encroachments of 1943, the escape we had concocted, this afternoon of momentary, illusory special and separate peace."
   Using the above quotes, answer the following questions:
   a. How does Leper escape from reality (the brutality of war)?
   b. Finny (who refused to accept the reality of evil) must finally confront it. What is his only escape?
   c. *Why* does only Gene survive?

3. How does your perception of Gene and Gene's perception of himself change due to different contexts of time? Refer to the following quotes:
   ". . . wars were not made by generations and their special stupidities, but that wars were made instead by something ignorant in the human heart."
   "Phineas alone had escaped this. He possessed an extra vigor, a heightened confidence in himself, a serene capacity for affection which saved him. Nothing . . . even about the war had broken his harmonious and natural unity. So at last I had."
   "Because my war ended before I ever put on a uniform; I was on active duty all my time in school; I killed my enemy there."

ORGANICISM

The interrelation of setting (not only places, but also times, societies, and individuals) with character, plot, and theme has combined to make *A Separate Peace* a unique experience. The result is a complete integration of feeling. In order to examine how each aspect reinforces and complements the other, and contributes to the final aesthetic experience, have students work with the following questions and activities:

1. How would you characterize Devon? In what kind of setting is it shown to exist? What changes has the war brought about in the school and its life? Is the nature of Devon important to the story?
2. What part does the war play in the story? How do the students feel about the war? Why?
3. If a war had not been going on, how might the story have been different? Does the war influence the action? The students' feelings? Their relations to each other?
4. Why does Gene spend so much time describing the places and people around him? Do his descriptions add to the book? How?
5. Gene sees a great change in Devon from the summer to the fall and winter. What seems to be the cause of this change? Do the seasons seem to affect the students' moods and feelings?
6. Read aloud the concluding passage of the book and discuss with the class the effect of the setting in causing the events of the story and the effect they and Finny had on Gene.
7. How much of Gene's idealized view of Finny was a result of the setting in which he knew him—that is, the war, the school, and so forth?

Critical Pluralism

The pluralistic approach outlined here has implications for curriculum building and methods of teaching. Pepper's four world views provide a basis for both individualizing and expanding learning experiences. Use of categories of formism and mechanism gives the student practice in applying quantitative evidence; use of the categories of contextualism and organicism gives the student practice in applying qualitative evidence. In *The Educational Imagination,* Elliot Eisner has argued that if we are to move beyond the present truncated curriculum of most high schools, we must teach students to use both quantitative and qualitative evidence, to approach art *and* science with rigorous tools of inquiry.[19]

In *Experiential Learning,* David Kolb has shown how Pepper's system can be used to support multiple learning styles (see Figure 12.9). To Kolb, these basic learning choices have implications not only for academic mastery but for career choices as well. Ideally, all students will gain facility in all learning styles, even though

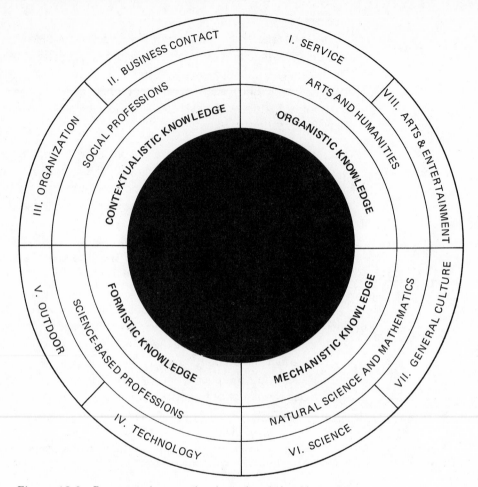

Figure 12.9 Root metaphors can be shown in relationship to careers.

one style will probably remain dominant for each individual. The chart at the end of the chapter provides a basis for planning lessons in the sciences and the humanities. By using this chart the teacher can build into her lessons key words and phrases derived from each world hypothesis. This approach to metaphoric teaching meets the needs of a variety of learning style preferences, provides optional ways of processing science and literature and allows one to explore relationships between disciplines. See, for example, the article in your bibliography by Arthur N. Geddis, "Teaching: A Study in Evidence," in which Geddis tells how to teach high school physics in terms of Pepper's four world hypotheses.[20] The same methods and the same modes of evidence that Geddis uses to teach physics can be used to teach high school literature, pointing to vital commonalities between science and literature. Metaphoric teaching is truly interdisciplinary.

Ernest Boyer, president of the Carnegie Foundation for the Advancement of Teaching, has said in his book *High School* that

> in addition to tightening requirements [for high school], we must bring a new interdisciplinary vision into the classroom and the total program of the school; . . . The content of the core curriculum must extend beyond the specialties to touch larger, more transcendent issues.
>
> Teachers must play a key role in making these connections between the disciplines. They must view the curriculum in a more coherent way . . . .[21]

Perhaps no disciplines are inherently incompatible. Compatibility may be a matter of locating useful metaphors to build bridges between disciplines.

■ *NOTES*

1. Carl Sagan, *Cosmos* (New York: Random House, 1980), 168.
2. Ibid.
3. Ibid.
4. William Gordon, *The Metaphorical Way of Learning and Knowing* (Cambridge, MA: Porpoise Books, 1973), 2.
5. Ibid., 2.
6. Mary Gerhart and Allan Russell, *Metaphoric Process: The Creation of Scientific and Religious Understanding* (Fort Worth, TX: Texas Christian University, 1984), 117–119.
7. Stephen C. Pepper, *World Hypotheses* (Berkeley: University of California Press, 1970), 91.
8. James Quina, "Root Metaphor and Interdisciplinary Curriculum: Designs for Teaching Literature in Secondary Schools," *The Journal of Mind and Behavior* *3*(4): 347–348 (Autumn 1982).
9. Gordon Peterson, "Paradigms, Puzzles and Root Metaphors: Georg Lichtenberg and the Exact Sciences," in *The Journal of Mind and Behavior 3*(3): 282 (Summer 1982).
10. Jacob Bronowski, *Science and Human Values* (New York: Harper & Row, 1965), 15.
11. Alfred North Whitehead, *Science and the Modern World* (Great Britain: William Collins Sons & Co. Ltd., 1975), 33.
12. Frank Seidel, *Pioneers of Science* (Boston: Houghton Mifflin, 1968), 13–14.
13. Ibid., 67.
14. Robert F. Gould, *Kekule Centennial* (Washington, DC: American Chemical Society, 1966), 10.
15. John Tobias, "Reflections on a Gift of Watermelon Pickle Received from a Friend Called Felicity." © 1961 by the University of New Mexico Press. Reprinted by permission of the author, 305 East 86th St., New York, NY 10028.
16. Jerome Dishman, *Music as a Tool in Teaching the High School Language Arts* (Master of Education Project, Wayne State University, June 3, 1987, directed by James Quina), 25. A copy of this project is on reserve in the Kresge Library,

Root Metaphor in Literature and Science

	Formism	Mechanism	Contextualism	Organicism
Root metaphor	Similarity	Machine	Changing historical event/ experiential moment	Integration (harmonious unity)
Images				
Theories of truth	Correspondence (absolute)	Causal adjustment (relativistic)	Instrumental/pragmatic (relativistic)	Coherence (absolute)
Key words	definition characteristics form plan classification ideal form participation norms standards normal comparison design pattern	cause effect stimulus response measurement quantity location physical laws sensations association space-time	quality purpose goal flux change point of view strands texture multiple realities conflict arbitrary presence (now) act event	relationship growth integration ideal cumulative truth nexus fragments unity wholistic organism appearance/reality complete

Root Metaphor in Literature and Science (*Continued*)

	Formism	Mechanism	Contextualism	Organicism
Literary manifestation	standards/norms genre character types literary period styles of writing	determinism in character motivation emotive and sensory response (cause and effect) in literary criticism	funded experience points of view conflict aesthetic quality purposive action	"reconciliation of opposite and discordant qualities" every image and concept supports every other image and concept
Standard of literary judgment	Conformity to a standard or norm (e.g., conformity to the requirements of an Elizabethan sonnet)	productive of the pleasures of sensory and emotive response; the pleasures of association	Rich in strands of experience; intense experience of quality	Appropriateness; fitting all parts to create a unified whole; organic unity
Scientific metaphors as root metaphors	Galen: "A physician needs to study anatomy as an architect needs to follow a plan." Newton: Noting the similarity between the falling of an apple and the orbiting of the moon suggested law of gravitation.	Archimedes: "Give me a place to stand and I will move the earth." Boyle: The rise of mercury in a column is caused by "the spring in the air."	Leonardo da Vinci: "Those sciences are vain . . . which are not born of experience." Thomas Edison: "There's a better way to do it . . . find it." Benjamin Thompson: Invention seems to be peculiarly the province of the many sciences . . . discovery his harvest; utility his reward.	Kekule:

Wayne State University, Detroit, Michigan 48202. Quoted by permission of the author.

17. Frank N. Magill, *Masterplots Annual* (New York: Salem Press, 1961), 226–227.

18. Elizabeth Joan Blaszczak, *Brain Research and Its Implications for Cognitive and Affective Learning in Literary Study* (Master of Education Essay, Teacher Education, Wayne State University, 1982, directed by James Quina), 35–41. A copy of this essay is on reserve in the Kresge Library, Wayne State University, Detroit, Michigan 48202. Quoted by permission of the author.

19. Elliot W. Eisner, "The Forms and Functions of Educational Connoisseurship and Educational Criticism," in *The Educational Imagination* (New York: Macmillan, 1979), 108–134, 190–226.

20. Arthur N. Geddis, "Teaching: A Study in Evidence," *The Journal of Mind and Behavior, 3*(4): 363–373 (Autumn 1982).

21. Ernest L. Boyer, *High School* (New York: Harper & Row, 1983), p. 115.

Homework as Multiple Skills Mastery

WRITTEN WITH KENNETH LONG

A family gathering can promote joy, relaxation, and a sense of belonging—
all foundational for learning.

The things you practice in private, you will be rewarded for in public.

—Anthony Robbins

Chance favors the prepared mind.

—Louis Pasteur

The Status of Homework

If students would be really honest with us about what they dislike most about being educated, I think homework would be at the top of the list. Yet educators know that homework is an important adjunct to the classroom experience. Homework can finish the task of gaining control over new information and concepts. It can anticipate classroom instruction and therefore promote more active participation and learning. In the long run it allows for the development of independent learning and the personal qualities that go with it—self-discipline, commitment, personal initiative. And the farther a student goes, the more important homework becomes. It is still a rule of thumb in college that two to three hours of private study should be spent for each hour of classroom study.

The importance of homework has not escaped debate in the current controversy over accountability in education. Many popular claims are made in this regard: American students are not doing enough. Oriental students do much more and that's why they do better on standardized tests. Whether these claims are true or not is beside the point. If the accountability challenge to education, vis-à-vis homework, is not to produce a mere face-saving, shallow response where more is erroneously associated with better, then teachers need to view homework with as much understanding and creativity as they do other aspects of teaching. Too often the nature of homework assignments richly deserves the negative response it receives from students. In these cases, homework is time-consuming busywork with little apparent relevance. It can cause a variety of negative feelings that generally impede real learning.

Consider the case of Ken, a timid first-year secondary student. At the end of a lesson in French grammar, the teacher assigned *two* exercises of 10 sentences each. The purpose of the dual exercises was to drive home the classroom instruction. Fair enough! But why two exercises when one would be plenty? Obviously displeasure showed on Ken's face because he was immediately challenged by the teacher.

"What's the matter with you, Ken?"

Shocked, and more than a bit intimidated, he stammered back, "I don't like having to do so much homework."

"You have to do the same as everyone else," came the reply.

"Yes, but I don't have to like it!"

With those uncharacteristically courageous words out of his mouth as if they had a life of their own, he cringed in anticipation of what was to come next. Surely he had gone too far. Thankfully, the only rejoinder was a quiet, "Sit down and do your work."

That night he dutifully did all 20 sentences, when 4 or 5 would have sufficed. He resented the infringement on time. He became bored long before finishing, and he learned to dislike the study of French a little more.

In a recent episode of the TV sitcom *Growing Pains,* Father Jason, a psychologist, is extremely concerned about son Mike's poor grades and lax attitude toward school. Mike is a senior and qualification for college is just around the corner. In an argument—so typical of parents and teens—Jason says in exasperation, "When is the last time you spent more than 14 minutes on your homework?" Mike's know-it-all reply is, "Dad, it's not how much time you put in, it's the quality of time."

Both father and son are right. As students progress through the education system, increasing amounts of time will have to be spent on homework. If it is not to be boring and counterproductive, then teachers need to initiate change. And they will benefit, too. The vast amounts of time teachers spend collecting, grading, and reprimanding for work not completed, and the disappointment they have about low-quality student work, can be alleviated. So, what needs to be done to ensure that homework time will have quality—so that students will know that they are learning and simultaneously develop skills that put them in control? Virtually every homework assignment is an opportunity to accomplish some of the above.

Purposes of Homework

The general purpose of all homework is to aid in the mastery of new learning. This involves the basic skills of reading and listening and note making and study for understanding and remembering.

Let's begin this section by talking about something that nearly everybody is good at—forgetting. Nearly all of us have been dismayed at having to study material over and over again, at having to reread chapters that seemed almost like new, and at laboring over notes that were only a month old. Forgetting plagues us all and is probably the source of the axiom "Goes in one ear and out the other." An experiment involving groups of students who were tested at various periods of time after listening to a lecture showed that forgetting mostly takes place almost immediately after listening (more than half in the first 24 hours) and then tapers off.[1] It follows logically that improvement in independent learning must bring the phenomenon of forgetting under control, both with respect to classroom material and homework. If this doesn't happen a student can begin to feel overwhelmed by the sheer bulk of material. Preventing this begins with clear communication. The importance of establishing and communicating clear objectives in the classroom was stated in Chapters 3 through 7. This should be doubly true of homework. Students need to know what (content), why (motivation), and how (method) when it comes time for homework.

■ *Teaching Note Making*

How does this apply to notes—the bulk of material that will be used for later study in preparation for tests and exams. Students should be taught a system of note making that has the ultimate purpose clearly in mind from the very beginning. One of the best systems is based on what F. P. Robinson calls the SQR[3] system—survey, question, read, recite, and review. Applied to notes, this system employs the following strategy. Each page of notes initially features a blank column on the left, approximately $2\frac{1}{2}$ inches wide, called the recall column. When a student finishes note making, the recall column should be filled in. Why and with what?

The recall column is a device to aid concentration and memory. It should be sparse, containing only key words or phrases that represent larger units of information. To do this it is necessary for the student to review the notes by skillful questioning. Students should be taught to use a question like, "What does my teacher want me to know from this?" The answer is drawn from the notes and represented in the recall column by a key word or phrase. Questions enable a student to stay engaged. They build a quest, a yearning for completion; they provide a focus. So, assist your students in creating questions and in filling out recall columns.

With very little practice, students will quickly master this technique. Then, in order to complete the process and effectively combat forgetting before it takes place, teach your students to use the recall column to recite their new understanding.

Why is this process so powerful? First, the student encounters material in three different ways: by making notes from reading, by listening and discussing, and by reviewing with a purpose—as well as by saying aloud. The whole person—mind and body—is involved, with the system acting as a device to ensure behavior that promotes learning memory and functional recall.

Strictly speaking, we never really forget anything—we just do not form workable mental models for organizing information. Johnson-Lairds' research on memory shows that we create two kinds of schemata: one similar to mind pictures, the other similar to a script that directs procedures.[2] These schemata overlap in millions of ways. We are constantly reconstructing schemata, embellishing them, deleting items, and adding others. Recall, then, is a creative problem, not merely a way of retrieving memory traces. Questions used in conjunction with concepts and facts assist us in producing organized and purposeful schemata and hence quality memories. Using this technique, study and remembering come much more easily.

■ *The Use of Symbols*

The act of note making itself, whether in class or from books or essays, can be made less taxing by the use of symbols.

Symbols from logic are useful to note relations between statements (propositions):

⊃	if . . . then
v	either/or
.	and
∽	not

Some symbols used in mathematics are useful:

>	greater than
<	less than

=	equals, is the same as
≠	not equal
∴	therefore

In addition, a few symbols from proofreading are useful:

℘	omit, delete
e.g.	for example
cf	compare
n.b.	note well, this is important[3]

These symbols can aid the student in taking classroom notes and in communicating with himself while working on assignments. You may also want to teach the following rules of thumb or experiment with some adaptations of the following:

1. Don't try to write down everything.
2. Focus on key points—listen for emphasized words, changes of pace in the teacher's voice. They are key points to jot down.
3. Use a mind map to take notes. Unlike an outline, you can keep adding beginning and middle information. An outline closes this possibility.
4. Associate doodles and pictures to the words.
5. Ask yourself questions about the material as you are making notes. Add questions to your mind map.
6. Use abbreviations along with the symbols above to speed up your note taking.
7. Keep your notes in a binder that is sectionalized for each subject.
8. Take your notes in only one section of the binder, the section designated for notes. Keep plenty of clean paper in this section.
9. A word of warning about dictionary use: interpret the use of the word in context before looking it up. The kinds of information given in dictionaries may vary depending on their purposes. Choose the one appropriate for your purpose.

■ *Reading Assignments*

The note-making system readily adapts to reading. Many students have unnecessary difficulty with reading assignments. Because of these difficulties students learn to dislike (even fear) reading. They feel defeated. Consider what happens when a student sets out to read a chapter in a text. More than likely it has been assigned with a vague directive, such as "Read the next chapter and be prepared to discuss it on Monday." The student plans to start reading at 7:00, but when 7:00 arrives he or she visits the bathroom (5 minutes), makes a quick call to a friend (5 minutes), gets an apple (2 minutes), and then sits down to work, but only after clearing the desk, sharpening pencils, and arranging some notes. Sound familiar? Delay avoidance plagues us all and is at its worst when we are faced with tasks that are distasteful as well as demanding. Even when reading begins, another problem with attention span arises. The student reads with eyes only; the mind has gone somewhere else. Many educators have commented on the impact of TV on reading ability and the short attention span so characteristic of today's student. So, how can you help to solve the problem of delay avoidance and attention span?

The system is divided into two stages. In the first stage, students are taught to plan to read. This begins with clear focused directives. What kind of discussion will be called for? What points will be emphasized? Is everything in the chapter of equal value? Armed with these questions, the student can create better advance organizers by quickly surveying the chapter looking for headings, key words, and important sentences. Students do not need to understand fully the meaning of advance organizers. Understanding comes later. The purpose of your clear directives and the survey is to warm up the mind and to create a map for the reading process itself.

Sizing the reading assignment is a technique based on the length of a student's attention span—how many pages can be read before the mind wanders. For example, a 20-page assignment might be divided into four 5-page reading segments, each to be done in 10 minutes, consecutively. Forty minutes is a long time to read attentively, but 10 minutes, four times, is very possible. For each, questions and advance organizers are established and then the second stage begins.

The second stage is the actual reading followed by recitation, similar to the strategy for listening and note taking. The active reader must have a pencil in hand and be prepared to underline, circle, draw arrows, and/or write brief notes in the margin as material is understood. The purpose is to identify and condense important material, which the reader cannot do unless he or she is concentrating. Once an appropriate-sized portion of text has been worked over in this fashion, the reader uses the markings to cue a brief recitation of what he or she has understood. The procedure can be repeated until the entire 20 pages have been read.

No student has ever read all of a textbook in one sitting because it was so interesting that it couldn't be put down. Even teachers don't do well for long periods of time. So it is not surprising that students need a powerful but simple strategy to help with this demanding but essential academic task. Just like note making, reading must produce a study aid that facilitates understanding, increases attention span, and facilitates later study.

Many creative versions of this system can be devised. Have students make a word mind map on the table of contents; then, working in groups, have them share their word mind maps with one another and create, as a group, a picture mind map. They create symbols and pictures for each word or group of words on the original mind maps. In the next stage, the students create a human sculpture representing their ideas and feelings expressed in the mind maps. Finally, as a group, they generate questions about the section of the text they have worked on.[4]

In the above process, the students have entered into a participation with one another and with the text on visual, auditory, and kinesthetic levels. The questions they generate will spring from an intense engagement with the material. And in the process, the teacher has taught them a reading skill that they can apply at home. If they can solicit the aid of friends, brothers and sisters, and parents to participate in the human sculptures they create, the support at home will intensify. And if they don't feel comfortable soliciting the aid of others, they can use imaginary partners in the manner of mime. At maximum, they can visualize themselves as human sculpture. The very act of transforming themselves into human sculptures will trigger some kinesthetic connections.

An embellishment of this technique is to tell about the material to be learned in the form of a delightful story. The Mad Hatter can explain debits and credits to Alice. Peter Pan can write out quadratic equations with a magic wand. Peter Rabbit can discover a new chemical symbol hanging from every tree in the garden.

Studying for Tests and Exams

Purposeful, systematic note making and active participation in class and out, featuring lots of recitation, leads to an ideal situation for test or exam preparation. But too few students accomplish this. Sabotaged by vague instruction and weak systemless study skills, they face a huge amorphous pile of material at test or exam time. Clean text pages all look alike. They will have to be reread and perhaps some notes will have to be made. This will take a lot of time. Notes, some more than a month old, appear strange—pages and pages of writing, one no different from the other. They, too, will have to be reread. Where will the time come from? Worse, understanding is not enough because everything has to be remembered, too. So these unfortunate students resort to reading short sections, and then turn away, close their eyes, and ask their minds to silently restate the material. For a while this works. But quickly the mind grows tired with this demand, and the students never can tell for sure if they will remember or not. Making it all worse is the ticking clock; time is running out, and feelings of desperation and panic take over. Homework is never so hateful as at this time. Certainly there students are not going to do their best.

But how much better can the students do because of your skillful direction supporting the development and use of learning skills? All notes have recall columns or mind maps; the same for readings. All have been recited or role played or actively discussed. Now, their study devices facilitate new recitation as understanding is sharpened for the exam. Each time the cues fail to trigger recitation the notes proper can be consulted until recitation comes easily. When students can recite, they know the material and they know they know it! So there is little reason for anxiety. An alternative but equally powerful system has students formulating their own exam questions. As we have said earlier, the ability to compose a question depends on high concentration and understanding.

Ideally, these methods of exam preparation are used on a daily basis. They give students practice in doing what they are asked to do on tests. The words in test questions stimulate responses similar to recitation. So the exam situation is really nothing new. Moreover, the essentials of this system can be adapted to meet the requirements of different kinds of exams.

Whether multiple-choice, short-answer, matching, or essay questions, the teacher must be aware that each type invites different kinds of study. For example, essay exams ask for organized bodies of thought focused on dominant themes. Sophisticated multiple-choice tests can test for comprehension, but also focus on recognition of specific facts and concepts. Students will be helped immeasurably if they can practice for the type of exam that you intend to give. Perhaps you could let them use old exams for this purpose, but in any case they should be shown how to adapt their study style to the style of the exam.

■ *The Essay Exam and the Mind Map*

A mind map functions like a giant recall column to cue a recitation on a particular topic—one that a student has decided is important enough possibly to be on an exam. The mind map represents detailed understanding of a logically related body of material. For example, a student may reduce 10 pages of notes to a single mind map. The mind map is then used to practice recitation. The student who accepts the task of producing a mind map ensures active, rather than lazy, involvement with material. And mind maps are particularly useful for review in the last hours and minutes before an exam, when anxiety is highest. It is impossible to work with books or notes at this time, but a good mind map facilitates quick, reassuring review.

Essay exams consistently feature certain key words. Students need help to know the precise (functional) meaning of those words and to see answers that have handled them effectively. Here is a list of frequently appearing exam terms described by Bird and Bird:[5]

Compare. When you are asked to compare, you should examine qualities, or characteristics, in order to discover resemblances. The term *compare* is usually stated as *compare with,* and it implies that you are to emphasize similarities, although differences may be mentioned.

Contrast. When you are instructed to contrast, dissimilarities, differences, or unlikeness of associated things, qualities, events, or problems should be stressed.

Criticize. In a criticism you should express your judgment with respect to the correctness or merit of the factors under consideration. You are expected to give the results of your own analysis and to discuss the limitations and good points or contributions of the plan or work in question.

Define. Definitions call for concise, clear, authoritative meanings. In such statements details are not required but boundaries or limitations of the definition should be briefly cited. You must keep in mind the class to which a thing belongs and whatever differentiates the particular object from all others in the class.

Describe. In a descriptive answer you should recount, characterize, sketch, or relate in narrative form.

Diagram. For a question which specifies a diagram you should present a drawing, chart, plan, or graphic representation in your answer. Generally the student is also expected to label the diagram and in some cases to add a brief explanation or description.

Discuss. The term *discuss,* which appears often in essay questions, directs you to examine, analyze carefully, and present considerations pro and con regarding the problems or items involved. This type of question calls for a complete and detailed answer.

Enumerate. The word *enumerate* specifies a list or outline form of reply. In such questions you should recount, one by one, in concise form, the points required.

Evaluate. In an evaluation question you are expected to present a careful appraisal of the problem, stressing both advantages and limitations. Evaluation implies authoritative and, to a lesser degree, personal appraisal of both contributions and limitations.

Explain. In explanatory answers it is imperative that you clarify, elucidate, and interpret the material you present. In such an answer it is best to state the "how" or "why," reconcile any differences in opinion or experimental results, and, where possible, state causes. The aim is to make plain the conditions which give rise to whatever you are examining.

Illustrate. A question which asks you to illustrate usually requires you to explain or clarify your answer to the problem by presenting a figure, picture, diagram, or concrete example.

Interpret. An interpretation question is similar to one requiring explanation. You are expected to translate, exemplify, solve, or comment upon the subject and usually to give your judgment or reaction to the problem.

Justify. When you are instructed to justify your answer you must prove or show grounds for decisions. In such an answer, evidence should be presented in convincing form.

List. Listing is similar to enumeration. You are expected in such questions to present an itemized series or a tabulation. Such answers should always be given in concise form.

Outline. An outlined answer is organized description. You should give main points and essential supplementary materials, omitting minor details, and present the information in a systematic arrangement or classification.

Prove. A question which requires proof is one which demands confirmation or verification. In such discussions you should establish something with certainty by evaluating and citing experimental evidence or by logical reasoning.

Relate. In a question which asks you to show the relationship or to relate, your answer should emphasize connections and associations in descriptive form.

Review. A review specifies a critical examination. You should analyze and comment briefly in organized sequence upon the major points of the problem.

State. In questions which direct you to specify, give, state, or present you are called upon to express the high points in brief, clear narrative form. Details, and usually illustrations or examples, may be omitted.

Summarize. When you are asked to summarize or present a summarization, you should give in condensed form the main points or facts. All details, illustrations, and elaboration are to be omitted.

Trace. When a question asks you to trace a course of events, you are to give a description of progress, historical sequence, or development from the point of origin. Such narratives may call for probing or for deductions.

■ *Essay Exam Strategy*

The strategies recommended here for building the skills of independent learning into your teaching are not about memorization. Too often memorization reflects only shallow understanding. The principles applied here require repeated attentive involvement leading to real understanding and the ability to demonstrate that new understanding. How else could students make and use recall columns or mind maps? But much can be lost if, in the last hour, students are not coached on how to adapt the system to meet the demands of different kinds of exams. Here is another suggestion to help you to help your students to avoid some common errors in exam strategy.

Most essay exams offer some choice and frequently not all questions are worth the same points. Students need to know such details in order to be able to develop a game plan. If they can't, good students who know some material very well may spend 30 minutes writing a brilliant answer to a 10-point question. Too much time for only one-tenth of the grade. Then, with time running out, they have too few minutes to spend on a really important question. They therefore earn a C when you know they are capable of better. So give them the information that they need to know.

■ *The Multiple-Choice Strategy*

A multiple-choice exam invites a different approach to study, but one still based on purposeful note making and daily active learning. A multiple-choice exam can literally touch on everything covered in a course of study. In fact, one of the best things about a multiple-choice exam is that it provides a final review of nearly everything. This is a key difference from the essay exam, which in turn invites a purposeful change in study strategy. It follows that the study system should be designed to support recognition of what is correct from what is not so correct—an exercise in careful reading where certain words cue the right response. You have coached your students to do this all along in making good notes, recall columns, and mind maps. Now, coach them to adapt to the demands of the multiple-choice exam by quick reading reviews of all required material several times rather than focused intense study applicable to the essay exam. Use the right independent study technique for the right challenge.

Of course, for both essay and multiple-choice exams there are additional strategies that should be applied during the exam itself. You can read about them in any of the recommended texts listed in the references at the end of this chapter. They, too, will contribute to your students' skills, enabling them to do as well as they can on tests and exams.

With basic skills in place, homework can become an experience that develops and reinforces a sense of power and control over the challenges of academic life. In this environment students can be encouraged to further personalize and empower their ability to learn.

■ *Music and Self-Study: A High-Tech Skill*

How long have we lived with the assumption that there must be absolute quiet for maximum learning to occur? And yet we know people who require some background music to be their most productive.

Classical, baroque, and romantic music can open up multiple channels of information processing and access long-term memory. The student can be taught to use technology as a standard procedure in doing homework. There are at least three ways the student can use the music. He can listen directly to music as background while he reads or recalls information. This, however, is the least efficient way of using the music. He can audiotape material to be memorized. These tapes can be made during parts of class time with the supervision of the instructor.

The equipment needed is a dual cassette tape recorder with a mixer. A separate tape is made of the material to be learned. Then the volume is turned down so the words are barely audible. This material is fed to a tape on the dual cassette system. At the same time, baroque or classical music is fed into the new tape. The volume of the music is turned up so that the voice is drowned out. And *voilà*! You now have a subliminal tape. There can be no rational fear of being brainwashed with this kind of subliminal tape. The student knows what is on the tape since he made the tape. The sounds of words are still on the tape and will be experienced on a level beneath the threshold of awareness. The music will open up long-term memory so that, later, when the student goes over the words, he will have great familiarity with them and learning will come easy. The rationale for using a subliminal tape is to circumvent the problem of resistance. If one resists, his or her energy is dissipated and learning is blocked. But if one can't consciously hear the words, then he or she can't resist—and the words are experienced at an altogether deeper level.

A third method consists of making a tape in which you hear the words. The material is read into a mixer along with baroque music. The music is slightly lower than the voice. *The words, phrases and sentences are read to conform to the music, not the meaning of the words.* This is the basis of what Lozanov calls a concert reading. It is as though the content, ordinarily thought of as neutral knowledge, is now being dramatized—presented as a concert.

The Homework Plan and Parents

In Chapters 3 through 7, we said that to communicate instructional intent fully, the purpose and specific objectives are stated. This is no less true of homework. The teacher, as we have seen, needs a curriculum plan, daily lesson plans, a disciplinary plan, and—yes—a homework plan. This plan is a general policy statement spelling out for parents and students the kinds of purposes for which you will assign homework. Following is a sample homework policy sent to the parent. It could be regarded as a "contract" between student, parent, and teacher.

Dear Parent(s):

I will be your (son's/daughter's) *English* teacher this year. In order to ensure your son/daughter and all the students in my classroom the educational opportunities they deserve, I will assign homework designed to promote growth in the following areas:

1. Assignments to stimulate students to think.
2. Assignments that will help them apply the knowledge they have.

3. Assignments that will provide for drill and practice with meaning.
4. Assignments that will call for thoughtful observation and searching out of knowledge.

All assignments will be based on one or more of the above purposes. The student will be given printed directions for the assignments and a statement of purpose for each assignment. The purpose of using printed homework directions is two-fold—to clearly communicate to the student what is expected *and* to clearly communicate to you, the parent, what is expected of your (daughter/son). I request that you and I work together to provide your daughter/son with the very best of educational opportunities and that you support your child in completing all assignments. If at any time you have any questions about the purpose or the direction of the assignment, I would very much appreciate your calling me (telephone number). In order for this plan to have its greatest effect, I need your cooperation. I have already reviewed this plan with your (son/daughter) and I would appreciate your discussing this letter with your (son/daughter), signing the form below before returning it to me.

I have read the homework plan outlined above and have discussed it with my (son/daughter).

_____   _____
                     Signature   Date

The above procedure will eliminate many of the questions about the purposes and directions for assignments. It also invites the parent and student to work with you in partnership. The parent is provided a set of expectations so that when the student brings home printouts of homework directions and stated purposes, a procedure is already established for working with and supporting the student. The parent is encouraged to discuss homework with the student, particularly the purpose of the homework. By becoming involved at the purpose level, the parent can act as a support person for the student, continually bringing the student back to the purpose when the going gets tough. Information, ideas, and strategies can flow back and forth between parent and student and teacher (see Figure 13.1).

■ *Grading Homework*

Some parents and students want the homework graded, but Langdon and Stout in *Homework* argue convincingly that homework is practice. The grade will come with class performance and examination. In this respect, homework is preparation for examination. This does not mean the teacher should not provide feedback to the student. The use of a plus sign can mean complete. A minus sign can mean a few details should be noted, and a double minus sign can mean that the assignment must be done over and done properly. Of course, it is not necessary to use these symbols. The teacher can provide specific comments whether or not symbols are used. Sample comments are: "Read this paragraph aloud to another person exactly the way you have written it. What changes would you make? What does the word mean to you?

Figure 13.1 Information, ideas, and strategies can flow back and forth between parent, student, and teacher.

Can you think of another to use in its place? Can you think of some more examples of 'comic relief'?" This kind of commentary will get far more reaction than vague tags like "Good," "Excellent," and "Needs more specifics." Such comments do not provide feedback to the student. Think through what will obtain maximum results. Put yourself into the role of the student. What do you need to hear to create change?

■ *Providing Speedy Feedback*

Use your time-management skills. Either return homework with comments or provide feedback in some other form. Not to act on the homework submitted communicates that you don't care. When teachers do not respect the homework, students stop respecting it also. How much damage is done to the instructional process when a student returns to school to get a belonging and finds all the homework papers, his included, in the wastebasket? Students sometimes test the teacher's reading of the homework by inserting something off the beaten path—a joke, an upside-down insert, a direct question to the teacher. Once it is discovered that the teacher is not reading the homework, the integrity of the class goes flat. Teacher and student enter into a covert pact to simulate the appearance of learning. A deadly ritual is the outcome.

■ *Memory Systems*

Retention can be measured through the use of multiple channels for the processing of information. The student can be taught in class how to process visually, auditorily, and kinesthetically. Periodically, the teacher can review how these techniques are working for the student at home.

Memorization is often discussed by educators as worthless, but there are ways of facilitating purposeful memorization. Listen to these directions:

> It is wise first to go through the whole section to get the feeling of it. Then go through to pull out the main ideas and get a mental picture of them in their consecutive order. Then notice the unusual, colorful, descriptive words associated with those ideas, and read it over as a whole, thinking about the ideas. Read again, and yet again, then look away from the written or printed lines, and think the first idea, then next, and so on.[6]

The focus here is on recalling ideas, the particular expression of the ideas being used to create context. But what is the purpose? As a teacher you can tell the students the purpose of memorizing as you see it: "You don't want to have to look up the formula for circumference every time you use it. Memorizing frequently used facts will save you time." The procedure of the assignment and the purpose are always given. The procedure provides clarity; the purpose provides meaning. Both are necessary for maximum effectiveness of the assignment.

The Memory Book by Harry Lorayne and Jerry Lucas contains many memory systems that can be adapted for instructional use. Gifted students often create their own learning strategies, including memory systems, but most students can profit from learning that such systems are available and that they can be empowered by them.

■ *A Home Work Space*

In many homes, space is very limited. The kitchen table may have to be cleared immediately after a meal so that several siblings can do homework. In other homes a private room with modern office equipment may be provided. It is useful for the teacher to try to visualize the students' work space and home conditions and to gear assignments to what can be realistically expected in the students' environment. Options for homework arrangements can be explored with student and parents. It may be possible for the student to make arrangements to study in a public library; ideal spots to study in the home may be assigned by the parent on a rotating basis. If noise is deafening in the home, the student may be able to use headphones in order to listen to music and read at the same time. It may be possible to teach the student concentration techniques that enable him to screen out distractions. Students may also wish to get together in groups to trade ideas and strategies. And, of course, the teacher's assignments will be shaped in part by these conditions. Later, coaching can be given in class, to provide the student with progressive skill in using a variety of study strategies.

Internalization of Broad Purpose	From time to time the teacher can make the broad purposes of homework explicit to the student. Brainstorming sessions are useful in getting students to realize how many subsidiary skills and values are being learned as they do homework. These insights best come from the student—as a discovery.

Some reported values may be patience, perseverance, concentration, and preparation for the world of work; indeed, they are doing *their* work just as the carpenter and architect continue to think about and plan their work for the next day. Some others may be observation, discovery, thinking skills, ability to follow directions, and ability to apply their knowledge to their environment.

Homework as Expansion of Creativity

Many students and some teachers hold to a mistaken notion of creativity—the idea that some people have it and others do not. Creativity, they think, is a magical thing that visits a person at odd times. It causes people to write songs or invent new cures for disease. To counter their resigned thinking, you can teach the student the stages of the creative process: (1) preparation, (2) incubation, (3) illumination, and (4) verification. You can take the students through an imaginary trip of discoveries made by creative geniuses and show how these stages came into operation. What often surprises students is the amount of preparation essential to creativity. They begin to see that even the genius hits a wall during most of his pursuits, and that recreation and play have a powerful function *if placed in the proper sequence.*

As we have said earlier, homework requires, but seldom receives, the same kind of planning and creativity that goes into other aspects of teaching. We wish to encourage and enable you to use homework to help students become powerful independent learners. They will benefit both academically and personally.

PROBES Design a homework plan to show students the importance of interpreting words in context. Example: Have students look up the word *run* in a standard dictionary. Then play devil's advocate by asking them how they can know the "real" meaning of the word. From a linguistic standpoint, there is no real meaning—meaning is determined by context. Can you think of another strategy for getting students to look at context?

Design a lesson to teach students how to proofread their papers before turning them in.

■ *SUMMARY*

This chapter explores techniques of making homework purposeful and effective. The SQR³ system (survey, question, read, recite, and review) is reviewed and applied for increasing retention and comprehension. The use of symbols borrowed from logic, mathematics, and proofreading are recommended as organizational devices for note making. The use of questions, mind maps, and recitation are explored as ways of preparing for examinations. Students can be coached in memory techniques and creativity strategies. Parent support for homework can be increased through systematic communication with parents.

■ *NOTES*

1. Walter Pauk, *How to Study in College* (Boston: Houghton Mifflin, 1974), pp. 34–36.
2. P. W. Johnson-Laird, *Mental Models: Toward a Cognitive Science of Language, Inference and Consciousness* (Cambridge, MA: Harvard University Press, 1983), 146–243.
3. Harry Maddox, *How to Study: Improve Your Reading, Thinking, Memorizing, Note-Taking* (Greenwich, CN: Fawcett, 1963), p. 104.
4. Peter Kline, Seminar on Photo Reading, Wayne State University, May 21, 1987.
5. C. Bird and D. M. Bird, *Learning More by Effective Study* (New York: Appleton-Century-Crofts, 1945), 195–198.
6. Langdon Grace and Irving Stout, *Homework* (New York: John Day, 1969), 87.

CHAPTER 14

Instructional Testing and Evaluation

DONALD MARCOTTE

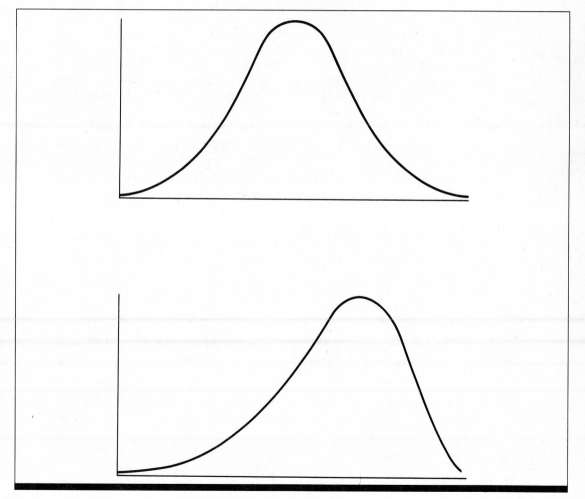

A bell curve and a skewed curve.

Evaluation is a two-edged sword which can enhance student learning and personality development or be destructive of student learning and personality development.

—Benjamin Bloom

Test Development

The development of a test is a bewildering experience if you are attempting this endeavor for the first time. It is bewildering because test construction is both an art and a science. The art component resides in the creative and imaginative ability of the instructor to write items that are interesting, challenging, and relevant. The science component requires a knowledge of the various facets of properly constructed tests such as representative sampling, reliability, and validity. This chapter will focus on the scientific aspects of test construction with an emphasis on delineating item types like true/false, matching, and essay. While reading through this chapter, you must remember that a lot of experience is required to construct good tests, and no experience to construct poor ones. It may be helpful for you to recall tests that you have taken while assimilating these technical components of test construction. Your observation of a "lousy" test may have had scientific merit.

The major tenet in test construction is to recognize the purpose of the test. Why do individuals have to be tested? For example, is it necessary for a person to recognize road signs while driving a motor vehicle? If the answer is yes, then the purpose of the test is clearly defined and items selected for the test should focus on road signs. The number of items selected, the item type used for presenting information, the manner of scoring, and the establishment of a passing score would be some of the components addressed in constructing the test (see Table 14.1); how the information is presented reflects the art component. A well-defined purpose for giving the test will eliminate many problems during the construction of the test; an ill-conceived purpose will generally lead to failure both in test construction and reported results.

Domain

A clear specification of purpose ultimately leads to a well-defined domain of interest, commonly referred to as the test's sample space. Since every test is a sampling of behavior, we should be cognizant of what sampling means in test construction. For example, if you were to construct a test that measures the ability of an individual to add, you would have to provide a limited sample of addition problems since there are an infinite number of such problems. This infinite number of addition problems would constitute the sample space, and the items you selected for inclusion on the test would be the sample. Since the purpose of the test is to determine if a person knows how to add, and since you will conclude that this is indeed the case based on the sample of items you selected, it is essential that this sample of items

TABLE 14.1 Measurement Model

Purpose of Measurement
(Issue of Validity)

Construction of Table of Specifications
(Issue of Validity)

Construction of Test
(Norm/Objective Referenced)

Administration of Test
(Issue of Reliability)

Analysis of Test
(Issue of Validity)
(Issue of Reliability)

Practical Use of Results
(Issue of Validity)

be representative of the sample space. The technical term used in making a judgment about the sample selected is validity. We state that the test has validity or, more specifically, that the test has *context validity* if the results lead to a proper conclusion that a student can add.

The issue of content validity when constructing standardized tests that can be used in many geographical settings is generally resolved by using panels of experts who, based on consensus, agree on the representativeness of each of the items. Content validity with teacher-made tests, however, usually depends on the teacher's selection of representative items. This is not an easy task, as any experienced teacher will freely admit. A method commonly used by test developers to aid in establishing validity is the construction of a table of specifications. This table essentially is an abstract of one or more of your plans of work.

Table of Specifications

A table of specifications will vary, contingent upon who is developing the table; however, there are several essential components that should be included in the table (see Table 14.2). Sample space, as mentioned earlier, is necessary, as is the level of cognition required of the student, such as knowledge, application, synthesis, analysis, and evaluation.[1] Other factors that are often overlooked but should be considered, especially with teacher-made tests, are time and importance. To spend a considerable amount of classroom time on a given topic and then have very few test items related to that topic is a frustrating student experience that can be avoided

TABLE 14.2 Test Specifications

COGNITIVE DOMAIN*					
Knowledge	Comprehension	Application	Analysis	Synthesis	Evaluation

True/False   Extended Response
Matching
Restricted Response

Multiple Choice

AFFECTIVE DOMAIN*				
Receiving	Responding	Valuing	Organization	Characterization

True/False   Extended Response
Matching
Restricted Response

Multiple Choice

*Taxonomy of Educational Objectives (1964).

by careful preparation of the table. A useful technique to circumvent this problem is to have the number of test items directly proportional to elapsed time. For example, if a test is covering a five-day period with three days of addition and two days of subtraction, then the number of test items should reflect this ratio; that is, for every three addition questions there should be two subtraction items.

The issue of *importance* of instructional material is not as clear-cut as time when planning a test. It is necessary, however, to ensure that there is a sufficient number of items to accurately assess the student's attainment of the material.

A table of specifications, as is evident, plays an important role in constructing a test. The specifics of the table is largely the responsibility of the teacher; yet adhering to such factors as sample space, level of cognition, time, and importance will enhance the development of a test that has content validity.

Closely associated with validity is the concept of *reliability*. Reliability can be looked at from two different viewpoints: test reliability and scorer reliability. In both instances the term means consistency in responses. With respect to test reliability, one must be concerned with how an individual responds to one or more test items.

The issue is *not* one of answering correctly; rather, it relates to how an individual responds to the item or items today, tomorrow, next week, or next month. If no learning occurs during this time period, one would expect that the student would respond to the items the same way each time; this is referred to as test reliability. On the other hand, if a student provides different responses to a test item on different administrations of the same item or items, the test would be lacking in reliability. Reliability from this point of view means response consistence. In general, a test that has content validity will be reliable; the converse, however, is not true—a reliable test is not necessarily valid.

Scorer reliability, unlike test reliability, refers to the consistency of different raters in scoring test items. If a group of raters arrives at the same answer for a test item, the item is said to have high scorer reliability. The degree of scorer reliability is a function of the type of response a student has to make in answering a question. If the required response is an essay, for example, scorer reliability will decrease; if the response is, true or false, for example, scorer reliability will increase.

It would be easy to say that all responses should be limited to ensure higher scorer reliability; however, this maxim would ignore the primary tenet in test construction, which is, What is the purpose of the test? Obviously, if the major purpose is to determine if a student can organize and present materials in a clear, succinct written communication, the limited student response is obviated. The balance between validity and reliability must be carefully considered when planning the test since, in many instances, one will be affected by the other. A good general rule to follow is ensure validity and maximize reliability. At no point should reliability be the major determining factor in the construction of a test.

Item Types

There are two major item types for most written cognitive tests: completion and supply. Completion-type items require a student to select a response from a given set of listed items. These item types traditionally are categorized as true/false, multiple choice, and matching. Supply-item types, on the other hand, require the student to provide an unlisted response such as a word, phrase, sentence, paragraph, or essay.

From the point of view of test construction, the supply-item type is easier to construct than the completion type; however, the supply-item type is generally more difficult to score.[2]

Supply and Completion Item Types

The differentiation among test types is based on the required response made by the student taking the test. If the student is required to provide a response from memory, then the item is referred to as a supply item; if the student has to recognize and select an answer, then it is a completion item. The supply type is often referred to as nonobjective, while the completion type is called objective. The distinction between objective and nonobjective is simply a case of reliability—more specifically, scorer reliability. It is easier to obtain consensus on a letter (T or F) or a number than it is on a word, phrase, sentence, paragraph, or essay. Both types of items are needed when evaluating students, since it is the purpose of the test, not the ease of scoring, that governs how items are to be written.

In order to facilitate your writing of test items, you should be familiar with several common item types. In the completion or objective area these items are true or false, multiple choice, and matching. In the supply, or nonobjective, area the item types are restricted and extended response. A complete discussion of test development is beyond the scope of this chapter; however, in the following sections of the chapter discourse several key points to be addressed in writing test items are presented.

■ *True and False*

The simplest form of a completion, or objective, type of test in terms of response is true and false. These items, generally, are declarative sentences. For example: A completion item is often referred to as objective. The major advantage of this item type is that it allows for sampling a considerable amount of content using a relatively small amount of space. Disadvantages, however, are (1) guessing, since there is a 50–50 chance of correctly answering he question, and (2) constructing items that are definitely true or false.

A commonly used approach to account for the guessing problem with true and false items is to require a student to correct an underlined word or phrase if the item is false. This requirement results in the item being both a supply and completion type of item, which reduces the guessing factor but introduces the scorer reliability issue. In any event, if students are to be exposed to this type of item they should be taught how to take this type of test. Written directions generally are not helpful if a student is unaccustomed to this item type.

If true and false items are to be used, ensure that there are an approximately equal number of true and false items. A test where all or most all answers are either true or false will affect the response set of the student. A series of T's or F's will likely be altered if the student is not quite sure of some responses and is uncomfortable with the extended repetition of a particular letter.

■ *Multiple Choice*

The most commonly used completion type item is multiple choice with more than two choices for each question. (In a restricted sense, it can be argued that true and false is a multiple-choice type of item.) The number of choices used generally is a function of the probability of correctly guessing the answer. The probability of guessing correctly is calculated by dividing 1 by the number of choices. For example, the probability of correctly guessing one choice from a set of three choices is 1/3, or 33 percent; one of four choices is 1/4, or 25 percent; and one of five choices is 1/5, or 20 percent. It can be seen that as the number of choices increases, the probability of guessing correctly decreases. The guessing factor, after five choices, begins to level off to the extent that guessing is not considered a problem. Have you seen multiple-choice tests with more than five choices?

The choices for a multiple-choice type of items are referred to by various names such as responses, alternatives, and distractors. Distractors are the incorrect choices for the question. Regardless of the terms used to identify the choices, it is essential that all choices being used for the question be equally plausible. "Equally plausible" means that if the student has insufficient information to answer the question, any of the choices will appear to be correct. Constructing equally plausible distractors is difficult and requires considerable trial and error; yet, if done properly, the results obtained regarding student performance are usually meaningful and accurate. Be careful in using "all of the above" or "none of the above" as distractors when you cannot think of another plausible alternative. These choices are meaningful if used in the proper context. Finally, make sure that your grammar is proper for each of the choices and the question.

■ *Matching*

The general format of matching items consists of having two or more columns of items that must be matched. Each column should consist of items that are relatively homogeneous. For example, if you want the students to match names of inventors and their inventions, then one column of items would contain the proper names and the other column the inventions. The complexity of this type of item could be increased by adding a third column of items that might relate to time period. It is clear that by using this type you can sample a considerable amount of information within a limited amount of space.

The major difficulty with this type of item is scoring, particularly if more than two columns are used. For example, if using three columns, should a student receive partial credit if only items in two of the columns are matched? Also, if there is an equal number of items in each column a student would provide an incorrect response simply because of a previous incorrect response. As with multiple choice, the construction of effective and meaningful matching items requires considerable experience.

■ *Restricted Response*

The simplest form of a restricted response type is the common fill-in-the-blank item. The response for the blank space could be either a word or phrase that must be provided from memory. In some instances, there is more than one blank space. The difficulty with this type of item is ensuring that there is only one correct response. If several words could be used to answer the question correctly, it is essential that the scorer be aware of these correct responses. In addition, it is essential that synonyms for the correct answer be considered when constructing the question. As in any situation where a student must provide a response, attention must be given to spelling and grammar. The student should know if spelling and grammar are factors in addition to the required response.

■ *Extended Response*

The extended-response type of item could be a sentence, paragraph, or essay. Of all the item types discussed, this has the lowest scorer reliability, particularly with respect to essays. To increase scorer reliability, structured formats are provided with the question, which show the student how to respond to the question. For example, rather than ask the student to discuss the construction of item types, which could lead to a lengthy treatise on true/false and multiple-choice items, you could specify direction by stating all of the item types and requiring an example of each. This not only indicates to the student what is required, but also indicates to the scorer what should be graded.

The greatest abuse in test construction occurs with extended-response items simply because the student or the scorer is not sure what is being requested. Careful consideration must be given to the construction of this type of item to ensure that both the student and scorer know what is needed for a satisfactory response. As with the restricted response, if spelling and grammar are factors in the grade, then this should be known; if organization, creativity, and content are factors, then these should also be known. Scorer reliability increases when all participants are aware of what is required.

PROBE Give advantages and disadvantages of the following test types: true/false, multiple choice, matching, restricted response, and extended response. What should be promoted in each type of test? What should be avoided in each type of test? Check your answers against Table 14.3. Distinguish test validity and test reliability. In a multiple-choice test, what are the characteristics of good distractors? What are the uses of Bloom's Taxonomy in designing test items? See Table 14.2.

■ *SUMMARY*

This chapter on test development is not intended to provide a definitive approach to the development of tests; rather, it is intended to make you aware of the use of these items, the advantages and disadvantages of each item type, and of what you should promote or avoid. Table 14.3 provides a summary of some of the major factors to be considered. More detailed information can be obtained from the references for Chapter 14 at the end of this book.

■ *NOTES*

1. B. S. Bloom, ed., et al., *Taxonomy of Educational Objectives: Handbook I, Cognitive Domain,* (New York: D. McKay, 1956.)
2. Norman E. Gronlund, *Measurement and Evaluation in Teaching,* 5th Ed. (New York: Macmillan, 1985.)

TABLE 14.3 Test Types (Comparison/Suggestions)

Type	Advantages	Disadvantages	Promote	Avoid
True/False	Large sampling of content Short administration time High scorer reliability	Guessing Measures low level of cognitive achievement	Equivalent number of T/F answers Clear unequivocal answer	Absolute terms Extraneous material Double negatives/ out of content items
Multiple choice	Large sampling of content (less than T/F, matching) Measures wide range of cognitive achievement High scorer reliability Allows for diagnosis Reduces guessing factor	Difficult to construct/ particular plausible alternatives	Equally plausible distractors Accurate use of problem statements Equal number of a,b,c,d answers Best answer	Unnecessarily long alternatives Multiple correct responses Extraneous material Nonplausible distractors
Matching	Large sampling of content Short administration time High scorer reliability	Guessing (due to elimination) Measures low level of cognitive achievement	Homogeneous material Proper ordering Variable size lists	Poor directions Repeated use of same answer
Restricted response	Large sampling of content No guessing factor High scorer reliability	Emphasis on memorization Scorer reliability (less than objective but greater than extended)	Direct questions Structured responses (guidelines for the response)	Multiple missing words Incomplete statements High degree of specificity
Extended response	Measures high levels of cognitive achievement	Scorer reliability at its lowest Sampling of content greatly diminished	Directions on how to respond Criteria for grading of essay	Vague and/or broad problem areas

NOTE: The focus of essay questions, particularly with respect to scorer reliability, should be clearly defined. In general, essays are used to look at the following categories: content, organization, creativity/originality, mechanics, and grammar. It is essential that the test taker be aware of the weight each of these categories is given in considering the final grade.

Management Skills

CHAPTER 15

Motivation of Self and Student

Motivation—a function of nonresistance.

For as we have members in one body,
    And all members have not the same office:
So we, being many, are one body . . .
    And every one member one of another.
Having then gifts differing . . .

—Romans 12:4–8

But excellence implies more than competence. It implies a striving for the highest standards in every phase of life. We need individual excellence in all its forms . . . Individual Americans—bus drivers and editors, grocers and senators, beauty parlor operators and ball players—can contribute to the greatness and strength of a free society, or they can help it to die.

—John Gardner

Science may have found a cure for most evils . . . it has found no remedy for the worst of them all—the apathy of human beings.

—Helen Keller

How do we get students to break through apathy, to create realistic dreams for themselves and to follow through on them? How do we communicate with students so that apathy and cynicism are converted to a search for meaningful work? Indeed, how do we connect schoolwork with the world of work?

Overcoming Resistance

The traditional approach to motivating students to study was to preach a great deal. Teachers moralized about the values and work skills to which students should aspire. Teachers used exhortation. And it didn't work very well. Aldous Huxley says it didn't work well because of what he called the principle of induction (or reversed effect):

> On all levels of our being, from the muscular and sensational to the moral and the intellectual, every tendency generates its own opposite. We look at something red, and visual induction intensifies our perception of green and even, in certain circumstances, causes us to see a green afterimage when the object has been removed. We will a movement; one set of muscles is stimulated and, automatically, by spinal induction, the opposing muscles are inhibited. The same principle holds good on the higher levels of consciousness. Every yes begets a corresponding no.[1]

Let's consider more examples of induction that you can readily test. If you are standing and I tell you in a commanding voice to sit, there will probably be some resistance in your response, whether you remain standing or actually follow my command and sit. And if you are sitting, the same will hold true if I command you to stand.

If I say, "Don't dare think about a purple turtle," you will very likely think about a purple turtle. And if you try to banish the idea, your very act of trying will create the image of the purple turtle.

On the moral level, adolescents often rebel against their parents as role models, adopting opposite lifestyles. This explains, says Huxley, why exhortation and physical punishment are so ineffective, often producing the very opposite of intended results. Huxley recommends a motivational strategy that bypasses resistance. Let's examine some basic motivational theories and see how they can be used to bypass resistance.

■ *A Behavioral Approach to Motivation*

B. F. Skinner's experiments called attention to the significance of reinforcement in learning. Organisms tend to repeat reinforced behavior. To maximize reinforcement for increasing learning, Skinner developed the technique of programmed instruction, a method that reinforces every correct response.[2] Behavioral modification expands the reward of being supplied the correct answer to include rewards of many types—grades and symbols of success such as medals and trophies.

Probably the most common form of reinforcement is the use of praise. Here Brophy's studies show that to be effective the teacher's praise should be sincere and specific, closely following the student's performance. Some of Brophy's examples of the effective and ineffective uses of praise are the following:[3]

Effective Praise	*Ineffective Praise*
1. Delivered contingently	1. Delivered randomly or or unsystematically
2. Specifies the particulars of the accomplishment	2. Restricted to global positive reactions
3. Shows spontaneity, variety, and other signs of credibility; suggests clear attention to the students' accomplishments	3. Shows a bland uniformity, which suggests a conditioned response made with minimum attention
4. Rewards attainment of specified performance criteria (which can include effort criteria, however)	4. Rewards mere participation, without consideration of performance processes or outcomes
5. Provides information to students about their competence or the value of their accomplishments	5. Provides no information at all or gives students information about their status
6. Orients students toward better appreciation of their own task-related behavior and thinking about problem solving	6. Orients students toward comparing themselves with others and thinking about competing

7. Uses students' own accomplishments as the context for describing present accomplishments

7. Uses the accomplishments of peers as the context for describing students' present accomplishments

8. Given in recognition of noteworthy effort or success at difficult (for *this* student) tasks

8. Given without regard to the effort expended or the meaning of the accomplishment (for *this* student)

9. Attributes success to effort and ability, implying that similar successes can be expected in the future

9. Attributes success to ability alone or to external factors such as luck or easy task

10. Fosters endogenous attributions (students believe that they expend effort on the task because they enjoy the task and/or want to develop task-relevant skills)

10. Fosters exogenous attributions (students believe that they expend effort on the task for external reasons—to please the teacher, win a competition or reward, etc.)

11. Focuses students' attention on their own task-relevant behavior

11. Focuses students' attention on the teacher as an external authority figure who is manipulating them

12. Fosters appreciation of and desirable attributions about task-relevant behavior after the process is completed

12. Intrudes into the ongoing process, distracting attention from task-relevant behavior

Critics say the behavioral approach stresses *extrinsic* motivation. The student is directed to focus on goals artifically paired with a subject when, ideally, the student will study for the sake of the subject itself. Moreover, over a period of time students may come to feel that they are manipulated through the use of extrinsic rewards. Student resistance may then curb learning. John W. Thomas's research indicated that educators should build a sense of *agency* in students; that is, the students should see themselves as the cause of their behavior. *Agency,* says Thomas, is the key factor in sustaining motivation over a long period of time.[4]

Thomas discourages giving tangible rewards for every type of activity. Excessive external rewards can create teacher dependency and diminish transfer to novel situations. In view of these limitations, one can gradually withdraw behavioral techniques, replacing them with techniques that develop a sense of *agency.*

■ *A Cognitive Approach to Motivation*

Cognitive psychologists explain motivation as a form of integrating experience, a way of resolving disequilibrium. Piaget maintains that human beings have a basic urge to maintain a sense of organization in their lives.

R. W. White maintains that motivation cannot be explained as a function of physiological drives since human beings engage in learning activities when all their physical needs are met.[5]

The cognitive view is applied by creating a sense of disequilibrium in the students by engaging them in questions, problem solving, and projects. The idea is to draw out the students' natural urge to integrate experience. In practice, these methods break down when the questions or problem-solving activities do not create a state of disequilibrium, when initial curiosity is not aroused, or when it is aroused but followed by tasks that are too difficult for the student.

■ *A Growth Approach to Motivation*

In *Motivation and Personality,* Abraham Maslow draws a distinction between growth needs and deficiency needs. He describes a hierarchy in which deficiency needs include (1) physiological needs, (2) safety needs, (3) belonging needs and love needs, and (4) esteem needs. Maslow argued that "the single, holistic principle that binds together the multiplicity of human motives is the tendency for a new and higher need to emerge as the lower need fulfills itself by being sufficiently gratified."[6] Only after the deficiency needs have been satisfied can the student go on to the higher growth needs. The growth needs include (1) need for self-actualization, (2) desire to know and understand, and (3) aesthetic needs.

In applying Maslow's principles, the teacher can do everything possible to satisfy the students' deficiency needs in order to create the emergence of growth needs.

Classroom Practices

Theories of motivation are useful in helping the teacher analyze why the student may be unmotivated and to design a strategy to counter resistance to learning. In *Psychology Applied to Teaching,* Robert F. Biehler and Jack Snowman present the following troubleshooting checklist:[7]

Why Student May Be Unmotivated	*Some Things You Might Do About It*
Subject is boring.	Try to make subject as interesting as possible; supply incentives to learn.
Subject is presented in a boring way.	Make a systematic effort to arouse and sustain interest.
Effort must be expended before mastery or enjoyment occurs.	Explain about delayed payoff, use behavior modification techniques to encourage perseverance, and provide short-term goals.
Pupil would rather not exert self.	Specify objectives, rewards; try to make lack of effort seem unappealing.

Pupil doesn't know what to do.	State specific instructional objectives; explain how these can be met, what rewards will be.
High school pupil has identity problems, lacks clear goals.	Urge pupil to select short-term goals, think about long-term goals.
Pupil lacks aptitude or ability.	Give less capable students individual help, more time to complete tasks; try different kinds of instruction.
Parents of pupil are neutral or negative about schooling.	Emphasize that learning can be enjoyable, that doing well in school opens up opportunities
Pupil comes from a disadvantaged background, has limited experiences. Pupil has had negative experiences in school or with a particular subject.	Check on range of experiences; supply necessary background information. Make experiences in your classroom as positive as possible; make sure reinforcement occurs frequently.
Pupil associates subject with a disliked individual.	Try to be a sympathetic, responsive person so that pupil will build up positive associations.
Pupil dislikes subject because of envy or jealousy of those who do well at it.	Play down comparisons between pupils; urge self-improvement.
Pupil feels tired, hungry, uncomfortable.	Try to allow for or alleviate discomfort.
Pupil feels insecure, anxious, scared.	Make your classroom physically and psychologically safe.
Pupil experiences little sense of acceptance, belonging, esteem.	Show student that you respond positively, that he or she is worthy of esteem.
Pupil has never earned high grades, has been "punished" by low grades.	Avoid public comparisons, stress self-competition and individual improvement.
Pupil has low level of aspiration.	Urge pupil to set and achieve realistic goals.
Pupil has weak need for achievement.	Try to strengthen pupil's self-confidence, stress values of achievement.
Pupil is afraid to try because of fear of failure.	Arrange a series of attainable goals, help student achieve them.
Pupil assumes failure is due to lack of ability and that there is no point in trying.	Try to strengthen pupil's self-concept, set up a series of short-term goals, and help pupil succeed after initial failure.

Pupil learns only when required or cajoled to learn.	Invite pupil to participate in selecting goals, deciding how they will be met; encourage pupil to become self-directed.
Pupil resents learning only what others say must be learned.	Invite pupil to participate in selecting instructional objectives.

Modeling

Teachers trained in whole-brain motivation can make use of subtle suggestions to motivate students—suggestions conveyed through body language, fantasy, metaphor, the visual arts, and music. These multidimensional, often nonverbal forms of communication bypass ordinary resistance. These approaches are more likely to motivate students to integrate learning with life goals than the use of prescriptive do's and don'ts. There is evidence, for example, that students who role play the lives of scientists, poets, and political leaders increase their capacity to learn. As they begin to imagine themselves as scientists, poets, and political leaders they break through limiting self-concepts; they discover powers and interests they did not know they possessed.

■ The Teacher as a Model

The most obvious model for the student is the teacher. The teacher models a knowledge of her subject, a sense of confidence in being an instructional leader, effective management, orderliness, spontaneity, enthusiasm, a sense of wonder in exploring her subject, respect for others, integrity, fairness, and flexibility. The teacher's speech habits, body language, board work, and presentations are all forms of modeling that speak the identity of the teacher. This is the invisible curriculum, the part that does not get advertised in course catalogs and syllabi, but may have the greatest impact on learning. Indeed, according to Lozanov, it is impossible not to use suggestion on this level. One's very choices, acts, presentations, and communication are powerful forms of suggestion.

■ Community Models

If you but take notice, you will find professional and nonprofessional persons all around you who represent a wide range of human accomplishment. These people are the doers and pathfinders, recognized by the community as leaders in their own right. You can make it a practice to interview these people, to discover how they became interested in their work, how they mastered the disciplines necessary to achieve their goals, and what satisfaction they have obtained. Then, with their permission, you can use this information together with photographs of the person as seeds to inspire your students to investigate a variety of vocations and avocations. The casual mentioning of personal discoveries made by local merchants and cooks, bankers and hairdressers, and mountain climbers and wine stewards can provide a valuable bridge for the students—a connection of content with vocation and avocation. Let's take a look at what some of these people say and see how their vision can be used for motivation.

*Vocation/Avocation: Selected
Profiles*[8]

PROFILE 1
David Brewster
Avocation: Mountain Climber

David lives in Boulder, Colorado. He is an accountant who has a passion for climbing. "The mountains are different," says David. "They care not whether you get an A on your exam or that your car is broken or that your idol was murdered by a terrorist . . . Rock, snow, ice, weather, climate, altitude, it is all there and doesn't really care what you are experiencing or going through. Climbing is the most 'be there' sport I've ever done. Like a demand it says 'Get present, now!' " David says that human problems are "like the 'alien,' always lurking in the background." But when he climbs he confronts fear and self-doubt directly and overcomes it. Ordinary problems then seem easy to handle.

David is inspired by the magnificence and the stark beauty of the mountains and by the quality of human relationships that arise from the life-supporting teamwork of climbing. He is committed to supporting his sister, Mary Kaye, a professional climber, to become the first American woman on Everest. Climbing, to David, is an "access point in life . . . access to what is genuine and real" in contrast to the human tendency to go through the motions.

PROFILE 2
Vicki Marinko
Vocation: Gemologist

Vicki lives in San Francisco, where she is a successful gemologist. She travels to various continents to purchase precious stones and designs and markets her own jewelry. "My first interest in gems," says Vicki, "was a romantic one. In high school I took a gemology course and would imagine myself traveling to far away places." Later she studied geology in college and became "fascinated with the way something so beautiful gets formed in the earth." When she finished college, she decided to take the training necessary to become a professional gemologist. She attended exhibits of precious stones, and there she met some of those persons who did in fact travel to faraway places, who evaluated and purchased gems.

From these persons Vicki learned the skills necessary to achieve a level of professional independence as a gemologist. What started as a romantic fantasy has become a practical career for Vicki.

*Vicky Marinko was fascinated with the way something so
beautiful gets formed in the earth.*

PROFILE 3
Philip Prohow
Vocation: Diver/Suicide Prevention Counselor

Mr. Prohow grew up in Miami where a high school friend introduced him to the joys of scuba diving. Looking at pictures of divers in action inspired Phil to take professional lessons with a leading diver in the area. Eventually he became good enough to teach others.

"When you are down very deep," he said, "the colors of the coral and the fish are brilliant. There are thousands of tiny fish swimming about. It's an underwater fantasy world. It is so silent and incredibly beautiful you can almost get hypnotized by it." The training Phil had in diving made him realize both the joys and the dangers of diving. "You must learn to do things right the first time; you can't count on getting a second chance. So you learn the safety procedures. You learn proper use of the equipment."

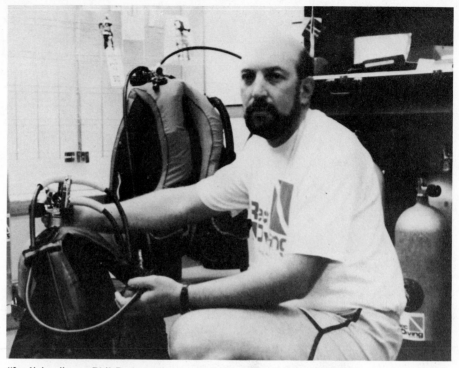

"In diving," says Phil Prohow, *"you must learn to do things right the first time; you can't count on getting a second chance."*

This training gave Phil a valuable foundation for his later work in the Coast Guard. Years later his respect for life carried over into work with suicide prevention. "I had worked with drown victims in the past," Phil explains. "And people can drown in many ways, drug abuse being one of them. When I stayed on the phone all night with potential suicide victims, or risked my own life going into dangerous dwellings to be with them, I recalled my experience in diving and in the Coast Guard. This got me through the night. I saved a few lives."

PROFILE 4
Angela Jones
Vocation: Hypnotherapist/Broadcaster

Angela Jones is from Detroit. She is both a hypnotherapist and a broadcaster. After earning an undergraduate degree in psychology, Angela spent two years training in a school of hypnotherapy.

"I wanted," says Angela, "to explore as many techniques as possible to render the best service to my potential patients. Hypnotherapy was one of the avenues explored as an adjunct to psychology." Since she was four years old, Angela recalls how the voices on radio and TV "were different from ordinary speech."

As a child Angela noticed that the voices on radio and TV "were different from ordinary speech." This observation inspired her to study hypnotherapy and broadcasting.

During her study of hypnotherapy Angela realized the power of the voice as a suggestive instrument. This led her to take training in one of Detroit's most prestigious broadcasting schools. As a result, Angela is now both a professional hypnotherapist and broadcaster.

PROFILE 5

Madeline Triffon

Vocation: Master Sommelier

Madeline Triffon is master sommelier (master wine steward) at Detroit's London Chop House, considered one of the best restaurants in the United States, if not the world. Madeline, a drama major, worked her way through the University of Michigan by waiting tables. She became fascinated with every aspect of the restaurant business and upon graduation applied for a position at the Detroit Renaissance Center while it was being built. She was offered a position as wine steward.

At first, her job was restricted to serving wine, but gradually she developed skills in cross indexing, tasting, food and wine compatibilities, marketing, and pricing, and she learned, in general, about wines in relation to all aspects of the restaurant business. She took over the responsibility for ordering wines and gradually developed into a self-taught expert on wines.

"I read some books," says Madeline, "but knowledge of geography and grapes is just a skeleton for you to hang the sensory experience on." Her knowledge expanded as she saw a need "to fill in the gaps to make the business work better." Madeline believes in "giving her all" to any situation she finds herself in, even if she did not choose the situation.

"You can learn from everybody and everything," says Madeline. "I enjoyed being a waitress. There are great wait persons who inspire trust. They treat people they serve like guests in their home. Each person served is a challenge."

Madeline believes that one should take risks, that the greatest limits are self-limits.

"Sure, I've got professional goals. People ask when I'll write a book or start my import/export business. But life's full of surprises. I never look back. I look *now.* Opportunities keep opening up and I step into them."

Madeline told about the master sommelier examination given in London, England, an exam passed by only 10 percent of the experts who take it. She decided that taking the exam was part of being in her chosen field.

"Hard work is never wasted. Work well done cuts across all class barriers."

"High school students," says Madeline Triffon, "should feel free to try many paths—to remain open to the possibilities of the moment."

The work paid off for Madeline when she was awarded the title of master sommelier, one of six Americans, the only American female, and one of two women in the world to hold the title. And yet Madeline places far more emphasis on the joy of working than she does on the rewards. According to Madeline, focus on rewards will almost surely lead to disappointment. But when one is totally engaged in projects, disregarding fears, "work becomes play."

"The best teachers," says Madeline, "are dynamic and fresh. They teach one to be fearless. I was fearless," Madeline said. "Then I lost it and became too cautious. Now I'm learning how to get it back again."

Madeline thinks it's absurd to worry about failure or to compare yourself with others. High school students should feel free "to try many paths, to remain open to the possibilities of the moment."

PROFILE 6
Rita and Chris Voukatieis
Vocations: Cosmetologists/Hair Salon Operators

"Being an effective hairdresser," says Chris, "requires creativity, technical talent, and many interpersonal skills." From a very young age, Chris's mother, Rita, enjoyed making people beautiful.

"It's really important that you enjoy your profession," says Rita. "It's very artistic work," Chris adds. "And it shows when you don't enjoy what you are doing because then the art doesn't come through."

Chris originally wanted to be a psychiatrist, but was also attracted to fashion. For her, hairdressing satisfied both of these interests.

Until ten years ago, Rita was primarily committed to her family; hairdressing had to take second place. Then with her family's basic needs in order, she committed herself to developing a family business—Hairlanding, a hair salon in Taylor, Michigan. Rita became committed to making the salon successful. Three years ago Chris finished beauty school and joined her mother's business.

"When I started working in it, it became our salon," said Chris. "I felt it was mine, too—to make it grow, to make it good."

Rita and Chris have some mutual advice for high school students seeking a career: "Whatever you do, do it with heart!"

PROFILE 7
Gurucharn S. Khalsa
Vocation: Yoga Teacher/Carpenter

When Gurucharn was 14 years old, he went with a friend to a yoga class and recalls that he had "never before met so many nice and simple people. The yoga," he said, "helped me to feel relaxed and radiant." He practices a form of yoga known as Kundalini yoga, "the yoga of awareness," from which all forms of yoga derive. A typical class

Mother and daughter build a business—Rita and Chris Voukatieis enjoy developing skills of cosmetology.

consists "of a combination of stretching exercises, holding certain yogic postures for a period of time along with a number of combined breathing techniques." According to Guru Charn, yoga "rebuilds the nervous system, balances the glandular system (which is the guardian of our health), strengthens the immune system, the heart and much more." The breathing, Gurucharn explains, creates a "powerful healing energy that dissolves stress and tension held deep in the body—commonly in the jaw, neck, shoulder, chest, and stomach. The breath creates the energy (prana) and the exercises direct the flow of this energy to nurture and relieve the stressed areas of the body."

Following the exercises, one lies on his or her back and covers the body from the shoulders down and is guided by the yoga master into a state of deep relaxation.

"Yoga," says Gurucharn, "means union. It is an ancient science that promotes union between body, mind and soul in which a Great Peace can be experienced, an escape from the limited mind into the universal mind or what some call the higher self. It is not a religion, but it will give you a direct experience of spiritual life rather than attempt to explain it.

"Yoga will help you become more calm, relaxed, alert, vibrant, alive and at peace within."

Gurucharn finds that yoga carries over into his life in many ways—in his work as a professional carpenter and in his relationship with himself and others.

PROFILE 8

Mary C. Furlette

Vocation: Clinical Psychologist

Mary Furlette says she intends to give up her profession when she finds two persons exactly alike. She loves working with small children in the area of testing and evaluation. Mary considers herself an "Aquarius conspirator." Although she is trained behaviorally and psychoanalytically, she has read every word of Maslow.

As a young girl Mary was fascinated with her father's ability to solve crossword puzzles in less than 15 minutes. Her interest in solving puzzles later led her to declare mathematics as her undergraduate major at the University of Michigan.

Mary received nurturing not only from her father but from several role models in the schools she attended—the priests and nuns who taught her.

Mary Furlette, clinical psychologist, says that she intends to give up her profession when she finds two persons exactly alike.

"They all had one characteristic in common. They let me be who I was and never expected anything more than that. I didn't have to change—I just grew."

"When I pray," says Mary, "I pray for one thing as a rule—wisdom. However, I often think if I become this wise person, I'll probably never be humble about it as was my father."

Teaching Self-Motivation

Many of the teaching strategies described in Chapter 8 are motivational techniques based on whole-brain processing. The use of role models to motivate can be heightened by presenting a description or picture of the role model through a Lozanov or NLP technique. For example, any of the above profiles can be used in role playing and fantasy activities. It is not always necessary to model famous persons. Photographs of community models can be placed on the walls of the classroom along with pictures of famous scientists, chief justices, and poets.

Instead of expending great effort on motivating students through primarily external means, it is useful to teach students how to motivate themselves. It comes as a shock to many students that there are actually technologies available that will assist them in doing what they want to do. Most hold the view that motivation is something you either have or you don't, that it may be a matter of willpower, or that it may even have something to do with morals and character. They are not sure what it is, but they are sure that they have absolutely no control over it. When it happens, it happens.

To these students it will come as a surprise that they are in control of their lives. Nevertheless, as they gradually gain mastery over specific motivational techniques and begin to see results in their own lives, they will want to expand their goals and depth of commitment. And once they begin to operate from commitment they will rapidly increase performance and the joy of performance.

Anytime is a good time to teach motivation. Teachers can model it, relate what worked for them in their career development, and integrate an anecdote or biographical sketch into any lessons, pointing to some real person who actually made use of the concept or content of the lesson.

Build up a repertory of role models cross-indexed for different topics. If you teach science, the human history of science is fascinating in its own right. You don't need long-winded formal expositions of the lives of the great explorers in science or any other field. All you need is some sharp images of real human beings working toward a goal and getting excited about it: Lavoisier needing to build three-dimensional models of scientific theories before they became real to him—why? Archimedes running naked through the streets of Sicily shouting, "I have found it! Eureka!" Why was he so excited about the displacement of water? Einstein gaining intuitive insight into what was to become his theory of relativity by imagining himself riding on a beam of light. Kekule discovering the structure of benzene in a dream about serpents. The message: Being a scientist is not a dry and stuffy affair; it is a highly imaginative adventure. It is but a short step to invite the student to imagine himself as a scientist, either one who has existed or one of the future.

Similar repertories of role models can be built up in any subject. Anthony Robbins, in *Unlimited Power,* advocates the use of living role models presented to the students in a film or video. A Supreme Court justice states his or her conviction in regard to a social problem, and then challenges the students to go out and solve certain social problems.[9]

Role models are all around you. By developing a keen ear and eye for specific anecdotal material, you can intersperse your lectures with rich stories from the lives of people you know. Of course, you need not mention their names.

PROBE Identify persons in your community who are perceived as leaders. Request an interview with them. If possible, you can audio- or videotape the interview and request permission to use it for instructional purposes. Some suggested questions to ask are:

1. How would you describe your profession to a layperson unfamiliar with your work?
2. How did you first become interested in your work?
3. Was there a point at which interest in your work became a commitment to the work? If so, please explore how this happened for you.
4. What disciplines and skill mastery were necessary to achieve your present level of competence? How did you feel about going through these disciplines?
5. Recall your high school experience. What was present (if anything) that has supported your motivation in your present profession? Were there role models given? Statements made? Field trips? Readings? Other factors?
6. What was missing from your high school experience (if anything) that *if present* would have supported your present motivation?
7. What suggestion would you offer high school students to assist them in expanding and applying their potentials?

NLP and Motivation

NLP (Neurolinguistic programming) offers a powerful refinement of modeling. After students view videotapes of famous persons engaged in various professional skills, the students work in groups of five. Each student selects a person from the film to model. The student assumes the physiology of the person being modeled: his or her facial expression, body stance, and movement. The other students act as coaches, giving the modeler correcting feedback. Then the modeler shares his experience of the state with the group.

Modeling past experiences sometimes reverses the procedure, challenging the group to guess what the modeler is experiencing as he recreates the physiology of a past experience. It is amazing how frequently the group will guess the exact state.

Suggestopedic and Optimalearning Approaches to Motivation

The general theory of Suggestopedia and Optimalearning approaches to motivation takes us back to the problem Aldous Huxley indicated earlier: the problem of overcoming resistance. Lozanov identifies the following *barriers* to learning:

1. *The moral-ethical barrier.* Social and cultural patterns will stop communication that is not acceptable to a group.
2. *The rational-logical barrier.* Communication perceived as illogical puzzles the listener and is rejected.
3. *The intuitive-emotional barrier.* Something said that is not liked, for whatever reason, is rejected.[10]

Lozanov presents three ways to use suggestion in the classroom to bypass student barriers:

1. *Psychological.* With appropriate training, the teacher organizes the lesson material psychotherapeutically, psychoprophylactically, psychophysically, and emotionally. Peripherally received communication is accepted noncritically.
2. *Didactic (instructional).* The teacher presents the material in different ways deliberately to promote learning.
3. *Artistic.* For example, the teacher uses artistic posters, uses classical music as background to globalize the lesson.[11]

A combination of de-suggestion and suggestion is used to integrate learning barriers:

1. *Authority (Nondirective Prestige)*
   Authority, says Lozanov, in the sense of nondirective prestige, "creates an atmosphere of confidence and intuitive desire to follow the set example. . . . Authority creates confidence in the reliability of expected results."[12]
2. *Infantilization (Childlike Learning State)*
   For Lozanov this process has nothing to do with the Freudian sense of infantilization, but is "a universal reaction of respect, inspiration and confidence which, without disrupting the level of the normal intellectual activity, considerably increases the perception, memory and creativity function." A liberation of the "plastic qualities of the earlier age periods," leading to "aesthetic experiences and intellectual conclusions, but in a more direct, spontaneous and convincing manner."[13]
3. *Dual-Planeness*
   Barzakov notes that the Bulgarian word *dvóen* has the sense of the English *dual.*[14] Dual means double, but in the specialized sense of being composed of

two *unlike* parts *(American Heritage Dictionary)*. In Lozanov's suggestology, dual-planeness refers to the "enormous signaling stream of diverse stimuli which unconsciously, or semiconsciously, are emitted from or perceived by the personality. . . . Imperceptible changes in facial expression, gait, speed, environment . . . can play a decisive role in the formation of the suggestive result."[15] The professional must be sincere in the practice of his or her discipline in order to master dual-planeness.

4. *Rhythms*

Regarded by Lozanov as a biological principle are the recurrence and patterns reflected by nature in days, seasons, years, and mental life.

5. *Intonation*

For Lozanov, "An expression—usually vocal—of an internal psychological content."[16] The use of sound, usually the voice, to influence one in respect to attitude.

6. *Concert Pseudo-Passiveness*

For Lozanov, ". . . A serene, confident attitude toward the suggestive program being presented . . . to be in the same state of mind as one would be in attending a [classical] concert."[17] "This state, says Ivan Barzakov," is "by no means limited to the concert session or to the use of music." Rather, says Barzakov, it is an "awakening of the reserve capacities of the individual, which creates the conditions for the mind to go as far as it can go."

In this sense, it is the "exact opposite of mind control," says Barzakov. It is a state students are in for most of the class period and is supported not only by music but by voice, movement and expression. The state is called *pseudo*-passive because the students only appear to be passive; actually they are in a very active learning state.[18]

"From a physiological point of view," says Barzakov, "the state is very relaxed, and at the same time, very concentrated. That is probably why, in his latest writing, Lozanov calls this state "concentrative psycho[logical]-relaxation."[19]

Ivan Barzakov's Optimalearning promotes a special unity between teaching and learning so that they are seen as different aspects of the same process. Special procedures and techniques are used to bring forth the "hidden teacher" in everyone. In the self-instructional process, for example, students are taught how to assume the viewpoint of a teacher preparing an imaginary lesson. "They learn to interact with the material," says Barzakov, "as if it were a game or an interesting puzzle."[20] "It is a fully creative process every step of the way," says Optimalearning instructor John Metric. "The point is that you're not trying to fill yourself like an empty bucket; you're a full bucket from the very start. It works because you give yourself the suggestion that you know the material already."[21]

Barzakov explains that the teacher within each person "inevitably finds the motivational hooks and the new connections which have real meaning to the learner." The outcome, says Barzakov, is comprehension, recall, heightened motivation, and a sudden burst of creativity. This burst of creativity is then used in a unique way to rekindle the acceleration of learning. Moreover, this special employment of creativity sets off a discovery process in the students' minds—a discovery of the rigor and scope of the subject matter, its relation to their personal lives and to the world, to their own powers of learning and to the nature of learning itself. "The result," says Barzakov, "is an upward spiral: the more you learn, the more creative you become. As you become more creative, you learn even more and perform better and better."[22]

Optimalearning is designed to support the teacher in becoming an "intimate part of the learning process during his/her actual instruction." There is a vigorous exchange between the students and the teacher—an exchange of "ideas, support and creative energy." All of these processes, together with the rapport between students and the teacher, are manifested on both conscious and unconscious levels. Both students and teacher discover the nature of learning and the implicit connectivity of learning and life. What they discover, says Barzakov, is power—"the power to be connected in the deepest sense to [their] fellow human beings and to the universe."[23]

The student and the teacher discover a process of progressive expansion: "This is where the real renaissance is. We believe there is a hidden Einstein and Rembrandt and Hemingway in everyone. My goal is not to re-create Hemingway. I consider it a limitation to work with an image and become another image. I think it is more essential that we bring something from everything and bring your own self to an optimal level."[24] This is achieved through the specialized uses of music and through suggestion in language, art, movement and voice. The teachers' "internal attitude of calmness, confidence and care for their students"—this way of being with their students is "projected *throughout* the instructional process." It is a way of being that plays a major role in activating the "reserve capacities of body and mind."[25]

"The beauty of the [Optimalearning] System," asserts John Metric, "is that it not only teaches you how to increase your efficiency but also how to keep increasing it as you go along in all areas of your life. It is not self limiting."[26]

Individual Differences

The effective teacher will use a variety of motivational strategies based on student need, always recognizing each student as an individual. Individual differences are the varying ways a student learns in or out of the classroom. It is a style that the student has adopted in the process of development. Mary Furlette puts it this way:

> . . . and what I have heard and what I have learned is this: that the phenomenon of individual differences is a phenomenon of perception. It is a question of how and what one perceives and the processing of that information and not what is spoken or shown. The phenomenon of individual differences defies being answered by the question of "WHY?" because why is so multiply determined. Individual differences go beyond A's and B's and even C's and D's or F's; beyond Nikes and Avias; beyond bluejeans and sweatsuits; beyond punk hairdos and bows and ribbons; beyond hightop [sneakers] and shoes and khaki shirts and pants. Individual differences answer the question of how a student is like no other

student and at the same time unlike no other student. The phenomenon goes beyond numbers and groups; beyond performance and behavior; beyond peers and siblings; beyond statistical significance and persons. Individual differences are beyond the bell curve and to encapsulate them within a hypothesis is to imprison them.[27]

■ SUMMARY

Motivation can be regarded as a function of overcoming student resistance to learning. Several approaches are reviewed as ways to decrease student resistance to learning: a behavioral approach, a cognitive approach, a growth approach, modeling, neurolinguistic programming, the Lozanov and Barzakov approach.

The behavioral approach emphasizes reinforcement of desired behavior through the use of praise, grading systems, and rewards. The cognitive approach makes use of states of disequilibrium to bring forth students' natural desire to maintain equilibrium and organization in their lives. Abraham Maslow's growth approach to motivation distinguishes between growth needs and deficiency needs. Only after deficiency needs, such as safety and basic physiological needs, are met can the individual pursue the development of growth needs, such as self-actualization. The teacher can model desired behavior for the student and can present community models to the class. Neurolinguistic programming makes use of multiple modes of processing (auditory, visual, and kinesthetic) to motivate. Lozanov's suggestopedia and Barzakov's Optimalearning focus specifically on the blocks (resistance) to learning and proceed to remove these blocks by creating conditions for the mind to function at its optimum level.

■ NOTES

1. Aldous Huxley, *The Devils of Loudun* (New York: Harper & Row, 1952), 29.
2. Robert F. Biehler and Jack Snowman, *Psychology Applied to Teaching,* 5th ed. (p. 469). Copyright © 1986 by Houghton Mifflin Company. Used with permission.
3. J. Brophy, "Teacher Praise: A Functional Analysis," *Review of Educational Research, 51*(1): 5–32 (1981). Copyright 1981, American Educational Research Association, Washington DC.
4. Robert F. Biehler and Jack Snowman, *Psychology Applied to Teaching,* 472.
5. Ibid., 472–473.
6. Ibid., 474–476.
7. Ibid., 478–488.
8. All quotations in the profiles are used with permission of the persons interviewed and are based on either tape-recorded transcriptions or letters provided by the persons interviewed.
9. Anthony Robbins, *Unlimited Power: The New Science of Personal Achievement* (New York: Simon & Schuster, 1986), 343–344.
10. D. H. Schuster and C. E. Gritton, *Suggestive Accelerative Learning Techniques* (New York: Gordon and Breach Science Publishers, 1986), 16.
11. Ibid., 17.

12. G. Lozanov, *Suggestology and Outlines of Suggestopedy* (New York: Gordon and Breach Science Publishers, 1978), pp. 187–188.

13. Ibid., pp. 191–192.

14. Ivan Barzakov, interview, June 1988. Quoted by permission of author.

15. G. Lozanov, *Suggestology and Outlines of Suggestopedy,* p. 193.

16. Ibid., p. 196.

17. Ibid., p. 198.

18. Ivan Barzakov, interview, June 1988. Quoted by permission of author.

19. Ibid.

20. Ibid.

21. John Metric in Hugh J. Delehanty's "Harnessing the Brain's Hidden Powers—Optimalearning: The Art of Learning Through the Arts," *San Francisco Focus* (San Francisco: KQED, PBS Television Station, April 1983), p. 85.

22. Ivan Barzakov, interview, June 1988. Quoted by permission of author.

23. Ibid.

24. Hugh J. Delehanty, "Harnessing the Brain's Hidden Powers—Optimalearning: The Art of Learning Through the Arts," *San Francisco Focus* (San Francisco: KQED, PBS Television Station, April 1983), p. 86.

25. Ivan Barzakov, interview, June 1988. Quoted by permission of author.

26. Hugh J. Delehanty, "Harnessing the Brain's Hidden Power . . .", p. 86.

27. Mary Finlette in a letter to the author by permission of Mary Finlette. Sept. 1988.

CHAPTER 16

The Organized Teacher: Time Management

Teacher using a time-management system.

We cannot put off living until we are ready. . . . The most salient characteristic of life is its coerciveness; it is always urgent, "here and now," without any postponement. Life is fired at us point blank.

—Jose Ortega y Gasset

The single biggest time waster in the world is not completing the work you start.

—John Garner

The effective teacher is an organized teacher. Organization here means much more than clear lesson plans and neat grade books. The high school teacher is responsible for many things. Reports must be properly completed and submitted on time. There are many meetings with parents, students, administrators, and supervisors. The teacher must have an organized agenda for these meetings. Depending on the union contract, there are a number of school activities the teacher is expected to supervise, such as school games, plays, and concerts. There may be committee meetings and financial records to keep. To be effective, the teacher needs a total commitment to the best use of professional and personal time. Such a commitment empowers one not only to be highly effective at work, but also to experience a high level of satisfaction in work and leisure.

In this chapter you will learn how to manage your time effectively. Specifically, you will learn to

1. Assess how you are presently managing your time
2. Work faster
3. Work "smarter"—that is, reduce work load, through setting priorities and delegating work
4. Use systems for organizing work
5. Increase energy sources, making work easier and more productive
6. Develop a personal philosophy of time management.

Your Time-Management Habits

Even if you have never read any of the literature of time management, you will habitually use time in certain ways. It is to your advantage to discover how you use time. Are you penny-wise and dollar-foolish when it comes to managing time? Do you rush through minutes and yet waste hours? Do you let things stack up and then become panicky and ineffective as deadlines approach? For the next week use the following chart to monitor your use of time. In this way you will identify a baseline. You will know where you are and what needs to be done. Then you can begin to increase your effective use of time.

In the left-hand column write in whatever you do in your waking hours. Each block represents a half hour. A version of the chart is located in Appendix D. In using this chart, be specific in writing down what you are doing. If you read, for example, write down the title of what you read and how much. If you grade papers, which papers were

Activity	Professional or Nonprofessional (P or Non-P)	A or B or C Priority	Notes
————	————————	————————	————
————	————————	————————	————
————	————————	————————	————
————	————————	————————	————

they and how many did you grade? Then, in column two, distinguish professional from nonprofessional activities. Only you can decide this. You may browse through the public library on the weekend and peruse 10 books, some of which tie into your professional goals and some of which tie into your leisure pursuits. You must decide this. In so doing, you may discover something of how you have set your goals.

Next, you get to prioritize your activity. Think back on your professional and life goals. Is there an activity that moves you toward your most important goal? If so, then place an A in the third column. If it is an activity that you think is important, but not aligned with your ultimate purposes in life, then rate that activity B. An example of a B activity for some may be running to stay in good shape. If, on the other hand, you plan to become a professional runner, then running is more appropriately recorded as A. If it is an activity that is not essential to your ultimate life's aim or profession, then give that a rating of C. An example for many persons may be washing the car or organizing the attic. But, again, this depends on one's life's goals. If the car and the contents of the attic are antiques, and one is in the antiques business, then these tasks have greater priority.

Finally, in column four you should record your notes—any feelings, observations, or thinking that doing the activity suggests to you. For example, you may perform the task grudgingly or with enthusiasm, with ease or difficulty. You may notice the frequency of performing a given task—and this information may come as a shock to you. If this is so, then you should record both your observation of frequency and your reaction to it. When you complete the 10 days, you are ready to take assessment.

PROBES

1. On what activity to you spend most of your time? What is your second priority? Your third? Did you know this in advance or did this pattern come as a surprise to you?
2. How many activities are professional? How many are nonprofessional? How much time do you spend on recreational activities, household chores, administrative duties, letter writing, social interaction, TV viewing, shopping, and other activities? Do you see any patterns?
3. Are your initial priorities (A,B,C) accurate, or do they need revision?
4. Do you notice any peak energy levels? Low energy levels?

5. Can you make distinctions between professional activities and nonprofessional ones?

6. What conclusion do you draw from these observations? What do you intend to do about it?

With your basic inventory of time use you are now ready to begin a plan of time management. If you noticed any fuzziness in setting priorities or in distinguishing professional and personal goals, you now have the opportunity to focus more clearly. Begin with goal setting. Many time-management experts recommend setting both short-range and long-range goals.

Most of us set very limited goals. We never allow ourselves, even in fantasy, to take the lid off, so to speak. In the following process allow yourself to let go, to think and feel all possibilities. Do not concern yourself with what is likely or how a goal is to be achieved. Create goals. Allow yourself to be a child again and let your imagination run free. Discover the life context in which you are becoming a teacher.

PROBES   Set a timer for 10 minutes. Think of five years in the future. Write down all the goals that come to mind as rapidly as possible.

Now switch hands. Write with your nondominant hand. Don't worry about your handwriting. Just write as fast as possible and let what comes up come up.

Repeat this process, generating goals for three years.

Repeat again and write goals for one year.

After you have finished setting down your goals, go through them and underscore recurrent patterns. There may be several goals related to academic achievement or teaching or to developing some personal skill. Underscore these and give them a label—academic, travel, and so forth. These are the major themes in your life. You can explore these even further by mind mapping.

The use of a mind map allows you to expand your interest in a nonlinear fashion. When you work with your students, you can teach them to mind map their own goals as well as the processes of their thoughts and feelings in relation to content and skills.

PROBES   Create a mind map of one of your goals. Now examine your associations in the mind map. What new pattern do you notice? Try color coding the different branches. Feel free to add to the branches, draw heavy or wavy lines. In short, personalize your mind map.

Goals for the Week, Month, and Year

Your next step will be to organize your long-range goals. Work backward and look for recurrent patterns in different time frames. How does teaching fit into the larger context of your life? Go back now and rank each goal A, B, or C. Do the same for each time span. You may want to move some items around, move up some three-year goals to one year. Feel free to change.

Look over your yearly goals and write out at the side of each how you will achieve them. What must you do to make them realistic? These are your interim objectives:

1. Complete educational psychology and philosophy of education courses
2. Complete analysis of teaching course
3. Complete TB (tuberculosis) test
4. Complete English proficiency test
5. Complete math proficiency test
6. Apply for student teaching
7. Complete cognate requirements
8. Complete the core requirements

A whole series of prior objectives must be completed for any one of the above goals to be completed. There will be term papers to complete, examinations to pass, and the skills of student teaching to master. These can be broken down into weekly and daily objectives. To keep track of your activities, purchase an organizer for daily planning. At minimum, you should acquire a notebook and a pocket calendar.

Daily Objectives

Set a time in the evening or morning to make up your daily list of objectives to be completed. By setting a definite time you will increase the chances of forming a firm habit. Do this for at least four weeks and you will see yourself develop worthwhile habits.

When you make out your list of daily objectives, draw from your lists of weekly and monthly objectives. If you can't think of specific objectives, try mind mapping them. Then, write them out as you think of them. Don't worry about listing them in the order you will complete them. Now go through your list and prioritize each task with an A, B, or C. Then go through all A's and firm up your priorities as A1, A2, A3, and so forth. Then go on to the Bs, and then the Cs. Now look at your list. You now have an order in which you will complete your list. If you must choose to leave some items incomplete, those items will be Cs.

Working Faster

By using your daily log you will automatically speed up your completion of daily tasks. Lack of organization is, in one sense, confusion over what to do next. Trying to hold in your head the acts and sequences of your daily routine is to place an unnecessary burden on yourself. You will have enough moment by moment mental bombardment from students, faculty, administration, and parents to keep your attention focused. Trying to retrieve a slipshod list of things to do from memory is a sure way to add to tension and confusion. But if by the time you depart for work you have your list clearly written and prioritized, all you need do throughout the day is refer to them. Just follow the list. If calling a parent is a high priority on your list, you will be more likely to make the call than you would had you not listed the call. Just follow the list and much of the struggle of completing the task disappears. As you complete a task, cross it off the list. The very act of crossing the item off the list will give you a sense of satisfaction. You will automatically speed up your work performance.

Using Wait Time

Another way of increasing your productivity is by using wait time. How many times have you allowed yourself to become bored and frustrated by placing yourself in situations where you have nothing to do? At a doctor's office or a hypnotic all-day drive on the freeway? Declare an end to wait time. Take a note pad to the doctor's office and plan some lessons, outline your ideas for the next departmental meeting, or, on the domestic side, make out a grocery list. There is no need to be bored when you drive. Take along plenty of audiotapes. In addition to music you can include tapes of lectures, workshops, and seminars. You can purchase or rent professional recordings of entire books.

Take a small tape recorder with you. As ideas come into your head—ideas for the next lesson, for the instructional material you want to check, for the next PTA meeting—put them on tape. If your interests turn to writing, this is a technique that will maximize your productivity. The author has written full-length articles while driving from Detroit to Atlanta, simply putting his ideas on tape as they come to him and later reorganizing them at the typewriter.

Overcoming Blocks

Sometimes when many tasks come at us at once, we become victims of overwhelm. The tendency is to shut down. After even a brief bout with flu it is easy to get behind. When papers get stacked up, you have many calls to return, or reports are due in the principal's office, you may feel that escape is the only solution. This reaction is based on an oversimplified interpretation of what confronts us. Either do all of it now or escape it—do nothing at all. The way out is neither of these approaches.

Try the "slice of cheese approach." Here you complete the major tasks a "slice at a time." This will get you back on track.

Take on the easy jobs first. Complete them quickly. Research shows that quickly completing a number of small tasks actually gives one energy to go on to larger tasks. This is a way of getting off living "on hold."

Organizing Your Work Space

Organizing your work space does not mean setting up a rigid environment; it does mean setting up an environment that supports you in your work. If you have to shuffle through countless papers each time you try to find an important letter, you are cheating yourself out of a support system that you can bring into being.

Set up a project for yourself to have an organized work space both at home and at school. Set a time for completion. Get your friends and fellow teachers to support you in this. Purchase organizers for important papers, secure a file cabinet, bookends, and in and out boxes. Sectionalize drawers in your desk for a supply of paper clips, rubber bands, colored markers, index cards, staples, and other necessary supplies (Figure 16.1). You should have a desk calendar that is large enough on which to write important forthcoming appointments.

As you complete forms, process them immediately. For memoranda, record the necessary information on your calendar or personal portfolio and throw away the memo. This way you can avoid clutter and stacks of paper. Some time-management experts say you should handle papers only once. The information gets stored on a calendar or computer as instructions to act on a particular date at a certain time. If the letter is not action oriented, if you can see no practical information forthcoming, then do not clutter your files with it. Put in your files communication and instructional materials that will further student learning and welfare, that have a bearing on your professional life, and that have possible legal implications.

Your work space should be comfortable. Some time-management specialists say you should face your desk toward a wall to avoid distraction, but facing a wall to work could completely close down people who work best with mild distraction. Research shows that music, particularly of the baroque type, can aid concentration in work.[1] Many persons, the author included, enjoy background music or even the busy chatter of a TV set. If you share an office, using a radio or cassette player with earphones could increase your productivity and work satisfaction. You must experiment to see

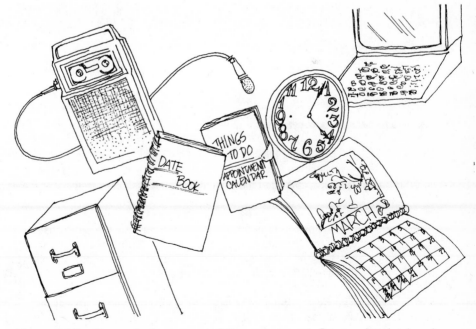

Figure 16.1 Master the instruments of time management. Set up a functional work space at home and at school.

what works for you. Remember, you want to do what supports your work—not to be a stereotyped image of a working robot.

| *Creating Projects* | You can create projects from your goals. As you decide to act on them, place them on your calendar and then translate them into daily activities. All of your projects should not be strictly professional, though they may be related. Projects can include |

camping, expeditions, travel, mastery of a new skill (such as photography, skydiving, or bridge), exploring rap music or a new opera, or mastering new software for your computer. Projects are ways of expanding your horizons through learning or recreation and preferably through a combination of both. They are ways of living to full capacity, of enriching your personal and professional life. Projects become self-created gifts to yourself and to your students and associates.

| *Systems That Support You* | Filing systems, tape recorders, dictaphones, computer storage systems, timers, stopwatches, appointment books, and time-management portfolios are all systems that can support you in keeping organized. There is no point in going out and purchas- |

ing all of these. Collecting equipment to look organized is not useful. Being organized is another matter, and as you become more organized you may perceive a need from time to time to make use of technology to support your new habits.

| *Eliminating Work: The Art of Delegating* | Whoever said you had to do it all? But isn't the teacher responsible for the work assigned—giving instruction, grading papers, keeping the room in order, taking roll, and the like. Yes, but this does not mean that you must physically do it all. You can train a paraprofessional or a willing student to help you. |

Delegate work. Teach a student assistant or aide to check the attendance using your seating chart. You can then use your time and energy to focus on quality teaching. Distractions caused by students coming in late can be handled systematically:

> . . . put a spiral tablet or a clipboard on a table or attach it somewhere near the door. When tardy students enter the room, they sign in before taking their seats. This preserves a record of tardy students and allows you to continue your instruction without interruption.[2]

This can eliminate any number of potential problems. If on February 3 the student claims he was not tardy during October and November, this student must confront the counterevidence of his own signature. You can have well-documented records, yet spend very little time handling these forms.

| **Increasing Energy Sources** |

You can increase energy sources in many ways. Instead of getting bogged down with a large, cumbersome task, choose a series of short, easy tasks. As you complete each task you will note that you are more motivated for the next one. There is nothing like completion of tasks to give you energy and momentum.

Many indefatigable workers like Thomas Edison and John F. Kennedy made a habit of taking short naps throughout the day. In this way, they virtually doubled and tripled their energy during work time. A 10-minute nap of "alpha rest" is deeply restorative and will give you a better energy boost at midday than pumping the system full of caffeine. Maintain a light daydreamlike state of consciousness. You don't want to actually go into deep "delta sleep." When you wake up from a "delta" nap, you may feel groggy all day. The trick is to control the *quality* of the rest and the duration—usually not over 10 minutes.

Alpha rest is like walking along the beach, looking at the waves coming in, hearing the sound of the gulls and feeling the sea breeze on your skin. Sit in a comfortable chair and close your eyes. Try it—continue your walk—and know that your daily walk takes just 10 minutes, for that is how long it takes to walk the length of beach up to the rock and return to the pathway that leads back to your home. Just 10 minutes. And during this time, it will be more like several hours have passed, for the waves coming in and the sound of the gulls take you back to a time in childhood when time was eternal and you walked on the beach and counted the waves coming in. So just stand now at the edge of the water and count the waves and listen to the sound of the tide and allow your mind to gain energy and freshness from the power of the waves coming in—and know that you will feel energy the rest of the day as you count the waves and gently walk down the beach. As the light comes up on the waves and the cry of the gulls increases, so does your energy. You quicken your pace and hurry down the beach toward the thought of the return path that is even now giving you an invigorating wakefulness. Open your eyes, stand up and stretch.

Try recording the above script on tape and play it at low volume. You can time the counting of the waves so that the wake-up part of the recording comes up in exactly 10 minutes from the beginning of the alpha process.

PROBE Create your own alpha process.

| **Create Your Own Time-Savers** |

You can spend your time very profitably by extracting general principles of time management from such paperbacks as Drew Scott's *How to Put More Time in Your Life*, Alexander Mackenzie's *The Time Trap*, and Alan Lakein's *How to Get Control of Your Time and Your Life*. The principles contained in these books have long been taught in business management seminars. With a little thought it is easy to adapt these principles to the work of teaching. For example, Parkinson's law, "Work expands to fill the time available for its completions," can be used to stress the necessity of stating educational goals and setting time lines for many teaching activities. Just notice what works for you and create.

Following are a number of time-savers created by student teachers and pre-student teachers:

1. Make "do lists" in specific behavioral terms. For example, don't just list "write term paper"; instead, put down "go to the library and check out specific books—make outline."
2. Cross off items on "do list" after they are complete. This gives one a psychological feeling of completion.
3. Do more than one thing at a time—for example, while cooking or washing dishes, make mental notes for a lesson plan.
4. Keep a journal and a calendar for agreements. This eliminates the energy drain of having to remember time that is promised.
5. Build in time for relaxation and recreation. Knowing that recreational time is built-in helps one to relax while working.
6. Get up earlier in the morning. Set aside a quiet time for yourself.
7. Think of time as distinct from space.
8. Use idle time to think ahead.
9. If you are organizing your office or home, tackle one section or room at a time.
10. Use boxes and folders to organize papers.

PROBE Put your time-savers on audiotape or on common bulletin boards to share them with fellow student teachers, students, and teachers. In *Space, Time and Medicine*, Larry Dossey reports the case of a young physician who controlled his migraine headaches by thinking of time as a circular river that flows in on itself rather than as a linear river—the most common way of representing time in Western culture.

When you are feeling overwhelmed by time, imagine time as a circular river and see what happens.

Effective Communication

All of your interaction with others will become smoother and more efficient when you master effective communication skills so that your intentions become clear to others. When you make a statement or a request, is your intention to persuade, to share, to demand, to avoid, to disregard, to reject, to help, to understand, to explore, or to clarify? Do others clearly know what you want? In Chapter 17 you will have an opportunity to master an effective model of communication, but for now it will be sufficient to notice how readily you are understood. Have your intentions clearly in mind. Don't waste your time and the administrator's or a fellow teacher's time by trying to decide what you want as you speak. Know what you want when you go into the conversation.

■ SUMMARY

Organization for effectiveness in teaching is much more than having organized grade books and lesson plans. It is being totally responsible for using time in the most productive and satisfying ways, both in one's professional and personal life. You can speed up your work by increasing energy sources and by actually working faster. Take notes by using key words or mind maps. Read rapidly by focusing on key words and key questions. You can increase the quality of your work production by generating life goals to which you are committed and by prioritizing your goals and daily tasks.

Learn to delegate and to train aides and students to perform tasks that can maximize their skills and learning opportunities and at the same time reduce your work load. You can learn to use wait time and to overcome blocks to productivity and feelings of "overwhelm" by using daily do lists and techniques such as the "slice of cheese approach." Daily interactions can be both speeded up and increased in quality by using clear communication. Quality of work and leisure can be enhanced through the creation of meaningful projects that are systematically translated into daily activities.

■ NOTES

1. Donald H. Schuster and Charles E. Gritton, *Suggestive Accelerative Learning Techniques* (New York: Gordon and Breach, 1986), 77.
2. Edmund T. Emmer et al., *Classroom Management for Secondary Teachers* (Englewood Cliffs, NJ: Prentice-Hall, 1984), 25.

■ PROGRAMS, SYSTEMS, AND SEMINARS

More Time: A Results Management Workshop
More Time Products
Order Department
240 Portland Avenue
Minneapolis, MN 55415
1-800-328-0324

Day-Timers, Inc.
Time Management Systems
P. O. Box 2368
Allentown, PA 18195-1551
1-215-395-5884 (Monday–Friday)

Evelyn Wood Reading Dynamics
c/o American Learning Corp.
Suite 800
200 S. Michigan Ave.
Chicago, IL 60604
1-800-447-7323

Coach Leatherware Co.
516 West 34th Street
New York, NY 10001
1-201-460-4716 (Monday–Friday)
(Leatherbound professional planners and
organizers)

CHAPTER 17

Communication as a Rhetoric of Inquiry

MARY C. FURLETTE

A teachers meeting: In an effective conference, issues are defined.

When we are working together at our best, we repudiate . . . the warfare of fixed positions; instead, we try out our reasons on each other, to see where we might come out. We practice a rhetoric of inquiry.

—Wayne Booth

I will not coerce you. Neither will I be coerced by you. If you behave unjustly, I will not oppose you by violence (body force) but by the force of truth—the integrity of my beliefs. My integrity is evident in my willingness to suffer, to endanger myself . . . seeing my intentions, sensing my compassion and my openness to your needs, you will respond in ways I could never manage by threat, bargaining, pleading, or body force. Together we can solve the problem. It is the opponent, not each other.

—Gandhi

Communication and Teaching

Ultimately, when a person speaks of effective teaching, methods of teaching, or teaching with excellence, the person is referring to the art of communication. Whether the communication is to define teaching, identify responsibilities, create a manageable environment, or organize time, one speaks of sending a message to another person:

> You are here today to participate in the educational process. You are here because someone cares about the transmission of knowledge from one generation to the next.

When one talks about motivating students, determining educational values, purposes, goals, or objectives, the person is setting criteria for evaluating whether a message is received by another person:

> This is what we are to learn. To share information, to acquire knowledge, to communicate, to think, and to act in light of the knowledge we understand for the benefit of ourselves and others.

Acquiring a teaching style, selecting video materials, or preparing a portfolio are all ways of presenting one's thoughts and images:

> This is who I am. These are the materials I have selected. I need to know who you are so that together we can learn through understanding of one another.

The communicator seeks to convey a message verbally or nonverbally, in written or oral form in such a manner that the communication is heard and received by another person and the intent of the sender is carried. A style of communication is effective when the message one sends is the same or equal to what is heard or received by the other person:

> Education is an active process. My participation is as important as the teacher's participation. I must be able to communicate who I am to this teacher.

The art of communication is an intricate balance between the message or communication sent and the message received:

> If you don't know the kind of person I am and I don't know the kind of person you are, a pattern that others made may prevail in the world and following the wrong God home, we may miss our star.*

Together we can make a difference.

■ *Adopting a Style of Communication*

Just as it is important to adopt a style of dress, a method of teaching, or a style of writing to convey "who I am," it is equally important to select a style of communication. Communication will help to convey who I am to others. Style of communication is a choice, perhaps one of the most crucial choices an effective teacher will make in his or her career. Style of communication is a prerequisite of excellence. It is a barometer of the degree of openness and interaction that one will create between students, parents, administrators, and other educators. The principles outlined in this chapter represent one style of communication that an effective teacher may choose to adopt. They are based on the work of Sherod Miller and associates with couples, families, and employers in business and industry (see bibliographical references for this chapter at the end of this book). In this chapter some of Sherod Miller's techniques and principles in his *Connecting with Self and Others* are applied to the educational process, specifically in the context of conferencing.

■ *Effective Communication Through Conferencing*

To facilitate the educational process and to create a state of understanding between home, school, and the community, schools have developed a process known as conferencing. Conferencing provides the opportunity for interpersonal interaction and solidifies the efforts to open communication to all care-givers for the socializing of the student. Conferencing is the framework for the process of communication. Messages are communicated between parents, students, teachers, counselors, administrators, guardians, and any other socializers. Conferencing is a means by which two or more persons gather to communicate and exchange their observations, perceptions, feelings, expectations, wants, desires, thoughts, or instincts about the student.

Simply stated, conferencing is communication or interpersonal interaction between parent and teacher; student, teacher, and parent; counselor and teacher; counselor and student; teacher and administrator; or any other combination of persons interested in the student's acquisition of knowledge. Conferencing is an exchange of information and relays the message that this is who I am, and I need to

*This quotation and the previous four are from William Stafford.

know who you are and what your expectations are for this student. Conferencing is for the benefit of the student. To communicate with excellence, the effective teacher needs to know what issues relate to a student, what other observations can contribute to the facilitation of the learning process, what is meant by all of these observations, and what solutions or alternatives can be created so that the student will be nurtured by the educational process. In this process, conferencing provides the framework to send and receive information pertinent to the student's growth and development. Ideally, for the effective teacher, conferencing is communication that extends the experience between student and teacher beyond the classroom to the home and the community. It is a means of building a relationship between other socializers for the purpose of understanding the student's strengths and needs. Ideally it coordinates and networks the efforts of education.

Historically and perhaps universally the word "conferencing" has been used within educational institutions to denote a period of time set aside for communication about a student's progress. Again, historically, conferencing has been understood more as a giving of information by a teacher to a significant other person than as a communication process in which all persons give and receive information. Take, for example, the classic parent-teacher conference. There is a general understanding that parent-teacher conferences are meetings in which parents learn about their children's progress. The teacher gives: the parent receives. The teacher relays the information about success-failure, about outcome rather than education process, about potential for success and how much better the child would do if effort were applied to his or her behavior problems that interfered with others in the classroom, and so on. Understanding is somewhat limited in the sense that the traditional parent-teacher conference has been a time set aside for the teacher to talk, to show and tell, to set objectives, to dictate, and to control.

This has led, unfortunately, to a negative view of parent-teacher conferences unless, perhaps, the student being evaluated is working to his or her full potential, is not a problem, and falls within the category of genius or "mostly likely to succeed." Over the years the word "conferencing" has led to many questions of accountability. Who is responsible for the student's acquisition of knowledge? The overtones of defensiveness and of misplaced judgment and displaced responsibility superseded building a unified network of members responsible for the transmission of knowledge. The relationship that should exist between teacher, parent, and child became a battleground of personalities and left communication closed rather than open.

If the teacher places conferencing within the context of communication and relationship-building, and uses the time set aside to discuss a student's progress as a time to learn and gather others' observations about the student, then conferencing can become effective. Conferencing can be used to build a relationship with the student, can be an equal exchange of information, and can create a unified experience in which parent, teacher, student, and administrator work together to accomplish the goals of education. Conferencing is talking *and* listening.

Conferencing has been a time for judging, evaluating, and analyzing behavior in terms of good and bad, right and wrong, and proper and improper. Perhaps one reason for the change in perspectives on conferencing relates to the statistic that children are better educated and have more educational opportunities than students did some 20 years ago. In any event, conferencing is becoming the process of communication and relationship building between homes, schools, and communities.

It is the experiences of the student with the parent as well as with the teachers and administrators that will shape the educational process, and these experiences will be shared through the conferencing process. Communication through conferencing is the life spirit of the classroom.

■ Issues for Conferencing

Because the conferencing process is a coordinated effort that addresses the strengths and needs of the student between home, school, and community, it requires communication between all socializers. The parents, the teachers, the students, the administrators, and all significant other persons contribute observations, perceptions, thoughts, feelings, and plans of action for the education of an individual student. Because each person contributing to conferencing will have a different experience of the student, come from a different relationship, and represent a different role in the life of the student, their thoughts will differ from person to person. Any difference in perception gives rise to an issue. Sherod Miller defines an issue as a difference between two persons. In respect to education, this can mean a difference in perception of strengths, weaknesses, or methods of teaching, as well as of many other features of the educational process.

The conferencing process as it exists today encompasses a multitude of issues. A student is no longer in school just for the purpose of learning to read and write. A student is viewed from a holistic perspective as a member of a family and as a member of the community in addition to being a student in the educational process. The goals of the educational system are expanded beyond the intellectual domain of the student. They include objectives that are aimed at generalizing beyond the classroom. The conferencing process has become a highly defined communication process—a kind of team planning. Together with parents and with input from the student, teachers set goals and objectives for the student.

The issues a teacher may initiate or be called upon to discuss through conferencing include intellectual, emotional, social, and physical issues. They may relate to the cognitive domain of growth and development or to independent functioning, social interaction, behavior, or performance. These categories are broad domains. They are presented here as a frame of reference.

Identification and specification of the area of growth and development is the first step in the conferencing process. Theoretically, anyone can call a conference. Anyone can ask to communicate. Anyone who has information that is relevant to the student's progress in school should call a conference. A parent may notice a child is resisting attending school. A teacher may observe a student sleeping in class, failing quizzes, or acting aggressively toward another. An administrator may receive a complaint from another parent regarding a student. A student may be noncompliant with respect to policy and standards set by the school. A medical doctor may want to conference regarding diabetes or epilepsy. If a learning disorder is discovered by a school psychologist, a program may be needed to address that problem. Anyone from the school, from the community, or in the home may observe a behavior that will affect the performance of the student in school. Complaints, self-referrals, and referrals by professionals, parents, or teachers are all ways of identifying a problem.

A problem, according to Sherod Miller, is nothing more than an issue that has not met with resolution. Issues build one upon another. They become complicated when there are so many issues that a conference alone will be insufficient to address them. In addition, a parent wants to hear about an issue occurring at school before it requires multiple interventions. Early identification can prevent an issue from becoming "out of control." A teacher wants to know if a child has a specific learning disability or a medical condition that requires adjustment of classroom activities for the student. The psychologist wants to know of emotional problems such as withdrawal, aggressiveness, moodiness, sleeping patterns, the frequency of behavior, and the like, so as to set up recommendations for smoothing the learning process. Issues are any observations within the intellectual, social, emotional, or physical domain that influence the student's behavior or performance in school.

The effective teacher resolves issues with the student first. As a teacher, your primary responsibility is toward that student. Your rapport will be with that student, and a relationship with that student should be established and maintained from the beginning of the school year.

■ General Approaches for Resolution of Issues

The purpose of conferencing is to create a state of understanding between home, school, and community through communication. Conferencing is communication. The student about whom we hold a conference is approached from a holistic view. The student is a member of the family, of the community, and of the educational system. Part of this holistic view is that the student's growth and development encompass many domains—intellectual, physical, emotional, and social development. While the teacher's responsibility focuses on intellectual development, the teacher will have the responsibility to predict issues in other areas of development. After identifying an issue, the teacher will need to determine who should be included in a conference. In any conference, the primary care-givers—the parents—should be advised and included in the conferencing process. The nature of the issue will direct the teacher to include others or identify others for conferencing.

Communication with others in a conferencing format is at best tricky. Each member of a conference will act as part of a team for the purpose of resolving the issue. Each member will have unique input—unique observations, thoughts, feelings, wants, or intentions—and will see the issue being resolved in several ways. Each member will have suggestions as to the possible cause of the issue. What the teacher views as aggressive behavior may be viewed as self-assertiveness by a psychologist. What a teacher sees as a learning disability may be viewed by another as related to physical problems. Each member will see or identify varying strengths, weaknesses, and needs for the student. Each member has input that is valuable for the resolution of the issue.

Conferencing is a combination of group process and individual planning. Conferencing usually centers on a particular student, not a group of students. Communication principles of both individual and group processing need to be considered.

All conferencing or communication is for a purpose. The purpose of the communication can and will vary. So, also, the principles can and will vary in the conferencing. On the one hand, each member of a conference will specify an issue, identify a possible cause, and offer solutions for the issue. On the other hand, each member is part of a team that has been pooled together for the purpose of planning for a student. There is, so to speak, both an "I" and a "we" in the process of communication in conferencing. The "I" part of the conference is the individual input. "I" observed the student sleeping in class; "I" observe a decrease in performance; "I" think this is the cause; "I" feel frustrated; "I" want to talk about the issue; "I" see this or that as the solution. The "we" part of the conference is the consensus of the group that the plan of action or program devised is to include certain elements.

Both the "I" and the "we" of conferencing are necessary components of communication. The "I" of conferencing allows for brainstorming ideas, solutions and the resolution of issues. The "we" of conferencing unifies understanding. The "we" is supportive for all members of the conference, suggesting a shared responsibility for the socialization and education of the student.

Conference Planning and Preparation

The first principle of social psychology goes something like this. In some ways, we are like all other persons; in some ways, we are like no other person; and in some ways we are unique. So, also, in the school setting some students will be like all other students; some students will be like some other students; and in some ways the student will be like no other student. It is the focus of the student as no other student that will aid in preparation for the conference.

There are many reasons why issues and problems arise in the educational process. Sometimes the parenting skills of moms and dads are ineffective, and as socializers we need to support any parenting efforts that are believed to benefit the child. Sometimes the methods of teaching chosen by a teacher are ineffective with a given student. Since one student is like no other student, a different methodology may be required; so, also, with management or administration. One standard or policy may address the organizational needs of many but fail for the student who is like no other student. Individual differences in students as persons give rise to issues or problems in the educational system. It is these individual differences that are conferenced most often.

If the conferencing process can be viewed as a support system for all socializers, communication will be effective and issues will be resolved. Adolescents often choose to take the path of least resistance when confronted with an issue: "My father is an alcoholic." "My mother is a hysteric." "My probation officer is a dud." "My teacher is demanding." "She doesn't like me." "He is unfair." "It is their fault (the socializers) that I am the way that I am." Teenagers may never assume responsibility for their own behavior and fail to grow and develop in a productive manner if they do not gain the support from teachers acting as socializers.

Your student is the focus of the communication during conferencing. Your team or other professionals are your support system. Together you will reach the best plan for the student who is like no other student.

The first step to planning for the conference, then, is to see those who will attend the the meeting as a support team. Next, view the student like no other student. Gather information from the past and the present, and develop alternatives for the future. Avoid labeling, which just states how the student is like some other students, but not how he is like *no* other student.

Identify the message you wish to send. Identify the message as it relates to the issue. Is the issue related to learning? Is it a cognitive problem? Does it have implications for social functioning? Are the issues related to performance? What are the strengths of the student? What are the needs of the student? Is the issue a behavioral issue, and does it interfere with the adjustment of others as well as the student? What has been the mood of the student? Have you observed any withdrawing behaviors, or is the student aggressive toward others? What have been past interventions for the issue? How were they handled, with what techniques? Were the techniques effective in controlling the issue? How do others relate to the student? How does the student relate to others? What are your recommendations? What plan of action do you wish to give the team? Are there inconsistencies in behavior or performance? Are there gaps in the information or assessment you have reviewed? What do you wish to say to other professionals about the issue? Can you identify areas where other professionals may be able to answer questions related to the issues?

When you are the initiator of a conference, identify the issues for others involved. This will allow them time to prepare to address the issue. It will allow them time to review and make observations relevant to the situation.

Be honest and open in approaching parents whether it be by phone, in writing, or in person. Let them know that you do not have all the answers, but that together you can reach solution. Emphasize the strengths of the student. Minimize the weakness. Look at all students as having the potential to learn and act as if you are looking for the key that will unlock that ability. Parents sometimes become hostile or negative because they are placated by teachers and other socializers. They worry about the influence they have over their children when they go to school. They see the school as substitute parents with differing philosophies and are often placed on the defensive.

Own the issue for the purpose of resolution. State to another: "I have an issue that I wish to discuss." "The issue is _____." This places the responsibility for communication on the person using the word "I" and frees the other person to examine the issue with you.

Avoid placing blame. Always be positive. Avoid interpretations. They are simply assumptions. Causation and interpretation belong to the group process of conferencing, not to an individual member alone. You may suggest causation, but leave this open for discussion.

Prepare for a conference as if you were networking the student to home, school, and community. View the conference as a support system and as a coordinating effort to socialize the student. Remember that the problems in the classroom might not be the problems in the home. Or the problems in the community may not reflect what is seen in school. Go to the conference prepared to identify issues related only to the school, then look and listen to others to see if the problem or issue is unique to the home, to the school, or to the community. The severity of an issue is identified by its occurrence in more than one setting. It is a diagnostic feature of a disorder. And treatment or intervention will need to be coordinated to resolve the issue.

Recognize your limits as a teacher. Your information is as valuable as any other in the conference. Prepare only those facts, observations, and assessments that relate to school and classroom behavior or performance.

■ About Observations

Observations are any bits or pieces of information received through the sensory organs and become processed as a thought. In this model, observations precede thoughts. The assumption is that we do not think before we receive sensory information. Observations may be information that a teacher has heard, seen, or discovered; or they may be larger pieces of information, such as an assessment of previous academic performance, school records, data-collection results, or verbal and nonverbal communication with the student or others. Before using an observation in a conference or as part of an issue, check that observation for characteristics of consistency or frequency. Checking out and clarifying information before the conference will help prevent labeling. It will also help keep the conference focused on the issue.

Sherod Miller has identified the sensory data—that which we see, hear, taste, smell, or touch—as the documenting factors for thought. Without observations there is no data. Observation leads to thought.

■ About Thoughts

Sensory data is processed by the act of thinking. An observation leads to thought. Thought gives meaning and context to the observation. Thoughts are interpretations of what is observed. They may lead to conclusions, assumptions (sometimes false), private opinions, images, or impressions. Expressing a thought at a conference does not make a statement true. It only leads to the discovery of the causes for the issue. Reserve your thoughts while expressing them in the conference. Reserve your judgments and conclusion. The team or other professionals will draw conclusions from the presentation of all possible causes as perceived by other members of the team. Judgmental attitudes come about when a teacher or any other professional acts upon a thought. A thought is a possible reason, but not necessarily *the* reason for the issue. Listening to others and hearing their observations and thoughts will give rise to the direction of the probable cause, but not necessarily *the* cause.

■ *About Feelings*

Feelings, perhaps more than any other component of communication, are subjective. They are valid because they belong to the person who experiences them, but unreliable because they belong *only* to that person. It is true that feelings have a role in communication but not in the decision-making process. Being subjective, they cloud the objectivity of the issue. Feelings arise from our observations. They are a natural consequence of the thinking process. Feelings may be positive or negative. A teacher might feel concerned about a student's progress or angry because a student is noncompliant. If there are strong negative feelings about a student, it is good to express them outside the conference to another professional so as to free oneself of the negative effect that could be produced in the conference. It is difficult for teachers to face an issue day after day with a student and remain calm. Recognize that difficulty and remember that feelings place others on the defensive, misdirect the communication of an issue, and sometimes prevent the creative solution of the issue.

■ *About Intentions*

Intentions are best defined as what a person wants to accomplish. A distinction is in order between an intention or want and a need. A need is a demand. A want is goal-related. What one wants for a student may not be what one needs for the student. In the school conference what is wanted is a resolution for the student, for the teacher, and for the educational process.

If one looks at the components of communication thus presented, we can begin to hypothesize that the observation provides input that creates a state of imbalance physiologically. The thought process attempts to resolve sensory input. Wants or intentions are the components of communication that give rise to homeostasis in communication. If wants are verbalized, then solutions can be generated. Knowing what you want and including it as part of the communication process in conferencing will lead to the setting of goals and objectives for the resolution of issues. In his research with communication between couples, Sherod Miller discovered that both men and women could express what they observed, what they thought or felt, but that both sexes had difficulty identifying what they wanted when they communicated on an issue. And the key to resolution is the intention.

Advanced preparation will give the effective teacher the opportunity to examine intentions and this will speed up the communication process while facilitating the conference.

■ *About Actions*

Actions are plans for resolution of an issue. Actions are the framework within which goals and objectives are defined in the resolution of an issue. The action part of communication belongs to the decision-making process. A plan of action should include means of implementation for goals and objectives set during the conference and the criteria to measure the outcome of the goals and objectives. While gathering observations for presentation in the conference, let your mind wander to solutions and interventions appropriate for the issue. Be able to give other professionals your alternative methods for interventions.

Sherod Miller in his work with couples has identified sensations, interpretation, feelings, intentions, and actions as the necessary components in sending a complete message. With one-on-one interaction or relationship-building, all components may and should be expressed. In the conferencing process where group interaction is the focus of an issue, all components are important, but feelings must be forfeited for the consensus of the group and the resolution of an issue.

Planning a conference will include such factors as setting the time and place and identifying the issues to be discussed. In addition, balancing and coordinating schedules will be of primary importance.

If possible, outline the issue by identifying your observations, thoughts, perceptions, and feelings, and be able to circulate, if possible, relevant data for others to review.

Teachers serve students. They are teaching to share information and disseminate knowledge that will be passed on for generations. Research verifies over and over again that there is no such thing as a bad parent. The student's first relationship was with his or her parents, no matter what your judgment of that may be. Always treat the parents as the primary caregivers of the child, and assume a strong positive relationship exists between that parent and child. The perceptions of parent and child may and do vary. The relationship does not.

When gathering information from past records, treat that information cautiously. Be influenced by the present, not the past. What is done is done, and students need grounds for developing new relationships. Put past information in its proper perspective. Nothing is more discouraging than to listen to teachers who have reviewed the records and discovered many problems and issues with students and then begin using the information to justify their judgmental attitudes about the student. Give the student the benefit of the doubt. You are new in their lives. You can make a difference. The trust the student failed to discover in another relationship does not imply that he or she is unable to develop a new relationship with trust. Let the conference be for the benefit, not to the detriment, of the student.

■ *Shared Meaning*

Sherod Miller has identified "shared meaning" as the key to successful communication. This process is attained when the receiver of a message hears exactly what the sender intends to say and in the same context and with the same meaning.

Shared meaning is a tricky concept. It requires that the receiver of the message understand the definition of all concepts and words presented. Ascertaining whether the message as heard is simple enough. Ask the receiver what he or she heard you say, and then correct any misinterpretations. In listening and clarifying statements from others, it is wise to know the meaning of the words and the context in which they are presented.

While there are many listening techniques for communication, listening is assured when shared meaning is targeted as the goal of communication. The process of shared meaning is simple enough. Each participant in a conference will have equal input into the discussion. Each will hopefully present his or her observations, perceptions, thoughts, interpretations, conclusions, assumptions, feelings, and wants and propose a plan of action. It is wise to listen with a little monitoring sheet divided into various components of communications. As each person speaks, jot down the person's thoughts, interpretations, and other information. If you see that a component of the communication is missing, formulate a question in that area and ask for the person's thoughts and impressions. Check each statement made for the intent of the statement. Clarify meanings. Ask the question, "What do you mean by aggressive, withdrawn, or manipulative?" This will prevent confrontation and prevent power plays in a meeting.

General Guidelines for Conferencing

All conferencing or communication is for a purpose. The purpose of communication can and will vary. Initial conferencing is for the purpose of establishing rapport, and all subsequent conferencing is for maintaining that rapport for the benefit of the student. Some reasons for conferencing are to explore, to search, to understand, to be responsive, to support, to approach, to share, to listen, to persuade, to be honest, to set goals and objectives, to plan, to follow up on previous conferences, to praise, to celebrate, to ponder, and to clarify. All conferencing or communication in the school system is for the intent and purpose of facilitating the educational process through the art of understanding a student wholly and within the environment in which the student functions.

■ *Social Conferencing (Establishing Rapport)*

Early in the school year, usually before the first marking period (reporting on performance), an administrator will set aside time for parents and other involved socializers to visit the school. This first meeting of the school year will set the tone for the remainder of the year. It will determine the direction of communication between the school and the community and home. Its purpose is to provide the opportunity to meet with other socializers and establish the structure of the organization and guidelines for policy. It usually sets forth the expectations, goals and objectives for the school year.

An effective teacher will utilize this opportunity to establish rapport with as many of the parents of students as possible. The effective teacher will seize the opportunity to open lines of communication and will send a message; "This is who I am. Who are you?"

At this first meeting of the school year rapport is established. This rapport will open lines of communication for discussion of issues throughout the school year. Encourage freedom of interaction with parents. Develop a sense of who the parents are as persons. Use the time to socialize, being pleasant, open, positive, receptive, available, and cooperative by visiting with parents, sharing information about your expectations, joking, smiling, reporting or sharing ideas about education in general. Listen for background information that may identify cultural differences or potential issues.

Set aside a time to meet with the parents of students for an initial contact. If parents do not attend the gathering, contact them and request to meet with them individually.

If during the course of this conference an issue arises that a parent wishes to discuss, schedule an appointment, but continue with the social conferencing process. Open up lines of communication and use this first meeting as social time for the purpose of establishing rapport. Let the parents or other socializers see a teacher who maintains an open-door policy, one who is approachable and concerned. In effect, establish your effectiveness as a teacher by encouraging freedom of interaction.

Social conferencing will establish rapport as well as open up alternative lines of communication with parents. It may be necessary to telephone a parent or send a written request for conferencing later in the school year. This social conferencing will give face-to-face communication in a nonthreatening setting that will later provide the groundwork for other communication. Be positive. Demonstrate effectiveness. Open up lines of communication.

■ *Maintaining Rapport with Parents or Guardians*

Establishing rapport has provided a groundwork for discussion of issues with parents and guardians throughout the school year. It is of vital importance, for the purpose of maintaining rapport and creating a state of understanding for the benefit of the student, to hold individual conferencing with a nonjudgmental attitude. Conferencing, if it is to be effective, must eliminate all elements of blaming, attacking, accusing, ridiculing, defending, complaining, placating, and labeling. While the teacher's effectiveness will include behaviors of directing, advising, or praising, it should omit intentions of authoritative, intrusive, coercive, depreciative, and negative behaviors. The intent and purpose of individual conferencing or communicating is to explore, search, speculate, formulate, and reflect on issues, and to be clear, direct, complete, responsive, open, and spontaneous. The individual conference is held to report, clarify, brainstorm, share, listen, present, resolve, assist, and allow communication. The role of the effective teacher in individual conferencing is to facilitate creative communication and resolution of issues in order to earn the respect of the parents as well as their trust; to be aware of their influence in the life of the student and the student's educational experience; to be empathetic and encouraging; and to be honest, open and supportive.

In individual conferencing or communication there is no room for judgment—just

The individual conference is held to report, clarify, brainstorm, share, listen, present, resolve, assist, and allow communication.

evaluation. There is no right or wrong, no good or bad, no correct or incorrect. There are messages to be sent for evaluation by another person, and that person can accept or reject, act or not act on the information provided. There are issues to be discussed and communicated. The observations, perceptions, thoughts, feelings, wants, or suggested actions for resolution by the effective teacher will be met with the observations and thoughts, the feelings, and the intentions and suggested resolutions of the parent or student. The sharing of information from both sides will facilitate the course of action to be initiated for resolution of the issue.

Generally speaking, creative conferencing, or communication on an individual basis, is limited to classroom behavior and performance. While other factors may be included in the communication behavior and performance, issues beyond the classroom are most effectively resolved by interdisciplinary team action. This guideline will give the effective teacher direction and focus if followed consistently. It will define the teacher's responsibility and role, thereby supporting the teacher's effectiveness. Limit creative conferencing to classroom behavior and performance. Use referral services if necessary for the resolution of issues that exceed classroom performance and behavior.

PROBES
1. What are the issues to be conferenced in creative or individual conferences?
2. What is the purpose of social conferencing or communication?
3. What are the purposes of creative conferencing?
4. Design a case study for conferencing. What are your thoughts, observations, feelings, and solutions for the issue? Project or imagine how the parents are going to respond by identifying their thoughts, observations, feelings, or resolutions.
5. What do you want for the student? What do you want for yourself? What is needed for the educational process to be effective?
6. What is the role of the effective teacher in creative conferencing? What does the teacher hope to accomplish? What are the limits of creative conferencing?

■ *Planning Through Group Process*

When an issue exceeds the limits of creative conferencing, when an issue includes more than performance and behavior, when an issue is global and requires attention by several experts, a group conference is scheduled to plan, evaluate, set goals, and objectives for the student. Usually such a conference will address issues in all areas of development: intellectual, emotional, and social. Such a conference is held when a student is discovered to have multiple handicaps. The student, for example, may be developmentally disabled as well as intellectually limited. The student may be emotionally disturbed and socially maladapted. Such a case might be discovered by an effective teacher. An effective teacher will recognize the limits of his or her expertise and will initiate such a conference for direction and guidance in communicating with the student in the classroom while providing additional educational services for the student.

The success of a group conference will depend upon the individual member's ability to compromise and be receptive to new information. An effective teacher will be able to present observations, perceptions, thoughts, and feelings, and will be able to offer solutions in conjunction with other professionals. In group conferencing, there are several observations, thoughts, feelings, and differing solutions to an issue. The needs, preferences, strengths, and weaknesses of the student are all presented by several professionals in the group.

The purpose of a group conference is to develop an educational plan from the ideas, thoughts, perceptions, knowledge, and expertise of these professionals. The effective teacher will share the responsibility and authority of group process as well as submit to the decisions of the group with respect to the student.

Group conferencing requires guidelines for ascertaining when an issue exceeds the limits of the classroom and requires input from several educational experts.

Group conferencing is utilized when a student requires more than weekly attention from a teacher or when the issues that the teacher experiences with the student are beyond the definition of performance and/or behavior. Utilize the group conferencing process for the benefit of the student's total adjustment within the educational system.

■ *Behavior and Performance*

No chapter on communication would be complete without reference to behavior and performance. In the educational system, the ideal is to resolve differences at an issue level; however, probably more often than not, issues are multiple and relate to several areas of development.

A good combination of effectiveness that allows students to assume responsibility for their behavior is empathy with and understanding of that behavior. Behavior occurs either individually or in a group. Group behavior is best known in the school system as peer interaction and delinquent behavior. Individual behavior is unique to the person and occurs across settings, with or without group interaction. All behavior is learned. All behavior is learned in a context or setting. All behavior will occur within a context. All behavior is communicative. And all behavior is connected with the reinforcement of that behavior. So behavior is communicative, reinforced to be maintained; it is learned, connected with performance, and occurs in a setting.

All behavior is connected with stress levels and with compliance. Research shows a connection between compliance or noncompliance, stress and environment. Some researchers have shown a connection between reinforcement of commands and performance and the reduction of noncompliant behavior. In fact, the idea is so popularized at this time that the researchers in the field have come up with a new form of differential reinforcement of other behavior (DRO) as part of behavior programming. The new term is differential reinforcement of communicative behavior (DRC). Communication is involved in behavior, the maintenance of behavior, and the reinforcement of the behavior. Learning is a crucial part of that behavior. With groups, behavior will have a communicative function most likely related to social issues or cultural stress. With individuals, communication will be a barometer of stress level. (See Chapter 19, on stress, for an in-depth discussion of this point.)

There are three general principles to consider in the interpretation of behavior:

1. The context in which the behavior occurs
2. The antecedent and consequent conditions
3. The communicative function

Context might include the environmental factors in which the behavior occurs, such as overcrowding, lighting, diet, physiological characteristics of the student, task difficulty or ability level, stress levels, and time and place. Remember we are looking for the occurrence of behavior across settings—in the home, the school, and the community. To correct the issue we must be able to generalize the program of action.

Antecedent conditions include those factors that led to the behavior. Was the student alone? With others? What is reinforcing to the student? For what will the student work—for social praise, grade, or leisure time?

Communicative functions are limitless. To determine the communicative function of a behavior is to place our thoughts or interpretations on the behavior. The following functions will help you to orient objectively in drawing your conclusions about behavior. Ask yourself:

Is the behavior for attention, social interaction, or both?

Is it for assistance or for testing the limits?

Is it to protest or be noncompliant?

Is it a statement about feelings such as anger, boredom, frustration, confusion, fear or pain, or perhaps pleasure?

Is the behavior an attempt to interact with others?

Remember, behavior occurs in the context of the person in a given situation.

■ *SUMMARY*

As an effective teacher you will need to combine the skills and principles of this chapter with your attitude. Your attitude will determine whether or not you can successfully apply these skills.

Attitude is a choice that you will make as an effective teacher. It will be reflected in the style of communication you choose. It will be demonstrated in your respect of the student, the parent, and the school system in which you work. As an effective teacher you will seek through communication skills to establish rapport with your students and together complete the goals of education. As an effective teacher you will seek to know not only yourself and your perceptions, thoughts, and intentions, but also seek to know the perceptions, thoughts, and intentions of your students, their parents, or guardians and your administrators. You will value and cherish the relationship you have with each of them. Communication through teamwork will produce the life-spirit of the classroom, and that spirit of integrity will spread to the homes and communities in which you reside.

The key to communication is empathy and understanding. These characteristics of the effective teacher will identify who the teacher is as a person. They will open lines of communication, and the teacher will experience who they are as persons. Together they will include others in their experience and will know who the parents and administrators are as persons.

Communication is the fruit of dedication and is the life-spirit of the classroom. It consists of a delicate balance between the experiences of the teacher and the experiences of the students. Out of these experiences and through communication the educational process is created.

Classroom Management

WRITTEN WITH JANET BOBBY

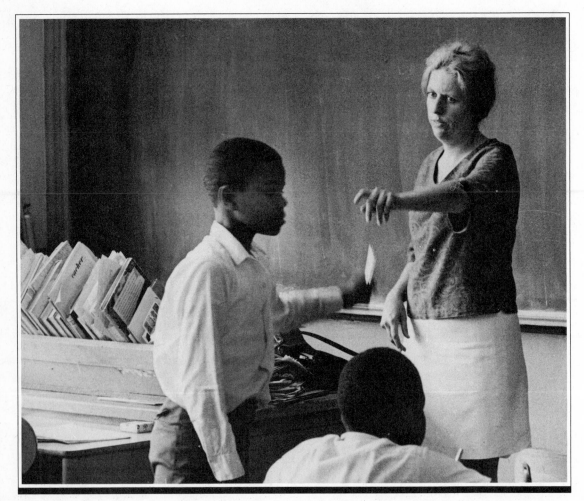

Teacher using body language to establish control.

Teachers must know what they want the students to do.

—Lee Canter

For him who has conquered the mind, the mind is the best of friends, but for one who has failed to do so his very mind will be the greatest enemy.

—Chapter 6, Text 6, *Bhagavad-Gita*

Lee Canter's assertion that "teachers must know what they want students to do" sounds simple enough on the surface, yet far too many teachers do not have a clear picture of the behavior they expect of their students. In working with over 350,000 K–12 teachers throughout the United States, Canter found that teachers often gave vague responses to the question "What do you want students to do?" Some typical responses were:

"I want kids to act good."

"I'm not sure what I specifically want, but I guess I want them to be good citizens and have a positive attitude."

"I want the children to respect me and each other."

"I don't want hassles from the boys who are troublemakers."[1]

What does a student acting "good" look like? What kinds of behavior represent "good citizenship"? What specific actions—verbal and nonverbal behavior—will be accepted as showing respect to the teacher and other students? What do "hassles" look like? Can you physically describe them?

Many beginning teachers feel insecure about discipline. Like Canter's teachers they have not examined what they really want their students to do. They find themselves wavering between competing popular approaches to class control, but unable to take a strong stand on the matter. Should they seek out the root psychological causes of deviant behavior? Should they reason with the student, drawing forth the student's understanding of the consequences of deviant behavior? Should they ignore deviant behavior and feed conforming kids M&Ms? Or should they send all "problem kids" to the office and "not smile till Christmas"?

Many of these views are distortions of some complete management systems based on the concepts of Freud, Glasser, Skinner, and perhaps Scrooge. For now, however, we shall begin our study of discipline with a system not included on this list—a system based on assertiveness training.

Assertive Discipline

Assertive training has been popularized by such books as Herbert Fensterheim and Jean Baer's, *Don't Say Yes When You Want to Say No,* Manuel Smith's *When I Say No I Feel Guilty,* Robert Alberti and Michael Emmons's *Your Perfect Right*, and Stanlee Philips and Nancy Austin's *The Assertive Woman.* Dr. Arnold Lazarus's *Behavior Therapy and Beyond* is useful in exploring the theoretical foundation of assertive training. The movement was adapted to a school setting by Lee and

Marlene Canter in their *Assertive Discipline* and assertive discipline workshop, which is available through many in-service programs throughout the United States.

Assertive training draws clear distinctions between passive, hostile, and assertive behavior. Much of the behavior that gets examined consists of verbal communication. Parallel cues such as eye contact, body position, and quality of voice are also examined (see Figure 18.1). In assertive training workshops one learns to reshape how one speaks to others. Passive and hostile communication is identified and replaced with assertive speech choices.

The *American Heritage Dictionary* defines *assert* as "to state; to defend or maintain one's rights; to express oneself forcefully or boldly." *Hostile* is defined as "feeling or showing enmity; antagonistic." *Passive* is defined as "accepting without objection or resistance; submissive, compliant." After considering these definitions, let us now turn to a few examples to clarify the distinctions.

Suppose you were in line at the bank and someone forced his way in front of you. Nonassertive responses would be:

1. Doing nothing
2. Avoiding the issue: "Long wait, isn't it?"
3. Leaving the line, holding the bank responsible for not noticing and disciplining the person

Hostile responses would be:

1. "What kind of crazy bank is this—waiting on guys who break in line?"
2. "You've got some nerve, mister—breaking into line."
3. Punching out the line breaker.

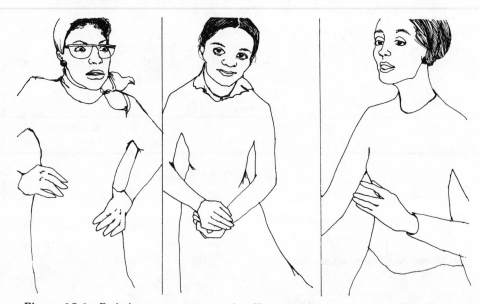

Figure 18.1 Body language can convey hostility, passivity, and assertion. The effective teacher practices an assertive use of the body.

Assertive responses would be:

1. "Sir, I was here first." (Eye contact, moving in front of him)
2. "Sir, the line begins back there. I am next."

PROBE   Recall a situation in which you were passive. How did you feel after the situation was over? Recall an incident in which you were hostile. How did you feel afterwards? Recall an incident in which you were assertive. How did you feel afterwards? How would you describe each way of communicating?

Let's spell out the technology implicit in the definitions and above examples and apply this technology to controlling a class.

Fensterheim and Baer describe three levels of assertion. The implication is that training should begin at the lower level:

1. *Nonverbal:* Eye contact, standing straight, firm voice
2. *Basic assertive skills:* Ability to say no and yes; ask favors; make requests; communicate feelings and thoughts in an open, direct way; handle put-downs; control work habits
3. *Complex situation:* Adaptive behavior in job situations, ability to form a social network, achieving close personal relations, parental relations[2]

Simple behaviors should not be overlooked. Nonverbal behavior is a powerful tool of class control. The effective teacher uses many nonverbal cues throughout the day to conduct the class. Progressively stronger degrees of assertion can be conveyed as follows:

1. The teacher stops speaking (silence).
2. The teacher establishes eye contact with the student.
3. The teacher uses a calming gesture.
4. The teacher stands near the student.

In one workshop, a participant had to work for 15 minutes to break through nonassertive habits. The task was to make a simple request like, "Raise the pencil, lower the pencil." But it was not so easy to make a request of a stranger without using nonverbal gestures that diluted the power of the request—like looking away, laughing, or smiling.[3]

The new teacher should note that developing assertive behavior may require more than simply recalling the behavior listed above; it may require habit change, in which case practice with a partner, corrective feedback, and modeling are very useful.

PROBE   Work with a partner, role playing the teacher and student. A third student observes the interaction and provides feedback. The teacher will give a simple request such as, "John, I want you to close your book." The third student notes body language that diminishes or supports the request (eye contact, gestures, facial expression, tone of voice). The process continues until each student plays each role and has successfully demonstrated assertive behavior.

Video- and audiotape playback is an excellent way for teachers to identify nonassertive behavior that may be such habitual parts of their repertory that they are unaware of them. The use of nonwords such as laughs, *uhs*, *know*, and *okay* as a tag to every teacher request are examples of nonwords and are tantamount to asking students for permission to make their request.

Behavior Modification

If you were to find yourself lost in a jungle, you would probably instinctively search for a clearing. In a school situation you must create the clearing. But to do so, you must know yourself; you must know what you expect. From Lee Canter's perspective you must, at minimum, be able to state what you want students to do. This means being able to state specific rules of conduct.[4]

Canter says that classroom rules should be limited to five. These rules should be straightforward, clear, and capable of being translated into behavioral terms. Typical rules for a secondary class are:

☐ Follow directions the first time they are given.
☐ Be in the classroom and seated when the bell rings.
☐ Bring books, notebooks, and pens to class.
☐ Raise hand to be recognized before speaking.
☐ Hand in all assignments on time.[5]

Canter recommends that these rules either be posted or handed out. One can make the rules a part of the instructional process by using them as a basis for teaching outlining or as examples of giving directions.

The teacher should be able to visualize how the rules will look when put into operation. The teacher and students discuss the rules, giving many examples and having students model the rules until they are clear.

Next, consequences for not following the rules must be given, usually in progressively more serious stages. A first infraction equals the name of the student on the board; a second infraction equals a check mark; a third infraction equals a call to parents; a fourth infraction requires a parental visit; and still another infraction requires a conference with the principal.

Positive consequences are spelled out also. This can mean earned free time for students consistently following the rules—being able to go to the game table or listen to music with headphones. Rewards are necessary in this system, and the students are regularly "stroked" for following rules. The way that teachers state rules, consequences, and rewards can make all the difference.

Stating consequences is direct and matter of fact. Let us assume that John is touching the student in front of him, distracting the student from his work. Here are some possible responses:

John, what are you doing?

John, why are you doing that?

John, what am I going to do with you?

John, do you think what you are doing is right?

Do you know you are violating a rule? You keep this up and I'll call your parents.

All of the above are passive responses. They are responses that are likely to be diversionary, leading to student-teacher exchange and rationalizations. Here are other possible responses:

Are you crazy, John? Keep your fruitcake hands to yourself.

These responses rely on put-down to stop deviant behavior. Name calling, loud demands, and threats are all forms of hostile responses. These tactics result in creating resentment and eventual rebellion.

Assertive responses are: "John, keep your hands to yourself." The teacher uses eye contact and body proximity. "John, stop touching. Put your name on the board."

In assertive training the phrase "I like the way" precedes an approved action such as "you are working." This phrase is more powerful than "You are doing good work." The "I" statement personalizes the stroking. Think about it. If someone complements you on your clothing, which statements are most effective?

1. I like the way your new suit looks on you.
2. I like your new suit.
3. Your new suit looks good on you.

Number 2 merely praises the suit. Number 3 praises the suit in relation to the person. Number 1 praises the person in relation to the suit and reveals the person's judgment in the matter.

In using verbal rewards with high school students, Canter recommends rewarding the group through the contribution of the individual.[6] "John just earned free class time for the class. I like the way you are working, John." This reinforces team spirit and avoids embarrassing a student by setting him apart from the group.

Canter argues that rewards should be instituted prior to issuing consequences. This emphasizes a positive class spirit, and calls attention to the role model and to the rule.

The fourth competency of Canter's system is the descriptive plan. Everything is spelled out: the rules, the consequences, and the rewards. The plan is first approved by the principal. The plan will also contain specific expectations of parents in respect to monitoring homework and following through on home consequences (e.g., TV becomes off-limits for a specified period of time). Parents receive a copy at the beginning of the term.[7]

Canter's plan is businesslike, procedural, and relentless. To ensure discipline, the teacher does whatever is necessary short of damaging the student. There is a consistent stand and a consistent behavioral repertory used throughout the system. The stand of the teacher is that he or she will not tolerate a student interfering with teaching or learning in the class. The rewards and consequences are assigned consistently and fairly, and all relevant parties are informed—parents, principal, aides, and students. There is consistency throughout, and there is evidence that it creates a clearing.

Canter's system is a type of behavior modification. It works through creating patterns of expected outcomes that are constantly reinforced: If you do A, then B happens; if you do C, then D happens. The consequences are enforced in a detailed nonpersonal manner. Rewards are given only as a consequence of approved behavior. In this system there is no way out but conformity. If the student tries arguing about the rules, he will encounter the "broken record," a powerful assertiveness technique.[8]

TEACHER: Marge, step out of line and go to zone 2.
  MARGE: I wasn't talking.
TEACHER: Yes, and step out of line and go to zone 2.
  MARGE: But Connie pushed me. It wasn't my fault.
TEACHER: Yes, and step out of line and go to zone 2.
  MARGE: But . . .
TEACHER: Step out of line and go to zone 2.
  MARGE: Oh, all right. (Steps out of line and goes to zone 2.)

The teacher never raises her voice. It is all delivered in an even businesslike tone.

Operant Conditioning

Canter's form of behavior modification is to be distinguished from operant conditioning, which is based on the pychological principles of B. F. Skinner. In operant conditioning, the negative behavior is ignored. The assumption is that if deviant behavior gets no attention, it will become extinguished—that is, disappear. Socially approved behaviors are reinforced, but one must wait for them to occur, then provide what looks like a natural consequence as a reward. Rewards are not announced in advance, and the student is rewarded without realizing he is the subject of an operant conditioning design. The teacher may simply give John more attention or smile more at John when he works hard. Since these rewards are not made public, many educators feel that operant conditioning is unethical, that it violates some basic principles of honesty, fair play, and self-disclosure—in short, that it is a manipulative strategy that, while working well with pigeons, leaves much to be desired as a design for human beings. Behavior modification, by contrast, is more Pavlovian, spelling out exactly what will cause what in advance.

Another criticism of operant conditioning as a method of control in classrooms is that the ignoring of a deviant behavior may bring about extinction of that behavior in animals or in persons who are isolated from peers, but in a classroom other factors are at work as well. Classmates take note that John was not reprimanded when he spoke without raising his hand. John thus becomes a role model for the students observing him. The assumption "Ignore it and it will go away" doesn't work very well in high school classes. Adolescents have a need for set limits. Abraham Maslow says that they need an organized world rather than an unorganized or unstructured one.

Ultimately, the teacher will want to assist the student in developing self-discipline, but it is the teacher's responsibility to provide an initial model of acceptable behavior. The teacher knows what will work for him in order to be maximally effective as an instructor. The teacher can hardly expect students to create standards of behavior that will match his uncommunicated expectations.

And, yet, assertive discipline and behavior modification have drawn criticism in recent years on the grounds that by emphasizing external control, the students internalize nothing. When the students leave the environment, go to another class, or go into a non-school setting, they will not be supported by the same reward and punishment system. If they depend on external control as a guide to behavior, they will find themselves at a loss. In short, nothing has been learned but a kind of dependency.

PROBES

1. How comfortable do you feel when you practice assertive communication? Do any statements or use of body language create discomfort for you? Which ones?
2. How do you feel about behavior modification? Is it compatible with operant conditioning? Why? Why not?
3. If neither behavior modification nor operant conditioning resulted in generalizing the students' behavioral norms to situations outside the classroom, how would you create a structure to increase internalization of behavioral norms?

Reality Therapy

If, as a teacher, you want to go beyond clearing a space for learning to the teaching of self discipline, then Glasser's model of reality therapy is useful. While Glasser's approach is still classified as a form of behavior modification, it focuses more on having the student create appropriate choices. Like Canter's system, it avoids dredging up the past. The teacher would never ask *why* a student was late for class. Like Canter's system, Glasser's approach focuses on consequences and future behavior. The difference is in the way the intervention is communicated. A typical Glasser question is: "What are you doing? Please stop." If the disruptive behavior continues, the teacher asks if the behavior is against the rules and what the student should be doing. The idea is to get the student to take responsibility for his own behavior.

In this paradigm of questions, the student is granted freedom of perception. The teacher avoids stating an interpretation of the student's behavior; rather, the interpretation is drawn forth from the student along with the connection of the behavior to the rules and consequences. Canter provides students with the choice of conformity with rewards or nonconformity with undesirable consequences, but the student gets practically no practice in processing the implications of his behavior.

In the event the student persists in his disruptive behavior, Glasser carries this focus on student autonomy a step further. Instead of asking "What should you be doing?" the teacher asks if the student can create a plan that will enable him to follow the rules. Both teacher and student can work on the plan, but the greater the student involvement, the better.

Glasser and Canter agree that if disruptions continue, the consequences should be progressively more severe: parental and administrator conference, followed by in-school suspension, followed by out-of-school suspension, followed by permanent exclusion from the school. They differ primarily in their mode of communication to the student and in the amount of latitude the student is given in creating the structure of his or her own discipline. Glasser's emphasis on assisting the student in building responsibility is summed up by him in the following:

> If a child misbehaves in class, the teacher must ask, "What are you doing?" If she is warm and personal, if she deals with the present and does not throw the child's past misdeeds in his face, he will almost always reply honestly and tell what he is doing. The teacher must then ask, in words appropriate to the age of the child and to the situation, whether his behavior is helping him, her, the class, or the school. If the child says, "No, what I am doing is not helping," the teacher must then ask the child what he could do that is different. This is exactly the opposite of what happens in almost all schools and homes when a child misbehaves. Ordinarily, the teacher or parent tells the child that he is doing wrong and that if he doesn't change he'll be punished. This traditional but ineffective approach removes the responsibility for his bad behavior from the child. The teacher makes the judgment and enforces the punishment; the child has little responsibility for what happens.[9]

Cooperative Learning/ Control Theory

Glasser has recently expanded his reality therapy to include considerations of the power needs of students. Glasser combines his control theory with David Johnson's cooperative learning to produce a unique synthesis set forth in his *Control Theory in the Classroom.*[10] In this book he explains how students' power needs can be satisfied by their working in learning teams. As their power needs are satisfied, they will become intrinsically motivated. The process of participating on the teams will replace the need to act out. Acting out, in this design, is an ineffective expression of a power need.[11]

In the learning team approach the students are dependent on one another, the goal being the success of all students for the good of the group as a whole. Following are some advantages of developing learning groups:

1. Students can gain a sense of belonging by working together in learning teams of two to five students. The teams should be selected by the teacher so that they are made up of a range of low, middle, and high achievers.

2. Belonging provides the initial motivation for students to work, and as they achieve academic success, students who had not worked previously begin to sense that knowledge is power and then want to work harder.

3. The stronger students find it need fulfilling to help the weaker ones because they want the power and friendship that go with a high-performing team.

4. The weaker students find it is need fulfilling to contribute as much as they can to the team effort, because now whatever they can contribute helps. When they worked alone, a little effort got them nowhere.

5. Students need not depend only on the teacher. They can (and are urged to) depend a great deal on themselves, their own creativity, and other members of their team. All this frees them from dependence on the teacher and, in doing so, gives them both power and freedom.

6. Learning teams can provide the structure that will help students to get past the superficiality that plagues our schools today. Without this structure, there is little chance for any but a few students to learn enough in depth to make the vital knowledge-is-power connection.

7. The teams are free to figure out how to convince the teacher and other students (and parents) that they have learned the material. Teachers will encourage teams to offer evidence (other than tests) that the material has been learned.

8. Teams will be changed by the teacher on a regular basis so that all students will have a chance to be on a high-scoring team. On some assignments, but not all, each student on the team will get the team score. High-achieving students who might complain that their grade suffered when they took a team score will still tend consistently to be on high-scoring teams, so as individuals they will not suffer in the long run. This will also create incentive regardless of the strength of any team.[12]

The general thesis of Glasser's control theory and reliance on team learning is that this model is self-regenerating. The students satisfy power needs through learning, gain satisfaction from doing so, and are inspired to learn progressively more. Learning itself becomes the motive force for directing behavior. And when the focus of interest is learning, discipline problems diminish.

Use of Humor as Behavioral Control

The student is angry. He or she has been silent for many days now, and queries about the student's silence have been ignored. No response. Now the student is responding. He or she hates the school, you the teacher, this stupid class, and is letting you know this in very emphatic terms—to quote: *!#@%! What do you do? This is a time for you to be most resourceful. Resourcefulness may take many forms, but for any strategy to work you have to stay in control. The more you feel out of control, the less effective you will be in handling the situation. Also, your stress may reach dangerous levels.

The means of attaining control is to put yourself there by an act of will. Recall a resourceful state you were in and recreate it immediately. If you can't recall one, imagine that the most resourceful person you know has immediately jumped into your body. What you will do then depends on what's needed. You may give the student choices, all of which lead to either following the rules and being responsible for the rules or being removed from class. You may break up the anger, using an interrupt pattern or humor (not ridicule): "I got that angry once and thought I'd have a heart attack. But then I decided I couldn't pay the doctor bills."

Humor is a way of breaking up fixed states of consciousness. It is also a way of integrating body and mind, and it is a great stress reducer. If you haven't yet learned to laugh at yourself, stand in front of a mirror and pretend you are Donald Duck. Make funny faces. Try anything. Mickey Mouse? Goofy? The point is that if you can laugh at yourself, you can deflect an abundance of negative energy that comes your way every day. It is also a way of building solid rapport with your classes. If you can laugh together, you can probably work together and plan together.

The author's first teaching assignment after he got his B.S. in science education was in chemistry. He always wore an open-neck shirt—never a tie. His rationalization with the administration was that the tie could interfere with chemical experiments. The truth was he simply didn't like wearing a tie. Nevertheless, one week, for business purposes outside school, he decided to break his routine and wear a suit every day.

Friday of that same week his first-hour students came to class early and somehow got into the room. The room was ominously quiet. As he walked in, they all greeted him in unison. They were sparkling. All of them, girls included, were wearing ties. Some wore long ties, some bow ties. Some of the boys had on suits. Most were wearing their Sunday best.

The author did a double-take and began to laugh. The whole class broke up. He walked over to the clothes hangers and took off his tie. They all did likewise. Learning accelerated after this. We were able to build strong projects in this class. Several class members won contests in the science fair that year. It was the year of Sputnik, and many students built good working model rockets. But the most astounding demo was put on by a young man who said that automobile brakes could be controlled so they wouldn't lock, preventing the car from going into a skid. He presented a model of how this would work. The author remembers well the demo, but he especially remembers the student in his blue suit and bow tie, sitting in the front row of class laughing.

The author interviewed a comedian who works with youth groups and suicide prevention. He asked him how he would diffuse the anger of a hostile student through the use of humor.

"You've got to take his mind off himself," he said. "Get him to see another point of view."

"What would you use as humor?" the author asked.

"I'd tell him a cannibal joke. Better yet, I'd confront him with a cannibal joke. Suppose the student is going into a rage about how he hates school, this class, me, and so on. First, I'd get his attention like this (response to angry student):

"You think you've got problems?" (Emphatic)

"I mean do you think you've got problems?" (More emphasis)

"I had dinner with a cannibal last night. The cannibal said, 'I hate my mother-in-law.' "

"So I said, 'Just eat the vegetables.' "

"And you think you've got problems? How would you like to have dinner with a cannibal? After all, I could have ended up as dinner!"

(Change of pace, mood and tempo)

"Now what was your problem?"

Humor is a way of breaking up fixed sets. It is important to use humor that shows the teacher laughing at himself or herself. Be careful not to ridicule the student. You may dominate the student but build deep and lasting resentments. The power of laughter can be therapeutic. In his *Anatomy of an Illness As Perceived by the Patient,* Norman Cousins demonstrated that he could laugh in the face of his doctor's dire prediction of failing health. He collected humorous movies and books and laughed himself back into good health.

Pamela Rand is a talented comedienne and trainer at Barzak Educational Institute. She has developed an exceptional training to increase creativity, confidence and skill in managing crisis situations, reduce stress, and improve the quality of self-expression—all through a unique exploration of comedy and humor.

Before working with Barzak Educational Institute, Pamela studied with the renowned Jacques Lecoq, Director of Movement, Mime and Theatre School in Paris. Through her course, "The Clown Within," Pamela has increased the effectiveness of many teachers, trainers, business managers and actors in the United States, Europe and South America. Listen to what she says about "The Clown Within": "There is another side of your personality—things you hide, even from yourself. Behind the confident adult, an innocent and naive character; behind the gentle and supportive person, a mischievous imp; behind the shy self, a brilliant show-off waiting to explode! Often, we hide these things because we are afraid that people will laugh at us."

We usually see the laughter as punishment. "But we can learn that the laughter is an offering of thanksgiving. It is a way for us to thank each other for showing life more truly. It is thanks for allowing our hidden persons to be remembered and freed. It is thanks for showing us your 'clown within.' "

This workshop is about finding and trusting that clown within. "It is not a course about jokes, gags, or stunts. It is not a course about 'acting' funny. It's about discovering your own, very natural, very unique sense of humor. It's about touching into your profound sources of creativity. It's about finding the courage to accept life more fully."[13]

Every comedian knows the power of humor to build rapport. If you can laugh at yourself and laugh with your students you will be on your way to building solid rapport. Remember, you may never be allowed to share your brilliant insights, your massive recall of facts, and your amazing deductions if you do not first establish rapport. Humor is a good way to do this and at the same time diffuse negative stress in the classroom.

Pamela Rand conducting a French demonstration during a training session at Barzak Educational Institute.

A more conservative way of interacting with an angry student is to walk toward the door and request that the student step outside to discuss the matter. This takes away the student's audience and also allows him to save face when you inform him outside that he has the option of doing his work or being removed. If in your judgment the anger is completely out of control, you may buzz security. Or when you step outside, if the student does not respond to your request to leave the room, you can go next door and have a teacher call security. There is no absolutely right way to handle this situation and each way will depend on your state of resourcefulness.

Organizational Strategies

It will be useful to reread Chapter 16 with the idea of creating an organized atmosphere in your classroom. If you are unprepared for teaching when you arrive, if your clerical homework is not in order, you will communicate your lack of order to your students. Many teachers allow their classes to drift while they sort through mail and administrative forms. Have all required forms organized in such a way that when you come to class you can give maximum attention to your students. Madeline Hunter points out that the beginning of the class period is quality time for learning; yet this time is often wasted by focusing on busywork.

Change the seating pattern in the room to whatever supports you and the students. There is no right pattern; it all depends on what you are trying to accomplish.

For example, if you are giving demonstrations, using maps, or lecturing, the traditional rows facing front is appropriate for the purpose. If you do lots of discussion work, and you want to give students an immediate sense of how each person is reacting, a semicircle is effective. If you work with projects, a clustered pattern is useful.

Feel free to experiment, to move students around until you get the most workable pattern. Some teachers alternate seating—boy-girl-boy-girl. Some teachers intentionally break up cliques; others find ways of converting the energy and rapport of the clique into teamwork that translates into successful school and community projects.

Handle all lower-order survival needs, such as ensuring proper lighting, ventilation, and appropriate spacing and seating arrangements in the room. Check the temperature. Is the room too hot? Too cold? If so, do you know the proper chain of command for getting the matter handled? If not, find out.

If you have written or printed material on the chalkboard, is it legible? And is it visible from any place in the class? Are all handouts legible? Have you checked all the equipment you are going to use? If you are doing a science demonstration lesson, check it in advance. This is not cheating. After all, your purpose is to demonstrate, not to hope Murphy's Law doesn't apply to you. If you are using a video monitor, a tape recorder, a projector, or slide equipment, you will do yourself and your students a great favor by rehearsing in advance.

If you don't know how to operate certain equipment, go in on your free period and get someone to show you. Memorize the procedure. Go through several trial runs. When you get before your class, all you should need to do is push buttons. Everything should flow like magic. No one should see the toil, the struggle to get it right. As Laurence Olivier says about the art of a great actor: one should never see the technique of the actor, only the illusion of reality. Teachers have the power to create a similar illusion—an illusion that inspires learning.

Make use of student assistants and aides to handle details in the room that you do not need to handle. Do you have sufficient supplies? Does the eraser work? If students are going to work with crayons, are there sufficient supplies? Do you have a plan for clean-up procedures after art work is completed?

The items mentioned in this section may appear trivial, but one only has to imagine the consequences of running out of chalk in the middle of demonstrating a math problem. Imagine turning down the lights with you and your students in eager anticipation of viewing the film *Amadeus,* only to discover that the film is not seated properly in the projector. Sharp clicking sounds emanate from the projector, and in your effort to seat the film properly the take-up reel becomes disengaged, and without your realizing it, mounds of film begin to stack up on the floor. Your class begins to protest in unison. You ask for the lights only to discover the film running onto the floor. Enough.

PROBE Try your hand at inventing some worst possible scenarios arising out of poor management and devise strategies of coping with them. Then go back to the initial management problem and say how you would have prevented the problem from the outset.

Suggestopedic, Integrative Learning, and Optimalearning Techniques

---

Many teachers, in applying the techniques of Georgi Lozanov, discovered as a by-product that they had far fewer classroom management problems.[13] Upon reflection, this is not surprising, for the techniques focus on physical and mental relaxation, on making learning a joyous experience, and on creating an atmosphere of trust and respect in the class. When these techniques take root, why should students want to act up?

Mental control techniques can be presented to students as a challenge: "How many of you can stop yourself from thinking about a green cow for the next 60 seconds?" After getting their attention with a humorous example, the teacher can go on to light but serious challenges. How many of you can become aware only of the sounds outside this room? Of the sounds inside the room? Of the sounds inside your own body?

During a "Reading with Music," the text is read to the students to the accompaniment of classical, baroque, or romantic music. As Ivan Barzakov explains:

> The teacher is trained to allow the music to gently conduct the phrasing of the written text. It is as if the voice of the reader surfs on the contours of the music. This special type of orchestration and synchronization of voice and music—with carefully selected composers and compositions—seems to activate and reactivate several layers of the brain *simultaneously.* The result is a marked flow of creative energy which in turn produces a highly conducive state for learning and well-being.[14]

Students have less need to act up, to participate in disruptive behavior, because they are already in a very pleasurable state of consciousness. Moreover, as the techniques are expanded, the students will take fantasy journeys in which they discover not only new concepts, but their relationship with these concepts. Self-concept, self-respect is strengthened, again reducing the need to act out for attention. They are getting maximum attention from peers and teacher in every lesson.

A specific class control technique using music is to have the volume of music slightly elevated at the beginning of a class and as the students take their seats gradually to lower the volume and at the same time move your hands in a downward motion.

Music can also be used to reinforce desirable behavior. Turn up the volume to *Rocky* theme music when the students en masse master a pronunciation or name all the planets in sequence. The music acts as an anchor to recall the learning state. When you play the music again, you can more easily re-create desirable learning states and hence desirable behavior. By learning to control the mind and body, the student is less likely to act as a victim of his or her imagination and/or random bodily reactions. (See Figure 18.2.)

The student also learns to control emotions through dramatic enactments. Peter Kline uses a process called "one to one hundred," in which two students are given a situation where they start off as two friends who meet after not having seen one another for a while. After initial rejoicing they experience a conflict, which they

Figure 18.2 In a relaxation process the student learns to control his or her mind and body, becoming less likely to act as a victim of imagination or random bodily reactions.

proceed to resolve. The catch is that they can only communicate in numbers. Student A begins, "One, two, three, four, five!" (happy, alert). B responds, "Six, seven, eight, nine, ten!" (equally happy, rejoicing). Then gloom and doom set in, and the students roar at one another using numbers to speak. The object is to resolve the conflict before they reach 100.*

The process can be used to teach dramatic structure or the short story; it can be used to explore body language and to note and investigate nuances of language—but one of the more powerful by-products of the technique is that it teaches students self-control. One can decide whether he wishes to be at 5, 45, or 95!

The suggestion is constantly embedded that learning is an adventure, that self-respect and respect of others is a desirable way to live, and that when one stays in quest of discovery he will discover something that only he can contribute.

Re-creation of past states of consciousness teaches the student how to control his states of awareness so that *by choice* he can be in a state of learning, a state of anger, or a state of laughter. No more "It just came over me," "He made me mad," or "He made me laugh."

Ivan Barzakov's Optimalearning adds further dimensions. It focuses on using conscious thought processes to increase comprehension and critical thinking. This is a necessary condition for understanding content that promotes the development of higher level concepts rather than the acquisition of language skills and vocabulary. Jean Lerede, a Canadian psychotherapist and researcher in Suggestology, states in his book, *Suggerer Pour Apprendre (To Suggest in Order to Learn)* that Lozanov's Suggestopedia derives its main strength from the unconscious. Barzakov's Optimalearning, however, adds a strong emphasis on conscious mental processing.

*Peter Kline demonstrated this technique at his Workshop, Summer 1987, Wayne State University, Detroit, MI.

Chris Myers-Baker, a methodology consultant from Tulsa, Oklahoma, says that Optimalearning adds to suggestology a strong emphasis on the conscious processes of analysis, deductive reasoning and dialectical thinking.

Nummela and Rosengreen make the same point in their article, "What's Happening in Students' Brains May Redefine Teaching," *Educational Leadership,* May 1986: ". . . teaching is done in a series of 'movements' where material to be learned is presented in a constant flow from the inductive to the deductive and back to the inductive."[15] Barzakov's instructors report that "increasing students' comprehension level with strong analytical thinking and inductive-deductive reasoning *reduces* disruptive behavior, the need to act up and discipline problems in general."[16]

The purpose is to bring forth not only the creative powers of the student, but autonomy, responsibility and commitment, and ultimately the creation of personal ideals. Discipline becomes self-discipline, and the mind becomes the best of friends.

Synthesis: A Teacher's View

So far in this chapter, various approaches to classroom management have been discussed. Perhaps reflection on these approaches has left you with some of the same questions the coauthor of this chapter (J. B.) has:

Yes, I understand each of these systems, but I'm not quite sure which one is best for me. I like some of the techniques for relaxation, but, if in the middle of a lesson, a student decides to be disruptive, it may not be expedient to stop the lesson and create a joyous and relaxing experience. I am not always comfortable being assertive, and Skinner's ideas of ignoring the negative behavior could result in a significant loss of instruction time if the student feels like continuing his disruptive behavior. When I actually have the responsibility of managing a classroom with real, not hypothetical, situations, which of these management approaches will work for me?

Your response could be, "None of the above." Perhaps your classroom management techniques will best be developed from a combination of these approaches, which are then integrated with your own personality and teaching style. Still, where does one begin?

Why not begin at the top?

Good classroom management often starts by aligning itself with overall school policy. If the principal has created a system of discipline, it makes good sense for the classroom teacher to build classroom management upon that structure. Students should be familiar with school guidelines and thus, the individual teacher need not re-create the wheel, but only reinforce the spokes. If all teachers in the building contribute to that same reinforcement, each teacher's job will be easier.

Joe Greene is a former high school principal who has been nationally acclaimed for his strong leadership qualities. Dr. Greene provides insight into the relationship of administration and staff in an effective school. The principal, he believes, must set the tone with strong, assertive leadership. Student achievement must be the first priority of administration and teachers. The principal, in addition to providing instruc-

DETROIT BOARD OF EDUCATION
CODE OF STUDENT CONDUCT

October 1986

Dear Parents,

The **Code of Student Conduct** identifies the rights and responsibilities of students. The administrative procedures outline the due process procedures which must be followed whenever infractions occur.

The Detroit Board of Education believes that the implementation of this policy will help to guarantee that every student in every school will be provided with a safe and secure environment in which to pursue the fine educational opportunities available in the Detroit Public Schools.

The full partnership of parents and students is essential in order to help ensure a safe and secure learning environment.

I urge you to spend the time necessary with your son or daughter to impress upon him or her the value of a good education and the importance of coming to school every day, fully prepared and ready to learn.

Sincerely,

Arthur Jefferson

Arthur Jefferson

POLICY ON DISCIPLINE AND STUDENT RIGHTS

I. INTRODUCTION

Students in the Detroit school system are guaranteed the right to a public education. If this right is to be guaranteed, regular attendance in classes is of vital importance for a student to succeed in school. The United States Supreme Court has held that a student may not be deprived of this right to a public education without adherence to procedural due process. It is the responsibility of the Detroit Board of Education and its staff to ensure that no student is arbitrarily denied the right to an education. It is the responsibility of each student to behave in a manner that does not threaten, interfere with or deprive other students of their right to an education.

The purposes of this conduct code are to provide regulations governing the behavior of students, to prevent actions or activities which interfere with the school program and/or are prohibited by law, and to provide for students' rights and responsibilities. Both the Board Policy and the Superintendent's Regulations reflected in this Code shall be mandatory and uniformly enforced in each Detroit public school. Each staff member employed by the School District of the City of Detroit is required to function in accordance with this Code.

It is the responsibility of all students and their parents to become familiar with the Student Code. Students and parents must recognize that when students engage in unacceptable conduct they will be subject to disciplinary action. (Whenever the parent is mentioned in the Code, it also means guardian.)

II. DELEGATION STATEMENT
Superintendent

The Board of Education hereby delegates to the General Superintendent the authority to develop administrative rules, regulations and procedures necessary for the implementation of this policy or necessary for the administration of student rights and discipline within the district.

The Superintendent's Regulations related to student rights, due process procedures, or appeal procedures shall be periodically published and disseminated to staff, parents and students. The Superintendent's Regulations related to internal administrative procedures shall be available for inspection by staff, students and parents in each school office.

Principals

The local school principal, vocational/technical director, or other administrator assigned responsibility for an educational facility may develop supplementary administrative rules, regulations, and procedures necessary to implement this policy and the Superintendent's Regulations, with written approval by the General Superintendent. However, such additional regulations may neither substitute for nor negate any Board policy nor the Superintendent's Regulations. A copy of the approved local school regulations must be filed with the Code Office.

III. STUDENT RIGHTS
Students have the following rights:

1. The Fair Administration of Discipline: The Board of Education of the School District of the City of Detroit does not illegally discriminate against any person, with regard to the administration of discipline, on the basis of race, sex, color, national origin, creed, religion or handicap.

2. Make-up Work: Students who are short term suspended must be given the opportunity to make-up academic course work assignments missed during their short term suspensions. The judgment of the principal and teacher shall be relied upon in both the content and scheduling of make-up assignments and examinations.

Students have the right to make-up assignments missed during excused absences. (Students are not entitled to make-up academic course work missed during absences due to truancy or long term suspension.)

3. The Rights to Freedom of Expression and Publication, Dissent and the Right to Petition: Students have the right to express their beliefs and opinions on issues orally, symbolically, and through publication, so long as such expression is made in a reasonable manner. However, freedom of expression does not include engaging in libel, obscenity, personal attacks on individuals and groups, defamation of character, commercial solicitations, or the distribution of materials of a racial,

---

The principal, in addition to providing instructional leadership, must implement an effective policy that is fairly and consistently enforced by all. The code of conduct is often a basis for such a policy.

tional leadership, must implement an effective discipline policy that is fairly and consistently enforced by all. As administrators and staff work together to achieve this goal, a school climate is achieved that allows teachers to teach and students to learn. Since high expectations are set for students, teachers must be able to focus on instruction.

According to Greene, the principal must give teachers the opportunity to teach by eliminating those things that have little or nothing to do with student achievement, such as classroom interruptions, unnecessary paperwork, and the like. The atmosphere in an effective school is calm and friendly, but carries the message that the business of this school is education. It is a place where administrators and teachers are not adversaries; rather, they work in concert to provide the best education possible for all students.

When the coauthor of this chapter (J.B.) taught in Joe Greene's school, she used his guidelines as a starting point and integrated them with her own philosophy in developing a personal style of classroom management. As an experienced classroom teacher, the coauthor believes that every teacher must develop a philosophy of education that can be used as a basis for all educational actions. This philosophy gives direction to professional decisions, whether the concern is content, teaching techniques, or classroom management. The fact that the coauthor's philosophy also permeates her decisions on all teaching matters gives a unity of approach that is transmitted to students and adds an underlying stability, a comfort zone, that is reflected in the students' ability to learn in a predictable and relaxed environment.

One guiding aspect of the coauthor's educational philosophy in the development of classroom management techniques is the principle that each student is a unique individual. Like Kolb (1984), she believes that "the learning process is not identical for all human beings."[17] Some learn effectively while working quietly in their seats; some do not. Since all students have the right to the best education they are capable of achieving, it is necessary to provide a structure that will allow students to eventually achieve freedom. Freedom does not mean that individuals can do what they want whenever they want. Rather, protecting the right of each student to learn implies that limits of conduct based on respect for all must be established. Then, working within the limits of the structure, each student can achieve not only freedom of movement but, as John Dewey (1938) says, "freedom of thought, desire, and purpose."[18]

Thus, the coauthor's initial planning for classroom management is based on the principal's guidelines and the philosophy of the individual's rights, structure, and resulting freedom.

Each teacher must make a personal decision about the atmosphere in which he or she can work most effectively. Realizing that order was important to her, the coauthor decided to start with an orderly classroom structure and work toward the goal of students' recognizing and internalizing the necessity for order in effective learning.

Order is not accidental. It takes careful planning. Thus, when students arrive in the coauthor's English class on the first day of school, she is ready. Not only has she planned her approach to classroom management, from structure to "structured freedom," but she has also organized an overview of the course content. Her plans are not only for this day, but will also lay the groundwork for the days to come. First on the agenda are classroom and course expectations:

"The following behavior is expected. . . ."

"The consequences of unacceptable behavior are as follows . . ."

"Grades will be calculated using the following method . . ."

And so on.

The first class period is used to clearly articulate the teacher's expectations for the students. All are reasonably high. The coauthor is friendly in her explanation, but makes it clear that all students will be treated equally. "If you do not live up to these expectations, you will receive exactly the same consequences as any other student. When I ask you to go to the Dean's office after three tardies, it is not because I don't like you, or that I am angry with you; it is because you have exceeded the number of tardies and school policy states clearly that you must then go to the Dean's office." Like Canter, the coauthor is assertive as she explains her basic philosophy that all students have the right to an education and that any behavior that interferes with that right is unacceptable and will not be tolerated.

She distributes a copy of the goals and expectations to each student. They are written in outline format. With a touch of humor, she instructs that students "Cling to the handouts," because they are done in correct outline form and will be used by them as a model when outlining is studied later in the class.

In the initial discussion of class expectations, the coauthor is careful to present only rules and consequences on which she can honestly follow through. She has approximately 150 students per day and realizes her limitations. She knows that good classroom management dictates that she follow through on her expectations with fairness and consistency. Anything else results in a breakdown of the system. Further, lists of rules tend to imply lack of flexibility and focus the student's and the teacher's attention on disciplinary concerns. Since learning is the primary focus in the classroom, the coauthor wishes only to begin building the necessary structure. In a classroom where students are busy learning, disruptive behavior is infrequent.

Needless to say, the plans for the second day must consist of activities that capture the students by involving them in both the discipline and excitement of learning.

There is, however, no such thing as a discipline-free classroom, and disruptive behavior is impossible to predict. Students, like all people, have bad days—many with good reasons. Because the coauthor has found herself to be uncomfortable when disruptive behavior arises, she has planned approaches to use in these instances:

(Teacher is passing back essays to students.)

ROB: Ms. M, you never get our papers back on time. If ours are late, you won't take them. A good teacher oughta practice what she preaches, and you don't!

TEACHER: (Without anger in her voice) You're right about that. You often don't get your papers back as fast as you should. (She wishes he could follow her around so he could know how many hours she spends correcting papers.) I will try to do better.

This is an approach that the coauthor thinks of as neutralization. She could confront the student, cite him for insubordination, or send him to an administrator for discipline; however, she allows him to express his anger. She realizes two things: first, confrontation often exacerbates the problem; second, the student has a legitimate complaint. In this situation, if the student is rebuked when he confronts authority, he learns that it is not wise to express his position, even though it is right. If a teacher wishes to recognize the individual student and his rights, she must sometimes admit that she is wrong.

Sometimes neutralization does not work. Suppose that the teacher's response does not end the behavior. Instead, when the disruptive student receives his paper, he notes that the teacher has instructed him to do a rewrite:

ROB: (Gets up and goes to the wastebasket, tearing up the paper) I'm not writing this stupid thing over. I hate this dumb class anyway.

TEACHER: That's your choice. Please return to your group and continue the discussion of today's lesson.

ROB: (Returns to his group but continues talking about the teacher and his paper, disrupting the work of the other students.)

In this situation, the teacher's basic rule of behavior has been violated. Rob is significantly interfering with the learning of other students. He knows that his behavior is not tolerated.

TEACHER: Rob, please come to my desk. (She prepares a note that objectively reports the behavior of the student.) Take this note to Ms. R. in the English Center. Do not return to class this period. We will discuss the problem later.

The teacher does not want an angry confrontation in full view of the class. Generally, it upsets the other students and diverts the attention of the students from the focus of the lesson. By removing the student from the situation, two things are accomplished: first, and most important, class time is not wasted; second, it gives both the teacher and the student a chance to gain composure. Later, the teacher can discuss the situation with the student on a one-to-one basis. If necessary, additional disciplinary steps may be taken. If this behavior is reflective of a pattern, the teacher will call the parent and, if serious enough, send the student to the dean of students for administrative action.

Most classroom management problems involve small infractions of rules. For example, two students are talking during instruction, or the class is inattentive for one reason or another. Some general guidelines to rely on when dealing with these types of management problems follow:

Don't see everything. Frequently, before the teacher has time to interrupt what she is saying in order to speak to the students, the behavior ends.

At all times, even in a disciplinary situation, always treat students with respect. They are people, no less than adults. It is never appropriate for a teacher to call a student a name or to insult or embarrass him in any way. An educator has the responsibility of helping students understand that they must accept each individual, with that person's strengths and weaknesses. It is especially important that today's young people learn that even though someone does something that they don't like, it does not mean that the person is bad. The teacher must show that there are methods of resolving conflict other than anger and the resulting physical or emotional violence. Serious disagreement does not mean that we must hate someone and want to hurt them. It means that an individual has a viewpoint differing from ours. Resolution is best found by hearing the student's point of view, stating ours, and seeking a solution. It is this behavior that the teacher must model.

Good classroom management is only one aspect of good teaching. Good teaching, according to Kounin (1970), involves "planning and preparation for effective instruction and group management."[19] A teacher who is spending a great deal of time on management should review what is being taught and the methods being used. Students are always ready to learn information that they perceive as relevant to them. When students are involved in classroom situations that stimulate them to learn things that have relevance to their lives in a relaxed and enjoyable way, and at a level which they can understand, classroom management is easy.

■ *SUMMARY*

There are a number of schools of thought on effective classroom management. In this chapter we took a look at management based on Canter's assertive discipline, Glasser's reality therapy, Skinner's operant conditioning, and Lozanov's suggestopedia. We also looked at space and time organization of the room and procedures. Finally, we considered a synthetic vision of classroom management, a view which incorporates many features of the foregoing theories.

Canter's assertive discipline is a form of behavior modification. The teacher's expectations are made clear through rules and role models. Rewards and consequences are spelled out in advance. Basic to Canter's method is emphasis on assertive communication. Desirable behavior is immediately reinforced; undesirable behavior is confronted with swift application of consequences. Neutral but firm language is used in addressing the student. Anger and passive responses are avoided. The emphasis is on shaping the student's external behavior through external means. Skinnerian techniques, though similar as a form of external behavior control, make use of covert strategies. The environment is manipulated in ways the student may not consciously recognize. Undesirable behavior is ignored on the grounds that if the student gets no attention, the undesirable behavior will disappear (be extinguished). Critics charge that this system is unethical because it is covert and that it is not as useful in controlling human behavior as it is with nonhuman animals.

Glasser promotes a method for internalizing desirable behavior by encouraging the student to reflect on his behavioral choices. Lozanov uses suggestopedic techniques to create a positive atmosphere that promotes self-respect, respect for others, and a passionate love of learning.

Barzakov adds to Lozanov's suggestopedia a "strong development of analytical skills, deductive-inductive reasoning and special use of creativity."[20]

It is possible to synthesize a personal approach to classroom management that is aligned with administrative policy in your school. This requires a thorough understanding of your principal's policies and attention to the development of a personal comprehensive philosophy.

■ *NOTES*

1. Lee Canter with Marlene Canter, *Assertive Discipline* (Santa Monica, CA: Canter and Associates, Inc., 1987), 62.
2. H. Fensterheim and J. Baer, *Don't Say Yes When You Want to Say No* (New York: Dell: 1973), p. 33.
3. Ibid.
4. Lee Canter, pp. 62–69.
5. Lee Canter, pp. 63–64.
6. Lee Canter, pp. 118–133.
7. Lee Canter, pp. 145–154.
8. Manuel J. Smith, *When I Say No I Feel Guilty* (New York: Bantam Books, 1975), see "Bill of Assertive Right," 24–71, and various self-defense techniques.
9. William Glasser, *Schools Without Failure* (New York: Harper & Row, 1969), 21–22.
10. William Glasser, *Control Theory in the Classroom* (New York: Harper & Row, 1986).
11. Ibid., 75–76.
12. Ibid.
13. Pamela Rand, interview, June 1988. Quoted by permission of author.
14. Ivan Barzakov, *Manual: How to Use Music Everywhere in Life* (San Rafael, CA: Barzak Educational Institute, 1988), p. 5.
15. Renate M. Nummela and Tennes M. Rosengren, "What's Happening in Students' Brains May Redefine Teaching," *Educational Leadership,* May 1986, p. 51.
16. Ivan Barzakov, interview, June 1988. Quoted by permission of author.
17. David Kolb, *Experiential Learning* (Englewood Cliffs, NJ: Prentice-Hall, 1984), 62.
18. John Dewey, *Experience in Education* (New York: Collier, 1938), 61.
19. J. Kounin, *Discipline and Group Management in the Classroom* (New York: Holt, Rinehart and Winston, 1970).
20. Ivan Barzakov; interview, June, 1988. Quoted by permission of author.

CHAPTER 19

Stress Management for Teachers

Kundalini Yoga: Breaking up tension blocks.

Personal stress as well as the collective stress of our age, the much-discussed future shock, can be agents of transformation once we know how to integrate them.

—Marilyn Ferguson

You are not the target.

—Laura Huxley

The mind is its own place, and in itself
Can make a heaven of Hell, a hell of Heaven.

—John Milton

As a teacher you will be expected to perform under pressure. Schools are volatile places. Students, parents, teachers, and administrators experience frustration and may express anger—anger which is sometimes not directed to its proper place. Whatever the case, teachers are often the recipients of misplaced aggression. There are student conflicts that if not controlled can erupt into physical confrontations. There are schedules to keep, work to organize and return, and meetings to manage.

There is the added problem of nonstudent entries into the school—entries that have resulted in violence, rape and homicide. There are students who need immediate attention because of illness, parental abuse, or drug involvement. Many of these situations create double binds for the teacher who wishes to support the student and at the same time uphold school policy and legal sanctions. The norms may be in conflict.

In this chapter you will learn techniques to control stress. Specifically, you will learn to control stress through (1) environmental means, (2) psychological means, and (3) physical means.

You will learn strategies appropriate for yourself and students.

Physiological Basis of Stress

Stress has many physiological correlates. Dr. Peter G. Hanson in his book *The Joy of Stress* lists 12 physiological responses to stress:[1]

1. Release of cortisone from the adrenal glands.
   Liabilities: If continued over a period of time, the body's resistance to disease is lowered, blood pressure can be elevated, bones made brittle.
2. Thyroid hormone is increased in the bloodstream.
   Liabilities: Burnout, shaky nerves, intolerance to heat.
3. Release of endorphin from the hypothalamus.
   Liabilities: Aggravates migraine, the pain of arthritis, backache.
4. Reduction in sex hormones.
   Liabilities: Decrease in libido for male and female. Anxiety and failure in sexual performance. Loss of self-esteem.

5. The shutdown of the entire digestive tract.
   Liabilities: Dry mouth, inability to digest food, diarrhea.
6. Release of sugar into the blood, along with an increase in insulin levels to metabolize it.
   Liabilities: Promotion of diabetes and hypoglycemia.
7. Increase of cholesterol in the blood, mainly from the liver.
   Liabilities: On a chronic basis can produce coronary arteries, heart attack.
8. Racing heartbeat.
   Liabilities: High blood pressure, heart attack.
9. Increased air supply.
   Liabilities: If you smoke, the toxicity level drastically increases under strain.
10. The blood thickens.
    Liabilities: Strokes, heart attacks, or an embolus.
11. The skin crawls, pales and sweats.
    Liabilities: Social leprosy.
12. All five senses become acute.
    Liabilities: The senses "burn out" and person's error rate increases.

You may not be able to notice all of these physiological changes when you are under stress. You may, in fact, feel no physical changes. High blood pressure, for this reason, has been called the silent killer. Many of these physiological changes, such as blood cholesterol level, require a medical test. There are, however, many behavioral signs of stress. These are usually present, and if you or a colleague notice a number of them, it's time to take action and deal with the stress on an ongoing basis.

■ *Burnout*

Burnout is a form of emotional exhaustion "occurring primarily within human service professions, where staff members spend a great deal of time in intense interaction with other people."[2] Caton's research indicates that burnout is characterized by "a loss of concern with whom the staff member is working."[3] Ganju and Mason's research with direct care staff in state schools for the mentally retarded showed no significant differences in burnout between sex, education, shift, and length of day. They did, however, find that blacks were more burned out than were Mexican Americans.[4] Harris found the following feeling states to be associated with burnout:[5]

1. Helplessness
2. Disenchantment
3. Hopelessness
4. Emotional exhaustion

Physical states associated with burnout are:

1. Physical exhaustion
2. Accident proneness
3. Increased susceptibility to illness

Organizational variables associated with burnout are:

1. Increased use of sick time
2. Decreased use of vacation time
3. Increased number of on-the-job accidents
4. Decrease in work quality
5. Increased use of overtime in small increments of time

■ *Some Signals of Stress*
Ask yourself if you are manifesting any of the following signals:

1. Snapping at colleagues, students
2. Doing things hurriedly that don't need rushing
3. Dropping things; accidentally breaking things
4. Losing keys, pens, glasses, articles of clothing
5. Breathing pattern changes
6. Going away: not noticing environment
7. Working in a slumped posture—looking downward
8. Feelings of being dominated by time
9. Feeling the victim; feeling oppressed by imagined student, peer, or administrative demands
10. Voice level varies—too loud or so soft you are often asked to repeat
11. Feelings of weakness, faintness
12. Cutting other people off, finishing their sentences for them
13. Dogmatic, argumentative, locked into fixed positions
14. Use of absolutes—all, never, must, can't, shouldn't; no room for possibility.
15. Not listening to others
16. Facial tics, nervous mannerisms
17. Inability to respond to humor or to laugh at oneself
18. Speaking too rapidly for others to follow comfortably

There are many other "signals" of stress; these are ones that may be most apparent to you and others. All of these signs are behavior patterns that can be changed; you don't have to live with them. There are definite strategies for changing each one of these, and if you clear up a few of them, then others will clear up in the process. For example, if you change your state of consciousness so that you feel more empowered in your environment, then you are more likely to act responsibly about noting your environment, communicating effectively, and organizing your personal possessions.

My own philosophy of stress control is, always set aside a time for yourself, no matter how brief, just to relax. I happen to relax by doing exercises in front of my favorite TV programs.

Student Teacher

. . . a certain amount of sleep every night, a good balanced diet with vitamin supplements and a program of exercise. These factors will lead to a sense of well-being and self-esteem which will automatically make a person more able to handle stress.

Student Teacher

I tell myself that a lot of what I feel in the way of stress and anxiety is absolutely, positively normal. It's a human thing. It's normal to sometimes think about quitting; it's normal to sometimes think about grabbing a disruptive student by the neck and twisting it a few times; it's normal to want to stick your head out the window and start swearing. It's normal to feel upset when things are upsetting. After all, an abnormal response to an abnormal situation is normal. And that's what stress is sometimes. Sometimes it is normal. It's born of real frustration. It's born of real fear. And it's there. It's a fact of life. Now after I convince myself that my feelings are not freakish, given my particular situation, then I aim at comforting myself by saying to myself such things as, "Look, Ray, you're doing the best that you can possibly do, you're trying the best that you can possibly try, and you're doing what you believe is right."

Raymond Pisani, Student Teacher

Reducing Stress in the Environment

If your classroom is drab and uninspiring, if you feel as though the walls reflect a prison atmosphere rather than the joy of learning, take steps to change your external environment. Make a project with your classes to paint the room and redecorate it. Of course, you will clear this with the administration first. And if you share the room consistently with another teacher, you will want to get agreements on color schemes and furniture arrangements. And don't get stuck with ho-hum colors of paint for the room. You must first decide what mood or moods you wish to create. Then you can support this mood by choosing appropriate colors. There has been quite a lot of research on the psychology of color. Certain shades of pink produce calmness; the yellows produce alertness. Make it part of the project to research the color you want. If your room is sectionalized, you may want to create a calming section for doing relaxation exercises and a section for high energy and alertness. Or, you may decide on a compromise. Your decision will be guided by what you wish to produce in yourself and your students and by the environmental possibilities.

If you are comfortable with a certain chair at home, you may wish to use it at your school desk or obtain a duplicate chair for school. Maximize your comfort.

Plants and flowers will bring a room to life. Studies have shown that the nurturing of plants (and animals) has a beneficial, stress-reducing effect on the person doing the nurturing. Each student can care for the plants on a rotating basis. Responsibility is taught right along with the opportunity to nurture and be nurtured.

Make use of music to introduce your lessons, as mood setters, as anchors to reinforce a productive state of consciousness, and as conduits to higher levels of learning. Mix up the use of popular and classical music and plan the use of the music.

Properly used this can enliven the class, increase learning, and reduce behavior problems. See the Appendix for a suggested list of popular, classical, and baroque music appropriate for classroom use. The use of music alone is a great stress reducer; used intelligently, music can transform a class.

Contextual Shifts

Recontextualization, sometimes called reframing, is a way of reinterpreting a problem so that it becomes a benefit. It is like seeing the other side of an optical illusion. In my graduate classes we work with optical illusions and spatial problems requiring the students to step outside their usual assumptions. Consider the nine dots on the left side of Figure 19.1. Using four straight lines, connect all the dots without removing your pencil from the paper once you begin. Try it. If you restricted yourself to an imaginary boundary formed by the dots, you were placing unnecessary limits on yourself at the outset. Contextual shifting or reframing allows you to step back and take another look. Then you can raise the question, What would it be like to draw lines away from or through this imaginary square and connect all dots? Your solution may look something like the image on the right side of Figure 19.1. By shifting perspective, a solution becomes possible. There was no possibility in the original set of assumptions, only dead-end options.

Similar boundaries are often placed on human relationships and on interpreting the behavior of others. One teacher may see only the anger a student is expressing; another may see the frustration and hurt behind that anger; yet another may see the potential of a budding actor in the way the anger is expressed; and another may see humor and may even get the student to laugh at him- or herself.

Stress Reduction for Teachers and Students

In a sense there is no such thing as separate stress-control techniques for teachers and students. Stress affects all persons, teachers and students alike. Most of the techniques that follow are addressed to the teacher. Nevertheless, wise teachers will from time to time teach some of these techniques to

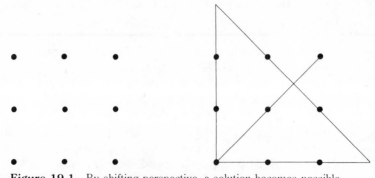

Figure 19.1 By shifting perspective, a solution becomes possible.

their students. The teacher must use his or her discretion as to what is workable in the specific teaching assignment. Some processes, such as visualization and deep breathing, can become consistent phases of learning. Others, such as sauna, massage, and specific aerobic exercise, are more individual preferences and can be casually recommended by the teacher.

Here are some useful general ideas to keep in mind when you are changing your habits in response to stress.

■ *Some Key Concepts*

1. Laura Huxley says in her book of the same title that "you are *not* the target." When you encounter sarcasm, hostility, and rudeness, remember that 90 percent of the time the proper target for the negative energy is not you; you happen to be a convenient target and you are not the appropriate target. Strategy: Think of the negative energy projected toward you as a misdirected arrow. Merely allow it to miss you.

   If you should allow the arrow to hit you, then convert the negative energy into positive energy. Allow the energy to become refocused in your body-mind and act accordingly:
   a. Use the energy to tone muscles of your body.
   b. Use the energy to suggest constructive alternatives for the person who has misdirected energy.

2. Become aware of what is going on in your body-mind when you get upset. Note:
   a. *Your intentions.* Were your intentions blocked or thwarted? Can you change the circumstances? If so, then do what you can. If not, then choose to live with what you have and immediately direct your energy to circumstances you can change.
   b. *Your expectations.* Did something happen which did not match your expectations? Can you change those circumstances? If not, what can you do?
   c. *Your communications.* Did you fail to communicate your intentions and expectations to someone who has the power or authority to help you actualize those intentions and expectations? If so, then communicate—completely, honestly, directly.[8]

3. According to Maltz, fear is the basis of most upsets and fear is based on the pictures (mental images) that one creates for himself/herself.[9] For example, you may have a picture of your critic teacher becoming angry or punitive if you tell him/her the truth. Your behavior is then controlled by your pictures rather than by your intent. Check (test) your pictures against reality. Also, create positive pictures for situations that can go the way you want them to go. For example, create an ideal lesson for your students. Imagine yourself doing everything right. Imagine yourself effectively handling all possible circumstances. See yourself as the source of your imagination, not the victim of it.

4. Don't allow work and responsibilities to build up. Act continuously so that this will not occur. If large, seemingly overwhelming, responsibilities confront you, try the slice-of-cheese-approach. Translated, this means work with and master a small portion at a time. Avoid the extremes of freezing, dropping responsibility or taking on more than you can handle. The rule of thumb is do what you can do. Do it completely and effectively.

5. Share your problems with a friend; don't hold things in.

6. Prepare in advance. Realize that there will be days when you will be down. If, however, you have well-organized handouts for those days, you can perform effectively even when you are down.

7. Develop and use your sense of humor.

8. Observe proper diet. A good breakfast is better than tons of coffee, which will lower blood sugar and ultimately lower your energy level. The same goes for existing on sugar. Rapid increase in energy is followed by a rapid decline. Also, a light lunch, as opposed to a heavy lunch, will help curtail afternoon drowsiness.

9. Proper rest is a must. Try going into alpha sleep, using the 10–15 minute nap—but no more than 15 minutes. If you go into delta sleep (the zombie state), you may as well sleep for several hours.

10. Be of good cheer. Develop or cultivate a hobby, sport or recreational activity. One of the beauties of teaching is that no matter what you are interested in, you can make it relevant to teaching. And you can enjoy the activity for itself. So you will get double value out of whatever you are doing when you are not teaching.

We will be exploring some of these in more detail and relating these strategies to specific situations in teaching. Some of these tips will work for your students, also.

■ Deep Breathing

Deep breathing is one of the most effective, yet easy to use of the stress reduction techniques. Long recognized by yogis as a general aid to health, it is a technique that can be used anywhere, whether in the office or walking down the street. Deep breathing does many things. The physical experience of it quietly translates into an invigorating mental boost. More oxygen is circulated in the bloodstream, the brain is nourished, and the lymph system is moved through the body, carrying away waste products. And all of these physical and mental shifts facilitate a shift in mental set. Whatever consciousness you are stuck in can be altered by this simple, healthful practice. You can give yourself "breathing space" in many ways—internally (physically), externally (environmentally), and mentally.

Yogic breathing is in a 1:4:2 ratio. Inhale for a count of one, hold four times as long as you took to inhale, and then exhale for a count of two. If your context or environment permits, you can increase the effectiveness of the breathing by raising your hands over your head as you inhale and lowering them as you exhale.

Another way of increasing the effectiveness of the breathing is to start with diaphragmatic breathing and then move on to filling up the thoracic region. You should notice a rise in your stomach at the beginning of your breathing. After you notice this, continue to fill your chest cavity.

We are energy transformers, but we forget to carry out our ability to transform.

It helps to do these breathing exercises in the morning, before every meal, and before bedtime. Since you should do them on an empty stomach, it makes sense to do them before meals. An added benefit of doing them before meals is that exercise prior to meals reduces hunger, so it will be easier to control your food intake. If you want a motivational source for acting on this, listen to the audiocassette tapes of Dr. Mark V. Hansen (Dr. Mark V. Hansen, Be Fit, Mark Victor Hansen & Associates, P.O. Box 7667, Newport Beach, CA 92658).

■ Visualization

Visualization in itself is a vast subject. Even as it applies to stress control there are entire books written on the subject, so here our examination will touch only on the highlights of this method.

When we visualize as we consciously breathe, we integrate mind and body, calling forth the function of the whole brain. Visualization is primarily a right brain process, and it can include left brain function, particularly if abstract relationships are visualized. It is a highly creative art. One can visualize in color, in black and white, at close range, as a participant, as an observer, with sound or without, with focus or without.

Those who wish to explore visualization in depth are directed to Adelaide Bry's book, *Visualization: Directing the Movies of Your Mind,* a concise study giving both practical uses and theoretical foundations for using visualization. Also see Hendricks and Roberts, *The Second Centering Book.* Dr. Johannes H. Schultz, the founder of autogenics in the 1930s, was one of the first to make systematic use of visualization in stress control. At present, any number of psychotherapists, exercise physiologists, and medical practitioners use visualization for a variety of purposes.

John Syer and Christopher Connolly use visualization to assist athletes to break through tension and fear prior to competition.[10] Visualization processes are a key component of the highly successful therapy developed by Bandler and Grinder—NLP (neurolinguistic programming).[11]

■ Visualization Techniques

The golden fluid visualization is a powerful technique that works on many levels— the visual, the kinesthetic, and the verbal. Visualize a golden fluid permeating your entire body. Visualize this liquid entering every tissue, every organ, every cell of the body. Think of it as a healing liquid, an energizing source. Then count down from 10 to 1. As you count down, imagine the liquid moving through your body and draining out of your toes and fingertips. Imagine it removing toxins, tensions, stress patterns from your body. Imagine it as a hybrid substance—sometimes moving like a golden fluid, sometimes as golden light. Imagine it has a faint sound that increases as it moves through the body, calming the body, converting tensions to useful energy, removing harmful toxins. Keep counting until the fluid has cleansed, calmed, and reinvigorated your entire body. End with the last bit of liquid draining from your toes. Then bring your hands together with a vigorous clap, stand up, and experience your change in mood, energy, and well-being.

Body-Mind Integration is another powerful visualization technique that will give you a sense of wholeness. It is useful when stress and tension arise from a conflict of values. Imagine a time in your past when you felt totally integrated, totally committed to a project, idea, or performance or a project that was a great success. Assume the physiology of that experience, using the same body position, facial expression, and breathing patterns. Imagine the location of your mental state. Imagine your mental state as a point of light. Give it a color and a sound. Now get in touch with your body. Locate a point in your body that represents your body. Give this point a color and a sound. Now very gradually bring together the mental point of light and the physical point of light. At the same time, recall the highest point of your successful project experience. Recall. Hold this state for 20 seconds, then bring your hands together in a loud clap and stand up. Allow yourself to experience the renewed integration of body and mind.

■ *Massage*

Ordinarily we think of massage as something that must be done for us. You may have a professional masseur. If so, you already know some of the benefits of massage. Or, you may have a willing friend—a fellow teacher perhaps. If not, you can make it a project to create a buddy system for massage trade-outs. But even if none of these possibilities are open to you at present, you can start by being your own masseuse.

Use kneading motions over your entire body. The only place you may not be able to reach very well is the center of your back. The good news is that you can wake up 99 percent of your body, create more circulation, and reduce body tension. Try this when you are waking up in the morning. It's a good way to gently complete the wake-up process. Try it before and after you exercise, and you may find less tightness in your muscles during and after the exercise. And, of course, when you are tense if you invest 3–5 minutes in personal massage, you will be able to break up much tension before you allow it to build up.

A variation of personal massage, recommended by Paavo Airola, the Swedish naturalist, is the dry-brush massage. For this you must have a natural bristle brush. It is important that the bristles be natural fiber; synthetic fiber can damage the skin. You can purchase these brushes with long handles so that you can reach everywhere on your back. For massaging when you are showering, a loofah brush is convenient and invigorating.

■ *Sauna and Steam Bath*

Some teachers join a health spa just to unwind in the sauna or steam bath. The author personally prefers the Finnish sauna. Here you can control the amount of steam by pouring water over heated rocks. And in most large cities, you can find Finnish saunas available at a reasonable rate per use. You do not have to join a club. Also, you have the option of a private sauna if you prefer to be alone.

In a sauna or steam bath you can practically feel your muscles melt, feel the tension draining from your body. Be sure to keep track of time, follow recommended time limits, and listen to your body signals (see Figure 19.2). Don't try to make a contest out of how much heat you can endure. Also, be sure to follow the steam with a warm shower gradually increased to cool, or cold, depending on what you can tolerate. This will close the pores of your skin and also change your body state again, assisting you in breaking up fixed states of consciousness. In short, it will wake you up, assisting you in projecting the mental-physical state you intend.

■ *Exercise as Stress Control*

For maximum stress reduction, aerobic exercise is recommended. Aerobic exercise is based on the amount of oxygen the body can utilize while under stress. The more oxygen the body can consume, the higher the level of fitness. Exercises like running, bicycling, aerobics, skiing, fast walking, tennis, badminton, and racquetball are excellent for this purpose (see Figure 19.3). These all force you to take in more oxygen than you normally use. A word of caution: Before starting one of these activities, and in particular if you have been sedentary, get a thorough checkup, including an EKG and stress test. Also, start out sensibly. Many people become discouraged with exercise because they overdo exercising, experiencing more pain than pleasure, and stop altogether. Others create serious injuries by going to fast too soon. Your body needs time to adjust.

The best approach for starting out is to join a group or sign up for a continuing education class taught by a qualified professional. The author recommends doing this through a university in your area, so as to ensure that you will get expert guidance

Figure 19.2 In using the sauna or steam bath, be sure to follow recommended time limits and listen to your body signals.

Figure 19.3 Fast walking and jogging are excellent forms of aerobic exercises.

in proceeding at optimal rate and correct information and feedback on cardiovascular improvement. If you join a commercial spa, remember that profit is usually the bottom line and instructors are often hired on the basis of how they look and present themselves, rather than on their training in exercise physiology. This is not to say that you will not find some excellent instructors with solid credentials; it is meant to say that you should check the training of the instructor.

Many persons complain that they can't exercise because they don't have time or they can't tolerate traffic or exhaust fumes or they don't live near a spa or university or YMCA/YWCA. They may also say that inclement weather is a barrier to exercising. If it's snowing out, this may be the time to head for the hills for a weekend of skiing. But if you are uncomfortable with outdoor exercise per se, there are any number of indoor exercises you can do on a routine basis. Invest in an indoor exercise cycle. Don't cut corners. Make sure the flywheel is at least 40 pounds or more and that the cycle is stable. This will minimize jerky movements, thereby reducing possibility of muscle and joint injury. A rebounder is also excellent. Here you can get the whole body involved without having to worry about excessive stress on the joints, a common hazard of running.

You may prefer a rowing machine or a skiing machine. These are usually more expensive than a cycle, but they give you a more total workout, working the arms and upper torso as well as the legs and cardiovascular system.

■ *Martial Arts*

The martial arts stress precision control over the body, timing, coordination, balance, and self-control (see Figure 19.4). From a discipline like tai chi you can discover new ways to move the body gracefully—ways that can translate stress into an art form akin to dance. Karate stresses generating and focusing energy for specific kinds of blocks and strikes. If you are tense or anxious, you probably won't be after

Figure 19.4 The martial arts stress precision control over the body—timing, coordination, balance, and self-control.

a full-scale karate workout. You will generate tremendous amounts of energy and control it. Again, pent-up tension gets transmuted.

Aikido is the perfect metaphor for deflecting unwanted forces being directed toward us. Circular movements are used to redirect the path of these forces. Judo stresses balance and the proper use of force at strategic moments in close sparring *(randori).* Most of these disciplines stress deep breathing. Karate is high on the list for cardiovascular conditioning, with judo running a close second, but much of this will depend on the instructor *(sensei).* Some martial arts, like tai jitsu (joint twisting), are useful for self-defense but do not provide cardiovascular benefit. All of the disciplines should be taken with a qualified instructor. Now many universities offer a variety of martial arts in their continuing education programs.

■ *Yoga*

Remarkable for stress control, transformation of energy, mind-body, and mood control, yoga is available in many forms—hatha yoga, kundalini yoga, and raja yoga, to name a few. Hatha yoga stresses breathing, relaxation, and body flexibility. There are a number of body positions one can get into which promote flexibility and strength in various parts of the body. Kundalini yoga stresses very deep and powerful breathing combined with exercise and sometimes stressful body postures. One of its aims is the breaking up of fixed body and mind patterns. It also aims to increase your tolerance for pain through conversion of pain into usable energy. It is a physically and mentally demanding form of yoga. All forms of yoga should be approached under the direction of a qualified instructor. This is particularly true of kundalini yoga. Finally, if you want to develop your ability to visualize, to control your thoughts and emotions through imagizing, you may wish to explore raja yoga.

- ## *Redirection*

Laura Huxley reminds us that human beings are constantly being charged with negative energy through a chain reaction that is largely an accident of time and place and misinterpretation of intention.[13] The paperboy accidentally breaks a flower in Mr. X's front yard—a plant Mr. X has taken great pride in cultivating. Mr. X assumes the boy across the street (the son of Mr. Y) broke his plant. Mr. X does not discuss this belief with Mr. Y. Had he done so he would have found out that Y's son had gone to camp two days before. Mr. Y comes into Mr. X's store. Mr. X is seething inside with anger but "congratulates himself on his self-control." His repressed hostility instead finds self-expression by "accidentally" shortchanging Mr. Y. Mr. Y later discovers he is shortchanged. He becomes angry, but instead of confronting Mr. X, he takes out his anger on his wife. Mrs. Y goes out to shop and takes out her frustration on the saleswoman. The negative energy has traveled through many persons, from the newsboy's accidental damage to a plant all the way to a salesperson. Our world, says Laura Huxley, is full of free-floating energy, some negative, some positive. Most of the time we are not the real target; we just happen to be present. Our task, then, is to deflect this energy, and insofar as we internalize it, to reconvert it. If, for example, one of your colleagues snaps at you in the lunch line, realize what pressure that person may be under and convert that energy. Anger can be converted into enthusiasm. Insofar as this negative energy enters your body, use it to tone the muscles of your stomach or to wake yourself up. Translate it into a Wagnerian opera. And let your colleague go ahead of you. You have the energy now and the good will to do so.

- ## *Nutrition and Stress*

Do you know the calorie content and food value of a typical fast-food meal? Do you know why you feel unsatisfied shortly after you eat? Here is the typical meal:

Hamburger	470
French fries (20)	310
Large Coke (12 oz.)	154
Ice cream cone (1 scoop)	174
Total	1,108 calories[14]

The calorie content is sufficient for a full day for most adults, yet it is consumed in one meal.

There are more diet books on the market than one can easily count, and they keep coming. Many of these books, written by authorities in medicine and nutrition, conflict on basic points—some are high-protein food plans, and others are high-carbohydrate plans. Some stress vegetarianism, and others the four basic food groups. What is one to believe? If we look for common denominators, there are a couple that stand out. While there is disagreement about the amount of protein intake, most of the leading food plans recommend a small intake of fat, and low sugar, particularly processed sugar. Most also recommend a plentiful supply of fresh vegetables and fruits.

Athletes increase energy levels and reduce stress by eating a diet high in carbohydrates and low in fats. Fresh fruits and vegetables and whole grains are the best sources of carbohydrates (not pizza and beer!). Fast foods and pop should be avoided because of the high fat content and excess sodium (from salt). These foods deplete your energy and over a period of time build up dangerous fat deposits in the arteries. The sodium causes water retention, contributing to excess weight, feelings of stuffiness and bloat.

The sugar in fruit is fructose. This sugar is readily converted to glucose and utilized by the body and does not create the insatiable craving that candy, chocolate and pop create. One way of curbing the excess eating of candy, cakes, and pies is to begin taking fruit as a dessert.

In our hectic culture we often feel that the fast-food hamburger or pizza or energy-booster candy bar is justified because it is quick and we need the energy now. It is just as easy to take a little fruit along to work to give you a solid nutritional energy boost throughout the morning. Instead of ordering that pizza, it may even be quicker to steam some vegetables—and think how good you will feel afterwards. You will know that your body is properly nourished and that you've avoided excess calories and you won't have that stuffy feeling. The lack of fiber results in your feeling hungry again very soon. And the excess sodium from the salt results in a stuffy bloated feeling and excess water retention.

If you want to alter teenage dietary habits, the first rule is not to lecture. Pictures of wholesome fruit, grains, nuts, and vegetables that are beautifully arranged and colorful are much more powerfully suggestive than a lecture. Verbal information is only about 7 percent effective. Visual information and suggestions of feeling are far more effective communication vehicles. Think of how advertising works. Think of how effective it is in selling fast foods. Using a parallel strategy, you might put up a poster of Michael Jackson or Brooke Shields eating a vegetarian meal, of a baseball star who likes fruit for breakfast. We need a whole new set of images that promote health as a counterculture (see Figure 19.5).

The Control of Stress

Throughout this chapter we have talked about controlling stress, not eliminating it. It may, in fact, be impossible, if not undesirable, to eliminate stress. Some people have higher stress needs and higher stress tolerances than others. According to Dr. Peter G. Hanson, we all need an optimum level of stress in order to function as healthy human beings. Some people actually thrive on stress.[15] Take Sir Edmund Hillary, for example. Not only did he conquer Mount Everest, he also went overland to the South Pole and drove jet boats up the Ganges all involving high levels of stress. And in Hillary's own words, "Life would have been rather boring without it."[16] We all know of people dying shortly after retirement, particularly those who had no

Figure 19.5 We need a whole new set of images that promote health as a counterculture.

projects. So it's not the amount of stress that counts; it's the way one uses the stress that counts. We must learn to use stress effectively.

■ *SUMMARY*

Stress is manifested both physically and psychologically. Peter G. Hanson's *The Joy of Stress* provides an excellent summary of the physiological bias. Hanson argues that stress if controlled can be a useful source of creative energy. Uncontrolled, it can be damaging, even fatal.

Burnout is distinguished from stress by many signs, behavioral, psychological, and organizational. Burnout is characterized by a loss of interest in fellow workers, increased accident-proneness, physical exhaustion, increased use of sick time, and by feelings of helplessness, disenchantment, and emotional exhaustion.

There are many ways of controlling stress so that it is shaped into a positive force: creating a pleasant physical environment; using music, humor, and contextual shifts; and maintaining good health habits, such as proper diet and rest, deep breathing, visualization, massage, sauna, and exercise.

■ *NOTES*

1. Peter Hansen, *The Joy of Stress* (New York: Andrews, McMeel and Parker, 1986), 22–35.
2. Deborah Jane Caton, Burnout and Stress Among Direct Care and Support Staff at a Large State Institution for the Mentally Retarded. Master's thesis, East Carolina University, 1986, page 7.
3. Ibid.

4. V. Ganju and M. Mason, *Job Satisfaction, Employee Turnover, and Burnout Among Direct Care Staff in Texas State Schools: Determinants and Implications for Administrative Policy.* (Paper presented to 106th Annual Meeting of the AAMD, Boston, Mass. 1982)

5. P.L. Harris, *"Assessing Burnout: The Organizational and Individual Perspective"* in *Family and Community Health* (vol. 6, No 4, 1984) p. 32–43.

6. Ibid.

7. Ibid.

8. Werner Erhard, founder of est training and the Forum, interprets upsets as a function of thwarted intentions, unfulfilled expectations, and withheld communications.

9. See Maxwell Maltz, *Psychocybernetics* (New York: Pocket Books, 1966).

10. See John Syer and Christopher Connolly. *Sporting Body, Sporting Mind: An Athletic Guide to Mental Training* (London: Cambridge University Press, 1984). Contains visualization exercises keyed to specific learning states desired.

11. See Richard Bandler and John Grinder, *Frogs Into Princes* (Moab, UT: Real People Press, 1979).

12. Paavo Airola, *How to Get Well* (Phoenix, AZ: Health Plus Publishers, 1974), 225–229.

13. See Laura Huxley, *You Are Not the Target,* 15–20.

14. Peter G. Hanson, *The Joy of Stress,* 255.

15. Ibid., ix-xxiii.

16. Ibid., ix.

PART FIVE

Professional Development

CHAPTER 20

Getting Hired

WRITTEN WITH JEANETTE H. PICCIRELLI

Some interviewers use a scattered approach—questions about feelings and values are interspersed with questions of fact.

You're a bunch of jackasses. You work your rear ends off in a trivial course that no one will ever care about again. You're not willing to spend time researching a company that you're interested in working for. Why don't you decide who you want to work for and go after them?

—Albert Shapero
in Richard Nelson Bolles'
What Color is Your Parachute?

I think most of us are looking for a calling, not a job. Most of us, like the assembly line worker, have jobs that are too small for our spirit. Jobs are not big enough for people.

—Nora Watson
in Studs Terkel's
Working

Preparing for Employment

Completion of a degree and of teacher certification does not guarantee employment. Throughout teacher education it is wise to devote a set amount of time to the preparation necessary for getting hired. Granted that you may have made straight A's in history and government courses, performed splendidly in professional education courses, including student teaching, and have amassed glowing recommendations, still you must compete with hundreds of teachers in your area or thousands across the nation who have similar qualifications. What are you going to do to distinguish yourself from them?

■ *Overcoming Destructive Beliefs*

Many new graduates from colleges of education are immobilized by destructive beliefs—beliefs that prevent them from getting hired. One such belief is that employment is owed them by virtue of having completed the required curriculum in a teachers college. The other is that the prospects of employment are dismal and purely a function of luck. Both of these beliefs promote abdication of responsibility; neither is based on evidence.

Completion of the required course of study means only that you have completed the required course of study. *In and of itself,* it means nothing beyond this. When it is reshaped and effectively presented to an employer, it may justifiably come to mean more, both to you and to an employer. But there is a great deal of work to be done in the meantime.

At the other end of the spectrum is cynicism. There are some students who drift into teacher education because they can't think of what to do with themselves. They tell themselves they will teach for a while, or if they can't get hired, they will drift into something else and try that for a while. Life is a series of stopgaps. Something may turn up, although it is not likely they will get hired soon. It is all chance, and luck is against them. Both of these beliefs are counterproductive. This chapter is about making an assault on these beliefs, about bypassing them, about approaching getting hired with purpose, planning, and aggression. For example, those who would place themselves at the mercy of luck may profit by considering the following:

1. Luck favors the prepared mind. If you've done all the homework on yourself . . . you will be more sensitive and alert to luck when it crosses your path.
2. Luck favors the person who is working the hardest at the job-hunt. . . .
3. Luck favors the person who has told the most people clearly and precisely what he or she is looking for. . . .
4. Luck favors the person who has alternatives up his or her sleeve. . . .
5. Luck favors the person who *wants with all their heart* to find that job.
6. Luck favors the person who is going after their dream—the thing they really want to do the most in this world.
7. Luck favors the person who is trying hard to be a 'special kind of person' in this world, treating others with grace and dignity and courtesy and kindness.[1]

To approach getting hired effectively you will find it useful to develop a network that leads to employment, develop a self-inventory to discern skills that distinguish you from others, make choices based on the region of the world or country you would like to work in and the kind of teaching you would like, prepare a portfolio including a curriculum vitae and representative sample of your work, develop interview skills, give attention to appropriate dress, develop interpersonal skills and practice using them, use resources such as college placement, and develop a substitute-teaching portfolio and plan.

■ *Knowing Your Options*

Persons trained as teachers can be valuable workers in business, industry, and government, as well as in a number of nonprofit foundations. You may have discovered in student teaching that although you like to teach, you are not comfortable in a school environment. Acknowledge this and move on. There are thousands of jobs that require making presentations, training personnel, or otherwise using teaching skills. Some places to look are:

1. Training academies (such as fire and police)
2. Corporate training and education departments
3. Local and state councils on higher education
4. Designers and manufacturers of educational equipment
5. Teachers associations
6. Foundations
7. Private research firms
8. Regional and national associations of universities
9. State and Congressional legislative committees on education.
10. Specialized educational publishing houses
11. Professional and trade societies[2]

| Substitute Teaching | In most large cities substitute teaching has become a rite of passage, a way to gain interim experience before settling into a permanent commitment and, above all, a way to demonstrate what you can offer as a teacher. If you can deliver consistent |

and outstanding work as a substitute teacher, the probability is that you will eventually be hired, usually within a two-year period. In most urban school systems there is a definite pattern of development for the substitute.

Anne Young, a successful inner-city secondary substitute teacher, offers the following advice:

> Substitute teaching can be a very positive way to launch a teaching career. You can pick up methods and approaches from a variety of experienced teachers that you can adapt to use in your own classroom later. Many school districts prefer the opportunity to observe how you function first-hand, and prefer to hire people as teachers who have substituted for them. To make a good impression, be sure to follow the lesson plan given to you, and to communicate clearly to the teacher you replaced as well as to the administrator in charge of the building. Hopefully, these tips will help you secure a permanent teaching position.[3]

In view of Anne Young's recommendations, consider the following substitute-teaching experiences:

> My beginning days of substitute teaching included a variety of classroom settings. I was usually substituting for a teacher who was out ill, mainly language arts, reading and math and some special education classes. Later, after I was told to give my classroom key to a teacher who had been offered a contract, I substitute-taught all over the school, including the girls' gym and typing. At the end of this year (1985) I was helping the librarian organize her card catalogue files. In the beginning weeks at Jackson my schedule consisted of staying in one teacher's room all day or possibly two to three days, and once I had put in about two and a half weeks here, the assistant principal asked me if I would be interested in teaching a seventh[-grade] math lab position with Chapter I Article 3 students. I accepted and worked in this room for 38 days and was one day replaced by a math teacher who more or less "bumped" me from the job. . . .
>
> . . . I became an ESRP substitute and would float around the entire building from room to room, subject to subject, and did what was called pay[ing] back other teachers' owed prep time. My areas of substituting were a large variety of subjects . . . special education classes, the girls' gym, typing, math, shop, etc. I was not the only employee hired to do this particular task and subbing. . . .
>
> . . . Most of the teachers I substituted for always left plenty of materials and because I was familiar with their styles I followed their directions left on notes and proceeded with the assignments. Everyone always used dittos, except the gym teachers. Some teachers were very organized, others left magazines or too many dittos. The special education classes were the most fun because the students were able to play games and solve complex puzzles. Usually, teachers did not expect me to correct their papers. However, two particular teachers felt that it was my responsibility to check the papers the students handed in while I followed through on the assignment these teachers left them. This ESRP role felt

more like baby-sitting the students since oftentimes the teacher was very happy to have another free hour in the day. I would always try to give individual attention for those students who wanted to do the work and needed help or assistance; however, the primary concern here was to make sure the attendance and paperwork were done without errors. Eventually I left that school. The Detroit Board needed me at Nolan Middle School to do the same assignment. I traveled farther and the job was the same, but the teachers here left easier assignments and lesson plans because it was so near to ending the year. There were usually charts on the board or magazines to read or fun games to play. This school had different school rules that applied and I was surprised to see students write notes of apology when they had a confrontation with the teacher.[4]

PROBES Analyze the substitute-teaching experience just described above.

1. What is important to this teacher?
2. What differences does she note as she moves from one position to another?
3. From the context of the passage, how would you interpret the job description of an ESRP (emergency substitute in a regular position) and an ES (emergency substitute)?
4. Can you think of alternative ways of approaching similar work situations?

The assertive substitute teacher will build a repertory of methods that can be used in any situation. Lessons planned for topics like "How to Get a Job" and "How to Take an Examination and Increase Your Scores" can be connected with any available subject matter or be taught independently. These topics will appeal to most students.

Research all your topics, even popular ones. Don't rely on giving information off the top of your head. An excellent resource for assisting teens in getting jobs are D. Mosenfelder's *Vocabulary for the World of Work* (New York: Educational Design, Inc., 1985) and Martin C. Douglas's *Go for It: How to Get Your First Good Job* (Berkeley, CA: Ten Speed Press, 1983). The wise teacher will collect other sources and create a number of usable methods. You cannot depend on the teacher for whom you are substituting to always leave a lesson plan.

What is important is that your performance as a substitute teacher be outstanding. This takes planning, creativity, flexibility, persistence, and hard work. The reward, aside from the intrinsic satisfaction of doing a job well, is often the offer of permanent employment.

Preparing a Resume

When the prospective teacher is approaching completion of degree requirements and appropriate certification, it is time to begin thinking where these skills will be put to use. In seeking any position, the most important tool is the resume. The resume has a single purpose—to get your foot through the door for an interview. An interview may go well or not, but you will not be hired without an interview, and normally you will not be considered for an interview without an effective resume.

■ *The Resume*

A good resume lays out all the key attributes about yourself that an employer uses in a hiring decision. Not only the background information but the very structuring of the resume itself will attest to such characteristics as the organizational ability, thoroughness, and neatness of the writer. A teacher just out of college and applying for that first position will necessarily have a much shorter resume than a seasoned veteran of the teaching profession. Resumes must be short—one page or at most two pages, especially for new graduates. School administrators, especially in large institutions with large staffs and large turnover, will not have time to read many paragraphs of detailed procedures that are common to all practice teaching and/or regular teaching positions. They will be thankful to you for your brevity. (If you ramble in your resume, will you also ramble in the classroom?)

Your college placement office will have samples of effective resumes and will help you construct yours, usually without charge. Your visit to the placement office will go much more smoothly if you have already seen what a resume should include and have taken the time to organize your own information. Libraries have many books devoted wholly or in part to the writing of resumes. While some of these are very helpful, some do not deserve the space they occupy on the library shelves, so be sure to scan several before you choose. Beware of the "complete" resume-writing handbook that is overly detailed, confusing, and intimidating. You are looking for guidelines—not a 3-credit course in resume writing. Do not heed the warning of some authors who advocate *not* sending a resume at all. Their argument is that if you send a resume, the administrator will know all he needs to know and have no need to interview you. The administrator theoretically would see your cover letter and then write or call you to request a resume. Nonsense. The administrator does not have time to play games and your cover letter would quite probably be relegated to File 13. Your approach might be: "If I were a school administrator, what would I like to know about a prospective employee?"

■ *Tips on Format Style*

There are many possible formats for a resume. The only ones that are not good are those which are confusing, difficult to read, or disorganized.

In any case, name, address, and phone number should be seen first, so these should appear at the top. They may be centered near the top of the page or alternatively be placed on the top left side.

The two most often used overall formats are the centered-heading format and the columnar format. The centered-heading format has the text under the heading beginning at the left margin and running across the page toward the right margin. Main headings—Education, Honors, Work Experience, and so on—are usually capitalized, set in bold, underlined, or any combination of the three. Subheadings, such as specific job titles, should stand out but be less noticeable than the centered headings. (See examples on following pages.)

The columnar format usually has the headings flush left, often with associated dates also flush left. This column is normally about one-third of the left portion of

FRANCES BROOKSTONE
23305 Wentworth Boulevard
Detroit, Michigan   48230
(313) 876-5432

JOB OBJECTIVE   Teaching position: Sciences/Mathematics, 9–12.

EDUCATION   **B.S.** in Secondary Education, May 1987
Wayne State University, Detroit, Michigan
    Major: Physics
    Minor: Mathematics

A.A., June 1979
Wayne County Community College, Detroit, Michigan
    Concentration: Science

CERTIFICATION   Thirty-Hour Continuing Certificate, August 1987
Grades 9–12 CE CX
State of Michigan, Department of Education

PROFESSIONAL PREPARATION

Student Teaching
☐ Physics, January 1981
    Polk High School, Wilmont, Michigan
☐ Precalculus, September 1980
    Tyler High School, Worthington, Michigan

Prestudent Teaching
☐ Algebra I, January 1980
    Woodstock High School, Woodstock, Michigan
☐ General Science, September 1979
    Dundee High School, Dundee, Michigan

HONORS   Mortar Board, Wayne State University
Charles C. Barnes Memorial Award

MEMBERSHIPS   American Association for the Advancement of Science
American Mathematical Association
National Education Association

WORK EXPERIENCE

Counselor, Summers 1985–87
Camp Gitchegoomi, Houghton, Michigan

Clerk (part-time), 1983–85
J. L. Hudson Co., Detroit, Michigan

Credentials available upon request from:
    Education Placement Office
    College of Education
    Wayne State University
    Detroit, Michigan   48202
    (313) 577-1635

FRANCES BROOKSTONE
23305 Wentworth Boulevard
Detroit, Michigan 48230
(313) 876-5432

JOB OBJECTIVE

Teaching position: Sciences/Mathematics, 9–12.

EDUCATION

B.S. in Secondary Education, May 1987
Wayne State University, Detroit, Michigan
Major: Physics   Minor: Mathematics

A.A., June 1979
Wayne County Community College, Detroit, Michigan
Concentration: Science

CERTIFICATION

Thirty-Hour Continuing Certificate, Grades 9–12 CE CX, August 1987
State of Michigan, Department of Education

PROFESSIONAL PREPARATION

Student Teaching
☐ Physics, January 1981
Polk High School, Wilmont, Michigan
☐ Precalculus, September 1980
Tyler High School, Worthington, Michigan

Prestudent Teaching
☐ Algebra I, January 1980
Woodstock High School, Woodstock, Michigan
☐ General Science, September 1979
Dundee High School, Dundee, Michigan

HONORS

Mortar Board, Wayne State University
Charles C. Barnes Memorial Award

MEMBERSHIPS

American Association for the Advancement of Science
American Mathematical Association
National Education Association

WORK EXPERIENCE

Counselor, Summers 1985–87
Camp Gitchegoomi, Houghton, Michigan

Clerk (part-time), 1983–85
J.L. Hudson Co., Detroit, Michigan

CREDENTIALS AND REFERENCES AVAILABLE UPON REQUEST

the page. The second column extends to the right margin and contains information called for by the headings at the left. Most other formats are variations of the centered and columnar formats.

For aesthetic impact, white space, quality of paper, and sharpness of print are important. White spaces are the unprinted areas of the page that balance and define the text. If the print is crowded or the margins are small, the resume will be difficult to read and will lose impact. One-inch margins are good, but they may be slightly more or less. The bottom margin should be equal to or slightly larger than the top margin. If necessary for appearance, it's better to continue on a second page, allowing greater vertical spacing and wider margins. Be sure to put your name on the second page. Your name here is usually on the top left and should be followed either by "(page 2)" or "(continued)."

A good-quality paper adds to the overall appearance of a resume. Textured papers such as linens, classic laid or woven papers have a good feel and print well. White is no longer the only color choice for paper, and off-whites and soft pastels are increasingly being used. Bright colors are never used.

■ *Professional Resume Services*

Should you type your own resume or have it done professionally? It is certainly acceptable to type your own if you have typing skills and have access to a good-quality typewriter or word processor with either a film ribbon or a new cloth ribbon. Erasures and white-outs are not acceptable. Dot matrix printers are acceptable if the print is near letter quality (not dotty). Laser printers by their very nature will produce top-quality print, assuming they have adequate toner and the drum does not need replacing.

You might consider having your resume done by a professional word-processing company. A resume service will be able to provide you with a typeset or at least very high-quality word-processed resume. Be sure to ask to see samples of the company's work before committing a significant amount of money for a resume. One- or two-page resumes should take an experienced typist or word processor anywhere from 20 minutes to an hour to enter (depending upon the complexity of the resume), so if you are paying a flat fee, decide whether it is a fair fee for the amount of work involved.

PROBES Remember that you will be coming to the professional with your resume well-organized and neatly hand written, so the amount of time to enter it will be a minimum. Questions to ask:

1. Will the professional be responsible for typos or give you the chance to proofread the first draft before copies are made? You will probably be charged for any changes other than typo corrections once it is entered.
2. Will the typist/typesetter save your resume on computer disk so that you can later have changes made without redoing the entire resume?

Even if your resume is kept on disk, it is important to keep the master copy and have extra copies on hand; otherwise if something happens to the disk and you have just given away your last copy, you'll have to rewrite your entire resume. Another reason to keep the master copy is to use it for any subsequent copies that you make. Copies of copies of copies will be progressively less sharp and spots will accumulate.

With the advent of better printers, especially the lasers, the availability of various font styles makes for professional-looking resumes without the expense of typesetting. However, a little restraint is in order when it comes to mixing font styles. Standard fonts such as Courier, Prestige Elite, Helvetica, and Times Roman are clean, attractive type styles when used by themselves, but the use of more than one or two fonts on a page can be distracting to the reader. However, using various sizes of the same type style can be very effective. There is *never* any excuse for using a font as elaborate and hard to read as Old English or as fancy as Calligraphic—not even for art majors.

The overuse of italic, bold, and underlining can result in so many words being emphasized that they all lose their importance.

Photocopies of resumes are acceptable *if* they are sharp and clean and essentially indistinguishable from the original. Spotty pages or faint print sends the message to the prospective employer that you don't care enough to invest a dime for a clear copy.

■ *Elements of the Resume*

Let us break down the information in the resume into logical elements in a logical sequence.

Name.   Use your legal first and last names (middle name or initial optional). If you dislike or have an especially difficult to pronounce first name, you may wish to designate an acceptable substitute—for example, Mihaeloviticus "Mike" Smith.

Address.   Include street address and apartment number (if applicable). Do not use a post office box number unless you will be moving and do not as yet know your new address. If you must use a box number, explain why in your cover letter. Write out in full the name of the city and the state, followed by the zip code. Include your home number or a number where messages can be left. If permitted by your present employer, you may also include your work number and the hours you can be reached there. Even if applying only in your own city, include the area code.

General Style.   Try to avoid use of personal pronouns such as "I," "me" and "myself." Since this resume is all about you, these words soon become very repetitive. In most cases it is not necessary to use whole sentences, and thus personal pronouns can be avoided entirely.

Job Objective.   What position are you applying for? You can use the exact wording of the job notice, or you might state you are seeking a position in one or more subject areas—for example, biology, physics, and/or chemistry. It is suggested that you not label this resume heading *Career Objective.* It sounds as if you expect your life aspirations will be fulfilled with your next job.

Education.   For the new graduate, *Education* will be the next heading because it lets the prospective employer know what degrees you hold, when and where you received them, and what your major and minor were. You may wish to include your grade point average (GPA); however, if it was less than 3.0, it is just as well to omit this information and hope your glowing references will make up for less than brilliant scholastic achievement. Any awards, scholarships, and other honors received during college should be included here.

If you have attended seminars or courses applicable to your profession, but over and above the normal curriculum, you may want to list them in this section. Post-degree courses now in progress should also be mentioned.

If significant, a line stating the approximate percent of college expenses earned by work or through scholarships is also appropriate here.

Certification.   Certification by the state attesting that you have met the necessary qualifications to teach certain subjects at stated grade levels should be included. Be sure to copy the certification statement exactly. Teaching professionals will know what they mean.

Work Experience.   It is the rare individual who has completed college without having at some time been gainfully employed. The prospective teacher, if nothing else, will have had practice teaching experience that can be mentioned here. It is important that you can account for your time from high school graduation to the present—further education, employment, absence from the work force to stay home and raise a family, military service, prolonged illness, and the like. Large time gaps are suspect.

It is good to list work experience in reverse chronological order—that is, the most recent job first and then backward as far as you feel necessary. The prospective employer can then quickly scan back as many years as he wishes. If done in chronological order, he must read through the (usually) insignificant early experiences before he reaches the "meaty" jobs you've held lately.

The elements of each work experience interval should include: (1) title of your position (dishwasher, bank president, etc.); (2) period of time you held this position (1985–1987, not 1987–1985 even though the resume is in reverse chronological order); (3) name of the organization employing you; and (4) city and state where this job was performed. (The street address, zip code and telephone number are *not* proper here because you are not at this point authorizing the company as a reference.) A very brief job description may be included. Here it is proper and effective to use phrases or enumeration rather than declarative story form. This is a resume, not the great American novel. Such jobs as dishwasher, busboy, or waitress, for example, do not need further clarification. If this position was a result of promotion from a previous job or if it resulted in promotion, mention that fact. If the job strengthened skills especially needed in the position being applied for, explain—for example, demonstrating the Handi-Dandy combination potato peeler and shoe polisher for the H. Mackeral Company may have promoted self-confidence in hostile group situations.

Use action words in your resume. Lists of suggested words can be found in books on resume writing—for example, *organized, reviewed, supervised,* instead of *did.*

If you presently hold a job, indicate by stating the work interval from the date of hiring to "present," rather than to the current month or year, which would lead the reader to assume termination at that time. It is always better to be employed when seeking another job than to be out of work—that is, lead from strength rather than from weakness.

Publications.   If you have publications to your credit, either alone or with coauthors, list them. Give the author(s), title, date of publication, place of publication and name of publisher, or name of journal or group responsible for publication.

Volunteer Work.   Even though the work has no direct bearing on the position for which you are applying, the fact that you have given of your time to a worthwhile cause is a plus. If your volunteer work was with an age group or special category of individuals you would be working with in the hoped-for job, you probably have a head start over other applicants. Volunteer work which might have a negative effect should not be mentioned; for example, having organized a teachers' strike will not make points with a school administration.

Interests, Hobbies, and Leisure-Time Activities.   Often what you do in your leisure time can have a direct bearing on your value to the school. For example, a computer buff on the faculty could be a plus for the administration when it comes time to lobby for more computers in the classrooms. Participation in sports usually shows an interest in personal health and the ability to compete. Although it is not necessary to include this category in your resume, it often tells much about what you do in your leisure time and could indicate acquired skills that do not appear elsewhere in the resume. But be brief.

Memberships/Honors.   Active memberships in professional or civic organizations identify you as a doer. If you have held offices in any of these organizations, mention them. If you have received civic or other awards, name them and the associated dates.

References.   Usually the phrase "Available upon request" is sufficient at this stage of your application. However, if you are a recent graduate, you may state "Credentials available upon request from . . ." (usually the education placement office). Include the complete address and phone number. If you are called in for an interview, you should have a list of references at hand in case you are asked for them. Be sure you have asked permission from the people on your reference list. It is essential that these people know you well and think highly of you. If they hesitate when you ask them, better ask someone else.

General Remarks. Perhaps the most important principle to observe in preparing your resume is *don't* ever write anything that is not true. A lie on a resume can result in instant dismissal without recourse. This does not mean that you cannot put yourself in the best possible light. For example, in the education segment of a resume, one student had stated "Ph.D. dissertation has not been completed." How much better it looked when it was changed to "All course work toward the Ph.D. degree has been completed."

■ *The Curriculum Vitae*

A curriculum vitae (CV) is similar to a resume, but is normally assembled by an individual with a considerable amount of experience in his profession. It has all the elements of the resume plus others that are specific to the individual. For instance, a music professor would also include participation in performances, guest appearances, compositions, and the like. The CV is often done in chronological order from college days to the present, as opposed to the reverse chronological that is usually used in a resume. In general, the same rules apply for both.

A resume or curriculum vitae should be revised when necessary. If you have been on interviews, take note of questions asked of you and incorporate those items into your resume if appropriate.

■ *The Cover Letter*

Whether you are answering an ad for a position or have heard about a possible job opening from a friend, as stated earlier it is essential that you send a cover letter with your resume.

The cover letter is a *brief* (three or four paragraph) explanation of why you are sending the resume. You need to state the job position for which you are applying (the school may have many job openings, especially in a larger organization) and how you heard about the opening. If someone you know is already with the school or organization and is in good standing, mention that in your letter. A familiar name in the letter will help the recipient remember *your* name.

Since you will be enclosing your resume, do not repeat all the details in your letter. However, if there is something in your past experience that would make you especially well qualified for the position, it is well to emphasize that in the letter.

If you are responding to an ad or posted call for applications, try to answer all the questions indicated. If a salary history is required, it is best to put that in the cover letter. However, if a salary requirement is requested and you are not familiar with the cost of living in the area and the going salaries for the position, you might state that salary is negotiable, depending on benefits and local living costs. It would be best, however, to have researched living costs for the area where the job is offered.

Your final paragraph should request an interview. The key word here is *request*—do not demand and do not grovel. If you are presently working and would have difficulty leaving during working hours, note the times when you are available. It is always a good idea to include your phone number under your signature in case your resume and cover letter become separated. Don't staple them together.

It is a nice touch but not essential to have the stationery of your cover letter and envelope match the paper used for the resume. Again, neatness and clarity count. A poorly written cover letter can undo all the effort you put into your resume.

As obvious as this may sound, remember to sign the letter, fold, seal, address, and put a stamp on your letter-resume combination. After signing the letter (in ink), place it on top of the resume and fold them together into thirds, insert them into the envelope, seal, address, and stamp. If you don't know how to fold something into thirds to fit a No. 10 business-size letter—and many college graduates, including engineers, don't—practice with similar-size sheets of scrap paper. It is permissible but not necessary to use a large manila envelope to eliminate folding of letter and resume.

■ *The Thank-You Note*

As soon as possible after you have had your interview, sit down and write a thank-you note to the interviewer. Even if the interview didn't go at all well and you don't think you will get the job, or you don't even want the job, it is an excellent idea to thank the interviewer for the opportunity to have spoken to him or her. It has been known to happen that the thank-you letter has tipped the scale favorably when several applicants were qualified for the job. And even if you were not quite the right person for that position, your letter will bring your name once again to the interviewer's attention. He may know another administrator who has an opening just perfect for you.

It is a good idea to keep a file of dated copies of all correspondence from your job search, including notes of telephone conversations. If you have not received a response to a submitted resume, it is not out of place to call the school or business and ask the status of your resume. If it is still being considered, fine. If you are not being considered, it is just as well to know now. If they have not received your resume and cover letter, you still have the opportunity to send another.

The Audio-Video Portfolio

In any job search, personal contact is premium use of time—no question about it. But what if you are completing your degree requirements in New York and you wish to teach in California? How will you present yourself personally? One way is to go there. But this may be prohibitively expensive, particularly if you want to interview in more than one place out of state. An alternative method is the use of the audio-video portfolio. In addition to sending the usual credential file from your university, you send under separate cover a presentation of yourself which includes the following:

1. Brief resume, emphasizing your career objectives that are perfectly aligned with the goals, objectives, and ambience of the school and system to which you will apply.
2. A sample lesson plan—your very best!

3. A video- or audiotape presenting you at your very best. This should be edited to delete dead silences, confusion, and other unwanted elements. Present only your best. One of my students added an introduction to his video in which he sings a song describing his educational philosophy. He was able to exhibit his skill at playing the guitar, song writing, singing, and succinctly stating his educational views in a dramatic and powerful way. The video showed him *doing* what he professed. Few interviews provide an employer with this much information.

4. Include a sample test and test scores showing student performance on the material presented in the audio-video. Another alternative would be to include products of the students' work—essays, drawings, science projects—all neatly assembled.

5. Organize all the above data in a portfolio, a folder with pockets for insertions. Label everything clearly. Provide a table of contents.

6. Provide a cover letter.

7. Package securely and send by certified mail. This last touch signals that you have sent something of value and that your intent is to ensure proper delivery.

When you are preparing your portfolio, make sure your appearance is exactly what you wish to project. According to Nelson Bolles, study after study shows that if you are male you will make a better impression if—

1. Your hair or beard is short and neatly trimmed

2. You have freshly bathed, used a deodorant and mouthwash, and have clean fingernails

3. You have on freshly laundered clothes and a suit rather than sports outfit, and sit without slouching

4. Your breath does not dispense gallons of garlic, onion, stale tobacco, or strong drink into the enclosed office air

5. Your shoes are neatly polished, and your pants have a sharp crease

6. You are not wafting tons of after-shave cologne 15 feet ahead of you.[5]

And, if you are a female, you will make a better impression if—

1. Your hair is newly "permed" or "coiffed"

2. You are freshly bathed, use a deodorant and mouthwash, and have clean or nicely manicured fingernails

3. You wear a bra, freshly cleaned clothes, a suit or sophisticated-looking dress, and sit without slouching

4. Your breath does not dispense gallons of garlic, onion, stale tobacco or strong drink into the enclosed office air

5. You wear shoes rather than sandals

6. You are not wafting tons of perfume 15 feet ahead of you.[6]

Many readers will, no doubt, regard some of these rules as absurd. The point is that they work, regardless of what one may think of them. Some are not germane to the making of a videotape; however, they are all germane to a direct interview.

The Interview

■ *Questions to Ask Yourself*

You can prepare for the interview in advance by learning as much as possible about the school and system for which you may end up working. Some questions to ask yourself are:

1. What are the organization's purposes and objectives in hiring?
2. What tasks, skills, content knowledge, and methodologies are they in need of?
3. How does my training, ability to perform match 1 and 2?
4. Do I really want to work for this principal, at this school; serve this population of students, parents; work with these colleagues? Can I find value compatibility here?
5. Can I persuade you to hire me?[7]

■ *Interview Styles and Visualization*

You can use visualization to prepare yourself for alternate interview styles. Visualize yourself performing splendidly regardless of the interview style used (see Figure 20.1). Some interviews are very much like filling out a questionnaire: What

Figure 20.1 Visualize yourself performing splendidly regardless of the interview style used.

training have you had in X? What community services have you contributed? How many hours have you had in subject Z? Some interviewers use a scattered approach—questions about feelings and values are interspersed with questions of fact. The interviewer may change the subject abruptly or become silent, in which case you may feel the need to shape the interview. Many of these factors are designed to see how you think on your feet, to test your integrity under pressure. It is possible, however, that you may run up against an inexperienced interviewer, in which case you had better have a prepared presentation of yourself. The interviewers may just sit there and ask you to tell them what you want and what you have to offer. The rest is up to you.

■ *SUMMARY*

Betty Doyle is a career counselor for a large employment agency in Alabama. She offers the following summary on preparing yourself to seek employment:

> It is important to define your career objectives. Where would you like to be, what would you like to be doing 5, 10, 15 years from now? Personnel specialists tell us that we do best that which we like most. The next step is to plan your marketing strategy. The bottom line is, of course, obtaining job offers. If you have more than one objective, your game plan might well be different for each objective.
>
> One thing is certain. Generating enough interviews to produce several offers will involve a substantial amount of activity and paperwork. This is a full-time job and will require every ounce of your ability and ingenuity, not to mention persistence.
>
> Develop a marketing strategy to develop job interviews by using the following:
>
> 1. Published openings (newspaper and magazine ads and trade journals)
> 2. Employment agencies or executive search firms
> 3. Target company mailings
> 4. Personal contact
>
> Prepare a good resume. Since resumes are seen by busy people who peruse many, the challenge is to get your key message across quickly, easily, and at the very beginning of your resume. Employers want to know most of all what you are seeking. One page is preferred, leaving references at either the first or second interview.
>
> Appearance is crucial at the interview. Unless yours is one of the flamboyant areas, dress should be tailored and businesslike. Most employers look beyond your skills and seek the real person within. They will be interested in your work ethic, your personality, and perhaps what you do after 5 o'clock.
>
> Good luck![8]

■ *NOTES*

1. Richard Nelson Bolles, *What Color Is Your Parachute? A Practical Manual for Job-Hunters and Career Changers* (Berkeley, CA: Ten Speed Press, 1988), 216–218.

2. Ibid., 237.
3. Interview with Anne Young, March 1987. Written statement quoted with permission.
4. Interview with Elaine Szwala, March 1987. Written statement quoted with permission.
5. Bolles, *What Color Is Your Parachute?* 190.
6. Ibid., 191.
7. Ibid., 187. This list is a modification of the questions suggested by Bolles.
8. Interview with Betty Doyle, October 1987. Written statement quoted with permission.

CHAPTER 21

Legal Rights and Responsibilities

JOSEPH M. WRIGHT

Teachers today must concern themselves with a diverse set of legal issues that, to a significant degree, control teaching environments as well as educational processes.

Human history becomes more and more a race between education and catastrophe.

—H. G. Wells

The statement "Good teachers cost more, but poor teachers cost most" may have originally referred to the tragic, intangible cost of ignorance, but today it is also true in terms of legal expense. Teachers today must concern themselves with a diverse set of legal issues that, to a significant degree, control teaching environments as well as educational processes.

Teachers do not need to become lawyers before they can teach, because appropriate legal assistance can and should be obtained by the school administrators in order to properly prevent or address a legal matter. Teachers must, however, keep abreast of legal developments regarding such issues as teachers' and students' competence; school security and student safety; environmental conditions; teachers' freedoms and restraints, the student as consumer and citizen; due process and procedural mandates; the Family Educational Rights and Privacy Act, as amended and commonly referred to as the confidentiality and freedom of information act; the redefinition of the school's authority; tort liability (a wrongful act, injury, or damage for which a civil action may be brought); disciplinary actions; the integrity of academic systems; and Title IX of the Education Amendments Act of 1972, which established certain antidiscrimination rules—to name some of the legal concerns.

Given the complex and diverse legal issues confronting the education profession, the question of how a teacher or school administrator can best legally protect the school, the students, the faculty, the staff, and himself is quite appropriate. The best general answer is to simply maintain a clear definition of *what* is to be accomplished, *how* it is to be accomplished, and *when* it is to be accomplished. Prudent legal-risk management is based on the understanding, firmness, efficiency, controls, and direction that exist within the organization. These, of course, are the same factors upon which the accomplishment of other specific tasks and institutional objectives is based.

Teachers' Legal Responsibilities to Students	**PROBES** What are the school's and teacher's legal responsibilities to students? What are the basic legal rights that teachers and schools accord students?

The complete inventory of the legal responsibilities of teachers to students cannot be fully discussed within the parameters of this chapter. However, there are certain basic legal rights that teachers must accord to students.

Basically, a teacher will need to have less concern for his legal rights than for his legal responsibilities. This is so because generally a teacher will have a subsequent opportunity to address a legal right that has been neglected, but if a teacher has neglected a legal responsibility, the opportunity to correct the problem wherein the responsibility arose may be gone forever, and irreparable harm may have been suffered by another person (student, colleague, or other).

Since courts have provided a more contemporary definition of *in loco parentis* (in the place of parents), it has become more important for schools and teachers to recognize that school authorities have a constructive, legal, educational mission with respect to the children who attend school. Furthermore, school authorities are authorized by parents, by an implied contract, to do whatever is reasonable and necessary within the learning environment, learning processes and content, and means and methods involving the education of children. In that regard, school authorities must appropriately control and take responsibility for the quality and quantity of teaching, the administration and management of the educational processes, and the safety of the children while they are in the immediate environs of the school.

> Education of children imposes three duties which teachers and other school officials owe to their students: (1) instruction; (2) supervision; and (3) safety. School officials necessarily must have a certain amount of authority in order to fulfill these duties. As a result, when acting in performance of these duties, school officials are recognized to have the authority to enact reasonable rules governing student conduct and to use reasonable disciplinary action in controlling students. In these matters, school officials' authority is much like that of the students' parents.[1]

Obviously, school authorities do not have unlimited powers. They must adhere to certain reasonable, yet clearly defined standards in most areas of administration, but particularly in the areas of disciplinary action, safety, teacher competency, and school facilities. In these areas, school authorities are solely responsible and should not let any peripheral people (for example, students or parents) adversely interfere with that obligation or the management thereof.

School authorities, however, must be cautious; they must not exceed their authority, engage in unreasonable actions, or implement unreasonable regulations by which the children cannot possibly abide. If care is taken to manage these areas properly, school authorities may avoid incurring certain legal liabilities.

Jurisdiction of School Authorities

PROBE When do students come within the jurisdiction of the school and school authorities acquire legal authority?

A student comes within the jurisdiction of the school system when that student is on school property or when the student is away from school premises but attending an activity or event that is conducted or sponsored by the school system. Therefore, as a matter of policy, parental authorization is needed in order to take a student away from the school premises. The jurisdiction and responsibility of the school system remain in effect until the student is returned either to the student's home or to the school (for subsequent transportation home in the student's customary manner). The school system is not liable for students or their conduct to and from school unless the school system provides transportation:

A student must be provided safe transportation if the school operates buses, and the student must be released at a safe bus stop. Nevertheless, if the school bus driver has deposited a student at a safe bus stop, the school will not be liable if the student is injured in an accident on his way home from the bus stop.[2]

As one may conclude, the legal responsibilities of a school system are quite varied, and the only appropriate means of properly addressing each responsibility is through strict and professional management. The most significant ingredient of legal-risk management is simple commonsense management with a constant view of actions that must be taken to correct certain deficiencies, minimize visible hazards, and negate possible risk conditions. As you may agree, good teachers and administrators are made rather than born.

| Records and Freedom of Information | **PROBES** What records should be kept? Who can have access to the records? What should I do if I am called to testify about the content of records, for example? Other than to tell the truth, how should I act when testifying? |

Schools and teachers are required to maintain precise and systematic records of any and all formal actions that may be taken on behalf of or used as a rationale for establishing and/or grading student performance, placement, and status. Schools must keep records of attendance, health, grades, addresses, test scores, and the like; access to said records is limited to the school authorities who possess a need to know, parents (with respect to minors), and the student. Records must be kept of any and all inquiries into a student's record. In order to properly handle freedom of information requests, a school should officially appoint a freedom of information officer and an alternate, with specific responsibility to handle all requests for student records.

Testifying in a formal context regarding student records, school policy, grades, and the like is a delicate matter. If not handled forthrightly, properly, and professionally, a teacher's testimony can cause inconvenience, personal strain, financial loss, and pain. In this context, all school personnel should be familiar with the amended Family Educational Rights and Privacy Act, commonly referred to as the confidentiality and freedom of information act.

Teachers and school officials who must serve as witnesses should be cognizant of the following information. First, you must know the contents of the records, how and where the records are kept, why the records are maintained, and the original source of the information therein. Obviously, if you are not expected, in the normal course of your duties, to be familiar with school records and storage processes, you shouldn't try to be an instant expert. If it is reasonable, however, for you to have some familiarity with the records the school maintains, you should find out as much as possible about your school's record-keeping policies and procedures.

With respect to your recollection of past events or incidents, you may need to constructively refresh your memory by revisiting the site of the event or incident; by discussing the event or incident with others who were there and can remember situations that you may not recall; and by simple personal concentrated thought on what took place and where it took place. However, the utmost care must be taken not to imply or create similar explanations or stories that are based upon something other than the facts. Also, remind yourself that your testimony can only reflect what you know. Hearsay is irrelevant, because under the rules of evidence, hearsay is not admissible in court proceedings.

Proper personal deportment is necessary when serving as a witness. You should be appropriately dressed. You should be alert and responsive. You should not, however, anticipate questions or volunteer information that has not been directly requested. Above all, remain calm and collected, and tell the absolute truth. Take reasonable care to talk in your normal manner, without exhibiting any form of staging or hesitation. It is advisable to be well rested so that you can adequately participate in the question-answer dialogue. Be patient and listen keenly to every question. Wait until you are sure you comprehend the question before you respond. It is appropriate to request that a question be asked again, and if you can't understand the question or don't know the answer, simply state that fact. Witnesses occasionally must struggle with a question that simply cannot be answered with a no or yes response. If that situation arises, you should merely say that you are unable to respond with a simple no or yes (see Figure 21.1).

A witness's answers should be formal, as direct and precise as possible. If you know the facts pertaining to the question asked, respond accordingly. Likewise, if you do not know, simply say so. A witness is not expected to know everything, and an honest admission of ignorance will keep your integrity intact. Remember, you can recall and testify about a situation without remembering all of the minute particulars surrounding the situation. By the same token, generalizations should be avoided.

Finally, if you realize that you have given a wrong or confusing response, take the initiative to correct it. If you do not do so, the improper answer may be revisited during the subsequent testimony, and the opposition can capitalize upon that situation.

As a matter of policy, a teacher or school authority should not testify unless his attorney is present and fully abreast of the proceedings.

Of course, legal counsel should be retained whenever you deem the legal process to be beyond your level of expertise, either substantively or procedurally, and also whenever the stakes are simply large enough to merit professional advice and the participation of a trained lawyer. School teachers and administrators are not expected to be legal strategists, as they generally do not have the legal training or experience necessary for adequately handling legal issues and jurisprudence.

Search and Seizure	**PROBES** Do school officials have the right to search and seizure? Is a search warrant necessary? What can legally be done to provide a safe school environment?

Search and seizure is currently a matter of concern in many urban high schools. This issue is a double-edged sword because the schools are mandated, by relevant laws of contracts and torts, to provide a safe learning environment, and simultaneously the

Figure 21.1 In serving as a witness, wait until you are sure you comprehend the question before you respond.

schools must protect the right of students pursuant to the Fourth Amendment of the Constitution of the United States of America, which states:

> The right of the people to be secure in their persons, houses, papers, and effects, against unreasonable searches and seizures, shall not be violated, and no warrants shall be issued, but upon probable cause, supported by Oath or affirmation, and particularly describing the place to be searched, and the persons or things to be seized.

The most current litigation regarding search and seizure in a public high school is the pending case before Judge Avern Cohn of the U.S. District Court, Eastern District, Detroit, Michigan,[3] wherein the City of Detroit high schools' use of metal detectors for the purpose of eliminating or minimizing the number of weapons brought into the high schools is being challenged.

Historically, the search and seizure issue has focused on the systematic search of school lockers. The effort now, however, is to detect and remove weapons before they are carried to and stored in lockers or some other school area that is controlled by the student(s).

Professor Yale Kamisar recently wrote, in an article in the *New York Times,* that

> whether and how to apply the Fourth Amendment to new conditions has generated great controversy . . . [because] . . . the epidemics of the 80's have put enormous pressures on the Fourth Amendment. Proposals that would require certain groups to submit to random urinalysis tests for drugs, or to blood tests for the AIDS virus, directly threaten the concept of "individualized suspicion" that lies at the heart of the amendment. In brief, this notion holds that the Government should not be able to interfere with someone's liberty or invade his privacy, unless officials can demonstrate that they have "probable cause" to believe that particular person is committing or has committed a crime. The amendment forbids the Government to issue search warrants unless officials can satisfy the "probable cause" requirement.[4]

The crisis of weapons being brought into schools has provoked a number of boards of education to establish various random, yet structured, student search and seizure policies and processes. Searching students without the accompaniment of a legal court order obviously presents a legal and political predicament of misfeasance. However, unsafe school environments are a reality. Accordingly, in order to avoid the malfeasance of being accused of not meeting the obligation to provide a safe learning environment, schools must be given the same liberal interpretation of the law that has been accorded with respect to the personal searches that take place in all major airports, federal courts, many state courts, and a host of quasi-governmental installations.

Let's summarize the status of search and seizure as it relates to students. Basically, schools have the privilege of search and seizure. Under proper circumstances, however, students have a Constitutional right against improper or unreasonable search and seizure. When a student attends school, he is obligated to follow any and all policies, processes, rules, and regulations that have been properly instituted by the school. In general, the law considers the school's need to carry out its educational mission superior to the rights of the student.

Educational Malpractice: Fact or Fallacy?

PROBES Is there malpractice in the education profession? What should be done to respond to competency and performance concerns pertaining to teachers?

The possibility of malpractice—the violation of established codes of professionalism with damage to another—is inherent in every profession. Nevertheless, insightful and prudent management can drastically reduce the risks of being sued for malpractice. To a large degree, the courts have given the educational entities and teachers almost carte blanche protection with respect to their policies and procedures in all academic matters. With respect to a possible tort action by a plaintiff against an educational institution for an academic matter of alleged misfeasance or malfeasance, at present most courts would not consider tort action appropriate. However, it is evident that during the next decade, a reasonable level of success will be achieved with regard to penetrating the implied public policy protection that, at present, schools have and courts presently respect. The Association for the Study of Higher Education addressed that issue in a recent report, wherein it was stated that

> . . . the current disposition of the courts is not to encroach into some areas of the fiduciary relationship, specifically academic decision-making, which includes, for the moment, educational malpractice. The courts refuse to recognize educational malpractice as a tort, because to do so would conflict with public policy. Several policy considerations seem appropriate:
>
> a. The process for peer review and evaluation by department heads and supervisory administrators should be reviewed to ensure that incompetence and poor performance are not swept under the rug.
> b. Institutions should ensure that diagnostic procedures must meet the practice and procedures accepted by professionals in the field when such standards are available.
> c. Review should be built into the process of awarding grades and certifying skills to protect against arbitrary and capricious decisions and, at the same time, to protect the academic integrity of the faculty evaluation process.
> d. Catalogs, bulletins, and other publications should be reviewed to ensure that they do not make guarantees beyond the institution's capabilities.[5]

Here again, teachers and school authorities can avoid alleged malpractice complaints by good management, evaluating what is taught and how it is taught. Concurrently, the administrative policies and procedures should be evaluated to ensure that they are consistent with sound public policy and prudent management, and that they are constructed to assist the school in maximizing its educational goals for students.

A number of courts are placing legal responsibility on third-party schools that have become party to a suit partially because of their perceived "deep pocket" (ability to pay). In order to reduce the risk, aggressive managerial efforts must be exerted, and even then, schools and their staffs remain in a state of high legal risk.

> [A school] may be held liable if it fails to correct a dangerous situation of which it is, or should be, aware. For instance, if experience teaches that certain circumstances are associated with behavior problems, such as rowdiness at parties and sporting events, the school can be held liable if it fails to provide adequate security. Likewise, schools have a responsibility to protect others from students known to be abusive.[6]

Although it is not necessary for a teacher to be able to evaluate a school situation or incident to establish whether negligence existed with some form of tort liability, the meaning of tort liability should be understood. Tort liability is based upon one's right to collect for damages incurred as a result of a school or educator not doing what should be done with respect to an alleged wrongful act, injury, or damage for which a civil action may be brought.

<table>
<tr><td>

Teachers, Schools, and Boards
of Education

</td><td>

PROBES What is the role of a board of education in developing educational policy? How can citizens effect appropriate change of a board policy? What is the authority of a board of education?

</td></tr>
</table>

A significant component in the educational system is the typical board of education. The board is generally a public body elected by the local citizens of the community. Operating as a public service administrative body, the board determines what administrative rules and regulations are to be used by the school system. Many educators, parents, and students consider the board a monolithic monster that simultaneously ill serves teachers, administrators, and students. That perception is widespread, but as a matter of law it is unfounded.

Whether formal or informal, board rules and decisions viewed as unwarranted incursions on protected private interests are increasingly subject to challenge in the federal courts.

According to H. T. Edwards and V. D. Nordin in *The American Legal System,* the traditional model of American administrative law is

> one in which judicial review operates as the mechanism for control of official intrusions on private interests. The focus of this review historically has been twofold: on whether administrative discretion has been exercised within statutorily authorized bounds, and on whether agency procedures have been adequate to insure the accuracy, rationality, and reviewability of agency implementation of legislative directives. Legislative and judicial controls, aimed at protecting individuals and regulated entities from the arbitrary exercise of agency discretion, were thought sufficient guarantees that agencies would act to advance the "public interest."[7]

Contemporary society mandates that the competing claims, concurrent needs, and interests of teachers, school administrators, students, and parents be considered essential elements in determining policies, procedures, and regulations. Courts have continuously indicated the desire to balance the needs of society and the multiple interests contained therein. Therefore, school authorities must strive to consider all of their constituents (staff, students, and others) and all of the essential elements in determining and articulating what must be both the right decision and the most reasonable. The decision-making process used by school systems is simple and efficient, but it sometimes fails to prevent individual discretion from overruling objective considerations and creating a risk situation that the school could have avoided.

Recent situations indicate that boards of education—whose members are quite conscious of their constituencies and of possible judicial review—have expanded their involvement in all aspects of teaching, school administration, and the educational transitions of students. This reality was verified by Professor Stewart of Harvard University, who outlined the following "doctrinal developments through which control of administrative action has been extended":

1. The establishment of an increasingly strong presumption of judicial review of agency action (or inaction);
2. The enlargement of the class of interests entitled under the due process clause to an administrative hearing before agency infringement of those interests;
3. The enlargement of the class of interests entitled by statute or regulation to participate in formal processes of agency decision;
4. The enlargement of the class of interests entitled to obtain judicial review of agency action.[8]

Therefore, teachers and all school authorities must be cognizant of the possibility that certain actions taken by a school board may be challenged in a court of law.

Legal-Risk Management

PROBES How can school administrators and teachers minimize their legal risk? What legal concerns should be specifically included in a disciplinary procedure?

Aristotle reportedly observed that "the roots of education are bitter, but the fruit is sweet." Modern educators would probably agree that this is a true statement, although the bitterness with which they are acquainted comes of an educational environment that is characterized by inertia, wherein the rewards and appreciation for superb teachers continue to be limited, while opportunities and benefits for students are deficient. Of course when a student successfully makes the transition, all agree the "fruit is sweet."

In order to bear "sweet fruit," administrators and teachers must cooperate in controlling the learning environment. Otherwise, they will not be able to provide the students with the necessary learning resources. One tool for controlling the learning environment is the systematic annual risk analysis.

Every school, through a systemwide process, should conduct an annual legal-risk analysis, which should serve to measure the school's ability to respond to new situations and new students. Part of the annual legal-risk analysis should include an evaluation of the effectiveness of its current management systems, teaching methods, administrative procedures, and personnel policies. This is necessary to identify any deficiencies that must be addressed and any changes or improvements that should be implemented.

Furthermore, each school and its various staff entities, as well as selected external entities and individuals, should annually be asked to provide input concerning the local education system and its specific components. This process must include an assessment of relevant internal and external legal and management issues that affect the school's ability to meet student and staff needs and expectations, as well as consideration of the legal implications of these issues as they affect the educational processes and objectives.

A subsequent written legal-risk analysis can be used as a framework for the creation of practices and policies that will serve to prevent specific legal issues and conflicts.

Such an analysis may show, for example, that a regularly contested legal issue is the discipline or expulsion of a student for breach of rules or regulations. In revising existing policies or creating new ones, one should keep in mind the need for due process, equal protection, and managerial accountability, as well as the points which follow.

I. In every student disciplinary hearing, the following documents should be made available to the parties involved:
A. A statement containing the compilation of the facts regarding the alleged misconduct, from the view of the witness(es).
B. A formal description of the procedure for resolution. The procedure must provide for the hearing and consideration of both sides in detail.
C. A written notice to the student that specifies the charges, describes the process of resolution, and specifies possible sanctions.
II. The disciplinary process should be consistent with the method of handling a typical adversarial proceeding. Nevertheless, care can be taken to maintain the normal and calm educational pursuits and interests of the school, so that the school and the parties subject to the proceedings can return to a normal conflict-free environment as soon as possible.
III. The student must be provided an opportunity to know the identity of witnesses against him. Also, upon request, he or she should be given a copy of any and all reports, affidavits, facts, and other items to which the witnesses testified.
IV. The student should be given the opportunity to present his or her defense and to submit written and oral evidence that supports it.
V. The decision of the hearing must be communicated to the student, and he or she should be advised of any existing appeal processes.

Likewise, the above elements of basic due process should be contained in all grievance hearings, disciplinary actions, and other actions involving school employees.

| *Due Process and Equal Protection* | **PROBE** What is due process? What are the due process issues that teachers must know? To define due process, let's use the *In re Coates* decision, wherein the court stated that the exact meaning and scope of the phrase "due process of law" cannot be defined with precision, but |

requires an orderly proceeding, adapted to the nature of the case, in which a citizen has an opportunity to be heard and to defend and protect his rights. A hearing or an opportunity to be heard is absolutely essential, but due process does not guarantee a citizen any particular form or method of state procedure.[9]

What are the crucial legal rights of which all teachers should be aware? Of course, due process and equal protection are fundamental Constitutional rights. More significant, however, may be the need of teachers to have some legal right (through a bargained-for contractual agreement and/or the school administration's desire to enhance the concept of participatory management) to help address certain school issues, such as disciplinary action, grading, attendance, textbook and curriculum decisions, and so forth. These concerns were verified in a survey conducted by the Carnegie Foundation for the Advancement of Teaching. The survey indicated teacher frustration owing to a dearth of professional authority. In contrast, if teachers have a legal responsibility to their constituents (students, peers, and administrators), teachers must have an implied legal right to participate appropriately in improving the work environment, conditions, methods, professional development, procedures, and program evaluations.

Let's revisit and further define what constitutes due process. There are two concurrent areas of due process. Substantive and procedural due process ensure objectivity, consistency, fairness, competency, and equality in procedure and substance with respect to the issue, the method of resolution, who resolves the issue, and all other relevant aspects. In *Cohen* v. *Hurley* the court stated that

> Whatever procedures are fair, what state process is Constitutionally due, what distinctions are consistent with equal protection, all depend on particular situations presented, and history is relevant to such inquiries.[10]

Due process and equal protection must be contained in all school procedures, policies, and regulations. Pursuant to the Fourteenth Amendment to the Constitution, due process of law is guaranteed to every U.S. citizen. The amendment states that a state cannot deprive any person of life, liberty, or property, without due process of law. As a rule, due process is a procedural process wherein mandated, fair, consistent rules are followed with respect to the enforcement, protection, and resolution of individual considerations.

The primary intent of due process is to ensure basic and consistent fairness. This includes a *fair* tribunal, a *fair* process, and a *fair,* or at least reasonable, conclusion. School authorities and agencies must be cognizant of the need to abide by all Fourteenth Amendment mandates and avoid action that may be considered arbitrary or capricious.

If the issue being addressed is quite serious, then the process used for resolution should be quite formal with respect to guaranteeing due process.

Due process is a right reserved to all parties within a school system. With regard to school employees, however, the due process rights of permanent staff are substantially more definitive than those for temporary staff. Many school systems allow administrators to terminate the employment of nontenured temporary teachers at will, but require complex hearings if the same action is taken against a tenured permanent teacher.

Due process requires appropriate procedural protections that must be honored in a substantive manner in all of a school's personnel actions and policies. This provides a means of stability for the school system, its personnel, and its constituency.

Teachers and the Collective Bargaining Process	**PROBES** What should a teacher know about collective bargaining? What is the role of a teacher in the collective bargaining process?

Collective bargaining is commonly understood as the method used to determine a teacher's salary. The collective bargaining process, however, can be used to determine any and all of the parameters of the learning environment (class size, disciplinary procedures, curriculum, instructional resources, and so forth). With respect to the collective bargaining environment, teachers and administrators are normally on opposite sides of the table and issues, and generally refuse to give appropriate consideration to the position of the other side until all of the preliminary psychological positioning has been buried.

Teachers should understand that the school authorities must maintain administrative and financial control. If presented in a reasonable manner everything else is bargainable. Teachers should be mindful of the significant impact parents and students can have on the collective bargaining agenda and logistics. It is incumbent upon both sides of the bargaining table to facilitate an environment in which students and parents are kept informed of the proceedings and progress.

All parties must recognize the human dynamics that exist in a bargaining strategy. Initially, all parties will approach the bargaining situation with positions based upon their particular vested interests. Those interests should never be items of surprise. That is why both sides must have experienced representatives to speak and bargain for them. This also ensures objectivity and negates conflict over trite issues.

There are five basic elements that will affect the operation of a collective bargaining environment. They are social interaction, economic conditions, legal and political forces, technological development, and educational changes. The ability of those involved in the collective bargaining process to control and influence these elements will, to a large degree, determine their success on certain issues. Bargainers must respond affirmatively to all forces that are brought to bear upon their clientele. The inability of a particular bargaining entity to influence the elements noted above, or a portion thereof, may eliminate that entity's usefulness as a bargaining unit. A case in point is *Crestwood Education Association* v. *Crestwood Board of Education (Dearborn Heights, Michigan),* wherein the board, with the backing of the court, discharged all of its teachers who were on strike. This action followed a long history of discord between the board and the teachers' association. One may conclude that the dismissal resulted from failure on the part of the teachers' representative at the bargaining table to adequately assess and systematically monitor the economic, political, and legal forces that were functioning while the bargaining was going on. A fine example of a contemporary view of human resource management and labor relations is the Career in Teaching Plan by the Rochester City School District and the Rochester Teachers Association (May 1988). The *Joint Statement of Intent Agreement* describes the Career in Teaching Plan as follows:

> In a radical departure from traditional career paths in education, teachers in the Rochester City School District will have career options that do not require leaving the classroom to assume greater responsibility in shaping and improving student attainment and performance.
>
> The intent of the Career In Teaching Plan is to help improve public education in Rochester by providing an opportunity for exemplary teachers to inspire excellence in the profession, to share their knowledge and expertise with others, and to actively participate in instructional decision-making. The success of the Plan will be measured by improved student outcomes and attainment.
>
> The Plan also establishes a method for developing and maintaining a corps of the highest caliber teachers in Rochester City Schools by incorporating into this agreement provisions from the previously negotiated Peer Assistance and Review Program, including both the Internship for new teachers and intervention for tenured teachers who are experiencing severe difficulties in the classroom. The Plan also calls for peer review in the evaluation of tenured, fully certified teachers. . . .
>
> All RCSD teachers will participate in the Career In Teaching Plan. The Plan provides for four career development stages: Intern, Resident, Professional and Lead Teacher. Assignment to the first three stages of the Career in Teaching Plan is based on teacher certification, tenure and experience in teaching. For example, newly hired teachers without New York State teaching experience will be Interns for their first year in the District. After successful completion of their internship, they will be Residents until they have received both permanent New York State certification and tenure in the District. Permanently certified, tenured teachers in the District will be Professional Teachers. Professional status is a prerequisite for applying for the new Lead Teacher positions.
>
> The selection of Lead Teachers is based on an open competitive process; teachers, administrators and others could be involved in the selection of Lead Teachers. To be considered for a Lead Teacher position, applicants must have a proven ability to work successfully with students who have the greatest needs and have demonstrated an ongoing commitment to improving student outcomes. Provisions for student and parent involvement in the selection of Lead Teacher will be developed and phased-in.
>
> A number of different Lead Teacher assignments will be developed by the Panel in response to identified District needs. Each position will have a job description outlining the position's organization placement; the responsibilities and intended accomplishments; the reporting, supervision, and evaluation procedures; and the appropriate compensation. Each assignment will include challenging teaching responsibilities, as well as profession related duties. All Lead Teachers must reapply for continued status every two years.[11]

As the problems that confront our educational systems escalate, it is becoming necessary to involve the total educational community in all aspects of educational management. External forces are having a substantial impact on educational management and on the school system. One may reasonably predict that the public may soon demand representation at all levels of educational management, including representation within the process of collective bargaining. Within the educational community, the bargaining adversaries may request "the cake and ice cream, too," without being accountable to those who provide "the cake and ice cream." Our society is very heterogeneous, and the educational community must respond to the distinctive needs of each homogeneous section of our society. This relationship in and of itself demands the involvement of all segments of an educational community. If such community interaction is not achieved, or realized, drastic program cuts and unrealistic bargaining demands may become the rule rather than the exception, and the continued deterioration of our educational system may be inevitable.

Future Perspectives

PROBE   How will the law change with respect to education?

The education profession and the operation of educational institutions are in the midst of dramatic change because of our changing society, environment, technology, resources, and human needs.

Schools should expect academic content to be increasingly challenged because of increasing pressure from organized religion and parents who want more accountability and better-educated children.

It is also likely that the success and quality of the educational experience will be questioned more definitively because of the growing number of teenagers who are failing to adapt to the traditional school environment or failing to acquire the necessary knowledge and skills. William Bennett, U.S. secretary of education in the Reagan administration, stated: "Our schools are teaching students how to think but not what to think about." Mr. Bennett's point is well taken. In most urban schools and many rural schools, students are simply not acquiring adequate basic knowledge. Accordingly, school authorities will be asked to manage and provide an educational environment that is safer, more goal-oriented, and better equipped to provide students with skills for employment. Courts will provide less protection in those areas wherein the schools have had a reasonable degree of immunity.

Teachers will probably be required to take more preemployment competence examinations and enroll in formal continuing education programs in order to maintain state-of-the-art skills and knowledge. Refresher courses are already badly needed by many grade school teachers who are grossly ignorant of the latest developments in science, math, foreign languages, and computer technology, but are nevertheless responsible for teaching those subjects. This deficiency must be addressed or school systems may become legally negligent for the shortfalls.

School systems must and will acquire more definitive and contemporary legal rights to control the school environment and unruly students. At present, school authorities are, as a matter of law, in a nebulous position in addressing unruly students. Usually, they expel such students from school, but subsequently the uncontrolled students become a greater burden to themselves and to society. Therefore, urban school systems are likely to be legally required to provide alternative education facilities for unruly students in the near future.

Teachers and administrators must modify their traditional methods in order to foster productive learning. Education is—and must be understood to be—a lifelong endeavor. As Sir William Haley stated: "Education would be much more effective if its purpose were to ensure that by the time they leave school, all boys and girls would know how much they do not know, and be imbued with a lifelong desire to know it."

■ SUMMARY

Teachers must keep abreast of legal developments regarding the following:

1. Teachers' and students' competence
2. School security and student safety
3. Environmental conditions
4. Teachers' freedoms and restraints
5. The student as consumer and citizen
6. Due process and procedural mandates
7. The Family Educational Rights and Privacy Act, as amended, commonly referred to as the confidentiality and freedom of information act
8. Redefinition of the school's authority
9. Tort liability—that is, a wrongful act, injury, or damage for which a civil action may be brought
10. Disciplinary actions
11. Integrity of academic systems;
12. Title IX of the Education Amendments Act of 1972, which established certain antidiscrimination rules

■ NOTES

1. R. D. Gatti and D. J. Gatti, *Encyclopedic Dictionary of School Law.* West Nyack, NY: Parker Publishing, 1975, 153.
2. Ibid.
3. *Jane Doe* v. *City of Detroit Board of Education et al.,* 85-CV-74256 DT, U.S. District Ct., Eastern District of Michigan.
4. Y. Kamisar, *New York Times Magazine,* Sept. 13, 1987, 109–114.
5. Association for the Study of Higher Education Reports, 1986, Report 7, Washington, DC
6. *National On-Campus Report,* June 23, 1986, vol. 14, no. 12; 1, Madison, Wisconsin.
7. H. T. Edwards, and V. D. Nordin, *The American Legal System,* Institute for Educational Management, Harvard University, 1980, 40.

8. Ibid.
9. *In re Coates,* 213 NYS 2d 74, 929 2d 242 173 NE 2d 797 (1961).
10. *Cohen* v. *Hurley,* 81 S. Ct. 954 (NY 1961).
11. Peter McWalters and Adam Urbanski, *Career in Teaching Plan: Joint Statement of Intent Agreement,* a pamphlet issued by Wilbur Gerst, Supervising Director for Labor Relations for Rochester School District, Rochester, NY, May 1988.

CHAPTER 22

Professional Goals and Development

The effective teacher transforms work into projects.

Most people encapsulate themselves, shut up like oysters, sometimes before they have stopped being undergraduates, and go through life barricaded against every idea, every fresh and unconceptualized perception. It is obvious that education will never give satisfactory results until we learn how to teach children and adults to retain their openness.

—Aldous Huxley

Aldous Huxley's favorite affirmation, *au'n aprendo*—loosely translated "keep on learning"—was to him more than a mere ideal; it was a declaration by which he lived. Between 1916 and the time of his death on November 22, 1963, Huxley published on average one major book a year. As his interest turned toward education, he researched his final novel, *Island,* by drawing from interviews with everyday workers as well as literary and scientific scholars. He completed his final essay, "Shakespeare and Religion," on his deathbed. He was committed to a continual expansion of consciousness, to staying open to new ideas. But how does one do this? In particular, how does the teacher keep on learning as a professional?

Areas of Professional Development

There are many areas in which teachers can develop professionally: by systematically generating professional goals, by exploring current teaching methods through reading, and by participating in seminars, in-service workshops, and conferences. They can build a professional library; secure travel grants for learning and research; create self-monitoring systems; become aware of and contribute to ethical standards for their profession; seek advanced degrees in specialized areas; publish their findings in professional journals; network with other professionals; develop workshops for teachers, business, and industry; serve on school committees; take a leadership role in co-curriculum activities, clubs, drama, sports, and social groups; and continue to explore ways of expressing their values as teacher through their professional dress and daily behavior.

Professional Well-Being

Staying alive professionally is not an automatic consequence of having a degree or a teaching certificate; it is a conscious, active process. A good place to begin is with your state of well-being. Gail Sheehy, in researching the basis of quality self-directed work for her book *Pathfinders* found five self-descriptions of well-being common to all socioeconomic groups interviewed. In rank order they are:

1. My life has meaning and direction.
2. I have experienced one or more important transitions in my adult years, and I have handled these transitions in an unusual, personal or creative way.
3. I rarely feel cheated or disappointed by life.

4. I have already attained several of the long-term goals that are important to me.
5. I am pleased with the personal growth of my development.
6. I am in love; my partner and I love mutually.
7. I have many friends.
8. I am a cheerful person.
9. I am not thin-skinned or sensitive to criticism.
10. I have no major fears.[1]

Sheehy found that persons who could honestly state most of the above became leaders in their communities. Most became very successful at their careers or changed careers and carved out new professional possibilities for themselves and others. You may find the 10 descriptions useful in designing projects that forward your professional growth.

For example, consider the first statement: "My life has meaning and direction." Rarely will one experience meaning and direction by sitting around and thinking about it. Nor is it likely that one will experience meaning and direction by going through the motions on the job. One is much more likely to experience work as meaningful by *re-creating work as a project*.

To Martin Heidegger the human being is distinguished from other creatures as the-being-who-does-projects. We have the capacity to move against the drift, to shape our futures. So look to see if you have begun to rest on your laurels, to fall into automatic habits of acting, thereby reducing your work to mere doing. If this is happening, you can break out of the drift by setting goals and creating projects.

Setting Professional Goals

In Chapter 10, "The Organized Teacher: Time Management," your focus may have been on organizing class time, developing operational work schedules, and the like. You will recall, however, that the creation of projects was given high priority in the chapter.

Projects are powerful vehicles for re-creating the joy of professional growth. Start with professional goals. Generate goals for six months, a year, five and ten years. Brainstorm these goals—you can always clean up inconsistencies and repetitions later. After you have developed goals for different time periods, plot them on a calendar or professional log. Create a section in your notebook called projects and demarcate several pages for each project. You can designate notebook space with colored labels, headings, and subheadings. On the first few pages of each project enter your brainstorms, mind maps, drawings and doodles. Then paste in any clippings or photos related to the project.

In stage two of project building, share your project idea with persons who can enrich your vision. Invite them to brainstorm the project with you. Stay open to possibilities. Don't try to spell out all the details and how-to's at this stage. Just explore and allow yourself to enjoy new openings. By sharing your goals with another person, you grant reality to those goals. Later, as you begin to spell out steps by which you will reach your goals, you will have built a relationship of support to get you through the tough spots.

In stage three, work backward, listing what will have to happen to realize your completed project by the target date. For example, if you are going to study or travel out of the country, what preparations will be necessary before you start. Consider finances, itinerary, language mastery, clothes, support groups, and—en route—methods of organizing experiences: camera, notebook, tape recorder, video, sketch pad, portable computer, calculator. Then ask how you will arrive at these goals. Keep working backward until you arrive at the present. The next step is to plot everything on a calendar, so that you will know what steps you have to complete and by when. In your project pages, you will spell out *how* you will accomplish each stage. List many alternatives. If one approach doesn't work, keep trying other approaches until something works—and keep creating projects.

Exploring Current Methods

Many teachers work on advanced degrees while they are teaching. As the guidelines of the Holmes Report and the Carnegie Foundation become more of a reality, this will become mandatory for teachers who plan to secure and hold leadership positions.

Many teachers take enrichment courses unrelated to an advanced degree. An English teacher may choose to learn more about reading, drama, history, or art; a math teacher may want to know more about engineering and drafting. A cluster of related knowledge becomes a base from which one continually expands. It is useful at times to draw a mind map of your content interests. If you do this at the same time every year, you should see significant growth.

Professional Reading

It is useful to familiarize yourself with several libraries in your area and get to know the librarians there and the resources available. Interlibrary loans, computer retrieval systems and printout of bibliographies, such as those available through ERIC, may save you the expense and the cost of purchasing books unnecessarily. On the other hand, it is a delightful experience to spend a Saturday afternoon browsing through shops that sell old and new books, looking for out-of-print publications in one's field. An old technique may be rediscovered, a piece of forgotten information revitalized.

Professional Organizations

While you are still in college, you will have the opportunity of joining professional organizations that disseminate research findings in your teaching field. For example, the National Council of Teachers of English (NCTE) disseminates research on the methodology of teaching English on the elementary, secondary, and college levels. NCTE publishes corresponding journals: *Elementary English, The English Journal,* and *College English.* These journals contain abstracts by teachers and professors who have developed new ways of teaching composition, literature, linguistics, or reading. Comparable organizations and publications exist for other subject areas. Both the National Council of Teachers of Mathematics (NCTM) and the National Council for Teachers of Social Studies (NCTSS) publish journals.

Both the NEA and AFT are national organizations. The NEA has a membership of over 1,830,000, organized into 12,000 local affiliates that work toward organizational vitality, improvement of employee compensation and work conditions. NEA student members can participate on review teams that regularly evaluate teacher accreditation policy. The NEA is older, and more established but the AFT, because of its affiliation with the AFL-CIO, has gained power in some large cities in recent years. The new teacher would do well to study the philosophy and by-laws of these organizations and discuss their objectives with more experienced teachers before making a professional decision about joining. The issues that they address and their tactics should be researched thoroughly, so that the committed teacher can make a rational decision and communicate that decision to the public. Teachers are often interviewed impromptu by the press. Parents want to know their reasons for striking, collective bargaining, and the like.

Professional Conferences, Workshops, and Seminars

Annual conferences are held for exploring new methodology in the content areas cited above. In addition, there are conferences devoted to the exploration of scholarships in a subject area, such as those of the Modern Language Association for English (MLA). MLA provides both regional and national conferences. Some conferences, such as SALT (Society for Accelerative Learning and Teaching), provide both content research and methodological research.

Conferences often provide small group workshops and seminars as well as book exhibits from the major publishing companies of the world. These exhibits often list discounted books that would be excellent additions to one's professional library.

Conferences also provide an opportunity to meet face-to-face the scholars and teachers who may have influenced your own teaching. It is a time to meet fellow professionals with shared interests. It is a time to network.

Networking

Get those business cards printed. Let persons of like interest know who you are and for what you stand. The card smooths out introductions and makes it easier for the person to recall your name while speaking to you or calling you on the tele-

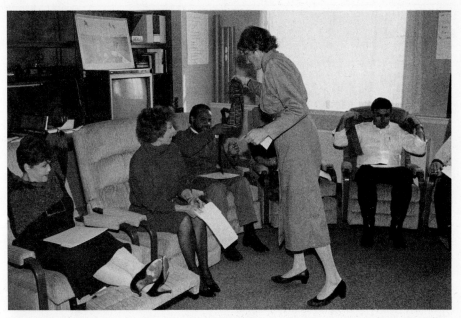

The first activation. The teacher is giving out costumes so that the students will more easily play roles as they read. On the walls there are posters with grammatical points that are presented peripherally.

A fellow professional may share your interest.

phone. Offer to share with those in your field ideas and techniques that have worked for you; you will find an abundance of ideas and techniques flowing back to you. Through networking you will also find persons who will gladly support you in projects, correspond with you, develop ideas for publication, and travel to other conferences with you.

The joy of discovery.

| **Study Grants** | Explore the possibilities of travel grants at your local universities. Ford Foundation grants enable teachers to study abroad for a summer. Some grants pay tuition for intensive courses in linguistics, mathematics, or the humanities, taught by top |

scholars on Ivy League campuses.

You will be using your time well if you take courses in writing for a grant. With this skill you can create funds to gain equipment and supplies for your school. You can design your own research project that can support you during a summer dry spell and you can expand your network base to include administrators and specialists who are necessary to help obtain the grant. Many excellent courses in grant writing are offered in evening sessions at community colleges.

| **Committee Work** | Complaints can be a source of action instead of a litany for inaction parroted in the teachers' lounge. Convert complaints into projects by joining committees that address the issues. If |

no committee exists to address an issue that interests you, create one. Committees work insofar as they are conversations for action. You can commit to this kind of speaking as a committee member.

| **Self-Assessment Instruments** | Video- and audiotapes are useful in giving you the raw data for our own teaching. How good are you? How good do you want to be? And how do you define *good?* We have returned to the |

central issue in this text—*effectiveness*. Each chapter in this book examines a different aspect of effectiveness. You can abstract from the summaries of each chapter to create a self-assessment instrument. To check your effective-

A teacher training process using a language game for activation.

ness it is useful to use a videotape with a split screen and two cameras. This setup will give you the student response at each stage of your teaching. Use the Effective Planning Instrument in Appendix D to check off the techniques you intend to use and the student responses you expect to elicit.

After you have checked off your expectations for teacher and student behavior and have taught the lesson, check off what actually happened from the video playback. Did you forget some techniques? Did you substitute others? Did the students respond as expected? What percentage of actual teaching behavior corresponded to your prediction? What percentage of actual student behavior corresponded to your prediction? Feel free to add teacher and student behaviors as you devise new ones. Also, if you changed your plan in the midst of teaching, do you know why you did so? Perhaps you had good reason for doing so.

Time-on-task studies show that the more time a student spends actually learning something, the more likely the student is to perform well on subsequent testing.[2] The teacher can use this as a rough measure of his own effectiveness by recording time spent on actual instruction. Audio and video playback are useful here. A word of warning, however: Time-on-task studies have tended to focus on the formal teaching of lower-level cognitive skills—perhaps because these kinds of skills are easily measured. Many techniques described in this text require the student to incubate ideas, to fantasize, and to explore new ways of solving problems. Time-on-task should include higher-level cognitive and affective learning.

The quality of the learning experience should be considered along with the time spent on learning. Quality will show up in the work produced, in the students' statements of interest, and in the kinds of questions asked. You can increase the quality of your instruction by periodically asking students to rate themselves. Use a scale from 1–5, with 5 denoting a high measure of interest, judgment of learning, and participation. Simply ask the student how he would rate his interest in this lesson on a scale of 1–5 (1 stands for very little interest and 5 for intense interest). Do the same for: How would you rate your participation? How would you rate your learning? Student judgments can then be checked against your own class observations and the actual test scores of students. The idea is to align the subjective and the objective and in the process fine-tune your instruction. At the same time, the student is gradually internalizing norms related to performance.

The big question you will ask along with the above is, What changes in instruction would support you in learning more and better, becoming more interested and participating at a higher level?

Ethical Issues

Most school boards have a printed code of ethics that addresses the general conflict of norms that may arise in the school. Most of the issues addressed by these codes are not strictly legal, although they may become legal over time. These codes should be studied by teachers, both individually and collectively. You may think some statements in these documents are not ethical, in which case you have another opportunity to create action through an appropriate committee.

The following are some statements from a sample code of ethics.[3]

CODE OF ETHICS FOR THE EDUCATION PROFESSION

Preamble

The educator believes in the worth and dignity of people. He/she recognizes the supreme importance of the pursuit of truth, devotion to excellence, and the nature of democratic citizenship. He/she regards as essential to these goals the protection of freedom to learn and to teach and the guarantee to equal educational opportunity for all. The educator accepts responsibility to practice the profession according to the highest ethical standards.

The educator recognizes the magnitude of the responsibility accepted in choosing a career in education, and engages, individually and collectively with other educators, to judge colleagues, and to be judged by them, in accordance with the provisions of this code.

Principle I
Commitment to the Student

The educator measures success by the progress of each student toward realization of potential as a worthy and effective citizen. The educator therefore works to stimulate the spirit of inquiry, the acquisition of knowledge and understanding, and the thoughtful formulation of worthy goals. In fulfilling his obligation to the student, the educator:

1. Shall not without just cause restrain the student from independent action in the pursuit of learning, shall not without just cause deny the student access to varying points of view.
2. Shall not deliberately suppress or distort subject matter for which he/she bears responsibility.
3. Shall make reasonable effort to protect the student from conditions harmful to learning or to health and safety.
4. Shall conduct professional business in such a way that the student is not exposed to unnecessary embarrassment or disparagement.
5. Shall not on the ground of race, color, creed, or national origin exclude any student from participation in or deny the benefits under any program, nor grant any discriminatory consideration or advantage.
6. Shall not use professional relationships with students for private advantage.
7. Shall keep in confidence information that has been obtained in the course of professional service, unless disclosure serves professional purposes or is required by law.
8. Shall not tutor for remuneration students assigned to his/her classes, unless no other qualified teacher is reasonably available.

Motivational Workshops and Tapes

There are any number of commercial companies that offer workshops throughout the country. Most of these courses are based on some form of applied psychology, philosophy, or communication system. The content of these courses is usually slanted toward business but can be easily adapted to education. Audio- and videotapes—on stress control, overcoming procrastination, goal setting, and the like—are usually available at the workshop or by mail order. Many of these tapes are suggestopedic; they contain imagery, guided fantasy, and suggestions of music and speech. The vocal suggestions may be subliminal, marked by music, ocean sounds, seagulls, or similar background effects. For some persons, the idea of being influenced by suggestion they cannot consciously evaluate is unacceptable. And, yet, to constantly hear the suggestion is to invite resistance to it. Fortunately, there is a middle choice. Many companies supply a listing of the implanted suggestions and, of course, it is always possible to create one's own suggestopedic tape. (See Chapter 13, "Homework as Multiple Skills Mastery," for the methodology of creating your own tape.) When you create your own tape, you know the suggestions you have implanted under the music, but since you do not hear the voice, you are not likely to build resistance to the suggestions One tactic, then, is to create your own tapes, using adaptations of concepts acquired in motivational seminars.

■ *SUMMARY*

Teachers can develop professionally in many ways, such as:

1. Systematically generate professional goals
2. Explore current teaching methods through reading

3. Participate in seminars, in-service workshops, and conferences
4. Build a professional library
5. Secure travel grants for learning and research
6. Create self-monitoring systems, become more aware of and contribute to ethical standards for their profession
7. Seek advanced degrees, publish in professional journals
8. Network with other professionals
9. Develop workshops for teachers, business, and industry
10. Serve on school committees
11. Take a leadership role in co-curricular activities: clubs, drama, and sports and social groups
12. Explore ways of expressing values as a teacher through professional dress and daily behavior
13. Build a collection of motivational audio- and videotapes.

Periodically, it is useful to take inventory—to assess one's professional well-being. Gail Sheehy's self-description of well-being can be used for such a review. To perform at maximum one must perform with purpose—to stay engaged and willing to act. This is not always comfortable or safe. But then listen to Vicki Aragon, the female jockey, who upon being asked how a good jockey confronts the fear of performance in riding said: "You either ride or you don't."

Periodically it is useful to take inventory to assess one's professional well-being.

■ *NOTES*

1. Gail Sheehy, *Pathfinders* (New York: Morrow, 1981), 25.
2. John B. Carroll, "A Model of School Learning," *Teachers College Record* 64: 723–732 (1963).
3. *Code of Ethics* (Ann Arbor School District, Ann Arbor, MI, September 17, 1975), 1–2. By permission of Ann Arbor Board of Education.

Teaching to the Whole Brain

. . . The most significant creative activities of our or any other human culture—legal and ethical system, art and music, science and technology—were made possible only through the collaborative work of the left and right cerebral hemispheres. These creative acts, even if engaged in rarely or only by a few, have changed us and the world. We might say that human culture is the function of the corpus callosum.

—Carl Sagan, *Dragons of Eden*

There are techniques that can help us name our dreams and dragons. They are designed to reopen the bridge between left and right to through traffic, to increase the left brain's awareness of its counterpart. . . .

—Marilyn Ferguson, *The Aquarian Conspiracy*

┌─────────────────────────────┐
│ *The Experience of Whole-Brain* │
│ *Processing* │
└─────────────────────────────┘

Carl Sagan points to the social and personal power of whole-brain learning and Marilyn Ferguson points to the development of instructional techniques that will bring forth this power. In this chapter we will explore both the physiological-psychological basis for whole-brain instruction and some special techniques for teaching wholistically.

If you have ever recognized someone in a crowd after not having seen the person for five to ten years, or recalled your "sense of direction" to find the home of a friend in a city you had not visited for five, or more years, or made use of figurative language to express an idea that was too complex to express literally, or solved a problem in plane or solid geometry by visualizing the dimensions, you were probably using *whole-brain processing.*

Have you ever looked at a picture, perhaps in a family album, and experienced a flood of memories? Have you remembered things that surprised you? Or have you ever struggled to remember a name, only to recall it when you stopped struggling?

Have you ever found yourself "on a roll" in respect to learning—everything came easy whether it was a sport, a science subject, or art—there was no stopping you? Did you reflect on how you got into such a state? Was it accidental or did you do something, say something to yourself, hear or see something, or feel something prior to your extraordinary performance? These are the kinds of questions that are interesting to many educators, particularly those drawing on recent brain research for clues to increasing learning capacity and creating effective teaching methods.

Brain Cell Development

The questions get even more interesting when we examine current brain research. For example, M. C. Cowan calculates that there are 100 million nerve cells in the human brain and another 10 million in the brain stem and spinal cord. These make up 98.3 percent of all the nerve cells in the body! As James Hand says, if we could create a nerve cell for every second that passed, it would take 32 years to form a million brain cells and 3200 years to form 100 million brain cells.[2]

By conservative estimate, one has 100 trillion possible brain cell connections in the human brain, each connection transmitting a portion of knowledge and awareness. James Hand calculates that if one were to create one connection per second, this would take 3,200,000 years to accomplish.[3] One would have to start at the very dawn of the human species! Barring organic damage, this is the reserve brain capacity of most human beings, including the students you will teach. Why, then, is this capacity not used by most people?

PROBES Do you think education can release the reserve capacity of the brain? If so, which methods would you predict as most effective? The research of Marian Dimond points to the abundance of glial cells in the brain of Einstein. Glial cells work like ladders enabling migrating cells to travel more efficiently to their destination. Check Dimond's research. Do you think human performance can be increased by increasing the generation of glial cells? Do any medical studies point to the possibility of such an increase? If it were possible to increase reserve capability through medical means, would it be ethical to do so?

As you read through each section, you will find it useful to generate your own questions regarding the educational use of brain research. Let us now look at cell migration and the formation of specialized areas of the brain.

■ *Specialization in the Brain*

The cells of the brain are highly specialized. Early in fetal development certain types of neurons cluster together to produce areas of specialized function. Cells migrate from the core of the brain outward to a home site. There they aggregate and form a specialized colony. Cells that get lost in migration usually die; those that reach their destination usually live.[4]

■ *Information Transfer*

Information is transmitted from nerve cell to nerve cell through axons and dendrites. Axons serve an output function; they send messages to the dendrites and cell bodies of other cells (see Figure A.1). The message is sent across a microspace via a chemical called a neurotransmitter. When information comes into the human organism it enters the visual, auditory, and peripheral nervous system in wave form; and it enters the olfactory system in chemical form; and it enters the gustatory system in both chemical and wave forms. The more of these systems are activated to transmit a consistent message, the greater the likelihood that the message will be (a) received in short-term memory and (b) stored in long-term memory.[5] If, for example, students are required to memorize the bones of the body or the elements of the Periodic Table, it will, as James Hand points out, facilitate memory to process the information through as many channels as possible, being careful not to cloud the message with extraneous input.[6]

Instead of merely sitting and silently reading the names of the bones of the feet, the student can read them aloud and at the same time allow himself to touch various areas of his feet as he calls out the name. He can visualize a giant walking through a village. Using his imagination's x-ray vision, the student can see all the bones in the giant's feet as he storms the village. When the student can name all the bones of the feet, the giant must leave the village. The student can proceed to play such a game for each set of bones in the body until he has memorized them all. When he wants to recall the names of bones, he can go back to the village and reenact his game with the giant, he can recall the sounds of the names and the tactile sensations of

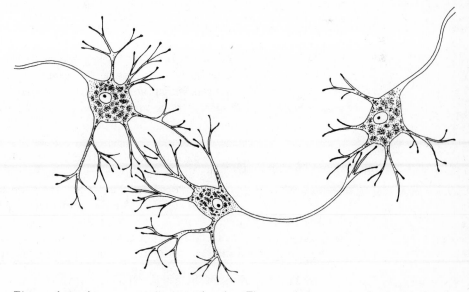

Figure A.1 Axons serve an output function. They send messages to the dendrites and cell bodies of other cells.

having experienced corresponding points of his own body, and he can recall the printed words in the book. This is a simple example of multiple channeling.

■ *Biofeedback*

Biofeedback research provides us with abundant data on the relationship between brain wave activity and human behavior. The speed of the electrical activity of the brain is measured in four wave forms: alpha, beta, delta, and theta. As you read the description of these wave patterns, reflect on experiences you have had that correspond to these patterns.

1. *Beta waves* (13–29 cycles per second). This is a rhythmic wave associated with active involvement. It can be positive and exhilarating. In learning situations, some report tension, alertness, and excitement.
2. *Alpha waves* (8–12 cycles per second). There are different alpha states of consciousness, depending on the average cycles per second over a time interval. The state is described by researchers and subjects as one of comfortable relaxation. Some report a flow of imagery, a daydreamlike quality. Subjects producing the highest levels of alpha describe losing all extraneous environmental awareness, of being absorbed into whatever they are focusing on.
3. *Theta waves* (4–7 cycles per second). According to the Menninger Clinic, the waves bring on a a very relaxed, twilight consciousness—reverie, associated with meditation by yoga masters.
4. *Delta Waves* (1–3 cycles per second). Delta waves occur in the various stages of sleep; this is an unconscious state.

One can learn to control states of consciousness that will generate more alpha or beta brain waves. This technology is useful pedagogically, for if one can learn to control the amount of alpha he or she is generating, the probability of controlling stress is enhanced, and if stress is controlled, the learning rate may be enhanced for certain tasks. Studies show that the increase of alpha significantly increases learning rate and retention.[7] We shall see that there is a physiological basis for this when we explore the next section—the triune brain theory.

The Triune Brain Theory

The main exponent of the triune brain theory is Paul MacLean, Senior Research Scientist, National Institute of Health, Animal Center, Poolsville, Maryland. The human brain, MacLean argues, "amounts to three interconnected biological computers," each with "its own special intelligence, its own subjectivity, its own sense of time and space, its own memory, motor and other functions."[8] MacLean points out the educational implications of his theory in the following passage:

In its development, the human forebrain has expanded to a great size, while retaining the basic features of three formations that reflect our relationship to reptiles, early mammals and recent mammals. Radically different in structure and chemistry, and, in an evolutionary sense, countless generations apart, the three formations constitute a hierarchy of three brains in one, or what may be called for short a *triune* brain. Such a situation indicates that we are obliged to look at ourselves and the world through the eyes of three quite different mentalities. As a further complication, there is evidence that the two older mentalities lack the necessary neural machinery for verbal communication. But to say that they lack the power of speech does not belittle their intelligence, nor does it relegate them to a realm of the "unconscious." Educationally, these are significant considerations, because it is usually assumed that we are dealing with a single intelligence. How much weight should we give to intelligence tests that largely ignore two of our ever-present personalities because they cannot read or write?[9]

The triune brain theory classifies the evolutionary development of the mammalian brain in three stages: the reptilian brain, the limbic system (paleomammalian brain), and the neocortex (neomammalian brain).

■ *The Reptilian Brain*

The reptilian brain is located in the bottom core of the forebrain, just above the brain stem. According to Carl Sagan, MacLean has shown that the R-complex, as the reptilian brain is called, plays a part in "aggressive behavior, territoriality, ritual and the establishment of social hierarchies."[10] We can easily observe these behaviors in teen students. Social hierarchies are formed in cliques, and ritual is readily observable in the affectionate slaps, strikes, and hugs teenagers exchange with one another as ritual greetings and as expressions of approval in sports.

Territoriality shows up in students in their attachment to *their* desk, *their* space, *their* locker, and *their* belongings. When extended to others, territoriality shows up in a drive to protect *their* in-group, *their* neighborhood, *their* school, *their* state, and *their* country.

The salient characteristic of the R-complex is a compulsion to conform to primitive genetic encoding as it is manifested in a particular social context. As Sagan puts it, "[the reptilian mind] is not characterized by powerful passions and wrenching contradictions but rather by a dutiful and stoical acquiescence to whatever its genes and brain dictates."[11] Sagan argues that bureaucratic behavior is a manifestation of the R-complex in adult life. This does not mean, however, that as human beings we are destined to rigid conformity. As Sagan points out, it is our plasticity that gave us the Bill of Rights and the Constitution.[12] We do not have to surrender to every impulse of the reptilian brain, *and* it is to our advantage as educators to acknowledge our primitive heritage. If and when teachers set out to break up ritualistic patterns, hierarchies, or cliques, they will at least know what they are up against. And if they use force to break up these patterns, they will probably be met with force (aggression and territoriality).

PROBE If the triune theory is correct, what strategies would you use to increase learning when you judge that certain ritual patterns, territoriality or hierarchies are interfering with the learning going on in your class? (*Hint:* Think of a Karate or Aikido master who never meets force with force, but instead deflects it or redirects it.)

■ *The Limbic System*

The limbic system surrounds the older reptilian brain and may first have appeared in mammalianlike giant reptiles of the Mesozoic Period. The limbic system functions as a unit to control emotions, memory, and many regulatory functions of the body, such as breathing. Although researchers have not yet agreed on exactly what features make up the limbic system, some of them are:

The *thalamus* is located near the center of the brain and sends sensory stimuli to the neocortex.

The *hypothalamus* lies beneath the thalamus and regulates body temperature, blood pressure, respiration, and long-term memory.

The *amygdala* controls rage and fear and is the basis of fight-flight responses. It adjoins the temporal lobe of the cortex.

The *pituitary gland* is located in the mid-brain and is responsible for growth.

The *hippocampus* controls short- and long-term memory, and it gauges expectation and actuality.

There is a feedback loop that transfers information from the senses through the limbic system and back to the neocortex. If the information is stopped anywhere in process, learning is stopped. For example, if a student is in a state of fear of being called on in class, the process of learning the information taught in that class may be stopped at the amygdala.[13] The amygdala sends a message of fear to the hippocampus, which gauges expectation against actuality. The resultant message is "I can't do it!" and the belief system is formed. And, true enough, the student can't perform, given this state of consciousness. We have here a physiological basis for the Pygmalion effect, the self-fulfilling prophecy.*

Rosenthal and Jacobson's research on the self-fulfilling prophecy has been difficult to replicate. Dozens of studies following the 1968 research led to contradictory results.[14] Carl Braun (1976) reviewed teacher expectation studies up to 1975[15] and agreed with J. D. Finn (1972), who in an earlier review accounted for the conflicting results of teacher expectation as a reflection of many influences on the teacher.[16] No matter what kind of expectations a teacher may desire to uphold, he can be influenced by such variables as name of the student, ethnic background, knowledge of siblings, physical characteristics, cumulative folders, sex, test results, and previous achievement.[17] The teacher's belief system can be expressed in very subtle ways—such as slightly hesitating when calling on a student that the teacher perceives as a slow learner.

If a teacher wants to set the conditions for positive expectations, he must do more than say the words or act the part of one who believes the student can perform well.

*The "self-fulfilling prophecy" or the "Pygmalion effect" refer to the phenomenon that people perform according to the expectations of important persons in their lives. It is documented by Rosenthal and Jacobson in *Pygmalion in the Classroom,* published by Holt, Rinehart and Winston, 1968.

What the teacher says must be aligned with body language, facial expression, timing, intonation, and so forth.[18] The teacher must be totally congruent in belief, actions, and sensibilities. This is what Lozanov calls "dual planeness." He must operate with consistency in both conscious and unconscious expression. If the integrity of his presentation is broken, then, according to Lozanov, students will become aware of the conflict, hesitancy, or tentativeness of the teacher and will begin to doubt the teacher's judgment about their ability to learn at optimal levels.[19] Nevertheless, the good news is that it can work in the opposite direction. If the student believes he can learn, it facilitates the probability that he will learn. As Hand says, "If you want to maximize learning you have to keep the limbic system happy."[20]

PROBES
1. What would a fight-flight pattern look like in a classroom? How would you communicate with a student experiencing this pattern?
2. How could you communicate standards, information about examinations and school rules, and at the same time keep the limbic system happy?
3. According to MacLean, the limbic system is the source of creative behavior. Given that MacLean's system is true, can you build a teaching strategy that would elicit creative behavior?

■ *The Neocortex*
According to MacLean, the neocortex primarily focuses on the outside world—on external environmental events.

Although abstract thinking, long-range planning, and transmission of cultural knowledge are primarily functions of the neocortex, the neocortex will not function optimally unless the more primitive brains are satisfied.[21] Traditional educational models that focus exclusively on the intellect attempt to bypass concern with primitive brain function; educational models based on whole-brain processing attempt to maximize learning by using primitive brain function—indeed, by using the functions of the entire brain.

Recent research in the neurosciences does not dispute MacLean's contention that the behaviors described actually occur; location specific to the three parts MacLean describes is, according to Hand, highly controversial. The neuroscientist, Lynn Nadel, writes, for example: "Anticipation of the future, anxiety, some language processing and many other indications of intellect are located *outside* the neocortex. Overemphasis upon the leading role of the neocortex in intelligence is but one of the many shortcomings of the triune brain idea."[22]

Hemisphericity

As early as 1836, Marc Dax, a country doctor living in Montpellier France, addressed his medical society, sharing with them his observation that damage to the left side of the brain (the left hemisphere) resulted in speech loss.[23] Dax argued that the two sides of the brain were specialized—the left being responsible for speech. Unfortunately, Dax's address fell on deaf ears. He died not knowing that he had anticipated scientific research focusing on the difference between the left and the right brain. This research was not to reach fruition until Phillip Vogel and Joseph Bogen performed split-brain surgery on epileptic patients.[24] Their primary purpose was to stop the flow of the "electric-storm" of the epileptic seizure from moving from one hemisphere to another. To contain the storm they cut the 200 million nerve fibers of the corpus callosum, which connects the two hemispheres. The surgery worked. The storm was contained. The seizure could be controlled. But this was only one consequence of the surgery. The truly revolutionary discovery that emerged from split-brain surgery was that the two hemispheres processed information differently.[25] Roger Sperry, a Nobel laureate in physiology, explained this as follows:

> Each hemisphere . . . has its own . . . private sensations, perceptions, thought, and ideas all of which are cut off from the corresponding experience in the opposite hemisphere. Each left and right hemisphere has its own private chain of memories and learning experiences that are accessible to recall by the other hemisphere. In many respects each disconnected hemisphere appears to have a separate "mind of its own."[26]

Some researchers take issue with Sperry's attribution of separate minds to the two hemispheres. To Sir John Eccles, also a Nobel laureate, the left brain is the source of language, thought, and culture, while the right brain is mere consciousness, representing a more primitive, animal nature.[27] And Donald McCay, a specialist in artificial intelligence, argues that before we attribute a concept of mind to each hemisphere, each hemisphere must be able to assign values to events, set goals, and establish priorities. And, yet, the distinction in perceiving and processing the world persists.

Some neurophysiologists, such as Ornstein, argue that the failure of American education is a result of excessive focus on left-brain processes. In his book, *Psychology of Consciousness* (1970) Ornstein asserted:

> We have learned to look at unconnected fragments instead of at entire solutions. . . . As a result of this preoccupation with isolated facts, it is not surprising that we face so many simultaneous problems whose solutions depend upon our ability to grasp the relationships of parts to wholes . . . Split- and whole-brain studies have led to a new conception of human knowledge, consciousness, and intelligence. All knowledge cannot be expressed in words, yet our education is based almost exclusively on its written and spoken forms . . . But the artist, dancer, and mystic have learned to develop the nonverbal portion of intelligence.[28]

Ornstein argued that our educational system is designed to train the left brain, that the emphasis in our current educational system is on quantitative and verbal knowledge at the expense of the arts, which are often relegated to extracurricular activities.

■ Left- and Right-Brain Function

There are a number of characteristics that distinguish left- and right-brain function. The two hemispheres process information differently. Following are some of these differences in processing:[29]

Left Hemisphere	Right Hemisphere
convergent	divergent
intellectual	intuitive
deductive	imagination
historical	timeless
analytical	holistic
explicit	tacit
objective	subjective
successive	simultaneous
verbal	nonverbal
logical	gestalt
digital	spatial
Western thought	Eastern thought
rational	metaphorical
vertical	horizontal
discrete	continuous
abstract	concrete
realistic	impulsive
directed	free
differential	existential
sequential	multiple

Some of the above characteristics, such as verbal or nonverbal, are experimentally verifiable; others such as successive or simultaneous are more inferential.[30] Researchers like Russell Whitman, a psychologist at Wayne State University, make a distinction between psychological description and molecular description—description based on physical tests.[31] Whitman, for example, finds that there are distinct physical differences in the way the left and right brain process visual information. The two hemispheres operate like special filters. The recognition of faces, for example, requires two kinds of visual information: low- and high-frequency spatial information.[32] High-frequency information is detailed information; low-frequency information is the overall configured pattern. In infrahumans, acceptance of high frequency information (details) is processed by X cells and acceptance of low frequency information (overall pattern) is a function of Y cells.[33] To function at optimum capacity, the brain must process for detail *and* for overall pattern.

■ Testing Brain Functions

There are other tests that distinguish the function of the left and right hemispheres for particular activities. Descriptions of these tests, taken from Marilee Zdenek's book *The Right Brain Experience,* follow:

The Wada Test. When either hemisphere is anesthetized, the functions of its partner become clearly observable. Doctors routinely use a procedure, called the Wada test, on brain-damaged patients prior to surgery to determine the [language] dominant hemisphere. Sodium amytal is injected into the artery that leads to either the left or the right hemisphere of the brain. This anesthetizes half of the brain and allows doctors to observe how patients use the unaffected hemisphere. Later they can reverse the procedure and observe how the other hemisphere performs. The results of their tests confirm the validity of the split-brain findings with regard to hemisphere specializations.

Tachistoscope. Using the tachistoscope, the researcher controls which hemisphere first receives specific information. Then, by measuring the time it takes for the person to react, the researcher can determine which hemisphere is specialized for that particular task.

Positron Tomography. The positron tomograph is an instrument that can photograph each half of the brain; it is activated by specific stimuli or specific activity. This device allows researchers to observe the healthy brain in action. It works by measuring hemispheric cerebral glucose utilization. Radioactive material, injected into the bloodstream, flows into the brain, allowing doctors to photograph metabolic activity in the hemispheres for as long as forty minutes after the injection is given.

Electroencephalograph (EEG). Electrodes are placed over the temporal and parietal lobe on both sides of normal subjects' brains before they are given various tests. The EEG records the type of brain activity during these mental tasks. High-voltage, slow alpha waves indicate a "relaxed" hemisphere; and low-voltage, fast beta waves indicate a "working" hemisphere.

Dichotic Listening Test. In dichotic testing, two channels of conflicting information are presented to a person simultaneously, one channel to each ear. Input to the right ear is conveyed to the left hemisphere and vice versa. The subject will report hearing only the information which was received by the hemisphere specialized for that type of input (for example, language in the left hemisphere, music in the right).[34]

It is important to keep in mind that "both hemispheres *share* in mental activities."[35] Hand, echoing the work of Kimura, states: "Scientists have not yet discovered any one higher intellectual function controlled entirely by one hemisphere."[36] Synthesis, for example, is not restricted to the right hemisphere as was earlier thought by many researchers and popularizers of left-right brain theory. In a 1985 interview, Levy, a protégé of Nobel laureate Roger Sperry, stated:

It seems possible that when a task is within the specialized domain of a hemisphere, then information is synthesized into some higher order configuration, and that feature-by-feature processing is compelled for the unspecialized hemisphere that lacks the capacity for deriving the emergent synthesis. The way each hemisphere deals with incoming information—how it encodes it—depends on what sort of information it is and what the hemisphere can do with it.[37]

Hand, following the lead of Levy, says we should now revise the popular listing of left and right domains; specifically, we should "now delete analysis of detail and sequence information from the list of left brain specialties, and synthesis and holism from the list of right brain specialties." Hand's revised list follows:[38]

Left Hemisphere	Right Hemisphere
Verbal, linguistic	Intonation, inflection
Ideation (abstractions)	Pictorial and pattern sense
Conceptual similarities	Visual similarities
Sense of time	Location in space
Controls right side of body	Controls left side of body
Numerics, quantities	Melodic perception
Logic	Poetic processing
Outlook	Insight
Geometric configurations	

■ Left and Right Hemispheric Learning

For right-handers, words are processed in the left hemisphere, whether for comprehension or spoken, but the emotional component of speech intonation, timing, use of body language is processed in the right hemisphere. Interpretations of facial expression, use of the eyes to "speak," and ability to grasp double meanings (respond to jokes) are more the function of the right hemisphere, although humor may also be a function of the hippocampus, which controls expectation versus actuality. In a joke, one expects one outcome but gets another. Imagine an extreme case of processing language entirely in the left brain. One would be able to receive and deliver information, but the information would be expressed literally, without expression, like the early state of computer speech.

Some patients who have damage to the right hemisphere are unable to comprehend jokes, to recognize members of their families, appreciate music, respond emotionally; yet they may be able to solve math problems efficiently. Conversely, if there is damage to the left hemisphere and the right is intact, the patient may be able to sing, even recalling song lyrics, yet be unable to read a newspaper, solve a math problem, or comprehend or use language in ordinary verbal communication.

To use the left- and right-brain theory as a model for developing teaching methods, it is useful to review the processing functions listed on pages 427 and 429 and construct strategies that you think would elicit these functions. In any lesson plan, make sure that both hemispheres are being activated by including a mixture of left- and right-brain processes. As was indicated earlier, some of the divisions are inferential and may not be the discrete domain of one hemisphere or another. Yet if teachers use a mixture of these dichotomies, they are more likely to elicit *whole-brain function.* For example, in 1976 Bordon and Schuster reported that "words presented rhythmically and with . . . baroque music as a background were learned and remembered significantly better than words merely given orally without such background."[39] Schuster and Mouzon (1982) reported that "different musical backgrounds while learning words affected this learning; baroque had the most effect, then classical as compared with no music as a control."[40]

Imaging, particularly picture imaging, appears to be another dominantly right-brain function that enhances learning.[41] Kimura's (1973) studies reported right-brain dominance in stereoscopic [depth] perception.[42] Pavio reported that information can be processed verbally or imagistically and that learning increased over separate processing when the information was processed both verbally and imagistically.[43]

PROBES

1. Recall primarily left-brain approaches to learning from your own school experiences. What could be done to convert these processes into a whole-brain approach?
2. Dreams are regarded by some researchers as primarily right-brain functions. Do dreams have any practical function for teaching and learning? (See Garfield, 1974.)

■ *Circadian Rhythms*

According to Dr. William Stroebel, a medical researcher on circadian rhythms, there is a shift in activity of the left and right hemisphere of human beings every 90 minutes throughout the day.[44] One can now purchase a biofeedback watch from Casio to check dominant hemisphere functioning throughout the day.* It operates with an electronic thermometer sensitive to .01 degree Fahrenheit.[45]

The watch registers minute temperature changes and provides a graph printout indicating when the brain shifts from left to right or right to left dominance in hemispheric functioning. By monitoring one's circadian rhythm one can graph high-energy cycles and states of efficiency and optimal creativity.[46] One can gain some mastery over predicting and therefore planning for maximum performance. Stroebel recommends using a diary to monitor optimum functions.

Whole-Brain Intelligence

In recent years IQ tests have come under attack from many quarters. One of the more popularized attacks argues that an intelligence test that has been standardized in terms of white middle-class norms cannot be a valid measure of intelligence as it is manifested in another culture—that is, black or Hispanic. The items on some tests were presented primarily verbally and were selected from the kind of reading matter and experiences that a white urban middle-class person would be expected to encounter.

Whole-brain research has led to an exploration of learning-style preference and ultimately to a redefinition of intelligence. If one does not define intelligence solely in terms of verbal mastery, what brain-processing components should be considered?

In *Frames of Mind: The Theory of Multiple Intelligences,* Howard Gardner invites us to consider cases of culturally acknowledged intelligence. Consider he says:

*Caveat! Hand notes that "since the watch thermometer is on one wrist, this effect is confounded by normal rise and fall in temperature due to exercise, eating/digestion, and relaxation [and] does not *necessarily* mean a switch in hemispheric activity." Personal communication with James Hand, Feb. 1988. By permission of James Hand.

The twelve-year-old male Puluwat in the Caroline Islands, who has been selected by his elders to learn how to become a master sailor. Under the tutelage of master navigators, he will learn to combine knowledge of sailing, stars, and geography so as to find his way around the hundreds of islands. Consider the fifteen-year-old Iranian youth who has committed to heart the entire Koran and mastered the Arabic language. Now he is being sent to a holy city to work closely for the next several years with an ayatollah, who will prepare him to be a teacher and religious leader. Or, consider the fourteen-year-old adolescent in Paris, who has learned how to program a computer and is beginning to compose works of music with the aid of a synthesizer.[47]

Gardner says that a moment's reflection reveals that, based on the accomplishment of each individual within his culture, these individuals should be regarded as exhibiting intelligent behavior. And, yet, we have no instruments that measure such competencies. It is not so much a limitation of technology, says Gardner; the problem lies in the limits we impose on our formulation of what counts as human intelligence. We must first expand our concept of intelligence, then look to technology to find ways of measuring it. Gardner expands intelligence to include (1) linguistic intelligence, (2) musical intelligence, (3) logical-mathematical intelligence, (4) spatial intelligence, (5) bodily-kinesthetic intelligence, and (6) personal intelligence.

Gardner uses several criteria to identify intelligence. A human competence must enable the individual to resolve genuine problems or difficulties *and* must also "entail the potential for *finding or creating problems*—thereby laying the groundwork for the acquisition of new knowledge."[48] The intellectual competence must be recognized as of value in the culture in which one lives. Many tests used by psychologists such as the recall of nonsense syllables fail Gardner's criteria. Gardner also says that the intelligence faculty should be capable of being destroyed by brain damage. This lets us know it is a basic capacity and is related to specific brain function. There must be evidence of the capacity in idiot savants, prodigies and other exceptional individuals; it must have its own core of operation, a developmental history, an evolutionary history, a possible symbol system, and it must gain support from psychological task studies.[49]

PROBES

1. Do you think that Gardner is correct in arguing for multiple intelligence, or do you think there is a core of competence/function common to all types of intelligence?
2. Drawing on whole-brain research, invent a theory that supports Gardner and one which discounts his position; then check your theories against what Gardner says in *Frames of Mind.* Does your theory still hold up?
3. If Gardner is correct, how would you identify multiple intelligence in the classroom? What steps could you take to nurture the development of multiple intelligences in a classroom?

Holographic Brain Theory

Instead of analogizing the brain as a computer, Karl Pribram in his *Language of the Brain* argues for a holographic analogy. The brain is like a hologram. A hologram is a plate or film with a recorded pattern. Gardner writes: "Information about any point in the original is distributed throughout the hologram, thus making it resistant to damage. Since waves from all parts of the object are recorded on all parts of the hologram, any part of the hologram (however small) can be used to reproduce the entire image."[50] Recent research points to limits, however. Clarity and specificity are damaged as size diminishes.

Nevertheless, the brain behaves much the same way when some portions are not used or are damaged. There are cases of massive brain damage wherein the remaining cells assume functions they do not ordinarily perform. Because of this plasticity, stroke victims can through training sometimes reroute the neural pathways and resume driving or other normal functions.[51]

Sex Differences

Jerre Levy has suggested that the left hemisphere may develop more rapidly in girls and the right hemisphere in boys. This, if true, can account for the developmental bias of verbal skills in girls and spatial skills in boys.

In defining vocabulary words, women use both hemispheres, front and back, while men tend to use the left hemisphere, front and back. Spatial ability in women has been found to vary with natural levels of sex hormones on a monthly cycle. When estrogen is lowest, women seem to function at their best on spatial tests. When estrogen is high, women excel in motor skills. In one major study, Kimura found that the corpus callosum was slightly larger in women than in men. Even so, all of these generalizations must be placed in a developmental context. At various stages in a person's life "structures are undergoing more or less rapid growth, and patterns of brain hemisphere will vary from time to time as a result."[52]

Ultimately individual differences must be taken into account. Despite the findings cited above, Kimura reminds us that

> . . . we can predict very little about an individual's mental capabilities based on his or her sex . . . biological sex itself has turned out to be much more variable and dynamic than we ever imagined. And brain organization patterns are even more variable from person to person, and probably even within the same person at different times. Further, on most tests of cognitive ability there is enormous overlap of men and women. We strain to look for differences and, of course, tend to emphasize the few we find.[53]

■ SUMMARY

In this appendix we examined some of the educational implications of modern brain research. Specifically, we examined human brain cell formation and the power of synaptic connection between brain cells. It is estimated that 100 trillion brain cell connections are possible in the human brain. Another way of saying this is that there are 100 trillion on and off switches in the human brain, 100 trillion possibilities of information transfer between cells. If we can increase the number of brain connections used, we can integrate experience in memory.

Are there methods of teaching and learning that will increase the use of brain capacity? We investigated the use of multiple channeling (learning through a number of sense factors) as a method for increasing connections made in the human brain. The research of Schuster indicates a higher learning rate and greater retention of learning when information is processed through multiple senses.

MacLean's version of the triune brain theory points to the necessity of controlling fear in the process of learning. Fear short-circuits learning in the limbic system. Fear can be minimized through positive suggestion, relaxation, and biofeedback techniques. Baroque and classical music are found to increase alpha waves in the brain, enhancing an attentive, yet relaxed, state that is conducive to learning.

Whole-brain processing can be enhanced by developing lesson plans in which students use both left and right hemisphere functions. Learning processes should be structured in the visual, auditory and kinesthetic modalities.

Howard Gardner's research on multiple intelligence calls for a redefinition of intelligence—a definition that is more in accord with whole-brain research. Gardner says intelligence must include the following types: (1) linguistic intelligence, (2) musical intelligence, (3) logical-mathematical intelligence, (4) spatial intelligence, (5) bodily-kinesthetic intelligence, and (6) personal intelligence.

Attention to circadian rhythms can make us more aware of optimum learning cycles, and Pribram's holographic theory calls our attention to the seemingly limitless plasticity of the human brain in its capacity to reorganize functional specialization— even after brain damage. Stroke victims have been taught to function again by rerouting the old neural patterns through new neural pathways.

Although Kimura and others have found patterns of differences in the brain function and in performance of males and females, these findings must be tempered with developmental studies and observations of individual differences.

■ *NOTES*

1. W. M. Cowan, "The Development of the Brain," *Scientific American,* 241(3), 1979.
2. James Hand, "The Mind/Brain Conjunction: Neurobiology, Psychology and Philosophy." Paper presented at the Society for Accelerative Learning and Teaching. Eleventh Annual Conference, West Palm Beach, Florida, Spring, 1986.
3. Ibid.
4. Ibid.
5. James Hand, "Brain Function During Learning," D. Jonassen, ed., in *The Technology of Text* (Englewood Cliffs, NJ: Educational Technology Publication, 1982).
6. James Hand, "The Brain and Accelerative Learning, Part III: How People Function and Suggestions for Educators," *SALT II* (3), Fall 1986, 283–249.
7. H. W. Gordon, "Hemispheric Asymmetry in the Perception of Musical Chords," *Cortex* 6: 387–398.

8. Paul MacLean, "On the Evolution of Three Mentalities," in *New Dimensions in Psychiatry, A Wordview* 2, Silbano Arieti and Gerard Chrzanowski, eds. (New York: Wiley, 1977), pp. 305–328.

9. Paul MacLean, "A Meeting of Minds: The Triune Brain Theory," *Dromenon: A Journal of New Ways of Being* 3(1):12–20. Fall Issue, 1980.

10. Carl Sagan, *Dragons of Eden,* 60.

11. Ibid.

12. Ibid., 61.

13. James Hand, "The Mind/Brain Conjunction: Neurobiology, Psychology and Philosophy." Paper presented at the Society for Accelerative Learning and Teaching, Eleventh Annual Conference, West Palm Beach, Florida, Spring, 1986.

14. Robert F. Biehler and Jack Snowman, *Psychology Applied to Teaching,* 4th ed. (Boston: Houghton Mifflin, 1982), 442.

15. Carl Braun, "Teacher Expectation: Sociopsychological Dynamics," *Review of Educational Research* 46(2):185–213.

16. J. D. Finn, "Expectations and the Educational Environment," *Review of Educational Research* 42:387–410.

17. Carl Braun, "Teacher Expectation," 185–213.

18. Anthony Robbins, *Unlimited Power: The New Science of Personal Achievement* (New York: Simon & Schuster, 1986), 140–155.

19. D. H. Schuster and C. E. Gritton, *Suggestive Accelerative Learning Techniques* (New York: Gordon and Breach, 1986), 89–90.

20. James Hand, "The Mind/Brain Conjunction: Neurobiology, Psychology and Philosophy."

21. Schuster and Gritton, *Suggestive Accelerative Learning Techniques,* 78.

22. L. Nadel, in a letter to James Hand, July 31, 1987.

23. Sally P. Springer and Georg Deutsch, *Left Brain, Right Brain* (New York: W. H. Friedman, 1985), 236–237.

24. Ibid., 26–30.

25. Ibid.

26. R. W. Sperry, "Lateral Specialization in the Surgically Separated Hemispheres," in *The Neuro-Sciences Third Study Program,* F. O. Schmitt and F. G. Warden, eds. (Cambridge: MA: MIT Press, 1974), 5–19.

27. Sir John Eccles, *The Brain and Unity of Conscious Experience: the 19th Arthur Stanley Eddington Memorial Lecture* (Cambridge, UK: Cambridge University Press, 1965).

28. Robert Ornstein, "The Split and Whole Brain," *Human Nature* 1 (1978): 76–83.

29. Sally P. Springer and Georg Deutsch, *Left Brain, Right Brain* (New York: W. H. Friedman, 1985), 236–237.

30. Russell Whitman, Creativity and Lateralization. Taped lecture, Wayne State University, College of Education, June 1986.

31. Ibid.

32. Ibid.

33. Ibid.

34. Marilee Zdenek, *The Right-Brain Experience: An Intimate Program to Free the Power of Your Imagination* (New York: McGraw-Hill, 1983), 240–241.

35. James Hand, "The Brain and Accelerative Learning," *Per Linguam* 2(2) (1986):6.

36. Ibid.

37. J. Levy, "Jerre Levy: Interview" *Omni* (Vol. 7, No. 4, 1985), pp. 68–70, 97, 99–102.

38. Ibid.

39. R. B. Bordon and D. H. Schuster, "The Effects of a Suggestive Learning Climate, Synchronized Breathing and Music on the Learning and Retention of Spanish Words," *Journal of Suggestive-Accelerated Learning and Teaching* 1(1): 27–40 (ERIC 180–234, 1976).

40. D. H. Schuster and D. Mouzon, "Music and Vocabulary Learning," *Journal of the Society for Accelerative Learning and Teaching* 7(1):82–108 (1982).

41. P. Russell, *The Brain Book* (New York: Hawthorn Books, 1979).

42. D. Kimura, "The Asymmetry of the Human Brain," *Scientific American* 228 (March (3) 1973):70–78.

43. A. Pavio, "Imagery and Long Term Memory," in A. Kennedy and A. Wilkes, eds., *Studies in Long Term Memory* (New York: Wiley, 1975).

44. Charles Stroebel, "Biological Rhythms and Accelerated Learning." Taped lecture, Society for Accelerative Learning and Teaching, Washington, DC, May 10–12, 1985.

45. Ibid.

46. Ibid.

47. Howard Gardner, *Frames of Mind: The Theory of Multiple Intelligence* (New York: Basic Books, 1983), 6.

48. Ibid., 61.

49. Ibid., 65–66.

50. Howard Gardner, *The Mind's New Science: A History of the Cognitive Revolution* (New York: Basic Books, 1985), 283.

51. James Hand, "The Mind/Brain Conjunction: Neurobiology, Psychology and Philosophy." Paper presented at the Society for Accelerative Learning and Teaching, Eleventh Annual Conference, West Palm Beach, Florida, Spring 1986.

52. James Hand, "The Brain and Accelerative Learning, Part III: How People Function and Suggestions for Educators," *SALT* 11(3) (Fall 1986), 233–249.

53. Doreen Kimura, "Male Brain, Female Brain, Hidden Differences," *Psychology Today,* November 1985, 51–58.

Music for Learning and Teaching

| Instrumental Music |
| Jerome P. Dishman |

The following are lists of suggested music for use in various classroom activities. The two major classifications are baroque and New Age music.

■ *Baroque Music*

English Madrigals—The Tallis Scholars (Angel AE-34483)

The Baroque Lute—Walter Gerwig (Nonesuch H-71229)

Concertos by Bach, Vivaldi, Handel—Bath Festival Orchestra (Angel AE-34466)

The Baroque Trumpet—Various artists (Nonesuch H-71002)

Pachelbel Canon, Albinoni Adagio, etc.—Baroque Chamber Orchestra (RCA AGLI-4218)

Bach: Toccata and Fugue—Karl Richter (Musikfest 415442-1)

Bach: Unaccompanied Cello Suites—Yo Yo Ma (CBS-IM39509)

Bach: Music for Two Harpsichords—Junghaus & Tracey (Nonesuch H-71357)

A Bach Celebration (Guitar & Orchestra)—C. Parkening (Angel DS-37343)

Bach: Goldberg Variations—Weissenberg (Angel Dsb-3926)

Bach on Wood—Brian Slawson (CBS M39704)

Bach: Brandenburg Concertos, One through Six—Pinchas Zukerman (Galleria 419465-1)

Handel: Water Music and Royal Fireworks Music—Stuttgart Chamber Orchestra (Jubilee 417273-1)

The Glory of Handel—Various artists (Musikfest 415441-1)

Handel: Four Concertos for Oboe and String Orchestra (Nonesuch H-71013)

An 18th Century Concert—London Harpsichord Ensemble (Nonesuch H-71004)

▪ *Classical, Romantic, Impressionist, 20th Century*

Beethoven: Sixth Symphony ("Pastoral")—Berlin Philharmonic (Galleria 415833-1)

Beethoven: Third Symphony ("Eroica")—Wiener Philharmoniker (Deutsche-Grammophon 419597-1)

Beethoven: Three Great Piano Sonatas—Wilhelm Kempff (MCA 25921)

Beethoven: Violin Concerto—Berlin Philharmonic (Galleria 419o521)

Beethoven: String Quartets—London Jubilee (414-080-1)

Bartok: Violin and Piano Concertos—Rudolf Serkin (CBS MP39057)

Chopin's Greatest Piano Works—Various Artists (Musikfest 413666-1)

Chopin: 26 Preludes—Martha Argerich (Galleria 415836-1)

Debussy: La Mer, Images—Los Angeles Philharmonic (Galleria 419473-1)

Mozart: Sonatas for Piano and Violin—Perlman & Barenboim (DG 419215-1)

Mozart: The Mozart Collection—London Sinfonia (American Gramophone AG586)

Classics in the Air—Paul Mauriat

Barber, Ives, Copland, et al.—Various artists (Argo ZRG845)

Holst: The Planets—Orchestra of Montreal (London 417553-1)

▪ *New Age Music*

William Ackerman: "Conferring with the Moon" (Windham Hill WH1050)

Ancient Future: "Natural Rhythms" (Philo 9006)

Daryl Anger/Barbara Higbie: "Tideline" (Windham Hill WH1021)

Checkerfield: "Water, Wind & Stone" (American Gramophone AG-700)

Wally Badarou: "echoes" (Island Records 90495-1)

Alex DeGrassi: "Southern Exposure" (Windham Hill WH1030)

William Goldstein: "Oceanscape" (CBS FM42226)

David Lange: "Return of the Comet" (DavLang Music DL101)

Mark Isham: "Vapor Drawings" (Windham Hill WH1027)

Ben Tavera King: "Desert Dreams" (Global Pacific GP301)

Gabriel Lee: "Impressions" (Narada N-61005)

Mannheim Steamroller: "Fresh Aire" (American Gramophone AG 355)

Vangelis: "Invisible Connections" (Deutsche Grammophon 415196-1)
Peter Seiler: "Flying Frames" (Innovative Communication KS80.057)
Andreas Vollenweider: "Down to the Moon" (CBS 42255)
George Winston: "Autumn" (Windham Hill WH1012)
Windham Hill Sampler '82 (WH1024)
Windham Hill Sampler '84 (WH1035)
Windham Hill Sampler '86 (WH 1048)

- *Miscellaneous Music*

Music for Instruments and Electronic Sounds—Donald Erb (Nonesuch H71223)
Computer Music—J. K. Randall (Nonesuch H71245)
Electronic Percussion—Max Neuhaus (Columbia MS7139)
Synergy: "Sequence" (Passport PB6002)
The Birds World of Sound (Folkways FX6115)
Pat Methany Group: "First Circle" (ECM 25008-1 E)

- *Program for Supplemental Tape*

Side A—Baroque and Classical Varieties. This side contains primarily baroque selections in addition to music of later periods. The pieces were selected to offer a sampling of various composers and styles. There is also some variety of instrumentation, although the string instruments are prevalent in most selections.

1. J. S. Bach, Brandenburg Concerto no. 1 in F, Minuetto-Polacca
2. Johann Pachelbel, Canon in D
3. Tomaso Albinoni, Concerto for Oboe and Strings op. 9 no. 2
4. Antonio Vivaldi, *The Four Seasons,* "Winter," Largo
5. George Frederich Handel, *The Water Music Suite,* Minuet, Air
6. Henry Purcell, Chaconne in G minor
7. Robert Schumann, Symphony no. 1 in B-flat major, op. 38
8. Johannes Brahms, Ballade in B-minor op. 10 no. 1
9. Maurice Ravel, *Bolero*

Side B—New Age Music, Jazz, and Rock. Quite a change from the first side, this music may be equally or even more appropriate for some lessons. Included are exemplary selections of New Age music, a mixture of classical and jazz. Also added are a jazz piece and an instrumental electronic rock music piece.

1. William Ackerman: "Remedies"
2. George Winston: "Blossom/Meadow"

3. Alex DeGrassi: "Clockwork"
4. Shadowfax: "Another Country"
5. Michael Mannering: "Welcoming"
6. Mike Marshall & Daryl Anger: "Dolphins"
7. Pat Methany Group: "First Circle"
8. The Who: "Quadrophenia"[1]

| *Thematic Music* |
| **John Gilboe** |

The author usually selects a song for a particular reading lesson or unit after the memory has been jogged by a line or two, or perhaps a single word, from the text material used in the unit. Once reminded of a song, other songs that are thematically similar come to mind, which results in a list of songs that can be roughly grouped—roughly, because even within a single group there are great differences in style, tone, and lyrical content. Once the lists are started, it's enjoyable to add to them, compare and contrast songs, find the songs that make points the loudest, determine which songs get the job done without a lot of noise, and devise other ways to pick the lists apart. It is important to note that many songs could be placed in different groups because their themes cut across other themes.

The lists that follow are excellent pools of information for use in the classroom. The lists are by no means finite, nor are their titles considered specific. The lists are starting points for gathering more information for lessons in a variety of subjects. Where a song is not identified by its record label number, its publisher is cited.

■ *Drug-Related Songs*

"Heroin" (APL 1-0472)	Lou Reed (1974)
"White Light White Heat" (APL 1-0472)	Lou Reed (1974)
"Needle and the Damage Done" (MS 2032)	Neil Young (1971)
"Medicine Jar" (McCartney Music Ltd.)	Jimmy McCulloch (1976)
"Waiting for My Man" (APL 1-0756)	Lou Reed (1975)
"Cocaine" (RS-1-4536)	Eric Clapton (1973)
"White Rabbit" (RCA LSP 4459)	The Jefferson Airplane (1967)
"Lucy in the Sky with Diamonds" (CAP 2835)	The Beatles (1967)
"Mother's Little Helper" (ABKCO Music)	The Rolling Stones (1966)
"Purple Haze" (RS 6261)	Jimi Hendrix (1967)
"Times Fade Away" (Silver Fiddle)	Neil Young (1973)

"Margaritaville" (Corral Reefer Music)	Jimmy Buffet (1977)
"Wino Junko" (McCartney Music Ltd.)	Jimmy McCulloch/Colin Allen (1976)
"Day Tripper" (Northern Songs Ltd.)	The Beatles (1965)

Contrary to what many parents or teachers may feel, most songs about drugs do not extol their use. Perhaps "Cocaine" (1974) comes closest to doing so with the line: "If your day is done and you want to ride on, cocaine." But even that line must be tempered by another line in the song: "Don't forget this fact, you can't get back, cocaine." Other songs warn of the dangers of addiction or of the problems associated with obtaining illegal drugs, as in "Waiting for My Man," "Heroin," "White Light White Heat," and "Needle and the Damage Done." Still others warn of addiction from legally obtained or prescribed drugs used with alcohol in "Mother's Little Helper," "Medicine Jar," and "Wino Junko." Information obtained from these songs about the desperation and ugliness of drug use and addiction is thought-provoking for youngsters at a time when they are confronted with making decisions about drug use.

■ *Famous and Infamous Characters*

"Abraham, Martin and John" (Roznique Music)	Dick Holler (1968)
"Pride in the Name of Love"	U2 (1984)
"So Long Frank Lloyd Wright" (Paul Simon)	Paul Simon (1969)
"Happy Birthday" (Tamla T8-373MI)	Stevie Wonder (1980)
"Empty Garden" (Big Pig Music)	Elton John/Bernie Taupin (1982)
"Vincent" (Mayday Music)	Don McLean (1971)
"Candle in the Wind" (MCA 2-10003)	Elton John/Bernie Taupin (1973)
"Cortez the Killer" (Reprise MS 2242)	Neil Young (1975)
"Hurricane" (From the album "Desire")	Bob Dylan (1976)
"Nostradamus" (Janus JLS 3063)	Al Stewart (1973)
"Sir Duke" (Tamla T13-34062)	Stevie Wonder (1976)
"Ballad of Billy the Kid" (CBS PC-32544)	Billy Joel (1973)
"A Simple Desultory Philippic" (Or How I Was Robert McNamara'd into Submission)	Paul Simon (1965)
"I Feel Like a Bullet (in the Gun of Robert Ford)" (MCA 2163)	Elton John/Bernie Taupin (1975)
"Payola Blues" (Geffen M5G 4013)	Neil Young (1983)

The songs listed are excellent biographical references to famous and infamous characters from a variety of backgrounds. From political life come the songs about Abraham Lincoln, Martin Luther King, Jr., John F. Kennedy, and Robert McNamara in "Abraham, Martin and John," "Pride in the Name of Love," "Happy Birthday" and "A Simple Desultory Philippic," respectively. It's interesting to note that three of the songs—"Abraham, Martin and John," "Pride in the Name of Love," and "Happy Birthday"—all deal with the life and work of Martin Luther King, Jr. Other songs recall heroes of the past: "So Long Frank Lloyd Wright," the famous architect; in "Candle in the Wind," the tragic life of Marilyn Monroe; in "Empty Garden," John Lennon; in "Vincent," the life and work of Vincent Van Gogh; in "Hurricane," the boxer Rubin "Hurricane" Carter; in "Sir Duke," the music of Duke Ellington; and in "Payola Blues," Alan Freed, who created "rock 'n' roll." Remembered too are some names from the distant past, including some that are not revered: Hernando Cortez, conqueror of the Aztec Empire, in "Cortez the Killer"; the Old West outlaw Billy the Kid in "Ballad of Billy the Kid"; Robert Ford, the man responsible for bringing Jesse James to justice by shooting him in the back as James was hanging a picture, in "I Feel Like a Bullet (in The Gun of Robert Ford)"; and the seer Nostradamus, author of *The Centuries*, in "Nostradamus." While some factual information can be taken from these songs, they are most useful for the impressions they create about the famous or infamous person described in the song.

■ *Against War and Destruction*

"2+2=?" (Capital 2143)	Bob Seger System (1969)
"Russians" (Magnetic Publishing Ltd.)	Sting (1985)
"Sky Pilot" (MGM K-13939)	The Animals (1967)
"Ohio" (Atlantic 2740)	Neil Young (1970)
"Eve of Destruction" (Dunhill 4009)	Barry McGuire (1965)
"It's a Mistake" (Columbia Records)	Men at Work (1982)
"Cost of Freedom" (Atlantic SD 2-902)	Crosby Stills Nash & Young (1970)
"Give Peace a Chance" (Apple 1809)	John Lennon (1969)
"Wooden Ships" (Gold Hill Music)	David Crosby/Steven Stills (1969)
"The Unknown Soldier" (Elecktra 45628)	The Doors (1968)
"Fortunate Son" (Capitol 2719)	Creedence Clearwater Revival (1969)
"Still in Saigon" (Dreena Music)	Charlie Daniels (1981)
"One Tin Soldier" (Trousdale Music)	Dennis Lambert/Brian Potter (1969)
"My Father's Gun" (UNI 1192)	Elton John/Bernie Taupin (1970)

"I'd Love to Change the World"   Alvin Lee (1972)
"Restless" (Big Pig Music Ltd.)   Elton John/Bernie Taupin (1984)
"Peace Train" (BMI)   Cat Stevens (1971)

The songs on this list come largely from the Vietnam era, but also include ideas about war that are still applicable to today's world. Sting, in "Russians," offers hope in this nuclear age by stating, "What might save us me and you, Is if the Russians love their children too." "One Tin Soldier" suggests that the most prized of possessions for any people is "peace on earth." Most of the songs follow the theme of a search for peace in a "restless" world.

■ *Troubled Youth*

"Authority Song" (Riva 7504)   John Cougar Mellencamp (1983)
"Wind Up" (Chrysalis 1044)   Jethro Tull (1971)
"Rebel Rebel" (Main Man 2-0771)   David Bowie (1973)
"Ticking" (MCA 2110)   Elton John/Bernie Taupin (1974)
"Think I'm Going to Kill Myself"   Elton John/Bernie Taupin (1972)
  (MCA 2017)
"Doctor My Eyes" (Asylum 5051)   Jackson Browne (1971)
"Saturday Night's Alright for   Elton John/Bernie Taupin (1973)
  Fighting" (MCA 2-10003)
"Street Kids" (MCA/Rocket   Elton John/Bernie Taupin (1975)
  2-11004)
"Remember" (Apple 3372)   John Lennon (1970)
"Working Class Hero" (Apple   John Lennon (1970)
  3372)
"Father and Son" (Freshwater   Cat Stevens (1970)
  Music Ltd.)
"The Laws Must Change"   John Mayall (1969)
  (Polydor 4004)
"Allentown" (Joel Songs)   Billy Joel (1981)
"DOO DOO DOO DOO   The Rolling Stones (1972)
  (Heartbreaker)" (Atlantic 79102)
"Motherless Children" (RSO 3023)   Eric Clapton (1974)
"I Am a Child" (ATCO 38-105)   Neil Young (1968)
"All the Girls Love Alice"   Elton John/Bernie Taupin (1973)
  (MCA2-10003)
"Dialogue" (Big Elk Music)   Chicago (1972)
"Old Man" (Warner Brothers   Neil Young (1972)
  0598)
"Hey, Hey, My, My" (Silver   Neil Young (1979)
  Fiddle)
"1999" (Controversy Music)   Prince (1982)
"Cut My Hair" (Guerrilla Music)   David Crosby (1970)

"Smokin' in the Boy's Room" (Big Tree 16011)	Brownsville Station (1974)

This collection contains a wide range of ideas upon the general theme of troubled youth. Songs like "Motherless Children," "Hey, Hey, My, My," "All the Girls Love Alice," and "Ticking" tell of the tragedy of death in the lives of the young. "I Think I'm Going to Kill Myself," "Saturday Night's Alright for Fighting," "Father and Son," and "Old Man" explore the difficulties young adults face when dealing with their parents. Conflicts with larger, more formal institutions are presented in "Authority Song," "Working Class Hero," "The Laws Must Change," "Dialogue," and "Wind Up." Apprehension about the future, in terms of employment and world peace is featured in "1999" and "Allentown." These songs are written with young people in mind and are excellent for promoting class discussions about issues that students need to discuss.

■ *God and Religion*

"Hymn 43" (Chrysalis 1044)	Jethro Tull (1971)
"My God" (Chrysalis 1044)	Jethro Tull (1971)
"Religion" (Geffen 4006)	Elton John/Bernie Taupin (1983)
"Wind Up" (Chrysalis 1044)	Jethro Tull (1971)
"God on Our Side" (Columbia 2105)	Bob Dylan (1965)
"Turn Turn Turn" (Melody Trails)	Book of Ecclesiastes; adapted by Pete Seeger (1962)
"Salvation" (MCA 2017)	Elton John/Bernie Taupin (1972)
"God" (Apple 3372)	John Lennon (1970)
"Presence of the Lord" (Polydor 3503)	Eric Clapton (1972)
"If There's a God in Heaven" (What's He Waiting For?) (MCA 11004)	Elton John/Bernie Taupin (1976)
"Tower of Babel" (MCA 2142)	Elton John/Bernie Taupin (1975)
"Have a Talk with God" (Tamla 34062)	Stevie Wonder (1976)
"Jesus Children of America" (Tamla 34062)	Stevie Wonder (1976)
"Only the Good Die Young" (Columbia 34987)	Billy Joel (1977)
"Knockin' on Heaven's Door" (Ram's Horn Music)	Bob Dylan (1973)
"Morning Has Broken" (Freshwater Music Ltd.)	Cat Stevens (1971)
"Sympathy for the Devil" (ABKCO Music)	The Rolling Stones (1968)

In the politically conservative atmosphere that extends to our schools, talk of God and religion is not totally out of the question. Fortunately, in parochial schools discussion of religion is part of the curriculum. "Hymn 43," "My God," "God on Our Side," "If There's a God in Heaven (What's He Waiting For)," "God," and "Tower of Babel" confront students with the idea of faith as the underlying strength of all religions. Questions of the validity of relying upon faith, in light of the hardships in the world, are presented in these songs. Other songs, though, like "Presence of the Lord," "Salvation," "Have a Talk with God," and "Jesus Children of America" simply praise the power of the Lord to direct the lives of His children. Perhaps the biggest contribution songs in this category make is to help young people clarify their values in the light of religious experiences.

■ *The Rat Race*

"Synchronicity" (A&M 3735)	The Police (1983)
"Too Many People" (Apple 3375)	Paul McCartney (1971)
"Money" (Harvest 11163)	Pink Floyd (1973)
"Smile Away" (Apple 3375)	Paul McCartney (1971)
"Living for the City" (Tamla 362)	Stevie Wonder (1976)
"Piano Man" (CBS PC-32544)	Billy Joel (1973)
"Moving Out" (Columbia 34987)	Billy Joel (1977)
"The Stranger" (Columbia 34987)	Billy Joel (1977)
"Penny Lane" (Capitol 2653)	The Beatles (1967)
"Eleanor Rigby" (Capitol 2653)	The Beatles (1967)
"A Day in the Life" (Apple SO-383)	The Beatles (1970)
"For What It's Worth" (Contillion Music)	Stephen Stills (1966)
"Holiday Inn" (UNI 93210)	Elton John/Bernie Taupin (1971)
"The Boxer" (Paul Simon)	Paul Simon (1968)
"Dirty Work" (American Broadcasting Music)	Steely Dan (1972)

Songs on this list comment negatively about the nature of society. "Synchronicity," "Too Many People," "Penny Lane," "Holiday Inn," and "The Boxer" comment on the sameness and boredom that pervade the lives of many seemingly happy and successful people. Other songs, including "Money," "Living for the City," "For What It's Worth," and "Smile Away," deal with difficulties and hardships brought on by social institutions. In "Money," "The Stranger," "Piano Man," "Dirty Work," and "Eleanor Rigby," individuals' losses in love, respect, or dignity is focused upon.

The lists of songs presented so far are based upon certain themes. There are, of course, other themes that provide students with an opportunity to search through albums and music books to find themes and compile lists of their own. Some suggested themes are:

Racial Prejudice in America. Songs for this theme can be found under other theme titles in this paper: "Troubled Youth," "God and Religion," and "The Rat Race."

Children and Suicide. This growing phenomenon is the number two killer of children in America and can be explored through many excellent song titles available. Related to this theme is that of child abuse, another pressing social problem.

The Classics in Popular Music. A great number of present-day song writers borrow from the classics.

Youth and the Automobile. Many songs exist that tell of the connections between youths and cars. Many excellent examples are given in *Christine,* the thriller by Stephen King.

Man and Outer Space. Man's fascination with space adventure spills over in many songs that glory in or question man's role in the cosmos.

Life in America. This theme could be divided many different ways. Songs about states, cities, American pride, accomplishment, ingenuity and generosity, geographical features of the United States, freedom, military and cultural history, and many others subjects are available.

Youth and Education. Many songs dealing with students, teachers, school administrators, attitudes toward education, and the responsibility of education bring the strengths and weaknesses of our educational system into view.

Human Relationships. Perhaps the largest group of songs falls into this category, which includes human emotions, especially love.[2]

■ *NOTES*

1. Jerome Dishman, Music as a Tool in Teaching the High School Language Arts (Master of Education Project, Wayne State University, June 3, 1987, directed by James Quina), 29–30. A copy of this project is on reserve in the Kresge Library, Wayne State University, Detroit, MI 48202.
2. John Gilboe, Recognizing Song Lyrics as Excellent Teaching Materials (Master of Education Project, Wayne State University, May 12, 1986, directed by James Quina), 24–33. A copy of this project is on reserve in the Kresge Library, Wayne State University, Detroit, MI 48202.

Instrumentation of Bloom's Taxonomy: Cognitive and Affective Domains

TABLE C.1 Instrumentation of the Taxonomy of Educational Objectives: Cognitive Domain

Taxonomy Classification	Key Words	
	Examples of Infinitives	Examples of Direct Objects
1.00 Knowledge		
1.10 Knowledge of specifics		
1.11 Knowledge of terminology	To define, to distinguish, to acquire, to identify, to recall, to recognize	Vocabulary, terms, terminology, meaning(s), definitions, referents, elements
1.12 Knowledge of specific facts	To recall, to recognize, to acquire, to identify	Facts, factual information, (sources), (names), (dates), (events), (persons), (places), (time periods), properties, examples, phenomena
1.20 Knowledge of ways and means of dealing with specifics		
1.21 Knowledge of conventions	To recall, to identify, to recognize, to acquire	Form(s), conventions, uses, usage, rules, ways, devices, symbols, representations, style(s), format(s)

TABLE C.1 (*Continued*)

Taxonomy Classification	Key Words	
	Examples of Infinitives	Examples of Direct Objects
1.22 Knowledge of trends, sequences	To recall, to recognize, to acquire, to identify	Action(s), processes, movement(s), continuity, development(s), trend(s), sequence(s), causes, relationship(s), forces, influences
1.23 Knowledge of classifications and categories	To recall, to recognize, to acquire, to identify	Area(s), type(s), feature(s), class(es), set(s), division(s), arrangement(s), classification(s), category/categories
1.24 Knowledge of criteria	To recall, to recognize, to acquire, to identify	Criteria, basics, elements
1.25 Knowledge of methodology	To recall, to recognize, to acquire, to identify	Methods, techniques, approaches, uses, procedures, treatments
1.30 Knowledge of the universals and abstractions in a field		
1.31 Knowledge of principles, generalizations	To recall, to recognize, to acquire, to identify	Principles(s), generalization(s), proposition(s), fundamentals, laws, principal elements, implication(s)
1.32 Knowledge of theories and structures	To recall, to recognize, to acquire, to identify	Theories, bases, interrelations, structure(s), organization(s), formulation(s)
2.00 Comprehension		
2.10 Translation	To translate, to transform, to give in own words, to illustrate, to prepare, to read, to represent, to change, to rephrase, to restate	Meaning(s), sample(s), definitions, abstractions, representations, words, phrases

TABLE C.1 (*Continued*)

| | Key Words | |
Taxonomy Classification	Examples of Infinitives	Examples of Direct Objects
2.20 Interpretation	To interpret, to reorder, to rearrange, to differentiate, to distinguish, to make, to draw, to explain, to demonstrate	Relevancies, relationships, essentials, aspects, new view(s), qualifications, conclusions, methods, theories, abstractions
2.30 Extrapolation	To estimate, to infer, to conclude, to predict, to differentiate, to determine, to extend, to interpolate, to extrapolate, to fill in, to draw	Consequences, implications, conclusions, factors, ramifications, meanings, corollaries, effects, probabilities
3.00 Application	To apply, to generalize, to relate, to choose, to develop, to organize, to use, to employ, to transfer, to restructure, to classify	Principles, laws, conclusions, effects, methods, theories, abstractions, situations, generalizations, processes, phenomena, procedures
4.00 Analysis		
4.10 Analysis of elements	To distinguish, to detect, to identify, to classify, to discriminate, to recognize, to categorize, to deduce	Elements, hypothesis/hypotheses, conclusions, assumptions, statements (of fact), statements (of intent), arguments, particulars
4.20 Analysis of relationships	To analyze, to contrast, to compare, to distinguish, to deduce	Relationships, interrelations, relevance, relevancies, themes, evidence, fallacies, arguments, cause-effect(s), consistency/consistencies, parts, ideas, assumptions
4.30 Analysis of organizational principles	To analyze, to distinguish, to detect, to deduce	Form(s), pattern(s), purpose(s), point(s) of view(s), techniques, bias(es), structure(s), theme(s), arrangement(s), organization(s)

TABLE C.1 (*Continued*)

| | Key Words | |
Taxonomy Classification	Examples of Infinitives	Examples of Direct Objects
5.00 Synthesis		
5.10 Production of a unique communication	To write, to tell, to relate, to produce, to constitute, to transmit, to originate, to modify, to document	Structure(s), pattern(s), product(s), performance(s), design(s), work(s), communications, effort(s), specifics, composition(s)
5.20 Production of a plan, or proposed set of operations	To propose, to plan, to produce, to design, to modify, to specify	Plan(s), objectives, specification(s), schematic(s), operations, way(s), solution(s), means
5.30 Derivation of a set of abstract relations	To produce, to derive, to develop, to combine, to organize, to synthesize, to classify, to deduce, to develop, to formulate, to modify	Phenomena, taxonomies, concept(s), scheme(s), theories, relationships, abstractions, generalizations, hypothesis/hypotheses, perceptions, ways, discoveries
6.00 Evaluation		
6.10 Judgments in terms of internal evidence	To judge, to argue, to validate, to assess, to decide	Accuracy/accuracies, consistency/consistencies, fallacies, reliability, flaws, errors, precision, exactness
6.20 Judgments in terms of external criteria	To judge, to argue, to consider, to compare, to contrast, to standardize, to appraise	Ends, means, efficiency, economy/economies, utility, alternatives, courses of action, standards, theories, generalizations

SOURCE: Tables C.1 and C.2 are reprinted by permission from Newton S. Metfessel, W. B. Michael, and D. A. Kirsner, "Instrumentation of Bloom's and Krathwohl's Taxonomies for the Writing of Educational Objectives," *Psychology in the Schools* 6(3): July 1969, 228–231.

TABLE C.2 Instrumentation of the Taxonomy of Educational Objectives: Affective Domain

Taxonomy Classification	Key Words	
	Examples of Infinitives	Examples of Direct Objects
1.0 Receiving		
1.1 Awareness	To differentiate, to separate, to set apart, to share	Sights, sounds, events, designs, arrangements
1.2 Willingness to receive	To accumulate, to select, to combine, to accept	Models, examples, shapes, sizes, meters, cadences
1.3 Controlled or selected attention	To select, to posturally respond to, to listen (for), to control	Alternatives, answers, rhythms, nuances
2.0 Responding		
2.1 Acquiescence in responding	To comply (with), to follow, to commend, to approve	Directions, instructions, laws, policies, demonstrations
2.2 Willingness to respond	To volunteer, to discuss, to practice, to play	Instruments, games, dramatic works, charades, burlesques
2.3 Satisfaction in response	To applaud, to acclaim, to spend leisure time in, to augment	Speeches, plays, presentations, writings
3.0 Valuing		
3.1 Acceptance of a value	To increase measured proficiency in, to increase numbers of, to relinquish, to specify	Group membership(s), artistic productions(s), musical productions, personal friendships
3.2 Preference for a value	To assist, to subsidize, to help, to support	Artists, projects, viewpoints, arguments
3.3 Commitment	To deny, to protest, to debate, to argue	Deceptions, irrelevancies, abdications, irrationalities
4.0 Organization		
4.1 Conceptualization of a value	To discuss, to theorize (on), to abstract, to compare	Parameters, codes, standards, goals
4.2 Organization of a value system	To balance, to organize, to define, to formulate	Systems, approaches, criteria, limits

TABLE C.2 (*Continued*)

	Key Words	
Taxonomy Classification	Examples of Infinitives	Examples of Direct Objects
5.0 Characterization by value or value complex		
5.1 Generalized set	To revise, to change, to complete, to require	Plans, behavior, methods, effort(s)
5.2 Characterization	To be rated high by peers in, to be rated high by superiors in, to be rated high by subordinates in	Humanitarianism, ethics, integrity, maturity
	and	
	to avoid, to manage, to resolve, to resist	Extravagance(s), excesses, conflicts, exorbitancy/exorbitancies

Self-Management Charts

Effective Teacher Planning

Name _____ Objective _____ Date _____

Subject _____

Planned Teacher Behavior	Planned Student Behavior	Actual Teacher Behavior	Actual Student Behavior
[ ] 1. Lecture	[ ] 1. Oral reading	[ ] 1. Lecture	[ ] 1. Oral reading
[ ] 2. Group process	[ ] 2. Note taking	[ ] 2. Group process	[ ] 2. Note taking
[ ] 3. Maps, diagrams, AV	[ ] 3. Confusion, noise	[ ] 3. Maps, diagrams, AV	[ ] 3. Confusion, noise
[ ] 4. Give directions	[ ] 4. Asks open questions	[ ] 4. Give directions	[ ] 4. Asks open questions
[ ] 5. Summarize	[ ] 5. Asks closed questions	[ ] 5. Summarize	[ ] 5. Asks closed questions
[ ] 6. Problem solving	[ ] 6. Student-to-student response	[ ] 6. Problem solving	[ ] 6. Student-to-student response
[ ] 7. Review	[ ] 7. Use of body language	[ ] 7. Review	[ ] 7. Use of body language
[ ] 8. Use games	[ ] 8. Solve problems	[ ] 8. Use games	[ ] 8. Solve problems
[ ] 9. Demonstration	[ ] 9. Resists directives	[ ] 9. Demonstration	[ ] 9. Resists directives
[ ] 10. Body language	[ ] 10. Factual recall	[ ] 10. Body language	[ ] 10. Factual recall
[ ] 11. Jokes/Humor	[ ] 11. Emotive response	[ ] 11. Jokes/Humor	[ ] 11. Emotive response
[ ] 12. Positive response	[ ] 12. High-cognitive response	[ ] 12. Positive response	[ ] 12. High-cognitive response
[ ] 13. Negative response	[ ] 13. Psychomotor response	[ ] 13. Negative response	[ ] 13. Psychomotor response
[ ] 14. Alter environment		[ ] 14. Alter environment	
[ ] 15. Ask open questions		[ ] 15. Ask open questions	
[ ] 16. Assign homework	[ ] 16. Other	[ ] 16. Assign homework	[ ] 16. Other
[ ] 17. Other	[ ] 17. Other	[ ] 17. Other	[ ] 17. Other

Record of Time Use

	Activity	Professional or Nonprofessional (P or NP)	A or B or C Priority	Notes
Hour 1:				
30 min.	_____	_____	_____	_____
30 min.	_____	_____	_____	_____
Hour 2:				
30 min.	_____	_____	_____	_____
30 min.	_____	_____	_____	_____
Hour 3:				
30 min.	_____	_____	_____	_____
30 min.	_____	_____	_____	_____
Hour 4:				
30 min.	_____	_____	_____	_____
30 min.	_____	_____	_____	_____
Hour 5:				
30 min.	_____	_____	_____	_____
30 min.	_____	_____	_____	_____
Hour 6:				
30 min.	_____	_____	_____	_____
30 min.	_____	_____	_____	_____
Hour 7:				
30 min.	_____	_____	_____	_____
30 min.	_____	_____	_____	_____
Hour 8:				
30 min.	_____	_____	_____	_____
30 min.	_____	_____	_____	_____

Glossary

acceptance of a value   In Bloom's taxonomy, consistency of response to the "class of objects" with which the belief or attitude is identified.

acquiescence in responding   In Bloom's taxonomy, compliance with the stimulus.

ACT   The American College Testing Program measures predictive ability in English, use of mathematics, the social sciences, and the natural sciences.

actions   In Sherod Miller's communication system, plans for the resolution of an issue—the framework within which goals and objectives are defined in the resolution of an issue.

affect/affective domain   In Bloom's taxonomy, the domain of feelings and values.

AFT   The American Federation of Teachers, a professional organization.

alpha rest   A state of focused relaxation in which an abundance of alpha waves are produced in the brain.

ambiguity   A term is ambiguous if it can mean more than one thing—if it has more than one referent. For example, the term "page" is ambiguous. It may refer to page of a book or a servant. A statement is ambiguous if it contains an ambiguous term(terms). Ambiguity is different from vagueness. (See *vagueness.*) [Harun-Ur Rashid]

amygdala   A mass of gray matter that controls rage and fear and is the basis of fight/flight responses. It adjoins the temporal lobe of the cortex.

antisuggestive barriers   Self-protection mechanisms that screen incoming information, but can reduce the effectiveness of learning: (1) the critical logical barrier rejects "everything which does not give an impression of well-intended logical motivation"; (2) the intuitive-affective antisuggestive barrier rejects "everything which fails to create confidence and a feeling of security"; and (3) the ethical barrier rejects "suggestions contradictory to the ethical principles of the individual. . . ." [Georgi Lozanov, *Suggestology and Outlines of Suggestopedy*]

approach response   For Robert F. Mager, movement toward a teacher or subject.

argument   An argument is a group of statements, one of which is the conclusion and the rest are premises. In an argument, we make a claim (conclusion) that is supported by reasons or evidences (premises).

Arguments are different from explanations in that they look for justifications or reasons, whereas explanations give us the causes. (See *causes and reasons.*)

Arguments are also different from verbal fights that do not follow any rules of logic. Verbal fights are more like nonevidential persuasions, whereas arguments are concerned with evidential support for the conclusions.

(See *deductive argument* and *inductive argument.*) [Harun-Ur Rashid]

assertive discipline Lee Canter's system of behavior modification, which is designed to warrant that no student will interfere with the teacher's instructional process or with the learning of another student. The system works through consistently using assertive responses as distinguished from passive or hostile responses, and through rewards and disciplinary consequences.

assertive training Training in making clear distinctions among passive, hostile, and assertive behavior.

authority (nondirective prestige) Authority, in the sense of nondirective prestige, "creates an atmosphere of confidence and intuitive desire to follow the set example. . . . Authority creates confidence in the reliability of expected results." [Georgi Lozanov, *Suggestology and Outlines of Suggestopedy*]

avoidance response For Robert F. Mager, movement away from a teacher or subject.

awareness In Bloom's taxonomy, apprehension of facts as distinct from being able to recall facts.

behavioral objective An educational objective that (1) states the expected behavior of students or expected student performance; (2) the conditions under which the student will exhibit the behavior; and (3) will sometimes include a criterion of acceptable performance.

behaviorism The psychological theory that excludes introspection and mental phenomena to account for behavior and that bases its conclusions on observable behavior.

behavior modification Shaping behavior through positive and/or negative reinforcement.

biofeedback The science and technology that studies states of consciousness in respect to four basic brain wave forms: beta waves (13–29 cycles per second), alpha waves (8–12 cycles per second), theta waves (4–7 cycles per second), and delta waves (1–3 cycles per second).

brainstorming An instructional technique used to generate the flow of ideas in a class. All answers, no matter how wrong they may seem to the teacher or other students, are accepted as possibilities to a solution.

breathing (yogic) Breathing in a 1-4-2 ratio. Inhale for a count of one; hold four times as long as it took to first inhale; exhale for a count of two.

burnout D. Caton defines burnout as "a form of emotional exhaustion occurring primarily within human service professions, where staff members spend a great deal of time in intense interaction with other people." Burnout is characterized by helplessness, disenchantment, hopelessness, emotional exhaustion, physical exhaustion, increased susceptibility to illness, increased use of sick time, decreased use of vacation time, increased number of on-the-job accidents, decrease in quality of work, and increased use of overtime in small increments of time.

causes and reasons If I ask you, "Why are you here in this world?" I am asking an ambiguous question—ambiguous because I did not make it explicit whether I am asking for the reasons for your being here or for the causes. You could either say, "I am here because my parents caused me to be here," or, following Jean-Paul Sartre, you might say, "I have been thrown into this situation." That gives us the cause of your being here. On the other hand, if you say, "I am here for serving humanity or serving my society," then you are giving the reasons why you are here. Critical thinking is more interested in the reasons for claims than in the causes of them. [Harun-Ur Rashid]

CAI Computer-assisted instruction. (See *PLATO* as an example.)

characterization In Bloom's taxonomy, one becomes a living emblem of the values he or she espouses.

characterization by a value or value complex In Bloom's taxonomy, values are organized into a world view.

circadian rhythms Periodicity over a 24-hour period. According to William Stroebel, M.D., there is a shift in activity of the left and right hemispheres of human beings every 90 minutes throughout the day.

code of ethics It states standards of general conduct covering possible conflicts of norms that may arise in a school. Most school boards provide a printed code of conduct.

cognitive handicaps Handicaps comprised of two groups: (1) the *retarded,* who generally lack intelligence, and (2) the *learning disabled,* who have difficulty processing information. [Paula Wood]

cognitive psychology A theory of psychology that focuses on mental phenomena—logical, linguistic, neurological, perceptual—to account for human behavior. In learning theory, the object is to account for what happens in the minds of students as they learn.

collective bargaining Commonly understood as the method used to determine a teacher's salary. The collective bargaining process can be used, however, to determine any and all of the parameters of the learning environment (class size, disciplinary procedures, curriculum, instructional resources, and so on). [Joseph M. Wright]

compare When you are asked to compare, you should examine qualities, or characteristics, in order to discover resemblances. The term *compare* is usually stated as "compare with," and it implies that you are to emphasize similarities, although differences may be mentioned. [C. Bird and D. M. Bird]

completion items Often called objective items on tests, the common types of completion items are true/false, multiple choice, and matching. [Donald Marcotte]

computing hardware The physical aspect of the computer. Modern hardware is compact, desktop, or portable.

computing software Software for instruction falls into three logical groupings: direct instructional delivery, indirect instructional support, and computing tools. [John W. Childs]

computing tools Both general-purpose and special-purpose systems, ranging from computer languages to special-purpose instructional design and support workstations. [John W. Childs]

conceptualization of a value In Bloom's taxonomy, the value is given symbolic import.

conceptual objective An objective that states learning goals in terms of concepts to be mastered rather than behavior to be performed. Conceptual objectives are abstract, nonobservable, and known through inference.

conferencing Communication or interpersonal interaction between parent and teacher; student, teacher, and parent; counselor and teacher; counselor and student; teacher and administrator; or any other combination of persons interested in the student's acquisition of knowledge.

concert pseudopassiveness "A serene, confident attitude toward the suggestive program being presented . . . to be in the same state of mind as one would be in attending a [classical] concert." [Georgi Lozanov, *Suggestology and Outlines of Suggestopedy.*] This state, says Ivan Barzakov, is "by no means limited to the concert session or to the use of music." Rather, says Barzakov, it is an "awakening of the reserve capacities of the individual, which creates the conditions for the mind to go as far as it can go."

In this sense, it is the "exact opposite of mind control," says Barzakov. It is a state students are in for most of the class period and is supported not only by music but by voice, movement and expression. The state is called *pseudo*passive because the students only appear to be passive; actually they are in a very active learning state.

"From a physiological point of view," says Barzakov, "the state is very relaxed and at the same time, very concentrated. That is probably why, in his latest writings, Lozanov calls this state 'concentrative psycho[logical] relaxation'."

conclusion   The claim made in an argument. When we make a logical argument, we make a claim that is supported by evidence (or premises). When we have one argument, we have exactly one conclusion. More than one conclusion gives us more than one argument. [Harun-Ur Rashid]

controlled or selected attention   In Bloom's taxonomy, a willing selection of stimulus among competing stimuli.

control theory   William Glasser's theory that recognizes students' power needs and provides a constructive use of power in group processes.

cooperative learning   David Johnson's approach to motivation and learning, which stresses interdependence and support for all members of a learning group.

contrast   When you are instructed to contrast, you should stress dissimilarities, differences, or unlikenesses of associated things, qualities, events, or problems should be stressed. [C. Bird and D. M. Bird]

convergent questions   Questions arranged in a series that progressively moves toward a conclusion. Convergent questions can be used to channel a student's thoughts toward a specific response.

corpus callosum   The bundle of nerve fibers connecting the two hemispheres of the brain that makes possible communication between the hemispheres.

criterion of acceptable performance   A description of "how well the learner must perform to be considered acceptable." [Robert F. Mager, *Preparing Instructional Objectives*]

criterion-referenced tests   Tests designed to specify standards students are expected to meet, usually expressed in terms of a minimum number of behavioral objectives. Students are judged with respect to performing the objectives rather than their relative performance in a group.

critical pluralism   A philosophical view that recognizes multiple modes of evidence.

critical thinking   Critical thinking is a Higher Order Thinking (HOT) skill that enables us to determine the validity (or invalidity) of a deductive argument, determine the strength (or weakness) of an inductive argument, and the goodness of a value judgment.

It is different from Lower Order Thinking (LOT), which involves basically memory and application, in that Higher Order Thinking (HOT) involves the special skill of analysis, synthesis, reflection, evaluation, and the like.

Critical thinking is a special kind of disposition which enables us to look at the universe and the events in it with a skeptical attitude—a questioning and inquiring mind. It is opposed to indoctrination and dogmatism. [Harun-Ur Rashid]

critical thinking and education   Critical thinking is relevant to education because it helps us to be a critical reader, a critical writer, a critical questioner, and a critical answerer. It helps us learn the effective strategies of thinking in education. It helps us in critical lesson planning and goal setting. It helps us in shaping an effective curriculum for the students.

Education ends up being dogmatic indoctrination if it is limited to Lower Order Thinking (memory, application). Critical thinking (Higher Order Thinking) helps us to be more inquisitive, more insightful, and more humane. Critical thinking helps us determine our standard of values in education. Planning a curriculum that promotes critical thinking can only be done if we develop a disposition of critical thinking and know how to apply it in appropriate situations. [Harun-Ur Rashid]

criticize   In a criticism you should express your judgment with respect to the correctness or merit of the factors under consideration. You are expected to give the results of your own analysis and to discuss the limitations and good points or contributions of the plan or work in question. [C. Bird and D. M. Bird]

CV (Curriculum Vitae)   Similar to a resume, but normally assembled by an individual with a considerable amount of experience in his or her profession. It includes all the elements of a resume plus—in the case of a musician, for example—performances, guest appearances, compositions, and the like. It is often organized in chronological order as opposed to the often-used reverse chronological order of the resume. (See *resume.*) [Jeanette H. Piccirelli]

deductive argument   An argument is deductive if it is, in principle, such that given all its premises are true, it is impossible for its conclusion to be false. In other words, in a deductive argument the conclusion necessarily follows from the premises. The premises provide 100 percent support (or conclusive reasons) for the conclusion.

The validity of this kind of argument depends on the very structure (or form) of the argument rather than the content of it. [Harun-Ur Rashid]

(See the examples of deductive argument in Chapter 8.)

define   Definitions call for concise, clear, authoritative meanings. In such statements details are not required, but boundaries or limitations of the definition should be briefly cited. You must keep in mind the class to which a thing belongs and whatever differentiates the particular object from all others in the class. [C. Bird and D. M. Bird]

delegation   In time management, extending one's power and effectiveness by distribution of power and responsibility.

describe   In a descriptive answer you should recount, characterize, sketch, or relate in narrative form. [C. Bird and D. M. Bird]

diagram   For a question that specifies a diagram you should present a drawing, chart, plan, or graphic representation in your answer. Generally, the student is also expected to label the diagram and in some cases to add a brief explanation or description. [C. Bird and D. M. Bird]

direct instructional delivery   Software commercially produced or generated by the teacher for direct instruction of the student may be categorized as follows: (1) drill practice, (2) tutorial, (3) game/simulation, (4) tutored problem solving, and (5) combination. [John W. Childs]

discuss   The term *discuss,* which appears often in essay questions, directs you to examine, analyze carefully, and present pro and con considerations regarding the problems or items involved. This type of question calls for a complete and detailed answer. [C. Bird and D. M. Bird]

divergent questions   Questions that are used to expand a student's specific thoughts to related concepts. These questions are designed to broaden a student's associations of an original concept.

domain of interest   The sample space of a test. [Donald Marcotte] (See *sample space.*)

dual-planeness   Ivan Barzakov notes that the Bulgarian term *dvóen* has the sense of the English "dual." Dual means double, but in the specialized sense of being composed of two *unlike* parts *(American Heritage Dictionary).* In suggestology, dual-planeness refers to the "enormous signaling stream of diverse stimuli which unconsciously, or semiconsciously, are emitted from or perceived by the personality. . . . Imperceptible changes in facial expression, gait, speed, environment . . . can play a decisive role in the formation of the suggestive result." [Gerogi Lozanov, *Suggestology and Outlines of Suggestopedy*] The professional must be sincere in the practice of his or her discipline in order to master dual-planeness.

due process   As a rule . . . a procedural process wherein mandated, fair, consistent rules are followed with respect to the enforcement, protection, and resolution of individual considerations. [Joseph M. Wright]

emotional handicaps   Handicaps comprised of *adjustment* problems and *behavioral* problems. *Adjustment* problems are usually situationally induced and relatively amenable to intervention. They occur in response to a specific stress either in family life, in community life, or from events such as death in the family. . . . *Behavioral* problems are well ingrained in maladaptive patterns. [Paula Wood]

encounter teaching   A method of teaching usually done in a group setting that stresses openness and honesty. Encounter teaching heightens self-awareness and facilitates effective use of personal capacities.

enumerate   The word specifies a list or outline form of reply. In such questions you should recount, one by one, in concise form, the points required. [C. Bird and D. M. Bird]

evaluate   In an evaluation question you are expected to present a careful appraisal of the problem, stressing both advantages and limitations. Evaluation implies authoritative and, to a lesser degree, personal appraisal of both contributions and limitations. [C. Bird and D. M. Bird]

expectations/expectancy   Peter Kline distinguishes *expectation* from *expectancy*. Expectation specifies learning outcomes in advance; expectancy invites one to remain open to emergent possibilities of learning.

explain   In explanatory answers it is imperative that you clarify, elucidate, and interpret the material you present. In such an answer it is best to state the "how" or "why," reconcile any differences in opinion or experimental results, and, where possible, state causes. The aim is to make plain the conditions that give rise to whatever you are examining. [C. Bird and D. M. Bird]

fallacy   A fallacy is a logical error in our reasoning. We commit various types of fallacies when we intend to make arguments. Some of these fallacies are deductive, some are inductive, and some are concerned with value judgments. For example, the fallacy of affirming the consequent is a fallacy in deductive logic, whereas the argument against the person is an inductive fallacy. [Harun-Ur Rashid]

feelings   In Sherod Miller's interpersonal communication system, feelings are positive or negative experiences that arise from observation. They have a role in communication, but not in the decision-making process.

generalized set   In Bloom's taxonomy, internal consistency is added to the value complex.

goal   The end toward which effort is directed. A condition or state to be brought about through a course of action. [*Webster's Third International Dictionary*]

hippocampus   Part of the brain that controls short- and long-term memory and gauges expectation and actuality.

holographic brain theory   According to Howard Gardner, "The brain is like a hologram. . . . Information about any point in the original is distributed throughout the hologram, thus making it resistant to damage. . . ."

illustrate A question that asks you to illustrate usually requires you to explain or clarify your answer to the problem by presenting a figure, picture, diagram, or concrete example. [C. Bird and D. M. Bird]

implication/inference An implication is a conditional statement. For example, if Bush becomes the president, there will be a drought next year. The if-clause is called the antecedent and the then-clause is called the consequent. Obviously, it is not an argument.

An inference, on the other hand, is an argument in which a claim is supported by reasons or evidence. An inference may have conditional statements as its premises and conclusion, but it might not as well. Inference is a process of getting to something new from something given. [Harun-Ur Rashid]

induction Physical and psychological reversed effect; the principle that accounts for every tendency generating its own opposite.

inductive argument An inductive argument is one in which the premises provide partial support for the conclusion. In this kind of argument, given that the premises are true, the conclusion need not necessarily be true, but it is probably true.

In other words, in an inductive argument the premises do not necessarily imply (or entail) the conclusion. In opposition to deductive argument, inductive argument deals with content rather than with structure. Inductive arguments obtain their premises from the world of experience and apply the principle of uniformity of nature and the law of causation to establish the conclusion. [Harun-Ur Rashid]

infantilization (childlike learning state) "A universal reaction of respect, inspiration and confidence which, without disrupting the level of the normal intellectual activity, considerably increases the perception, memory and creative function." A liberation of the "plastic qualities of the earlier age periods," leading to "aesthetic experiences and intellectual conclusions, but in a more direct, spontaneous and convincing manner." [Georgi Lozanov, *Suggestology and Outlines of Suggestopedy*]

intelligence According to Howard Gardner, competence that enables an individual to "resolve genuine problems or difficulties" *and* also entails "the potential for *finding or creating problems,* thereby laying the groundwork for the acquisition of new knowledge." Gardner expands the general concept of intelligence to include (1) linguistic intelligence, (2) musical intelligence, (3) logical-mathematical intelligence, (4) spatial intelligence, (5) bodily-kinesthetic intelligence, and (6) personal intelligence.

intentions In Sherod Miller's interpersonal communication system, that which a person wants to accomplish.

interest For John Dewey, an interest is an attitude toward a possible experience.

interpret An interpretation question is similar to one requiring explanation. You are expected to translate, exemplify, solve, or comment upon the subject and usually to give your judgment or reaction to the problem. [C. Bird and D. M. Bird]

intonation "An expression—usually vocal—of an internal psychological content." [Lozanov, *Suggestology and Outlines of Suggestopedy*] The use of sound, usually the voice, to influence one in respect to attitude.

justify When you are instructed to justify your answer, you must prove or show grounds for decisions. In such an answer, evidence should be presented in convincing form. [C. Bird and D. M. Bird]

list Listing is similar to enumeration. You are expected in such questions to present an itemized series or a tabulation. Such answers should always be given in concise form. [C. Bird and D. M. Bird]

loco parentis/in loco parentis (in place of the parents) . . . school authorities are authorized by parents, via an implied contract, to do whatever is reasonable and necessary with respect to the learning environment, learning process and content, and means and methods involving the education of children." [Joseph M. Wright]

mandala A visual geometric pattern designed to stimulate the right hemisphere of the brain. The right brain becomes fascinated with exploring the spatial configuration of the mandala.

mind map An instructional technique in which the student puts a word, short phrase, or picture in the center of a circle representing the main topic to be explored. The student then draws lines away from the circle, writing associative words and phrases on the lines. Subconcepts are placed on lines branching from the original lines. When the central circle branches to other circles, the technique is often called clustering.

minimum competency Testing of basic skills so as to warrant that students who graduate from public high schools have these skills.

modus ponens A valid form of deductive argument. It is also called the principle of affirming the antecedent. In this argument, the structure of the argument matters, not the content of it. For example: If Team X wins the seventh game, they will be world champions. *Team X wins.* Therefore, Team X is the world champion. [Harun-Ur Rashid]

modus tollens A valid form of deductive reasoning. Also called the rule of denying the consequent. The validity of this type of argument depends on the structure of it rather than the content. For example: (1) If Senator Smith finishes second, then he'll be the vice-presidential candidate. (2) Senator Smith is not the vice-presidential candidate. Therefore, Senator Smith did not finish second. [Harun-Ur Rashid]

multicultural education "The process by which persons acquire knowledge, abilities, habits and attitudes regarding those values that prevailing sectors of society have imposed on the social fabric. This educational enterprise enables the student to distinguish between values established to deny access and those intended to become productive members of the social order." [Rodolfo Martinez]

NAEP (National Assessment of Educational Programs) A survey of student achievement in various subject areas: art, career and occupational development, citizenship, literature, mathematics, music, reading, social studies, and writing.

NCATE (National Council for Accreditation of Teacher Education) An evaluative body that reviews standards and performances of teacher education institutions.

NEA (National Education Association) A professional organization for teachers.

neocortex In Paul MacLean's triune brain theory, the part of the brain representing the latest stage of brain evolution. For MacLean, the neocortex primarily focuses on the outside world—on external, environmental events.

networking A group of persons forming a system for the purpose of exchanging information and mutual support. The ongoing development of such a system.

NLP (Neurolinguistic Programming) The theory and practice that posits relationships between the nervous system and language, both verbal and nonverbal.

nonprojected media Delivery devices such as the on-demand audiotape, the display, the exhibit, the bulletin board, and the still picture. [John W. Childs]

norm-referenced test A test that sets standards for individual student performance relative to group performance.

observations In Sherod Miller's communication system, any bits or pieces of information received through the sensory organs and which become processed as thought.

objective Something toward which effort is directed: good or object; boundary. [*Webster's Third International Dictionary*] An educational objective is measurable, occurs in time, and may be observable.

operant conditioning Developed by B. F. Skinner, a form of conditioning that reinforces voluntary desirable responses.

organization In Bloom's taxonomy, systematic arrangement of values.

organization of a value system In Bloom's taxonomy, disparate values are brought into a coherent relationship.

other-hand writing A technique that elicits right-brain function through writing with one's nondominant hand.

outline An outlined answer is organized description. You should give main points and essential supplementary materials, omitting minor details, and present the information in a systematic arrangement or classification. [C. Bird and D. M. Bird]

physical handicaps Handicaps that include disorders of vision, learning, the brain, bones, muscles, the nervous system, chronic illness, or orthopedic deficits such as missing limbs. [Paula C. Wood]

pituitary gland Located in the midbrain and responsible for growth.

PLATO Programmed Logic for Automated Teaching Operations.

portfolio (audio/video) Contains a brief resume, sample lesson plans, a video- or audiotape presenting one's best work, sample student work or test scores, table of contents, a cover letter, and a folder with pockets that organize the above exhibits.

precision (as in scope and precision) Stephen Pepper's term for the rigor and discriminatory power of world hypotheses. As applied to instructional objectives, stating exactly and unambiguously what one intends the student to perform.

preference for a value In Bloom's taxonomy, acceptance and commitment to a value.

premise A reason or piece of evidence for a claim. When we make an argument, its premises are supposed to support or justify the conclusion. The very support or justification (or evidence) is called the premise. We use premises in all kinds of arguments in critical thinking. [Harun-Ur Rashid]

prioritize In time management, assigning relative value to tasks to be completed.

project method An instructional method whereby students explore possibilities for future planning, which includes feasibility checks, assessment of resources, delegation of responsibility, setting of time lines for completion, and criteria for evaluation.

prove A question that requires proof is one that demands confirmation or verification. In such discussions you should establish something with certainty by evaluating and citing experimental evidence or by logical reasoning. [C. Bird and D. M. Bird]

psychomotor domain In Anita Harrow's taxonomy, the classification of human movements on a continuum ranging from the simple to the complex.

purpose Something that one sets before himself as an object to be attained; an end to be kept in view in any plan, measure, exertion, operation. Synonym: intention. [*Webster's*

Third International Dictionary] Purposes are inexhaustible sources of generating goals and objectives.

Reading W/Music, or "Reading with Music" Barzakov's term for the reading of a text so that the voice "surfs" on the music. One reads according to the expression of the music. The voice becomes another instrument in the concert. The integration of voice and music is designed to integrate the function of the whole brain.

reality therapy William Glasser's personality theory that promotes self-worth and responsibility through nonjudgmental discussion of academic and personal problems.

recall column A device to aid concentration and memory. The use of key words or phrases placed in the margin of one's notes for the purpose of study or review.

reframing Also called recontextualization, it is a way of reinterpreting a problem so that it can become a benefit. A contextual shift.

relate In a question that asks you to show the relationship or to relate, your answer should emphasize connections and associations in descriptive form. [C. Bird and D. M. Bird]

reliability (1) Test reliability—the consistency of individual response over time; (2) scorer reliability—consistency in scoring test items by different raters. [Donald Marcotte]

reptilian brain Located in the bottom core of the forebrain, just above the brain. Paul MacLean says it plays a part in "aggressive behavior, territoriality, ritual and the establishment of social hierarchies."

reserve capacities Capacities that under special circumstances are, for the ordinary human being, an extraordinary phenomenon. Hypermnesia (supermemory) is an example. (See Georgi Lozanov, *Suggestology and Outlines of Suggestopedy.*)

resume Usually organized in reverse chronological order, the resume "lays out all the key attributes about [oneself] that an employer uses in a hiring decision." Elements of a resume are (1) name, (2) address, (3) phone number, (4) job objective, (5) education, (6) certification, (7) volunteer work, (8) interests, hobbies, etc., (9) memberships/honors, and (10) references. [Jeanette H. Piccirelli]

responding In Bloom's taxonomy, a participation with the stimulus phenomenon.

review A review specifies a critical examination. You should analyze and comment briefly in organized sequence on the major points of the problem. [C. Bird and D. M. Bird]

rhythms Regarded by Lozanov as a biological principle: the recurrence and patterns reflected in nature in days, seasons, years, and mental life.

role playing An instructional technique designed to release untapped potential of students through their identification with real or imagined scientists, artists, or inventors.

sample Items selected from the sample space for inclusion in a test. [Donald Marcotte]

sample space In a test, the well-defined domain of interest from which sample items are selected. For example, the items on a test that measures a person's ability to add will be drawn from an infinite number of addition problems, the *sample space*. [Donald Marcotte]

SAT (Scholastic Aptitude Test) A multiple-choice test originally designed to predict students' ability to do college work.

satisfaction in response In Bloom's taxonomy, a voluntary response accompanied by a feeling of satisfaction or pleasure.

scope (as in scope and precision) Stephen Pepper's term for the universal application of world hypotheses. As applied to instructional objectives, stating everything one intends.

shared meaning In Sherod Miller's interpersonal communication system, a process in which the receiver of a message hears exactly what the sender intends to say and in the same context and with the same meaning.

slice of cheese approach Completing major tasks a "slice at a time" in order to increase management effectiveness.

state In questions that direct you to specify, give, state, or present, you are called upon to express the high points in brief, clear narrative form. Details and usually illustrations or examples may be omitted. [C. Bird and D. M. Bird]

statement Not all sentences in the English language are statements. Only those that are in the indicative mood (those that have assertive elements in them) are statements.

In other words, only those sentences that are either true or false are statements in the English language. A sentence like "Alas! I am undone" is neither true nor false. It is a meaningful English sentence because it follows the syntactic and semantic rules of the English language. But since it does not have the property of truth, it is not a statement (logically). [Harun-Ur Rashid]

stress Physiologically, a human response is characterized by "(1) release of cortisone from the adrenal glands; (2) thyroid hormone increases in the bloodstream; (3) release of endorphin from the hypothalamus; (4) reduction in sex hormones; (5) the shutdown of the digestive tract; (6) release of sugar into the blood; (7) increase of cholesterol in the blood; (8) racing heartbeat; (9) increased air supply; (10) [thickening of the blood]; (11) ['crawling' skin, paleness], sweats; and (12) all five senses become acute." [Peter G. Hanson, *The Joy of Stress*]

suggestion According to Lozanov, "a constant communicative factor which chiefly through paraconscious mental activity can create conditions for tapping the functional reserve capacities of personality." [Lozanov, *Suggestology and Outlines of Suggestopedy*]

suggestology According to Lozanov, the science of the art of liberating and stimulating the personality both under guidance and alone.

summarize When you are asked to summarize or present a summarization, you should give in condensed form the main points or facts. All details, illustrations, and elaboration are to be omitted. [C. Bird and D. M. Bird]

supply items Often referred to as nonobjective test items in which the student is required to supply a test from memory. [Donald Marcotte]

table of specifications A table specifying sample space, levels of cognition, time, and relative importance, used to plan and construct a test. [Donald Marcotte]

term The word "term" has a unique meaning in logic and critical thinking. A *term* is a word or a group of words that can be used as the subject or the predicate of a logical proposition. That means not every word in the English language is a term. Only those words are terms that are capable of being used as the subject (about which we say something) or the predicate (what we say about the subject) of a logical statement. [Harun-Ur Rashid]

terminal behavior In behavioristic learning theory, terminal behavior is learning; the observable actions that the student is expected to perform at the termination of his instruction.

thoughts In Sherod Miller's interpersonal communication system, thoughts are interpretations of what one observes.

trace When a question asks you to trace a course of events, you are to give a description of progress, historical sequence, or development from the point of origin. Such narratives may call for probing or for deductions. [C. Bird and D. M. Bird]

transitional objects Objects such as old photographs or autographed baseballs that elicit memories associated with these objects.

triune brain theory The human brain, says Paul MacLean, "amounts to three interconnected biological computers," each with "its own special intelligence, its own subjectivity, its own sense of time and space, its own memory, motor and other functions."

unit An instructional plan spanning in time from one to eight weeks designed to unify global purposes and the mastery of specific concepts and skills that will enable the student to realize those purposes.

vagueness A term is vague if its meaning is unclear or imprecise—if it does not have any clear definition. In other words, a term is vague if we do not know the exact essential properties of it.

   For example: the term "love" is vague. It has various meanings in various contexts. Some people might define love as attraction toward beauty, some might not. Everyone has his own conception of love but probably no one can give a complete list of the characteristics (or properties) of love.

   Any statement containing one or more vague terms must be vague. [Harun-Ur Rashid]

validity "In a test, the items selected must be representative of the sample space. . . . More specifically . . . a test has *context validity* if the results lead to a proper conclusion that the student can perform [whatever he or she is tested on]. *Content validity* with teacher-made tests . . . usually depends on the teacher's selection of representative items." [Donald Marcotte]

value The quality or fact of being excellent, useful or desirable; worth in a thing. [*Webster's Third International Dictionary*]

valuing In Bloom's taxonomy, internalization of ideals or standards.

visualization Conscious control of inner images; specifically, "A method of developing inner awareness and control of the body's autonomic functions. A way to bring to consciousness what you really feel and to understand the meaning of the things that occur in your life. A way to get in touch with your imaginative powers. A source of information much vaster than words. A channel, for many, to personal and universal truth. And, most important, it is an act of conscious and deliberate creating." [Adelaide Bry, *Visualization: Directing the Movies of Your Mind*]

wait time In time management, the unproductive time arising from situations in which one is in between productive activity and is "waiting" for the next productive activity.

whole-brain processing Techniques that stimulate the left and right hemispheres and subcortical areas of the brain and are designed to maximize human performance.

willingness to receive In Bloom's taxonomy, a willingness to attend, but a suspension of judgment in regard to what is attended.

willingness to respond In Bloom's taxonomy, a voluntary dimension of response.

world hypothesis Unrestricted production of knowledge; hypotheses that cannot reject anything as irrelevant.

yoga *Hatha yoga* teaches breathing, relaxation, and body flexibility. *Kundalini yoga* teaches deep and powerful breathing along with combinations of exercise designed to break up fixed states of body and mind. *Raja yoga* teaches control of thoughts and emotions through visualization.

Bibliography

CHAPTER 1

Bloom, Allan. 1987. *The Closing of the American Mind: How Higher Education Has Failed Democracy and Impoverished the Souls of Today's Students.* New York: Simon & Schuster.

Boyer, Ernest L. 1983. *High School: A Report on Secondary Education in America.* New York: Harper & Row.

Costa, Arthur L. 1984. A Reaction to Hunter's Knowing, Teaching and Supervising. In *Using What We Know About Teaching,* edited by Phillip L. Hosford. Alexandria, VA: Association for Supervision and Curricular Development.

Ferguson, Marilyn. 1980. *The Aquarian Conspiracy: Personal and Social Transformation in the 1980's.* Los Angeles: J. P. Tarcher.

Hirsch, E. D., Jr. 1987. *Cultural Literacy: What Every American Needs to Know.* Boston: Houghton Mifflin Company, 1987.

Hosford, Phillip L., ed. 1984. *Using What We Know About Teaching.* Alexandria, VA: Association for Supervision and Curricular Development.

Hunter, Madeline. 1984. Knowing, Teaching and Supervising. In *Using What We Know About Teaching,* edited by Phillip L. Hosford. Alexandria, VA: Association for Supervision and Curricular Development.

Kounin, J. 1970. *Discipline and Group Management in the Classroom.* New York: Holt, Rinehart and Winston.

Leonard, George. 1968. *Education and Ecstasy.* New York: Delacorte Press, 1968.

CHAPTER 2

Anderson, Beverly, and Pipho, Chris. 1984. State Mandated Testing and the Fate of Local Control. *Phi Delta Kappan* 66.

Bobby, Janet. 1985. Minimum Competency Testing: A Review of Literature. Unpublished manuscript.

Boyer, Ernest L. 1987. *College.* New York: Harper & Row.

Cooper, Charles R. 1981. Competency Testing: Issues and Overview. In *Nature and Measurement of Competency in English,* edited by Charles R. Cooper. Urbana, IL: NCTE.

Fine, Michele. 1983. Perspectives in Inequity: Voices from Urban Schools. In *Applied Social Psychology,* edited by Leonard Bichman. London: Sage.

Hosford, Phillip L. 1984. The Art of Applying the Science of Education. In *Using What We Know About Teaching.* Urbana, IL: ASCD.

Husen, Torsten. 1983. Are Standards in U.S. Schools Really Lagging Behind Those in Other Countries? *Phi Beta Kappan* March 1983.

Lanier, Judith L. 1986. *Tomorrow's Teachers: A Report of the Holmes Group.* East Lansing, MI: The Holmes Group, Inc.

Mecklenberger, Jim. 1978. Minimum Competency Testing: The Bad Penny Again. *Phi Delta Kappan* 66.

Raywid, Mary Ann; Tesconi, Charles A., Jr.; and Warren, Donald R. 1984. *Pride and Promise: Schools of Excellence for All the People.* Burlington, VT: American Educational Studies Association.

Simpkins, Edward J., and Gibson, Dennis L. 1985. The High School Dropout Problem: Strategies for Reduction; a Report of the High School Dropout Prevention Network of Southeast Michigan. Detroit, MI: The High School Dropout Prevention Network of Southeast Michigan.

CHAPTER 3

Bayles, Ernest E., and Hood, Bruce L. 1966. *Growth of American Educational Thought and Practice.* Harper's Series on Teaching. New York: Harper & Row.

Bruner, Jerome. 1960. *The Process of Education.* Cambridge, MA: Harvard University Press.

Butts, R. Freeman. 1955. *A Cultural History of Western Education: Its Social and Intellectual Foundations.* 2d ed. New York: McGraw-Hill.

Cole, Luella. 1950. *A History of Education: Socrates to Montessori.* New York: Holt, Rinehart and Winston.

Dodgson, Charles Lutwidge (Carroll, Lewis). 1969. *Alice's Adventures in Wonderland: A Critical Handbook.* Belmont, CA: Wadsworth.

Drake, William Earle. 1967. *Intellectual Foundations of Modern Education.* 2d ed. Englewood Cliffs, NJ: Prentice-Hall.

Eby, Frederick. 1967. *The Development of Modern Education.* 2d ed. Englewood Cliffs, NJ: Prentice-Hall.

Karier, Clarence J. 1967. *Man, Society, and Education.* Glenview, IL: Scott Foresman (paperback).

Lee, Gordon C. 1965. *Education and Democratic Ideals: Philosophical Backgrounds of Modern Educational Thought.* The Professional Education for Teachers Series. New York: Harcourt Brace Jovanovich (paperback).

Power, Edward J. 1970. *Main Currents in the History of Education.* 2d ed. New York: McGraw-Hill.

Rippa, S. Alexander. 1967. *Education in a Free Society: An American History.* New York: McKay (paperback).

Tanner, Daniel. 1972. *Secondary Education: Perspectives and Prospects.* New York: Macmillan.

Thut, I. M. 1957. *The Story of Education: Philosophical and Historical Foundations.* New York: McGraw-Hill.

CHAPTER 4

Aristotle. *Nicomachaean Ethics.* Trans. by W. P. Ross. Oxford: Clarendon Press. 1925.

Bloom, Benjamin. 1956. *Taxonomy of Educational Objectives: Cognitive Domain.* New York: Longmans, Green.

Carroll, Lewis. 1969. *Alice's Adventures in Wonderland.* Edited by Donald Raukin. Belmont, CA: Wadsworth.

Dewey, John. 1933. *How We Think.* Lexington, MA: Heath.

Hunter, Madeline. 1982. *Mastery Teaching: Increasing Instructional Effectiveness in Secondary Schools, Colleges and Universities.* El Segundo, CA: TIP Publications.

Kibler, Robert J., et al. 1970. *Behavioral Objectives and Instruction.* Boston: Allyn and Bacon.

Kryspin, William J., and Fieldhusen, John F. 1974. *Writing Behavioral Objectives: A Guide to Planning Instruction.* Minneapolis, MN: Burgess.

Mager, Robert F. 1962. *Preparing Instructional Objectives.* Palo Alto, CA: Fearon.

Pepper, Stephen. 1942. *World Hypotheses.* Los Angeles: University of California Press.

CHAPTER 5

Bogen, Joseph E. 1975. The Other Side of the Brain. VII: Some Educational Aspects of Hemispheric Specialization. *UCLA Educator* 17.

Dewey, John. 1902. *The Child and the Curriculum.* Chicago: University of Chicago Press.

———. 1933. *How We Think.* Lexington, MA: Heath.

Harrow, Anita J. 1972. *A Taxonomy of the Psychomotor Domain: A Guide for Developing Behavioral Objectives.* New York: McKay.

Kaplan, Leonard. 1978. *Developing Objectives in the Affective Domain.* Columbus, OH: Collegiate Publishing, Inc.

Krathwohl, David R.; Bloom, Benjamin S.; and Masia, Bertram B. 1964. *Taxonomy of Educational Objectives. Handbook II: Affective Domain.* New York: McKay.

Lorber, Michael A., and Pierce, Walter D. 1983. *Objectives, Methods, and Evaluations for Secondary Teaching.* Englewood Cliffs, NJ: Prentice-Hall.

Lozanov, Georgi. 1979. *Suggestology and Outlines of Suggestopedy.* New York: Gordon and Breach.

Mager, Robert F. 1984. *Developing Attitude Toward Learning or SMATS "n" SMUTS.* Belmont, CA: Pitman Management and Training.

Maslow, Abraham. 1968. *Toward a Psychology of Being.* New York: Van Nostrand.

Roberts, Thomas B. 1977. *The Second Centering Book.* Englewood Cliffs, NJ: Prentice-Hall.

Sagan, Carl. 1977. *The Dragons of Eden.* New York: Random House.

Zdenek, Marilee. 1983. *The Right-Brain Experience: An Intimate Program to Free the Powers of Your Imagination.* New York: McGraw-Hill.

CHAPTER 6

Armstrong, David G.; Denton, John J.; and Savage, Tom V. 1978. *Instructional Skills Handbook.* Englewood Cliffs, NJ: Educational Technology Publications.

Boyer, James. 1987. Models of Student Lesson Plans. Edited compilation of submitted student lesson plans (unpublished). Wayne State University.

Gayler, Anne Richardson. 1973. *Planning in the Secondary Schools.* New York: McKay.

Hoover, Kenneth H. 1976. *The Professional Teacher's Handbook,* Chapter 3. Abridged 2d ed. Boston: Allyn and Bacon.

Hosford, Phillip L., ed. 1984. *Using What We Know About Teaching.* Alexandria, VA: ASCD.

Hunter, Madeline. 1982. *Mastering Teaching: Increasing Instructional Effectiveness in Secondary Schools, Colleges and Universities.* El Segundo, CA: TIP Publications.

Joyce, Bruce, and Weil, Marsha. 1986. *Models of Teaching.* Englewood Cliffs, NJ: Prentice-Hall.

Locker, Michael A., and Pierce, Walter D. 1983. *Objectives, Methods and Evaluation for Secondary Teaching.* Englewood Cliffs, NJ: Prentice-Hall.

Popham, W. James, and Baker, Eva L. 1970. *Systematic Instruction.* Englewood Cliffs, NJ: Prentice Hall.

Posner, George J., and Rudnitsky, Alan N. 1986. *Course Design: A Guide to Curriculum Development for Teachers.* New York: Longman.

Schuster, Donald H., and Gritton, Charles E. 1986. *Suggestive Accelerative Learning Techniques.* 1986. New York: Gordon and Breach.

Smith, Douglas. 1987. A Strategy for Effective Teaching. Unpublished monograph. Copyright 1987.

———. 1987. Course Syllabus: College Prep Chemistry. Unpublished monograph, copyright 1987. Reprinted by permission of author.

CHAPTER 7

Armstrong, David G.; Denton, John J.; and Savage, Tom V. 1978. *Instructional Skills Handbook.* Englewood Cliffs, NJ: Educational Technologies Publication.

Armstrong, David G., and Savage, Tom V. 1983. *Secondary Education.* New York: Macmillan.

Clark, Leonard H., and Starr, Irving S. 1986. *Secondary and Middle School Teaching Methods.* New York: Macmillan.

Jacobson, David; Eggen, Paul; Kanchah, Donald; and Dulaney, Carole. 1985. *Methods for Teaching: A Skills Approach.* Columbus, OH: Merrill.

Joyce, B., and Weil, M. 1972. *Models of Teaching.* Englewood Cliffs, NJ: Prentice-Hall.

Kim, E., and Kellough, R. 1976. *A Resource Guide for Secondary School Teaching.* New York: Macmillan.

Posner, George J., and Rudnitsky, Alan. 1986. *Course Design.* New York: Longman.

CHAPTER 8

Barzakov, Ivan. 1982. The Singing School: Means of Suggestion in Suggestology and in Optimalearning. *Journal of the Society for Accelerative Learning and Teaching* 7(2):173–184.

Bry, Adelaide. 1976. *Visualization: Directing the Movies of Your Mind.* New York: Barnes & Noble.

Buzan, Tony. 1983. *Use Both Sides of Your Brain.* New York: Dutton.

Dhority, Lynn. 1984. *Acquisition Through Creative Teaching: The Artful Use of Suggestion in Foreign Language Instruction.* Sharon, MA: Center for Continuing Development.

Education Network. *For Education.* A newsletter published bimonthly by the Education Network, Sawsalito, CA; Laura Holmes, Executive Editor.

Gardner, Martin. 1978. *Aha! Insight.* New York: W. H. Freeman.

Garfield, Patricia. 1982. *Creative Dreaming.* New York: Ballantine Books.

Galyean, Beverly-Colleene. 1983. *Mind Sight: Learning Through Imaging.* Long Beach, CA: Center for Integrative Learning. This book contains a wide range of visualization techniques useful for enhancing alternate learning states.

Gendlin, Eugene T. 1982. *Focusing.* Toronto: Bantam Books.

Harper, Linda. 1984. *Classroom Magic.* Troy, MI: Twiggs Communications.

Huxley, Aldous. 1956. Knowledge and Understanding. In *Adonis and the Alphabet,* pp. 39–72. London: Chatto & Windus.

———. 1977. Integrate Education. In *The Human Situation: Lectures at Santa Barbara, 1959.* New York: Harper & Row.

Key, Wilson Bryan. 1976. *Media Sexploitation.* New York: New American Library.

Kline, Peter. *Super Accelerated Learning Workshop.* This workshop is available in many major cities of the United States.

Lorayne, Harry, and Lucas, Jerry. 1974. *The Memory Book.* New York: Ballantine Books.

Merritt, Stephanie. 1987. *Successful, Non-Stressful Learning* San Diego, CA: Merritt Learning Systems.

———. 1988. *Unearthing the Treasures of Your Mind.* San Diego, CA: Merritt Learning Systems.

Maley, Alan, and Grellet, Francoise. 1981. *Mind Matters: Activities and Puzzles for Language Learners.* Cambridge: Cambridge University Press.

Nummela, Renate, and Rosengren, Tennes. 1986. What's Happening in Student's Brain May Redefine Teaching. *Educational Leadership* 43(8):49–53.

Optimalearning Foreign Language Audio Cassette Courses (Kits) for Tots and Care-takers. "Learn Along with Your Children (2½ to 6 year olds) and Stimulate Their

Giftedness." French, Spanish, and English. Contact: The Optimalearning Co. 409 Tamarack Place, Novato, CA 94947. (415) 459-4474

Quina, James, and Greenlaw, M. Jean. 1975. Science Fiction as a Mode of Interdisciplinary Education. *Journal of Reading* 19(2):105–111.

Rico, Gabrielle L. 1983. *Writing the Natural Way: Using Right-Brain Techniques to Release Your Experience Powers.* Los Angeles: J. P. Tarcher.

Robbins, Anthony. 1986. *Skills of Power Seminar.* Robbins Research Institute, Inc.

———. 1986. *Skills of Power: The New Science of Personal Achievement.* New York: Simon & Schuster.

Sagan, Carl. 1978. *Broca's Brain: Reflections on the Romance of Science.* New York: Random House.

Steinhaus, H. 1983. *Mathematical Snapshots.* Oxford: Oxford University Press.

Thomas, Lewis. 1986. *The Medusa and the Snail: More Notes of a Biology Watcher.* Toronto: Bantam Books.

Wood, Evelyn. 1969. *Evelyn Wood's Reading Dynamics.* Diversified Education and Publishing Corporation (institutes in principal cities throughout the world).

Woodyear, Ocie Posener. 1982. Suggestopedy. *Journal of the Mexican Association of Teachers of English to Speakers of Other Languages* 6(1):23–28.

Zdenek, Marilee. 1983. *The Right-Brain Experience.* New York: McGraw-Hill.

CHAPTER 9

Bitter, Gary, and Camuse, Ruth. 1988. *Using a Microcomputer in the Classroom.* Englewood Cliffs, NJ: Prentice-Hall.

Hannafin, Michael, and Peck, Kyle. 1988. *The Design, Development, and Evaluation of Instructional Software.* New York: Macmillan.

Heinich, Robert; Molenda, M.; and Russell, J. 1986. *Instructional Media and the New Technologies of Instruction.* New York: Wiley.

Miller, Harold. 1988. *An Administrator's Manual for the Use of Microcomputers in the Schools.* Englewood Cliffs, NJ: Prentice-Hall.

Owston, Ronald D. 1987. *Software Evaluation: A Criterion-Based Approach.* Scarborough, Ontario: Prentice-Hall Canada Inc.

Roberts, Nancy; Carter, R.; Friel, S.; and Miller, M. 1988. *Integrating Computers into the Elementary and Middle School.* Englewood Cliffs, NJ: Prentice-Hall.

Saettler, Paul. 1968. *A History of Instructional Technology.* New York: McGraw-Hill.

CHAPTER 10

Brown, Julia. Multicultural Lesson Plan: *Maria Concepcion.* Unpublished.

Joyce, Bruce, and Weil, Marsha. 1986. *Models of Teaching.* Englewood Cliffs, NJ: Prentice-Hall.

Schutz, William. 1967. *Joy: Expanding Human Awareness.* New York: Grove Press.

———. 1973. *Elements of Encounter.* Big Sur, CA: Joy Press.

Wiggins, Shielia. Multicultural Lesson Plan: *The Women of Brewster Place.* Unpublished.

CHAPTER 11

Gearheart, B.R., and Weishahn, M.W. 1980. *The Handicapped Student in the Regular Classroom.* St. Louis: Mosby.

Glass, R. M.; Christiansen, J.; and Christiansen, J. L. 1982. *Teaching Exceptional Students in the Classroom.* Toronto: Little, Brown.

Lewis, R. B., and Doorlag, D. H. 1987. *Teaching Special Students in the Mainstream.*

Marsh, G. E., and Price, B. J. 1980. *Methods for Teaching the Mildly Handicapped Adolescent.* St. Louis: Mosby.

McCoy, K. M., and Prehm, H. J. 1987. *Teaching Mainstreamed Students: Methods and Techniques.* Denver: Love.

Moran, M. R. 1978. *Assessment of the Exceptional Learner in the Regular Classroom.* Denver: Love.

Pasanella, A. L., and Volkmor, C. B. 1981. *Teaching Handicapped Students in the Mainstream: Coming Back or Never Leaving.* 2d ed. Columbus, OH: Merrill.

Stephens, T. M.; Blackhurst, A. E.; and Magliocca, L. A. 1982. *Teaching Mainstreamed Students.* New York: Wiley.

Wood, J. 1984. *Adapting Instruction for the Mainstream.* Columbus, OH: Merrill.

CHAPTER 12

Alexander, Lloyd. *The Chronicles of Prydain.* New York: Holt, Rinehart and Winston. *The Book of Three,* 1964; *The Black Cauldron,* 1965; *The Castle of Llyr,* 1966; *Taran Wanderer,* 1967; *The High King,* 1968.

Boyer, Ernest. 1983. *High School: A Report on Secondary Education in America.* New York: Harper & Row.

Bronowski, J. 1956. *Science and Human Values.* New York: Harper & Row.

Costa, Arthur L. 1984. A Reaction to Hunter's Knowing, Teaching and Supervising. In *Using What We Know About Teaching.* Alexandria, VA: ASCD.

Dewey, John. 1934. *Art as Experience.* New York: Minton, Balch & Co.

Dishman, Jerome. 1987. Music as a Tool in Teaching the High School Language Arts. Master of Arts essay, Wayne State University.

Fergusson, Marilyn. 1980. *The Aquarian Conspiracy: Personal and Social Transformation in the 1980's.* Los Angeles: J. P. Tarcher.

Garfield, Patricia. 1974. *Creative Dreaming.* New York: Ballantine Books.

Geddis, Arthur N. 1982. Teaching: A Study of Evidence. *Journal of Mind and Behavior* 3(4):363–373.

Gerhart, Mary, and Russell, Allan. 1984. *Metaphoric Process: The Creation of Scientific and Religious Understanding.* Fort Worth: Texas Christian University.

Gordon, William. 1973. *The Metaphorical Way of Learning and Knowing.* Cambridge, MA: Porpoise Books.

Gould, Robert F., ed. 1966. *Kekule Centennial.* Washington DC: American Chemical Society.

Joyce, Bruce, and Weil, Marsha. 1972. *Models of Teaching.* Englewood Cliffs, NJ: Prentice-Hall.

Kolb, David A. 1984. *Experiential Learning: Experience as the Source of Learning and Development.* Englewood Cliffs, NJ: Prentice-Hall.

Macy, Rudolph. 1944. *Organic Chemistry Simplified.* Brooklyn, NY: Chemical Publishing Co.

Pepper, Stephen C. 1963. *The Basis of Criticism in the Arts.* Cambridge, MA: Harvard University Press.

————. 1966. *World Hypotheses.* Los Angeles: University of California Press.

Peterson, Gordon. 1982. Paradigms, Puzzles, and Root Metaphor: Georg Christoph Lichtenberg and the Exact Sciences. *Journal of Mind and Behavior* 3(3):282.

Quina, James. 1971. World Hypotheses: A Basis for a Structural Curriculum. *Educational Theory,* 21 Summer, pp. 311–319.

————. 1982. Root Metaphor and Interdisciplinary Curriculum: Designs for Teaching Literature in Secondary Schools. *Journal of Mind and Behavior* 3(4):347–348.

Rico, Gabriele Lusser. 1983. *Writing the Natural Way.* Los Angeles: J. P. Tarcher.

Roberts, Douglas A. 1982. The Place of Qualitative Research in Science Education. *Journal of Research in Social Teaching* 19(4):277–292.

Sagan, Carl. 1977. *The Dragons of Eden.* New York: Random House.

————. 1980. *Cosmos.* New York: Random House.

Samples, Bob. (1978). *The Metaphoric Mind.* Reading, MA: Addison-Wesley.

Seidel, Frank, and James, M. 1986. *Pioneers in Science.* Boston: Houghton Mifflin.

CHAPTER 13

Bird, C., and Bird, D. M. 1945. *Learning More Effective Study.* New York: Appleton-Century-Crofts.

Grace, Langdon, and Stout, Irving W. 1969. *Homework.* New York: John Dury Company.

Kline, Peter. 1988. *The Everyday Genius: Restoring Children's Natural Joy of Learning.* Arlington, VA: Great Ocean Publishers.

Lorayne, Harry, and Lucas, Jerry. 1974. *The Memory Book.* New York: Ballantine Books.

Johnson-Laird, P. N. 1983. *Mental Models: Toward a Cognitive Science of Language, Inference and Consciousness.* Cambridge, MA: Harvard University Press.

Maddox, Henry. 1963. *How to Study: Improve Your Reading, Thinking, Memorizing, Note-Taking.* Greenwich, CT: Fawcett.

CHAPTER 14

Ahmann, J. S., and Glock, M. D. 1981. *Evaluating Pupil Growth.* 6th ed. Boston: Allyn and Bacon.

Anastasi, A. 1982. *Psychological Testing.* 5th ed. New York: Macmillan.

Bloom, B. S., et al. 1956. *Taxonomy of Educational Objectives. Handbook I: Cognitive Domain.* New York: McKay.

Brown, Frederick G. 1983. *Principles of Educational and Psychological Testing.* 3d ed. New York: Holt, Rinehart and Winston.

Cronbach, L. J. 1970. *Essentials of Psychological Testing.* 3d ed. New York: Harper & Row.

Mehrens, W. A., and Lehmann, I. J. 1978. *Measurement and Evaluation in Education and Psychology.* 2d ed. New York: Holt, Rinehart and Winston.

Thorndike, R. L., and Hagen, E. P. 1977. *Measurement and Evaluation in Psychology and Education.* 4th ed. New York: Wiley.

CHAPTER 15

Atkinson, J. W., and Raynor, J. O., eds. 1974. *Motivation and Achievement.* Washington, DC: Holt, Rinehart, and Winston.

Bandler, Richard, and Grinder, John. 1979. *Frogs into Princes.* Moab, UT: Real People Press.

Buzan, T. 1971. *Speed Memory.* London: David & Charles.

Erickson, M. H. 1980. *The Collected Papers of Milton H. Erickson on Hypnosis.* 4 vols. New York: Irvington Publishing.

Ferguson, M. 1973. *The Brain Revolution.* New York: Taplinger.

Jones, R. A. 1977. *Self-fulfilling Prophecies.* Hillsdale, NJ: Erlbaum Associates.

Lozanov, G. 1978. *Suggestology and Outlines of Suggestopedy.* New York: Gordon and Breach.

Maslow, Abraham. 1970. *Motivation and Personality.* New York: Harper & Row.

———. 1968. *Toward a Psychology of Being.* Princeton, NJ: Van Nostrand.

Satir, V. 1983. *Conjoint Family Therapy.* Palo Alto, CA: Science and Behavior Books.

Schuster, D. H., and Gritton, C. E. 1986. *Suggestive Accelerative Learning Techniques.* New York: Gordon and Breach.

Wlodkowski, R. J. 1978. *Motivation and Teaching: A Practical Guide.* 1978. Washington, DC: National Education Association.

CHAPTER 16

Barzun, Tony. 1983. *Use Both Sides of Your Brain.* New York: Dutton.

Dossey, Larry. 1982. *Space, Time and Medicine.* London: Shambhala.

Emmer, Edmund T., et al. 1984. *Classroom Management for Secondary Teachers.* Englewood Cliffs, NJ: Prentice-Hall.

Fanning, Tony, and Fanning, Robbie. 1980. *Get It All Done and Still Be Human.* New York: Ballantine Books.

Lakein, Alan. 1980. *How To Get Control of Your Time and Your Life.* New York: New American Library.

Mackenzie, Alec R. 1972. *The Time Trap.* New York: McGraw-Hill.

Schuster, Donald H., and Gritton, Charles E. 1986. *Suggestive Accelerative Learning Techniques.* New York: Gordon and Breach.

Scott, Dru. 1980. *How To Put More Time in Your Life.* New York: Harper & Row.

Shipman, Neil J.; Martin, Jack B.; McKay, Bruce A.; and Anastasi, Robert E. 1983. *Effective Time-Management Techniques for School Administrators.* Englewood Cliffs, NJ: Prentice-Hall.

Steinmetz, L. 1976. *The Art and Skill of Delegation.* Reading MA: Addison-Wesley.

Tec, Leon. 1980. *Target: How to Set Goals for Yourself and Reach Them.* New York: Harper & Row.

CHAPTER 17

Carium, Carole. May 1984. Quality Assurance. Workshop presented at Kinston, North Carolina.

Dores, Paul; Bird, F.; Monig, D.; and Robinson, J. 1987. A Comparison of Direct and Collateral Effect of the Differential Reinforcement of Other Behavior (DRO) and the Differential Reinforcement of Communicative Behavior (DRC). Paper presented at Association for Behavior Analysis, 13th Annual Convention, May 25–28, 1987.

Furlette, Mary C. 1983. Like No Other Child. Unpublished manuscript, 1983.

Higgins, Thomas. 1971. Non-Verbal Communication. Seminar presented at Flint College, Winter 1971.

Miller, Sherod, et al. 1988. *Connecting With Self and Others.* Littelton, CO: Interpersonal Communication Programs, Inc.

———. 1981. Working Together. Workshop in Chicago, July 19–20.

Wilkik, Joseph. 1987. Group Process. Workshop at Caswell Center, Kinston, North Carolina, May 22.

CHAPTER 18

Alberti, Robert E., and Emmons, Michael L. 1970. *Your Perfect Right.* San Luis Obispo, CA: Impact.

Canter, Lee (with Marlene Canter). 1976. *Assertive Discipline.* Santa Monica, CA: Canter and Associates, Inc.

Cuervo, Amalia G., ed. 1984. *Toward Better and Safer Schools: A School Leader's Guide to Delinquency Prevention.* Alexander, VA: National School Boards Association.

Dewey, John. 1938. *Experience in Education.* New York: Collier.

Dreikurs, Rudolf, and Grunwald, Bernice Bronia. 1982. *Maintaining Sanity in the Classroom: Classroom Management Techniques.* 2d ed. New York: Harper & Row.

Fensterheim, Herbert, and Baer, Jean. 1975. *Don't Say Yes When You Want to Say No.* New York: Dell.

Glasser, William. 1969. *Schools Without Failure.* New York: Harper & Row.

————. 1970. *Reality Therapy: A New Approach to Psychiatry.* New York: Holt, Rinehart and Winston.

————. 1985. *Control Theory.* New York: Harper & Row.

————. 1986. *Control Theory in the Classroom.* New York: Harper & Row.

Johnson, David W. *Circles of Learning.* Alexandria, VA: The Association of Supervision and Curriculum Development. Glasser recommends a new version of this book published by Interaction Book Co., 7208 Cornelia Dr., Edina, MN 55435.

Joyce, Bruce, and Weil, Marsha. 1986. *Models of Teaching.* Englewood Cliffs, NJ: Prentice-Hall.

Kolb, David. 1984. *Experiential Learning.* Englewood Cliffs, NJ: Prentice-Hall.

Kounin, J. 1970. *Discipline and Group Management in the Classroom.* New York: Holt, Rinehart and Winston.

Lazarrus, Arnold A. 1971. *Behavior Therapy and Beyond.* New York: McGraw-Hill Book.

Slavin, Robert E. 1982. *Cooperative Learning.* Washington, DC: National Education Association.

CHAPTER 19

Airolo, Paavo. 1974. *How to Get Well.* Phoenix, AZ: Health Plus Publishers.

Alpert, Richard (Baba Ram Dass). 1978. *Be Here Now.* Albuquerque, NM: Modern Press.

Barker, Sarah. 1976. *The Alexander Technique: The Revolutionary Way to Use Your Body for Total Energy.* St. Louis, MO: Singing Bone Press.

Brown, Barbara B. 1975. *New Mind, New Body.* New York: Bantam Books.

Bry, Adelaide (with Bair, Marjorie). 1978. *Visualization: Directing the Movies of Your Mind.* New York: Barnes & Noble.

Burns, David D. 1980. *Feeling Good: The Mood Therapy.* New York: New American Library.

Caton, Deborah Jane. 1986. Burnout and Stress Among Professional Direct Care and Support Staff at a Large State Institution for the Mentally Retarded. Master's thesis, East Caroline University.

Dossey, Larry. 1982. *Space, Time and Medicine.* Boulder, CO: Shambholm.

Gendlin, Eugen T. 1982. *Focusing.* New York: Bantam Books.

Hansen, Mark. *Be Fit!* Audiotape cassette by Mark Victor Hansen & Associates. P.O. Box 7665, Newport Beach, California, 92658–7665. Telephone: (714)759–9304.

Hanson, Peter G. 1986. *The Joy of Stress.* New York: Andrews, McMeel and Parker.

Hendricks, Gay, and Roberts, Thomas B. 1977. *The Second Centering Book.* Englewood Cliffs, NJ: Prentice-Hall. More awareness activities for children, parents, and teachers.

Hendricks, Gay, and Wilk, Russel. 1975. *The Centering Book.* Englewood Cliffs, NJ: Prentice-Hall.

Huxley, Aldous. 1942. *The Art of Seeing.* New York: Harper & Row.

Huxley, Laura. 1963. *You Are Not the Target.* New York: Farrar, Straus & Giroux.

Robbins, Anthony. 1986. *Unlimited Power: The New Science of Personal Achievement.* New York: Simon & Schuster.

Lutke, Wolfgang. 1969. *Autogenic Therapy.* New York: Grune & Stratton.

Maggs, Margaret Martin. 1980. *The Classroom Survival Book: A Practical Manual for Teachers.* New York: New Viewpoint.

Maltz, Maxwell. 1966. *Psycho-Cybernetics.* New York: Pocket Books.

Pritikin, Nathan (with Patrick M. McGrady, Jr.). 1984. *The Pritikin Program for Diet and Exercise.* New York: Bantam Books.

Syer, John, and Connolly, Christopher. 1984. *Sporting Body, Sporting Mind.* London: Cambridge University Press. An athletic guide to mental training.

Wagner, Jane. 1985. *The Search for Signs of Intelligent Life in the Universe.* New York: Harper & Row.

CHAPTER 20

American Historical Association. 1977. Careers for Students of History. 400 A St., SE, Washington, DC 20003.

Biegeleisen, J. I. 1982. *Job Resumes: How to Write Them, How to Present Them, Preparing for Interviews.* New York: Grosset & Dunlap.

Campbell, David. 1974. *If You Don't Know Where You're Going, You'll Probably End Up Somewhere Else.* Niles, IL: Argus Communications.

Crystal, John C., and Bolles, Richard N. 1974. *Where Do I Go from Here with My Life?* Berkeley, CA: Ten Speed Press.

Jackson, Tom. 1981. *The Perfect Resume.* Garden City, NY: Anchor Press.

Lathrop, Richard. 1980. *Who's Hiring Who?* Berkeley, CA: Ten Speed Press.

McLagan, Patricia A. 1983. *Training and Development Competencies.* Alexandria, VA: American Society for Training and Development.

Medley, H. Anthony. 1981. *Sweaty Palms: The Neglected Art of Being Interviewed.* Berkeley, CA: Ten Speed Press.

Molloy, John T. 1975. *Dress for Success.* New York: Warner Books.

O'Brien, Barbara, ed. *Summer Employment Directory of the United States.* Cincinnati, OH: Writers Digest Books. Published annually.

Ontario Society for Training and Development. 1983. *Competency Analysis for Trainers: A Personal Planning Guide.* O.S.T.D., Box 537, Postal Station K, Toronto M4P 2G9, Ontario, Canada.

Stump, Robert W. 1983. *Your Career in Human Resource Development: A Guide to Information and Decision Making.* Alexandria, VA: American Society for Training and Development.

Terkel, Studs. 1972. *Working.* New York: Pantheon.

Williams, Eugene. 1982. *Getting the Job You Want with the Audio Visual Portfolio.* Washington, DC: Comptex Associates.

Woodworth, D. J., ed. *Overseas Summer Jobs: Where the Jobs Are and How to Get Them.* Cincinnati, OH: Writers Digest Books. Published annually.

CHAPTER 21

Association for the Study of Higher Education. 1986. ASHE-ERIC Higher Education Report no. 7, One Dupont Circle, Suite 630, Dept. 7D, Washington, DC 20036.

Edwards, H. T., and Nordin, V. D. 1980. *The American Legal System.* Cambridge, MA: I.E.M., Harvard University.

Gatti, R. D., and Gatti, D. J. 1975. *Encyclopedic Dictionary of School Law.* West Nyack, NY: Parker Publishing.

Hollander, P. 1978. *Legal Handbook for Educators.* Boulder, CO: Westview Press.

Hudgins, H. C., and Vacca, R. S. 1979. *Law & Education: Contemporary Issues and Court Decisions.* Charlottesville, NC: Michie Co.

Kamisar, Yale. 1987. *New York Times Magazine,* Sept. 13, pp. 109–114.

Laudicina, R. A., and Tramutola, J. L., Jr. *A Legal Overview of the New Student.* 1976. Springfield, IL: Charles C. Thomas.

Stewart, Richard. 1975. The Reformation of American Administrative Law. *Harvard Law Review* 88:1669.

CHAPTER 22

Armstrong, David G., and Savage, Tom V. 1983. *Secondary Education.* New York: Macmillan.

Bedford, Sybille. 1974. *Aldous Huxley: A Biography.* New York: Harper & Row.

Clark, Leonard H., and Starr, Irving S. 1986. *Secondary and Middle School Teaching Methods.* New York: Macmillan.

Lorber, Michael A., and Pierce, Walter D. 1983. *Objectives, Methods, and Evaluation for Secondary Teaching.* Englewood Cliffs, NJ: Prentice-Hall.

Sheehy, Gail. 1981. *Pathfinders.* New York: Morrow.

APPENDIX A

Bogen, J. E., and Gazzinga, M. S. 1965. Cerebral Commissurotomy in Man. Minor Hemisphere Dominance for Certain Visuospatial Functions. *Journal of Neurosurgery* 23(4):394–399.

Braun, C. 1976. Teacher Expectations: Sociopsychological Dynamics. *Review of Educational Research* 46(2):185–213.

Brown, Barbara B. 1975. *New Mind, New Body.* New York: Bantam Books.

Bruner, Jerome. 1962. *On Knowing: Essays of the Left Hand.* Cambridge, MA: Harvard University Press.

Cowan, W. M. 1979. The Development of the Brain. *Scientific American* 241(3).

Dimond, S. I.; Farington, L.; and Johnson, P. 1976. Differing Emotional Response from Right and Left Hemispheres. *Nature* 261:690–692.

Edwards, Betty. 1979. *Drawing on the Right Side of the Brain.* Los Angeles: J. P. Tarcher.

Finn, J. D. 1972. Expectations and the Educational Environment. *Review of Educational Research* 42:387–410.

Gardner, Howard. 1983. *Frames of Mind: The Theory of Multiple Intelligences.* New York: Basic Books.

———. 1985. *The Mind's New Science.* New York: Basic Books.

Garfield, Patricia. 1974. *Creative Dreaming.* New York: Ballantine Books.

Gazzinga, Michael S. 1970. *The Bisected Brain.* New York: Appleton-Century-Crofts.

Hand, James. 1982. Brain Function During Learning. In D. Jonassen, ed., *The Technology of Text.* Englewood Cliffs, NJ: Educational Technology Publications.

———. 1986. The Mind/Brain Conjunction: Neurobiology, Psychology and Philosophy. Paper presented at the Society for Accelerative Learning and Teaching, Eleventh Annual Conference, Fort Lauderdale, FL.

Hart, Leslie. 1975. *How the Brain Works.* New York: Basic Books.

———. 1983. *Human Brain, Human Learning* New York: Longman.

Kimura, D. 1964. Left-Right Differences in the Perception of Melodies. *Quarterly Journal of Experimental Psychology* 16:355–358.

Ornstein, Robert F. 1975. *The Psychology of Consciousness.* New York: Penguin Books.

Ornstein, Robert F., and Sobel, David. 1987. *The Healing Brain.* New York: Simon & Schuster.

Rosenfield, Israel. 1988. *The Invention of Memory.* New York: Basic Books.

Rosenthal, R., and Jacobson, L. 1968. *Pygmalion in the Classroom.* New York: Holt, Rinehart and Winston.

Sagan, Carl. 1977. *The Dragons of Eden.* New York: Random House.

Schuster, D. H., and Gritton, C. E. 1986. *Suggestive Accelerative Learning Techniques.* New York: Gordon and Breach.

Springer, Sally P., and Deutsch, Georg. 1985. *Left Brain, Right Brain.* New York: W. H. Freeman.

Syer, John, and Connolly, Christopher. 1984. *Sporting Body, Sporting Mind.* New York: Cambridge University Press.

Zdenek, Marilee. 1983. *The Right-Brain Experience.* New York: McGraw-Hill.

Name Index

Airola, Paavo, 360, 367n
Alberti, Robert, 329
Alexander, Lloyd, 231
Anderson, Beverly, 28n
Aragon, Vicki, 416
Archimedes, 228, 292
Arieti, Silbano, 434n
Aristotle, 48, 49, 55n, 398
Austin, Nancy, 329

Baer, Jean, 329, 331, 350n
Bandler, Richard, 359, 367n
Banish, Mary, 230–231
Barzakov, Ivan, 142–143, 152, 165–168, 172n, 294–296, 298n, 342–344, 350n
Beckman, Leonard, 28n
Bennett, William, 403
Biehler, Robert F., 281–283, 297n, 434n
Bird, C., 256, 264n
Bird, D. M., 256, 264n
Blaszczak, Elizabeth, 237–243, 248n
Bloom, Allan, 11, 12, 23–24, 71
Bloom, Benjamin S., 52–54, 56n, 59–61, 67, 69n, 154, 266, 272n, 446–451
Bobby, Janet, 41–42, 43n, 328–350
Bogen, Joseph E., 63, 69n, 426
Bolles, Richard Nelson, 387n
Booth, Wayne, 312
Bordon, R. B., 429, 435n
Boyer, Ernest L., 10–11, 14n, 19, 20, 24–26, 27n, 28n, 100n, 102, 174, 245, 248n
Boyer, James, 100n
Boyle, Robert, 228
Bramsen, B. M., 193, 204n
Braun, Carl, 424, 434n
Brewster, David, 284
Brewster, Mary K., 284
Bronowski, Jacob, 228
Brophy, J., 279–280, 297n
Broudy, Harry S., 40–41, 43
Brown, Julie, 205n
Bruner, Jerome, 40, 43n
Bry, Adelaide, 152, 359
Buzan, Tony, 152, 171n

Canter, Lee, 329–330, 332, 335–336, 350n
Canter, Marlene, 330, 350n
Carroll, John B., 417n
Carroll, Lewis, 34, 45
Caton, Deborah Jane, 353, 366n
Childs, John W., 173–188
Chrzanowski, Gerard, 434n
Cohn, Avern, 394
Combs, Arthur, 281
Connolly, Christopher, 359, 367n
Cooper, Charles R., 21, 28n
Copperman, Paul, 20, 28n
Costa, Arthur L., 4, 8, 14n
Cousins, Norman, 339
Cowan, W. M., 420, 433n
Crump, W. D., 220n

Darwin, Charles, 223
Dax, Marc, 425–426
Delehanty, Hugh J., 298n
Deutsch, Georg, 434n
Dewey, John, 51, 56n, 58, 64, 65, 69n, 346, 350n
Dhority, Lynn, 164, 169, 172n
Dimond, Marian, 420
Dishman, Jerome P., 245n, 436–439, 445n
Dossey, Larry, 308
Douglas, Martin C., 375
Doyle, Betty, 388n
Dunn, L. M., 220n

Eccles, Sir John, 426, 434n
Eckartsberg, Rolf von, 222
Edison, Thomas, 228, 307
Edwards, H. T., 397, 404n
Einstein, Albert, 292
Eisner, Elliot W., 52, 56n, 243, 248n
Ellison, Ralph, 196
Emmer, Edmund T., 309n
Emmons, Michael, 329
Erhard, Werner, 34, 161, 367n
Escher, M. C., 160, 224, 225

Fensterheim, Herbert, 329, 331, 350n
Ferguson, Marilyn, 222, 352, 419
Fieldhusen, John F., 55n

Fine, Michelle, 22, 28n
Finn, J. D., 424, 434n
Fletcher, Hal, Jr., 148
Freud, Sigmund, 150
Furlette, Mary C., 291–292, 296–297, 311–327

Galyean, Beverly-Colleene, 153
Gandhi, Mahatma, 312
Ganju, V., 353, 367n
Gardner, Howard, 430–432, 435n
Gardner, John, 26, 278, 300
Garfield, Patricia, 150, 430
Garrett, M. K., 220n
Gatti, D. J., 404n
Gatti, R. D., 404n
Geddis, Arthur N., 244, 248n
Gerhart, Mary, 245n
Gibson, Dennis L., Jr., 28n
Gilboe, John, 439–445, 445n
Glasser, William, 335–337, 350n
Goethe, Johann Wolfgang von, 140
Gordon, H. W., 433n
Gordon, William, 223, 245n
Gottlieb, J., 220n
Gould, Robert F., 245n
Greene, Joe, 344–346
Greenlaw, M. Jean, 172n
Grinder, John, 359, 367n
Gritton, Charles E., 100n, 172n, 297n, 309n, 434n
Gronlund, Norman E., 272n

Hand, James, 420, 421, 425, 428–430, 433n, 434n, 435n
Hannibal, 140
Hanson, Mark V., 359
Hanson, Peter G., 352–353, 365, 366n, 367n
Harris, P. L., 353, 367n
Harrow, Anita J., 66–67, 69n
Harvey, William, 223
Hawthorne, Nathaniel, 233
Heidegger, Martin, 408
Hendricks, Gay, 152–153, 359
Hesse, Hermann, 231
Hillary, Sir Edmund, 365
Hirsch, E. D., Jr., 12, 14n, 23–24
Hosford, Philip L., 14n, 23, 28n, 100n
Hunter, Madeline, 4, 7–8, 14n, 45, 55n, 84–85, 100n
Husen, Torsten, 20, 28n
Huxley, Aldous, 6, 147, 170, 171n, 172n, 278, 279, 297n, 407
Huxley, Laura, 352, 357, 364, 367n

Ibanez, Ricardo Marin, 189–204

Jacobson, Lenore, 424
James, William, 58
Johnson, D. W., 220n
Johnson, R., 220n

Johnson-Laird, P. W., 252, 264n
Jonassen, D., 433n
Jones, Angela, 286–287
Jones, R. L., 220n
Joyce, Bruce, 190, 195–196, 204n, 205n

Kamisar, Yale, 395, 404n
Kaplan, Leonard, 64, 69n
Kekule, Stradonitz von, 228–230, 292
Keller, Helen, 3, 207, 278
Kennedy, John F., 307
Khalsa, Gurucharn, 289–291
Kibler, Robert J., 56n
Kimura, Doreen, 429, 432, 435n
Kirsner, D. A., 54, 449
Kish, Brian, 233
Kline, Peter, 52, 56n, 161–164, 171n, 264n, 342–343
Knowles, John, 237–243
Kolb, David, 243, 346, 350n
Kounin, J., 5, 14n, 350n
Krathwohl, David R., 59–61, 67, 69n
Kryspin, William J., 55n

Lakein, Alan, 307
Langdon, Grace, 260, 264n
Lanier, Judith, 29n
Lavoisier, Antoine Laurent, 292
Lazarus, Arnold, 329
Lecoq, Jacques, 339
Leonard, George, 14, 14n
Leonardo da Vinci, 228
Lerede, Jean, 343
Levy, Jerre, 428, 432, 435n
Leyser, Y., 220n
Lichtenberg, Georg C., 227–228
Long, Kenneth, 249–263
Lorayne, Harry, 262
Lorber, Michael A., 69n, 100n
Lortie, Dan, 16
Lozanov, Georgi, 64, 69n, 152, 259, 283, 294–295, 298n, 342, 425
Lucas, Jerry, 262

McCay, Donald, 426
Mackenzie, Alexander, 307
MacLean, Paul, 422–423, 425, 434n
McWalters, Peter, 405n
Maddox, Harry, 264n
Mager, Robert F., 49–50, 55n, 56n, 58, 69n
Magill, Frank N., 245n
Malcolm X, 6
Maltz, Maxwell, 357, 367n
Marcotte, Donald, 265–273
Marinko, Vicki, 284–285
Martinez, Rodolfo, 189–204
Masia, Bertram B., 59–61, 69n
Maslow, Abraham, 64, 69n, 281, 334–335
Mason, M., 353, 367n
Mecklenberger, James, 21

Metric, John, 295, 296, 298n
Michael, W. B., 54, 449
Miller, Sherod, 313, 315, 316, 319–321
Milton, John, 352
Mitfessel, Newton S., 54, 449
Mosenfelder, D., 375
Mouzon, D., 429, 435n
Myers-Baker, Chris, 344

Nadel, Lynn, 425, 434n
Narkiewicz, Geralyn, 135n
Newton, Sir Isaac, 228
Nordin, V. D., 397, 404n
Nummela, Renata M., 167, 172n, 344, 350n

Olivier, Sir Laurence, 341
Ornstein, Robert, 426, 434n
Ortega y Gasset, José, 300

Pasteur, Louis, 250
Pauk, Walter, 264n
Pavio, A., 429–430, 435n
Pepper, Stephen C., 55n, 224–226, 237, 245n
Peterson, Gordon, 245n
Philips, Stanlee, 329
Piaget, Jean, 280
Piccirelli, Jeanette H., 371–387
Pierce, Walter D., 69n, 100n
Pipho, Chris, 28n
Pisani, Raymond, 355
Popper, Karl, 51
Pribram, Karl, 432
Prohow, Philip, 285–286

Quina, James, 172n, 245n, 248n

Ramirez, S. Z., 169
Rand, Pamela, 339, 340, 350n
Rashid, Harun-Ur, 155–158, 223
Raywid, Anne, 27n, 29n
Retton, Mary Lou, 68
Rico, Gabrielle L., 152, 171n
Robbins, Anthony, 154–155, 171n, 250, 293, 297n, 434n
Roberts, Thomas B., 64, 69n, 152–153, 359
Robinson, F. P., 251–252
Rosengren, Tennes M., 167, 172n, 344, 350n
Rosenthal, Robert, 424
Russell, Allan, 245n
Russell, Bertrand, 55n
Russell, P., 435n
Ryle, Gilbert, 223

Sagan, Carl, 63, 69n, 164–165, 172n, 222, 245n, 419, 423, 434n
Schultz, Johannes H., 359
Schuster, Donald H., 100n, 172n, 297n, 309n, 429, 434n, 435n
Schutz, William, 194–195, 204n, 205n
Scott, Drew, 307

Seidel, Frank, 245n
Shakespeare, William, 58
Shapero, Albert, 372
Sheehy, Gail, 407–408, 417n
Simpkins, Edward, 28n
Skinner, B. F., 279, 334
Smith, Doug E., 88–89, 91–100, 100n
Smith, Manuel, 329, 350n
Snowman, Jack, 281–283, 297n, 434n
Snygg, Donald, 281
Socrates, 7
Sperry, Roger, 426, 434n
Springer, Sally P., 434n
Stafford, William, 313
Stone, Samuel, 51, 55n–56n
Stout, Irving, 260, 264n
Stroebel, Charles, 430, 435n
Sullivan, Annie, 3
Syer, John, 359, 367n
Szwala, Elaine, 388n

Tanner, Daniel, 43n
Terkel, Studs, 372
Tesconi, Charles A., 27n, 29n
Thomas, John W., 280
Thomas, Lewis, 150–152, 171n
Thompson, Benjamin (Count Rumford), 228
Tinker, I., 193, 204n
Tobias, John, 232, 245n
Topous, Colleen Carol, 109–135, 135n
Triffon, Madeline, 287–289
Tyler, Ralph, 41

Urbanski, Adam, 405n

Valle, Ronald S., 222
Vannan, D. A., 170
Vogel, Philip, 426
Voukatieis, Chris, 289
Voukatieis, Rita, 289

Warren, Donald R., 27n, 29n
Watson, Nora, 372
Weil, Marsha, 190, 195–196, 204n, 205n
Wells, H. G., 390
White, R. W., 280–281
Whitehead, Alfred North, 65, 104, 228
Whitman, Russell, 427, 434n
Whitman, Walt, 102
Wiggins, Shielia, 205n
Wood, Paula C., 206–220
Woodyear, Ocie Posener, 168–169, 172n
Wright, Joseph M., 389–404

Young, Anne, 374, 388n

Zdeneck, Marilee, 69n, 148, 150, 171n, 427–428, 434n
Zukav, G., 140

Subject Index

Abstractions in a field, knowledge of, 447
Abstract relations, derivation of a set of, 449
Acquisition Through Creative Teaching (Dhority), 164
Acting out, 336
Actions, conferencing and, 320–321
Addition, rule of, 158
Adequacy, 281
Adjustment problems, 214–215
Advanced degrees, 409
Affection, 195
Affective objectives, 58–68
  approach and avoidance behaviors and, 58
  fusion with cognitive objectives, 65–66
  relationship between cognitive objectives and, 63–65
  resistance to, 63
  statement of, 65
  taxonomy of, 59–61, 450–451
Affirming the consequent, 156, 157
Agency, 280
Aikido, 363
Aims, educational, 36–38. *See also* Purposes, educational
Alpha rest, 307, 358
Alpha waves, 422
American College Testing Program (ACT), 19
American Council on Educational Studies, 37, 42n
American Educational Studies Association, 24, 26
American Federation of Teachers (AFT), 410
Amygdala, 424
Analysis, 53, 154, 448
Anatomy of an Illness As Perceived by the Patient (Cousins), 339
Antecedent conditions, 326
Anticipation set, 85
Application, 53, 154, 448
Approach behavior, 58
Aquarian Conspiracy, The (Ferguson), 222, 419
As-if thinking, 164
Assertive discipline, 329–332
Assertive Discipline (Canter and Canter), 330
Assertive Woman, The (Philips and Austin), 329
Association for the Study of Higher Education, 396, 404n

Attending behavior, 59
Attention, controlled or selected, 59, 61, 450
Attitudes, 58–63
  in conferences, 319, 323–324
  toward handicapped students, 217–218
  identification of, 61–62
  stating affective objectives and, 65
  taxonomy of, 59–61
Audiotapes
  instructional, 182–183
  motivational, 415
  teacher portfolio, 384–385
  teacher self-assessment, 412–413
Audiovisual education. *See* Technology
Auditory handicaps, 210–211
Authoritative teacher, 218–219
Authority
  legal. *See* Legal rights and responsibilities
  motivation and, 294
Avoidance behavior, 58
Awareness, 59, 61, 450
Axons, 421

Barzak Educational Training Center, 340
Basic Principles of Curriculum and Instruction (Tyler), 41, 43n
Behavior, interpretation of, 326–327
Behavioral lesson plan format, 85–87
Behavioral objectives, 48, 50–52
Behavioral problems, 215
Behavior control. *See* Classroom management
Behavior management, nonintrusive, 219
Behavior modification, 279–280, 332–34
Behavior Therapy and Beyond (Lazarus), 329
Beta waves, 422
Bhagavad-Gita, 329
Biofeedback, 422
Blacks, dropout rates of, 22
Boards of education, 397–398
Body–mind integration, 360
Body posture of speaker, 141
Brain cell development, 420–422
Brain function tests, 427–428
Brainstorming, 145–146, 262
Brain waves, 422

Broca's Brain (Sagan), 164
Burnout, 353–354

Cardinal Principles of Education (U.S. Bureau of
  Education), 39, 42*n*, 43*n*
*Career in Teaching Plan: Joint Statement of
  Intent Agreement,* 402, 405*n*
Careers, root metaphors in relationship to, 243,
  244
Carnegie Foundation for the Advancement of
  Teaching, 12, 24–26, 400
Categories, knowledge of, 447
Centering, 64
Cerebral palsy, 211
Certification, 381
Characterization, 61, 62, 451
Chronic illnesses, 212
Chronicles of Prydain (Alexander), 231
Circadian rhythms, 430
Citizenship, cardinal principle of, 39
Classifications, knowledge of, 447
Classroom management, 329–350
  assertive discipline, 329–332
  behavior modification, 332–334
  cooperative learning/control theory, 336–337
  humor and, 337–340
  integrative learning and, 342–344
  legal-risk management and, 398–399
  operant conditioning, 334–335
  optimalearning technique and, 343–344
  organizational strategies, 340–341
  reality therapy, 335–336
  students' views of, 4–5
  suggestopedic technique and, 342–343
  synthesis of personal approach to, 344–349
Closing of the American Mind, The (Bloom), 11
Code of Ethics (Ann Arbor School District),
  417*n*
Codes of ethics, 414–415
Cognitive approach to motivation, 280–281
Cognitive handicaps, 212–214
Cognitive objectives, 45–55
  behavioral, 48, 50–52
  comprehensive, 51–52
  fusion with affective objectives, 65–66
  relationship between affective objectives and,
    63–65
  statement of, 46–52
  taxonomy of, 52–54, 154, 446–449
Cohen v. *Hurley* (NY 1961), 400, 405*n*
Collective bargaining, 401–403
Commission on the Reorganization of Secondary
  Education, 38
Commitment, 62, 450
Committee work, 412
Communication, 312–327
  behavior interpretation, 326–327
  conferencing. *See* Conferencing
  style of, 312–313
  time management and, 308

Communications, production of, 449
Communications media, 181–183
Communicative functions, 327
Community role models, 283–292
Completion-type test items, 269–271, 273
Compliance, 326
Comprehension, 53, 154, 447
Computer-assisted instruction (CAI), 183
Computer literacy, 186–187
Computer science, 187–188
Computing instruction, 186–188
Computing technology, 177, 183–188
Computing tools, 186
Concept development, unit, 103–104
Concept of Mind (Ryle), 223
Conceptual objectives, 48
Concert pseudo-passiveness, 295
Concert reading, 259
Conduct, rules of, 332
Conferences, professional, 410
Conferencing, 313–326
  defined, 313–315
  general approaches for resolution of issues,
    316–317
  general guidelines for, 322–327
  group, 325–326
  issues for, 315–316
  planning and preparation, 317–322
  social (establishing rapport), 322–323
Confidentiality and Freedom of Information Act,
  392
Conjunction, rule of, 158
Content
  versus method, 12
  unit, 103–104
Content validity, 267, 269
Context, 326
Contextualism, 246–247
  careers and, 244
  curriculum building and, 243
  defined, 224–227
  explanatory power of, 241–242
  in literature, 233, 247
  in science, 228, 247
Context validity, 267
Control, 195
Control theory, 336–337
Control Theory in the Classroom (Glasser),
  336
Conventions, knowledge of, 446
Convergent questions, 155
Cooperative learning, 218, 336–337
Core curriculum, Carnegie Foundation Report
  recommendations on, 24
Course structure and content sample,
  109–112
Course syllabus example, 92–100
Cover letters, 383–384
"Creating" (Banish), 230–231
Creative Dreaming (Garfield), 150

Crestwood Education Association v. *Crestwood Board of Education (Dearborn Heights, Michigan)*, 401
Criteria, knowledge of, 447
Critical thinking as method, 155–158
Cross-age tutoring, 218
Crossword puzzles, 159
Cultural Literacy (Hirsch), 12
Culture
  challenge of unity versus cultural pluralism, 192
  globalization of, 192–194
  lower versus higher, 191–192
  meaning of, 190–192
Curriculum building, metaphor as method and, 243–245
Curriculum guides, as sources of educational purposes, 41
Curriculum specialists, as sources of educational purposes, 41
Curriculum vitae (CV), 383

Daily objectives, 303
Decision making, 45–46
Declaration for a New World Information Service, 193
Declaration of the Principles of International Cultural Cooperation, 193
Deductive arguments, 155–158
Deep breathing, 358–359
Delegation of work, 306
Delta waves, 422
Dendrites, 421
Denying the antecedent, 157
Denying the consequent, 156
Department heads, as sources of educational purposes, 41
Design for General Education, A (American Council on Educational Studies), 37
Desk organization, 305
Developing Objectives in the Affective Domain (Kaplan), 64
Dichotic listening test, 428
Diet, 358, 364–365
Differential reinforcement of communicative behavior (DRC), 326
Differential reinforcement of other behavior (DRO), 326
Direct corrective feedback, 219
Direct instructional software, 185
Direct instruction using computing, 184
Discipline. *See also* Classroom management
  assertive, 329–332
  behavior modification and, 332–334
  legal-risk management and, 398–399
  operant conditioning and, 334–335
  self-, 335–337
  students' views on, 5
  synthesis of personal approach to, 344–349

Disjunctive syllogism, 157
Divergent questions, 155
Domain of interest, test, 266–267
Don't Say Yes When You Want to Say No (Fensterheim and Baer), 329
"Dr. Heidegger's Experiment" (Hawthorne), 233
Dragons of Eden (Sagan), 63, 419
Dramatic enactments, 342–343
Dramatization, 146–147
Dreams as methods, 150
Dropout problem, 22–23
Dry-brush massage, 360
Dual-planeness, 294–295
Due process, 399–401

Education, defined, 6
Educational Imagination, The (Eisner), 52, 243
Educational malpractice, 395–397
Educational Policies Commission, 40–41
Educational purposes. *See* Purposes, educational
Education Amendments Act of 1972, Title IX of, 390
Education heading, resumé, 381
Education Network, The, 171*n*
Education planning committee, 217
Effective Teacher Planning Chart, 452
Effective teaching, 4–14
  dictionary definitions of, 6–7
  documentary interpretation of, 10–11
  personal synthesis and, 11–12
  professional views of, 7–8
  recall of teachers' learning experiences and, 8–10
  self-assessment instruments, 412–414
  student definitions of, 4–5
  teacher definitions of, 5–6
Electroencephalograph (EEG), 428
Elements, analysis of, 448
Embedded world views, questions as, 155
Emotionally disturbed students, 214–216
Empathy, 326
Employment seeking, 372–387
  audio-video portfolio, 384–385
  interviews, 386–387
  options, 373
  overcoming destructive beliefs, 372–373
  resumé preparation, 375–384
  as substitute teacher, 374–375
Encounter teaching, 194–196
Energy sources, increasing, 307
Enrichment courses, 409
Environmental changes, 355–356
Equal protection, 399–401
Equipment checks, 341
Erhard, Werner, and Associates, 171*n*
Essay exams, 256–258
Ethical character, cardinal principle of, 40
Ethical issues, 414–415
Evaluation, 54, 154, 449

Evelyn Wood Reading Dynamics, 152, 171*n*
Exam preparation, 255–259
Excellence (Gardner), 26
Exercise, 361–362
Expectations
  versus expectancy, 52
  positive, conditions for, 424–425
Experiential Learning (Kolb), 243
Expressive objectives, 52
Extended-response tests, 272, 273
Extrapolation, 448
Extrinsic motivation, 280
Eye contact, 143

Family Educational Rights and Privacy Act, 390, 392
Fantasy
  cultural exploration and, 196–204
  teaching root metaphors with, 235–237
Fear, 357
Feedback, 8, 141, 219, 261, 424
Feelings, 58–63
  in conferences, 320
  identification of, 61–62
  taxonomy of, 59–61
Fill-in-the-blank tests, 271
Finnish saunas, 360
Ford Foundation grants, 412
Formism, 246–247
  careers and, 244
  curriculum building and, 243
  defined, 224–226
  explanatory power of, 241
  in literature, 231, 247
  in science, 227–228, 247
Fourteenth Amendment, 400
Fourth Amendment, 394, 395
Frames of Mind: The Theory of Multiple Intelligences (Gardner), 430–431
Free association, 149
Fundamental process command, cardinal principle of, 38

Gallup Poll, 19
Games as method, 159–161
Gandhi (film), 196
Generalizations, knowledge of, 447
Generalized set, 61, 62, 451
Globalization of culture, 192–194
Glossary, 455–466
Goals
  Carnegie Foundation Report recommendations on, 24
  defined, 38
  professional, 408–409
  time management and, 302–303
Go for It: How to Get Your First Good Job (Douglas), 375
Golden fluid visualization, 359–360

Grading homework, 260–261
Group behavior, 326
Group conferencing, 325–326
Group work, 144–145
Growth approach to motivation, 281
Guided practice, 85

Handicapped students
  cognitive handicaps, 212–214
  complicating factors in instruction of, 207–208
  emotional handicaps, 214–216
  general classroom adaptations and procedures for, 217–219
  physical handicaps, 209–212
  teacher role in education process, 216–217
Hardware
  communications, 181
  computing, 184–185
Harmonious unity. *See* Organicism
Hatha yoga, 363
Health, cardinal principle of, 38
Hearing-impaired students, 210–211
Hemisphericity, 425–430, 432
Hierarchy of needs, 281
Higher culture, 191–192
High School (Boyer), 20, 24–26
High schools
  academic expectations and, 19–20
  Carnegie Foundation Report recommendations on, 24–26
  dropout problem in, 22–23
  improvement of standards of, 23–26
  minimum competency testing and, 20–22
Hippocampus, 424
Historical moment, world as. *See* Contextualism
Holmes Group, 12, 24
Holographic brain theory, 432
Home membership, cardinal principle of, 39
Homework, 250–263
  as expansion of creativity, 263
  feedback on, 261
  grading, 260–261
  homework plan, 259–260
  internalization of broad purpose, 262–263
  memory systems and, 261–262
  purposes of, 251–255
  space for, 262
  status of, 250–251
  studying for tests and exams, 255–259
Hostile responses, 330, 333
How to Get Control of Your Time and Your Life (Lakein), 307
How to Put More Time in Your Life (Scott), 307
Humanities sample unit, 112–135
Humor
  behavior control with, 337–340
  as method, 150–152
Hypothalamus, 424

Imagery
  as language, 161–164
  visualization. *See* visualization
Imaging, 429–430
"Imperative Needs of Youth of Secondary School
    Age, The," 40, 43*n*
Inclusion, 195–196
Independent practice, 85
Indirect instructional software, 185–186
Individual behavior, 326
Induction, principle of, 278–279
Inert knowledge, 104
Infantilization, 294
Inference, rules of, 156–158
Information, freedom of, 392–393
Informational transfer, neural, 421–422
In loco parentis, 391
Input, in Hunter lesson plan format, 85
In re Coates (1961), 405*n*
Instruction. *See also* Teaching styles and
    strategies; Technology
  Carnegie Foundation Report recommendations
    on, 25
  defined, 6
  of handicapped students. *See* Handicapped
    students
  homework. *See* Homework
  legal duty of, 391
  lesson plans. *See* Lesson plans
  test development. *See* Test development
Instructional objectives. *See* Objectives,
    instructional
Instrumental music, list of, 436–439
"Instrumentation of the Taxonomy of
    Educational Objectives: Cognitive Domain"
    (Metfessel, Michael, and Kirsner), 54, 449
Integrated whole, world as. *See* Organicism
Integrate education, 170
Integrative learning, 161–170
  classroom management and, 342–344
  imagery as language, 161–164
  love, 168–170
  music, 165–168
  optimalearning. *See* Optimalearning
  puppets and as-if thinking, 164
  science fiction, 164–165
  suggestopedia. *See* Suggestopedia
Intelligence, whole-brain, 430–431
Intentions, conferencing and, 320
Interests, 58–65
  Dewey on, 65
  identification of, 61–62
  stating affective objectives and, 65
  taxonomy of, 59–61
Interpersonal training, 194–196
Interpretation, 448
Interviews, job, 386–387
Intonation, 295
Intuition, 8

Intuitive-emotional barrier to learning, 294
Invisible Man, The (Ellison), 196

Jane Doe v. *City of Detroit Board of Education et
    al,* 404*n*
Job objective, 380
Jobs. *See* Employment seeking
Joy: Expanding Human Awareness (Schutz),
    194–195
Joy of Stress, The (Hanson), 352–353
Judgmental attitudes, 319
Judgments, 449
Judo, 363
Jurisdiction of school authorities, 391–392

Karate, 362–363
Knowledge, 53, 154, 446–447
Kundalini yoga, 363

Language centrality, Carnegie Foundation Report
    recommendations on, 24
Language of the Brain (Pribram), 432
Language teaching, 168
Learning-disabled students, 213–214
Lectures, 140–143
Left brain, 425–430, 432
Legal rights and responsibilities, 390–404
  boards of education, 397–398
  collective bargaining, 401–403
  due process, 399–401
  educational malpractice, 395–397
  future perspectives, 403–404
  jurisdiction of school authorities, 391–392
  legal-risk management, 398–399
  records and freedom of information, 392–393
  search and seizure, 393–395
  teachers' responsibilities to students, 390–391
Legal-risk management, 398–399
Leisure time use, cardinal principle of, 39
Lesson plans, 71–100
  attitudes toward, 88–89
  basic format, 71–73
  behavioral format, 85–87
  Hunter format, 84–85
  myths about, 90–91
  self-designed, 88
  sources for, 91–100
  Suggestive Accelerative Learning Techniques
    (SALT), 87–88
Limbic system, 424–425
Literature, root metaphors in, 231–234, 247
Love as integration of learning, 168–170
Lower culture, 191–192
Lozanov trainers, 152

Machine, world as. *See* Mechanism
Mainstreaming, 217
Malpractice, 395–397
Management skills. *See* Classroom management;

Communication; Motivation; Stress management for teachers; Time management
Mandala, 148
Martial arts, 362–363
Massage, 360
Matching-type tests, 271, 273
Meaning, shared, 321–322
Mechanism, 246–247
  careers and, 244
  curriculum building and, 243
  defined, 224–226
  explanatory power of, 241
  in literature, 232, 247
  in science, 228, 247
Medusa and the Snail, The (Thomas), 150–152
Memory Book, The (Lorayne and Lucas), 262
Memory systems, 261–262
Menninger Clinic, 422
Mental control techniques, 342
Metaphorical Way of Learning and Knowing (Gordon), 223
Metaphors, 222–247
  basic. *See* Root metaphors
  contextual. *See* Contextualism
  critical pluralism and, 243–245
  formistic. *See* Formism
  in literature, 231–234, 247
  mechanistic. *See* Mechanism
  organic. *See* Organicism
  in science, 227–231, 247
  suggestopedic teaching of, 234–237, 239–243
  as ways of knowing, 222–227
  world hypotheses, 237–244
Metaphors of Consciousness (Valle and von Eckartsberg), 222
Method. *See also* Teaching styles and strategies
  versus content, 12
  defined, 140
Methodology, knowledge of, 447
Microcomputers, 177, 183–188
Mind maps, 152, 153
Mind Sight: Learning Through Imaging (Galyean), 153
Minimum competency testing, 20–22
Minorities, dropout rates of, 22
Modeling
  lesson plan, 85
  role, 283–293
Moderator, 145
Modern Language Association for English (MLA), 410
Modus ponens, 156
Modus tollens, 156
Mood set, 72–73
Moral-ethical barrier to learning, 294
Motivation, 278–297
  behavioral approach to, 279–280
  classroom practices, 281–283

cognitive approach to, 280–281
growth approach to, 281
individual differences and, 296–297
NLP (neurolinguistic programming) and, 293–294
overcoming resistance, 278–281, 294–296
role modeling and, 283–293
self-, 292–293
suggestopedic and optimalearning approach to, 295–296
Motivational workshops and tapes, 415
Motivation and Personality (Maslow), 281
Multicultural methods, 194–204
  encounter teaching, 194–196
  fantasy, 196–204
  music, 204
Multiple-choice tests and exams, 258, 270–271, 273
Music
  as aid to teacher concentration, 305
  classroom management and, 342
  hemispheric learning and, 429
  instrumental, list of, 436–439
  as integration of learning, 165–168
  multicultural methods and, 204
  self-study and, 258–259
  stress reduction with, 355–356
  teaching root metaphors with, 233–237
  thematic, list of, 439–445

Nap taking, 307, 358
Narcissus and Goldman (Hesse), 231
National Assessment of Educational Programs (NAEP), 19
National Council for Accreditation of Teacher Education (NCATE), 24
National Council for Teachers of Social Studies (NCTSS), 410
National Council of Teachers of English (NCTE), 409–410
National Council of Teachers of Mathematics (NCTM), 410
National Education Association (NEA), 16, 410
National On-Campus Report, 404n
National Science Foundation, 40
Nation at Risk, A, 23
Nationwide Teacher Opinion Poll (1980), 16
Needs, hierarchy of, 281
Neocortex, 425
Networking, 410–411
Neurotransmitters, 421
New World Economic Order, 193
NLP (neurolinguistic programming), 141, 152, 293–294, 359
Noncompliance, 326
Nonintrusive behavior management, 219
Nonobjective-type test items, 270–273
Nonprojected media, 182–183
Nonverbal behavior, 331

Nonverbal methods, 147–154
Note-making system, 251–253
Nutrition, 358, 364–365

Objectives, instructional
affective domain. *See* Affective objectives
cognitive domain. *See* Cognitive objectives
defined, 38
in lesson plans. *See* Lesson plans
psychomotor domain, 66–67
purposes as framework for generating, 37–39
purposes distinguished from, 34–36
time management and, 302–303
in units. *See* Unit design
Objective-type test items, 270–271, 273
Observations, 319
One-on-one sharing, 144, 145
One-Semester Course on Supernatural Literature,
A (Topous), 109–135
Operant conditioning, 334–335
Operations, production of a plan or proposed set
of, 449
Optimalearning, 165–170
classroom management and, 343–344
motivation and, 294–296
Organicism, 246–247
careers and, 244
curriculum building and, 243
defined, 225–227
explanatory power of, 243
in literature, 233–234, 247
in science, 228–231, 247
Organization, 60, 450
Organizational classroom management strategies,
340–341
Organizational principles, analysis of, 448
Organizations, professional, 409–410
Other-hand writing, 149
Overhead projectors, 143, 176

Paper management, 305
Parental authorization, 391
Parent-teacher conferences. *See* Conferencing
Parkinson's law, 307–308
Passage to India, A (film), 196
Passive responses, 330, 333
Pathfinders (Sheehy), 407–408
Peer tutoring, 218
"Perspectives on Equality: Voices from Urban
Schools" (Fine), 22
Physical handicaps, 209–212
Physical Science Study Committee (PSSC), 40
Physiological responses to stress, 352–353
Pituitary gland, 424
Planning, as decision making, 45–46. *See also*
Lesson plans; Objectives, instructional;
Purposes, educational; Unit design
PLATO (Programmed Logic for Automated
Teaching Operations), 183

Positron tomography, 428
Praise, 279–280
Precise objectives, 46–51
Precision, questions and the teaching of, 154–155
Preparing Instructional Objectives (Mager),
49–50
Preservice teachers, technology and, 179
President's Commission on Higher Education,
36, 37, 42n
Pride and Excellence: Schools of Excellence for All
the People, 26
Principles
educational, 34, 36, 38
knowledge of, 447
Professional development, 371–416
areas of, 407
committee work, 412
conferences, 410
employment seeking. *See* Employment seeking
ethical issues, 414–415
exploring current methods, 409
goal setting, 408–409
legal rights and responsibilities. *See* Legal
rights and responsibilities
motivational workshops and tapes, 415
networking, 410–411
organizations, 409–410
reading, 409
self-assessment instruments, 412–414
seminars, 410
study grants, 412
well-being, 407–408
workshops, 410, 415
Project creation, 306, 408–409
Projected media, 181–182
Project method, 146
Psychological set, 73
Psychology Applied to Teaching (Biehler and
Snowman), 281–283
Psychology of Consciousness (Ornstein), 426
Psychomotor domain, 66–67
Public commitment, Carnegie Foundation Report
recommendations on, 26
Puerto Ricans, dropout rates of, 22
Puppets, 164
Purposes, educational, 34–42
defined, 38
Educational Policies Commission and, 40–41
as framework for generating specific
objectives, 37–39
in Hunter lesson plan format, 85
objectives distinguished from, 34–36
Seven Cardinal Principles of Secondary
Education and, 34, 38–40
sources of, 41–42
test development and, 266
in unit design, 102
as values, 36–41
Puzzles as method, 159–161

Pygmalion effect, 424
Pygmalion in the Classroom (Rosenthal and Jacobson), 424

Questions as method, 154–155

Raja yoga, 363
Rapport with parents and guardians, 322–325
Rationale, unit, 102–103
Rational-logical barrier to learning, 294
R-complex, 423
Reading, professional, 409
Reading assignments, 253–255
Reading-with-music technique, 165–168, 235, 342
Reality therapy, 335–336
Receiving behavior, 59, 61, 450
Recitations, 143–144
Recontextualization, 356
Recorder, 145
Record of Time Use Chart, 453
Records, 392–393
Redirection, 364
References, 382
Referrals, 216–217
"Reflections on a Gift of Watermelon Pickle" (Tobias), 232
Reframing, 356
Reinforcement, 279–280, 326, 333–334
Relationships, analysis of, 448
Relaxation techniques, 342, 343
Reliability, test, 267–269
Reptilian brain, 423
Resistance, overcoming, 278–281, 294–296
Resource units, as sources of educational purposes, 41
Responding behavior, 60, 61, 450
Rest, 307, 358
Restricted-response tests, 271, 273
Resumé preparation, 375–384
Resumé services, professional, 379–380
Retarded students, 212–213
Reversed effect, principle of, 278–279
Rewards, 279–280, 333, 334
Rhythms, 295
Right brain, 426–430, 432
Right-Brain Experience, The (Zdeneck), 148, 150, 427–428
Risk, legal, management of, 398–399
Rochester City School District, 402
Rochester Teachers Association, 402
Role models, 283–293
Role playing, 146–147
Root metaphors
    changing historical event/experiential moment. *See* Contextualism
    critical pluralism and, 243–245
    defined, 224–227
    integration (harmonious unity). *See* Organicism
    in literature, 231–234, 247

machine. *See* Mechanism
rational extension of (world hypotheses), 237–244
in science, 227–231, 247
similarity. *See* Formism
suggestopedic teaching of, 234–237
Rosemont High School, 10–11

Safety, legal duty of providing, 391
SALT (Society for Accelerative Learning and Teaching) Conference (1987), 170, 410
Sample space, 266, 267
Sauna, 360–361
Scholastic Aptitude Test (SAT), 19
School authorities, jurisdiction of, 391–392
Science, root metaphors in, 227–231, 247
Science fiction as integration of learning, 164–165
Science sample unit, 104–109
Scope of objectives, 46
Search and seizure, 393–395
Seating patterns, 340–341
Second Centering Book (Hendricks and Roberts), 152–153, 359
Self-assessment instruments, 412–414
Self-fulfilling prophecy, 424
Self-instructional packages, 158
Self-management charts, 452–453
Self-motivation, 292–293
Seminars, 410
Sensory stimulation, 150
Separate Peace, A (Knowles), 237–243
Sequences, knowledge of, 447
Service requirement, Carnegie Foundation Report recommendations on, 24
Seven Cardinal Principles of Secondary Education, 34, 38–40
Shared meaning, 321–322
Sharing, one-on-one, 144
Similarity, world as. *See* Formism
Simplification, rules of, 157
Social conferencing (establishing rapport), 322–323
Software, computing, 185–186
Space, Time, and Medicine (Dossey), 308
Space design problem, 159, 160
Special education. *See* Handicapped students
Special learning programs, 218
Specifications, test, 267–269
Specifics, knowledge of, 446
Spider/Fly problem, 159
Spina bifida, 211–212
SQR3 (survey, question, read, recite, and review) system, 251–252
Steambaths, 360–361
Still Life and Street (woodcut) (Escher), 224, 225
Story of the Great Rock, 235–237
Stress management for teachers, 352–366

Stress management for teachers (*Continued*)
applied to students, 356–357
burnout, 353–354
contextual shifts, 356
deep breathing, 358–359
environmental changes, 355–356
exercise, 361–362
key concepts, 357–358
martial arts, 362–363
massage, 360
nutrition, 358, 364–365
physiological responses, 352–353
redirection, 364
sauna and steam bath, 360–361
signals of stress, 354–355
stress control versus stress elimination,
365–366
visualization, 359–360
yoga, 363
Structures, knowledge of, 447
Students
definitions of effective teaching of, 4–5
management of. *See* Classroom management
minimum competency testing and, 20–22
rights of. *See* Legal rights and responsibilities
test performance of, 19–20
Study grants, 412
Substitute teaching, 374–375
*Suggerer Pour Apprendre (To Suggest in Order to
Learn)* (Lerede), 343
Suggestive Accelerative Learning Techniques
(SALT) Plan, 87–88
Suggestopedia, 152, 165–170
classroom management and, 342–343
motivation and, 294–296
teaching root metaphors with, 234–237
teaching world hypotheses with, 239–243
Supervision, legal duty of, 391
Supply-type test items, 269–273
Support systems, 306, 309, 310
Symbols, in note making, 252–253
Synthesis, 53, 449

Table of specifications, test, 267–269
Tachistoscope, 428
Tai chi, 362
Tai jitsu, 363
Tapes. *See* Audiotapes; Videotapes
*Taxonomy of Educational Objectives, Handbook
II: Affective Domain* (Krathwohl, Bloom, and
Masia), 59–61
Teachers
authoritative, 218–219
Carnegie Foundation Report recommendations
on education of, 25
classroom management by. *See* Classroom
management
definitions of effective teaching of, 5–6
effective. *See* Effective teaching

legal responsibilities of. *See* Legal rights and
responsibilities
recall of learning experience of, 8–10
role in special education process, 216–217
as role models, 283
styles and strategies of. *See* Teaching styles
and strategies
technology and. *See* Technology
Teaching
defined, 6
effective. *See* Effective teaching
styles and strategies of. *See* Teaching styles
and strategies
to the whole brain. *See* Whole-brain
processing
"Teaching: A Study in Evidence" (Geddis), 244
Teaching profession
Carnegie Foundation Report recommendations
on, 25
popular views of, 16
realities of responsibilities in, 16–19
Teaching styles and strategies, 140–171
brainstorming, 145–146
classroom management and, 342–344
critical thinking, 155–158
dreams, 150
games and puzzles, 159–161
group work, 144–145
for handicapped students, 218–219
humor, 150–152
imagery as language, 161–164
integrative, 161–170
lectures, 140–143
love, 168–170
mandala, 148
metaphors. *See* Metaphors
mind maps, 152, 153
multicultural. *See* Multicultural methods
music, 165–168
nonverbal methods, 147–154
one-on-one sharing, 144, 145
optimalearning. *See* Optimalearning
other-hand writing, 149
project method, 146
puppets and as-if thinking, 164
questions, 154–155
recitations, 143–144
role playing, 146–147
science fiction, 164–165
self-instructional packages, 158
sensory stimulation, 150
suggestopedia. *See* Suggestopedia
traditional methods, 140–147
transitional objects, 149
visualization, 152–154
Technology, 174–188
audiovisual history, 176–177
Carnegie Foundation Report recommendations
on, 25

communications media, 181–183
computing technology, 177, 183–188
current schooling challenges and, 178
current teacher practices, 178
current teaching problems, 178–179
future, expectations for, 179–181
as object, 176
as process, 175–176
as product, 176
students and, 178, 180
teacher's role and, 177–178
Terminology, knowledge of, 446
Territoriality, 423
Test development, 266–273
completion-type items, 269–271, 273
domain of interest, 266–267
measurement model, 267
purpose of measurement, 266
supply-type items, 269–273
table of specifications, 267–269
Testimony, 392–394
Testing, minimum competency, 19–20
Test preparation, 255–259
Test reliability, 267–269
Test validity, 267, 269
Textbooks
as sources of educational purposes, 41
as sources of lesson plans, 91
Thalamus, 424
Thank-you notes, 384
Thematic music, list of, 436–439
Theories, knowledge of, 447
Theta waves, 422
Thoughts, conferencing and, 319–320
Time management, 300–309
communication and. See Communication
daily objectives, 303
delegation of work, 306
habits, 300–302
increasing energy sources, 307
long-range goals and, 302–303
overcoming blocks, 304
programs and seminars, 309
project creation, 306
self-created time savers, 307–308
support systems, 306, 309, 310
using wait time, 304
working faster, 303–304
work space organization, 304–306
Time-on-task studies, 413
Time Trap, The (Mackenzie), 307
Tonality of speaker, 141
Training, defined, 6
Transitional objects, 149
Transitions, Carnegie Foundation Report
recommendations on, 24
Translation, 447
Transparencies, 143
Transportation, 391–392

Trends, knowledge of, 447
Triune brain theory, 422–425
True/false tests, 270, 273
Tutoring
defined, 6
of handicapped students, 218

Understanding, checking for, 85
Unit design, 102–135
concept development, 103–104
culminating activity, 105–106
evaluation, 106
humanities sample, 112–135
materials, 105
procedures, 104–105
purpose, 102
rationale, 102–103
related themes, 109–112
science sample, 104–109
time span, 109
United Nations Education, Scientific, and Cultural
Organization (UNESCO), 193
United Nations (UN), 193
U.S. Bureau of Education, 39, 42n, 43n
Universal Declaration of Human Rights, 193
Universals in a field, knowledge of, 447
Unlimited Power (Robbins), 293
Use Both Sides of Your Brain (Buzan), 152

Validity, test, 267, 269
Value(s), 58–63, 190. See also Culture
acceptance of, 60, 62
characterization by, 60, 451
conceptualization of, 60, 62, 450
educational purposes as, 36–41
identification of, 61–62
internalization of, 59–61
preference for, 60, 62
stating affective objectives and, 65
Value system, organization of, 60, 62, 450
Valuing, 60, 450
Videotapes
instructional, 181–82
motivational, 415
portfolio, 384–385
teacher self-assessment, 412–413
Visual handicaps, 209–210
Visualization
job interview styles and, 386–387
as method, 152–154
raja yoga and, 363
teacher stress control with, 359–360
Visualization: Directing the Movies of Your Mind
(Bry), 152, 359
Vocabulary for the World of Work (Mosenfelder),
375
Vocation, cardinal principle of, 39
Volunteer work, 382

Wada test, 427–428
Wait time, using, 304
Weapons, 393–395
Well-being, professional, 407–408
"What's Happening in Students' Brains May
    Redefine Teaching" (Nummela and
    Rosengren), 344
When I Say No I Feel Guilty (Smith), 329
Whole-brain processing, 419–433
    brain cell development, 420–422
    experience of, 419–420
    hemisphericity, 425–430, 432
    holographic theory, 432
    intelligence, 430–431

sex differences in, 432
    triune theory, 422–425
Witnesses, 392–394
Woods Hole Conference, 40
Work experience, 381–382
Workshops, 410, 415
Work space organization, 304–306
World hypotheses, 237–244
World Hypotheses (Pepper), 224
Writing the Natural Way (Rico), 152

Yoga, 363
Yogic breathing, 358
Your Perfect Right (Alberti and Emmons), 329